M000160019

Stereotype P.105

MCGILL-QUEEN'S STUDIES IN
ETHNIC HISTORY
Donald Harman Akenson, Editor

Such Hardworking People

Italian Immigrants in Postwar Toronto

FRANCA IACOVETTA

McGill-Queen's University Press
Montreal & Kingston • London • Buffalo

© McGill-Queen's University Press 1992
ISBN 0-7735-0874-0
Legal deposit first quarter 1992
Bibliothèque nationale du Québec

Printed in Canada on acid-free paper

This book has been published with the help of a
grant from the Social Science Federation of Canada,
using funds provided by the Social Sciences and Humanities Research Council of Canada. Publication
has also been supported by Multiculturalism Canada
and by the Canada Council through its block grant
program.

Canadian Cataloguing in Publication Data

Iacovetta, Franca, 1957–
    Such hardworking people

    (McGill-Queen's studies in ethnic history; 12)
    Includes bibliographical references and index.
    ISBN 0-7735-0874-0

    1. Italian Canadians – Ontario – Toronto – Social con-
    ditions. 2. Alien labor, Italian – Ontario – Toronto.
    3. Immigrants – Ontario – Toronto – Social condi-
    tions. I. Title. II. Series.

    FC3097.9.I8I33 1992   971.3′54100451   C91-090623-8
    F1059.5.T68918 1992

This book was typeset by Typo Litho composition inc.
in 10/12 Palatino.

For Ian

Contents

Preface

I grew up in the 1950s and 1960s in a crowded southern Italian immigrant household in an ethnic neighbourhood in downtown Toronto. Some of my earliest and most vivid recollections are of the evenings when my parents would come home from work. My mother used to arrive first, following a day's shift in the industrial laundry where she repaired tablecloths, hotel sheets, and towels. Having spent the day under Nonna's watchful eyes – my grandmother spent much of her adult life in Canada helping to raise her children's children – my brothers and I would rush Ma at the door, begging to be allowed to play outside until Papa came home. In summertime the answer was usually yes, because my father, a bricklayer (and, later, a subcontractor), would not be home until dark. Soon after my mother's arrival, the other women of the household came home: my aunt, who lived upstairs with my uncle, cousin, and grandparents; and then "the lady downstairs," whose family rented the basement flat. It was not until Papa arrived and emerged from the basement shower that Ma, having tended to my baby sister, served supper. Afterwards, we children were sent to bed. I shared my bedroom – the main-floor living room – with two younger brothers and the family TV set. My parents slept in the dining room, and two older brothers occupied a third-floor attic room. At night, I would listen in on my parents' conversations. I can still hear the adults gathered around the kitchen table, endlessly discussing how to get jobs, the daily grind at work, and the struggle to get ahead. Amid the talk was the constant refrain: "*siamo lavoratori forte*" ["we are such hardworking people]." It is a refrain that in the years between 1946 and 1965 was also heard on the lips of sympathetic outsiders who marvelled at the remarkable capacity the Italians had for hard work.

Doubtless, thousands of women and men of my generation – the Canadian-born children of the postwar immigrants who left the rural towns and villages of southern Italy for a better future here – have heard their parents describe themselves as hardworking people. Most of us grew up acutely conscious of our immigrant heritage, and we were inundated with countless stories of the hardships our elders endured as newcomers. To be sure, we felt a sense of genuine pride in their accomplishments, even if we, as children, did not always appear to appreciate fully the sacrifices they had made on our behalf. As their children, we also understood, if only instinctively, that while decades later our immigrant parents could reflect positively, even nostalgically, on early life in Canada, the years of settlement and adjustment had been challenging indeed. The late 1940s, the 1950s, and early 1960s were a time when, as this book documents, our parents, as newcomers to this land, performed the dangerous or low-paying jobs that others shunned, spoke little English, and sometimes found themselves the victims of abuse. At the same time, they proved immensely resourceful, exhibiting a tremendous capacity for hard work and a talent for enjoying life, and each other's company, even in adversity.

When, many years later as a doctoral candidate, I began to seek out the men and women of my parents' generation to record the stories of their experiences as newly arrived immigrants, many of them readily agreed. They expressed the hope that their own children, and others, would more fully appreciate the choices they had made in their lives, the particular hardships they had faced, and the sense of triumph they now feel at having secured for themselves, and their children, a stable life. In this spirit of recording the experiences of men and women who might not otherwise leave behind a written record, I have examined the initial immigrant experiences of the large wave of southern Italians who entered Toronto during the two decades before 1965. The end product reflects not only a personal involvement with the subject but also my concern as a social historian to document the everyday struggles and triumphs of ordinary people. By offering both an internal and external perspective on the Italian immigrant experience in early postwar Toronto, I have sought to reconstruct the history of a specific era. My study pays particular attention to the ways in which class, gender, and ethnicity shaped the immigrant experiences of southern Italian men and women. In taking as my subject a group of former peasant farmers and rural artisans who in the period immediately following the Second World War became immigrant wage-earners in urban Toronto, and in making the stuff of their lives in that era – the workplace, household, church, club, and union – the subject of my historical analysis, I join a growing number of scholars, among them ethnic and labour historians and historians of women, who share a commitment to discovering the hidden or obscured aspects of our past and to appreciating the resourcefulness and resiliency of the disadvantaged and the richness of the every-day world of ordinary people.

Ordinary people, it has often been said, face extraordinary challenges, and certainly it is true of the Italian immigrants who entered Toronto during the two decades after the Second World War. Today, from the perspective of the 1990s, most people quite rightly look upon the Italians as one of Canada's best established immigrant groups. The economic advancement and growing influence of the community is evident in the important positions that Italians from all regional backgrounds now occupy in Canadian political parties and government, in the Catholic church, and in business and trade-union organizations. But, as history teaches us, things were not always this way, and today's successes should not lead us to forget or distort the past. To the tens of thousands of Italians and other immigrants who came in these years, the Toronto of the early postwar era could be an extremely cold and unfriendly place. The southern Italians were particularly unwelcomed by the Canadians who misjudged them. Italian-Canadian readers, especially the southern Italian men and women whose past lives I have tried to recapture, should be forewarned they may find it painful to read about the hardships, conflicts, and prejudices of an earlier period. As a historian, I believe it is essential that the past be remembered as accurately as possible and documented in all its complexity.

Out of respect for the privacy of the men and women who are not public figures accustomed to having their lives exposed or statements published, but who openly and frankly shared with me their private past experiences and perceptions, I have used pseudonyms whem citing matters they related in interviews. The same rule holds for the six interviews that were conducted by student researchers whose oral informants proved equally frank and helpful. The real names of people appear only where the individuals were public figures and/or engaged in public activities that are a matter of public record. Thus, political figures, community leaders, trade-union organizers, parish priests, and the other men and women whose lives have appeared in the historical record do appear on these pages. But when some of these same people have told me things in private, their confidences, too, have been respected. As a final caution, I also ask my non-academic readers to remember that this study is first and foremost a history book, and that, like any historical study, it rests on the interpretive skills of the scholar. Moreover, as a study in social history, the book is informed by the conventions of my profession and discipline, and issues crucial to the field, such as class formation (or more precisely, the transition from peasants to proletarians), gender relations within the family, and women's paid and unpaid work, occupy a central importance in the study. No doubt some readers will wish I had left some things out, while others will be disappointed about the stories and issues that do not appear in these pages. In the end, however, I hope they will appreciate that this is one scholar's honest effort to reconstruct a past time and place.

Of the many debts I have incurred in the course of completing this project, I am most pleased to acknowledge the help of the men and women who welcomed me into their homes, offered plenty of food and wine, and generously shared with me the stories of their past. While they may not always agree with what I have written, I trust they will respect that I have tried to do justice to their lives, even when I discuss the more agonizing or sensitive aspects of immigrant life. Several of my informants consented to more than one interview and patiently answered my follow-up questions on the phone and at the door-step. Special thanks goes to Frank Co-lantonio, a former Brandon Union Group organizer, who made available to me, and other historians, his written account of the early union history of Italian construction workers in postwar Toronto. For arranging several interviews with the women of her neighbourhood, I am indebted to my cousin, Antonietta, whose special talent for encouraging women to discuss their private lives enabled me to record intimate stories that in a less trustful environment might never have been told.

I have also incurred plenty of debts in the scholarly community. When I first considered doing work on the postwar Italians, but worried that it might not be perceived as a legitimate historical project, several teachers – Ramsay Cook, Susan Houston, Tom Traves, Tom Cohen, and Jack Granatstein – assured me that the topic offered an opportunity to combine my interests in immigration, working-class, and women's history. In a previous incarnation, this book was a PhD thesis prepared for the history department at York University. Various people on my committee – Roberto Perin, Clifford Jansen, Livio Visano, and Craig Heron – offered constructive suggestions for improving the study. Bruno Ramirez was an exemplary external examiner whose perceptive and demanding questions forced me to sharpen my arguments.

As a supervisor, Ramsay Cook allowed me the freedom to establish my own research priorities – and then took the time and effort to plough his way through long, rambling drafts and promptly give cogent advice on how to turn them into respectable chapters. For his encouragement and moral support – not to mention much hand-holding and phone-calling during the traumatic final stages of completing the dissertation – I am truly grateful.

Like many immigration historians in this country, I owe a great intellectual debt to the late Robert F. Harney, who, as an enthusiastic scholar and a friend, first inspired me to embark on this project. And by cajoling me into presenting conference papers, he also encouraged me to begin writing. Bob was one of those rare intellectuals whose brilliant scholarly interventions in the field of migration and immigration history were underscored by a passionate, and compassionate, respect for the world's ethnic peoples. He will be sorely missed.

Other friends who, like me, share both a personal and scholarly interest in Italian immigration generously lent me their research materials and allowed me to read their unpublished work: Enrico Cumbo, Franc Sturino, Nick Forte, and especially Luigi Pennachio. My good friend Allan Greer kindly read on earlier version of the entire manuscript and provided valuable suggestions for improving the text. Warm thanks go to Carl Goldenberg for his comments on my chapter on militancy, and to my new colleagues at the University of Toronto's Scarborough Campus for making a newcomer feel right at home.

Several archivists and librarians gave me invaluable assistance. I thank in particular Bennet McCardle, then of the National Archives of Canada, and Don Macleod of the Archives of Ontario. At the Multicultural History Society of Ontario, Lilian Petroff, Gabriel Scardellato, and, here too, Luigi Pennachio referred me to valuable archival sources. I also appreciated the initial enthusiasm and on-going support of Donald Akenson and Philip Cercone at McGill-Queen's University Press and the fine editing skills of Rosemary Shipton. The research for this project was aided by the considerable financial assistance of several funding agencies: the Fellowships Division of the Social Sciences and Humanities Research Council of Canada, the Mariano A. Elia Chair in Italian-Canadian Studies at York University, and the Ethnic Studies Research Program, Secretary of State for Multiculturalism. Some of the material in chapter 4 appeared in Jean Burnet, ed., *Looking Into My Sister's Eyes: An Exploration in Women's History* (Toronto 1986). Two sections, one appearing in chapter 2, the other in chapter 6, were published in a different format in *Canadian Woman Studies*, volumes 7 and 8, while an earlier version of my discussion of contract workers, also appearing in chapter 2, will be published in the *Journal of American Ethnic History*. Every effort has been made to identify, credit appropriately, and obtain publication rights from copyright holders of illustrations in this book. Notice of errors or omissions will be gratefully received and corrections made in any subsequent editions.

As someone who has enjoyed the luxury of belonging to two successful study groups, I am particularly pleased to acknowledge the significant contributions that several friends and allies made to the writing and rewriting of this book. The long-standing Toronto Labour Studies Group, which I joined in 1987, has been a valuable forum for lively intellectual and political debate. Patricia Baker, Ruth Frager, Charlene Ganage, Chris Huxley, Jim Naylor, Mark Rosenfeld, Ian Radforth, Ester Reiter, Robert Storey, Lynne Marks, and, here too, Craig Heron, have heard my tales of Toronto's Italian workers in several instalments over the years. I am grateful to them for their constructive criticisms of various portions of the manuscript. To the group of women who since 1983 have acted as my toughest critics and my most supportive feminist colleagues, I offer my deeply felt thanks. Without the constant encouragement of my friends in the Toronto women's history group, I would have produced an inferior product. For the good-natured way with which they waded through several long and rough drafts, and for the compassionate manner with which they debated the material, I am grateful to former members Marg Hobbs, Joan Sangster, and Kathy Arnup, and to Karen Dubinsky, Janice Newton, Carolyn Strange, Mariana Valverde, Cynthia Wright, and here too, Ruth Frager and Lynne Marks. I also owe a special debt to five women who have offered me intellectual comradeship and friendship: Daphne Read, who read an earlier version of the book and spent many hours discussing my project, Donna Andrew, whose passion for scholarly debate is contagious, Elizabeth Ewen, who offered me a home-away-from-home, the brilliant and warm Brenda Gainer, and my long-time friend Tracy Stewart, who graciously helped me to compile the tables.

My brothers and sister know well both the joys and strains that come with growing up in a large immigrant family. Tragedy has struck us more than once, sometimes threatening to sever the ties that bind us to each other, but we have persevered and even triumphed. No one of us has shown more resiliency than my mother, a peasant woman from the hills of southern Molise, who has given birth to seven children and watched one die, seen another suffer from a debilitating illness, nursed a sick husband, and spent more than three decades punching a time-clock. While she has not understood the choices I have made in my life, I have always felt secure in her utterly selfless love for me. My father, whose death in 1983 was the catalyst that initially prompted me to consider undertaking this study, was one of those uneducated but ambitious immigrants who, having made plenty of sacrifices in his own life, expected great things from his pampered children. Fortunately, he showed fine judgment in making the same demands of his daughters as of his sons. My brother David, whose recurring illness has irrevocably affected my life, has taught me that a person's mental anguish is as painful, and real, as any physical disability. That insight has helped shape my analysis of the immigrant experience.

Ian Radforth has lived with Toronto's postwar Italians for almost as long as I have. Without him this book might never have been completed. During the course of researching, writing, and revising, Ian performed many roles – critic, editor, housekeeper, chauffeur, cook, proofreader, partner, confidant, and friend – and he performed them admirably. For the hours spent listening to me drone on about my work (and obsess about my "brilliant career!"), the hours discussing my research findings, the hours pouring over drafts and redrafts – for these things, and much more, I am deeply grateful. He has helped ease my own sometimes painful transition from student to scholar, and helped me to meet the challenges of academic life by offering his unfailing support, his respect, and a healthy dose of humour. This book, with much love, is for him.

Introduction

Since the mid-nineteenth century, generations of immigrants from Europe, Asia, and elsewhere have entered the growing industrial cities and towns of North America. This extraordinary movement of people has been remarkably wide-ranging, encompassing peasants, artisans, shopkeepers, and industrial workers from diverse homelands. Whatever the time or place, most immigrants have confronted profound social transformations both at home and in the towns and cities to which they moved. Many were residents of agrarian villages and towns deeply affected by changes in economic organization that, in turn, challenged or threatened the customary ways of work and life in their communities. Usually, the immigrants were not destitute; rather, they tended to be yound adult men and women for whom immigration was one among a number of options.

In moving from less developed rural economies to more advanced industrial urban centres, immigrant newcomers to North America have encountered a radically different economy and, often, different social, political, and ideological structures. The immigrant experience has been largely a matter of families – of men, women, and children – reorienting themselves to the new realities of an industrializing or already fully industrialized economy. While compelled to reorder their lives in substantial ways, and often limited in the choices they could make, the immigrants have not been mere pawns in the process. As John Bodnar observes, generations of immigrants have shown a steadfast desire to preserve their pre-migration traditions and values – even while acquiescing in a changing economic order. The immigrant encounter with North American capitalism, he adds, has involved a series of compromises; the immigrants' response has included both an acceptance of the unfamiliar and a resistance to change.[1]

Beyond the impact on the immigrants' own lives, immigration has had a profound affect on the development of Canada and the United States. In the past, as today, immigrants have provided much-needed skills and talents, or they have provided large pools of un-skilled and semi-skilled labour for expanding industries. Large-scale immigration has often kept wages lower than they might otherwise have been, while the arrival of ethnically and racially diverse peoples has often engendered a nativist backlash and created serious chal-lenges for local and national political leaders. A vast array of ethnic neighbourhoods, churches, synogogues, stores, and other institu-tions have become permanent features of the landscape of countless cities and towns. Immigrant leaders of diverse ideological orienta-tions have emerged at various points; while some have enjoyed power within their ethnic colony, others have broken through the barriers, gaining success in the wider society, though often with the support of their old constituencies. Finally, immigrants have made an impact on the history of unions and the labour movement in North America, and on the evolution of both left- and right-wing political movements in both countries.

For more than a century, Italy has been a major exporter of its people. While the emigrants have originated from every region of Italy, the immigrant flows have been dominated by peasants – mostly smallholders and tenant farmers from the hilltop towns and villages of the south. The movement of Italians to North America has been part of a larger diaspora that has seen literally millions of people leave their hometowns for diverse locales around the world. Between 1876 and 1976, more than twenty-six million Italians have migrated, temporarily or permanently, to countries outside Italy. The first major wave of overseas migration occurred at the turn of the century and, by 1915, more than fourteen million people had left home. While many of them were men on seasonal sojourns, there were also entire families that sunk permanent roots outside Italy.

Well before the Great Depression put a temporary stop to immi-gration movements, Italian colonies had sprouted up in places as diverse as the mining regions of Switzerland and Belgium; the cities of Melbourne, Australia, and São Paulo, Brazil; California's orchards and vineyards; and the northern Ontario steel town of Sault Ste Marie. By 1930 the United States, which had been the most popular transatlantic destination among Italians, boasted numerous Little Italies located in a wide range of locales – from New York and Boston on the northeastern seaboard, to Chicago and other centres of the Midwest, and to the Deep South. In these years, Canada was not the preferred North American target of Italian immigrants: the majority of those who did arrive were male migrants who filled seasonal jobs as railway navvies, miners, and construction workers and, after accumulating a small nest egg, they hastily returned home to their families. Nonetheless, small Italian colonies did emerge across the country, the fastest growing of which were in Canada's two largest cities, Montreal and Toronto.[2]

While Toronto's association with immigrants has been enduring, it was not until the era after the Second World War that the volume of non-British immigrants, mostly Europeans, seriously challenged the city's predominantly Anglo-Saxon and Protestant character. Nevertheless, many of the postwar arrivals could point to an earlier generation of compatriots who settled in Toronto before 1930. This was certainly true of the Italians. As John Zucchi has documented, the Little Italies of Toronto began to be formed at the turn of the century, as various groups of townspeople arrived, gravitating to particular neighbourhoods of the city and giving rise to an extensive network of ethnic stores, services, and voluntary organizations. While the majority of Italian men toiled out of doors, their wives laboured inside the house. The colony's elite, composed mostly of labour agents, immigrant bankers, shopkeepers, mutual-aid society officials, and professionals, created an elaborate array of social and political associations. Before the Second World War resulted in the internment of several hundred Italians, and forced others to withdraw from the public arena, Toronto's Italian colony boasted a rich institutional life. Still, the community had never been large and, in 1941, it stood at fewer than 18,000 people. This prewar colony would be engulfed by the postwar Italian immigrants even as it helped to give shape to the new community.[3]

The Italian invasion of postwar Toronto, as some observers dubbed it, was part of a larger diaspora that saw seven million Italians migrate, temporarily or permanently, to countries in Europe, the Americas, and elsewhere during the three decades after the Second World War. Italy's earliest migrants tended to be northerners who headed for other countries in Europe, but they were soon joined, and then outnumbered, by central and southern Italians. Among those who headed for the continent were thousands of young migrant men on temporary work permits. Labelled as the "sweatbacks of Europe," some of them would spend years travelling throughout the continent, performing back-breaking work at low wages and tolerating poor living conditions. Eventually, however, many of them would plant roots in a new country or return home with the financial means to secure a more stable life. A parallel

Map 1 Italy

movement to emerge in the turbulent years immediately after the war saw thousands of southerners, among them impoverished agricultural labourers, migrating to Italy's few southern cities and to the crowded industrial centres of the golden triangle – Milan, Turin, and Genoa. In the poetry of Pier Paolo Pasolini, this mass of unskilled workers is tagged Italy's new "lumpenproletariate," a harsh term that nevertheless captures the harsh realities of urban life for the more disadvantaged rural populations of the postwar Italian south, and of the denigration that such men and women suffered at the hands of employers, landlords, and others. As in the past, however, migration to northern Italy, or Europe, gradually resulted in the permanent and successful resettlement of many Italians.[4]

Overseas migration from Italy, a phenomenon that has often been associated with the movement of the landed peasantry, followed closely on the heels of continental migration. By 1957 transoceanic immigration from Italy had topped one million persons. The United States emerged as a popular target among overseas migrants, but the country's national quota system kept a lid on the annual Italian admissions. Hundreds of thousands of Italians from every region of the country also left for Latin America, especially Argentina, Venezuela, and Brazil, and for Australia. Following a slow start, Canada after 1951 became one of the largest receivers of Italian overseas immigrants, and the country enjoyed one of the lowest repatriation rates among overseas targets. By 1971 more than 460,000 Italians had arrived in Canada, and three out of every five of them came to Ontario, the most popular province of destination (see appendix, tables 1, 2, and 3).

But it was Toronto[5] that emerged as the single most important Canadian target for immigrants from Italy. While the earliest arrivals came in the late 1940s, the first major influx of Italians arrived during the 1950s. Between 1951 and 1961, close to 90,000 Italians, or 40 per cent of the more than 240,000 Italians who entered Canada in these years, settled in Toronto. Another 33,000 Italians came to Toronto by 1965; and by 1971, 38,760 more had come. By 1961 the Italians had replaced the Jews as Toronto's largest non-British ethnic group, and Toronto had replaced Montreal as the home of the largest Italian population in a Canadian city. Since 1941 the Italians had quadrupled their numbers in the City of Toronto to 78,000; another 60,000 lived outside the city limits (see appendix, tables 5, 6, and 7).

The vast majority of Toronto's adult Italians are immigrants who arrived after 1945. Southern Italians, especially former peasants with sufficient means to finance their migration, dominated the Italian flow to postwar Toronto. They were joined by significant numbers of southern artisans and merchants, many of whom similarly possessed the means to resettle themselves across the ocean. Thousands of northern and central Italians, many of them from rural hometowns and occupational backgrounds that resembled those of their southern compatriots, also came. Many northern Italians were landed peasants and artisans who came from the agro-towns and villages of the economically hard-pressed areas of the northeastern regions of Friuli and Veneto, while numerous central Italians came from among the farm and artisanal families of the southern, rural portions of Lazio province (see map 1). Eager to escape the *miseria*[6] (misery) of the postwar south, attracted to urban jobs and the chance for a more secure life, and pulled by the logic of chain migration, tens of thousands of southern Italians flocked to Toronto in the years immediately following the Second World War. Italians who hailed from the southern agricultural regions of Abruzzi, Molise, Basilicata, Campagnia, Puglia, Calabria, and Sicily accounted for nearly 60 per cent of the total Italian immigration to Canada in the period 1951–61.[7]

The two worlds of the immigrants contrasted sharply, at least on the surface. During the twenty years after the Second World War, there were few signs that the nightmare of southern Italy's decline would ever end. After the war, farm incomes continued to tumble, local industrialization failed to materialize, and agro-towns remained unhealthy and overcrowded. In comparison, Toronto looked like a dream. Once the early postwar labour shortages were alleviated, the city's economy boomed. Manufacturing plants rose and expanded, head offices relocated in what was fast becoming Canada's premier financial centre, and expressways and suburbs sprawled outwards. The construction of a subway system began in earnest, and by 1965 several lines were built. Immigration, migration, and natural increase pushed Metro Toronto's population to the 1.8 million mark in 1961. The city could already lay claim to being a cosmopolitan metropolis, having attracted hundreds of thousands of newcomers from Italy, Ukraine, Poland, the Balkans, Hungary, and elsewhere. Despite the continuing influx of British arrivals, the number of Torontonians claiming a British heritage dropped markedly from 73 per cent in 1951 to 59 per cent in 1961.[8]

Like most immigrants, the postwar Italians were predominantly young, healthy men and women eager to secure jobs and prepared to work hard and make sacrifices to secure a better future for themselves and their children. They came to Toronto as members of families; networks of family, kin, and *paesani* (co-villagers) directed them to their destination and acted as buffers against the alienating features of urban industrial life. In the early years, many men preceded their families to Canada, but as wives and children joined them they sparked off the largest movement of sponsored families the country has ever witnessed. This movement was most closely identified with the southerners who dominated the Italian flow into Canada.

On migrating to Toronto, many southern Italians underwent a transition from being peasants in an underdeveloped rural economy to becoming proletarians in an urban industrial economy. For former peasants, and even artisans and shopkeepers who had once laboured in their own homes, the nature of the family economy changed profoundly on their arrival in Toronto. Here, men and women became immigrant wage-earners selling their labour power outside the home, and their lives were deeply influenced by the demands and rhythms of their work and family worlds. External factors also impinged on their lives, since they were forced to adjust and adapt not only to the occupational world, but also to the city's other residents, including the Italian oldtimers who belonged to the prewar community and the Catholic clergy, and to the institutions and social caretakers of the host society.

How best, then, do we understand the immigrant experience of southern Italian peasants who settled in the industrial metropolis of postwar Toronto before 1965? In addressing this central concern, this study combines an internal history of the immigrant group with an external examination of the views and responses of the host society.

To date, little work has been done by historians on the immigrant experience in postwar Canada.[9] The absence of scholarly, historical works in the field is particularly glaring given the enormous volume of the postwar influx. This is especially true for the Italians, who now make up Canada's fourth largest ethnic group. With few exceptions, the current research on the postwar Italians exists in the form of unpublished theses and a few articles.[10] Part of the explanation for this dearth of historical works lies in the reluctance of historians to tackle the postwar era, although in recent years several excellent studies of refugee policies and the immigration security system have appeared.[11]

Social scientists have dominated the writing on postwar immigrants, including Italians, and their works have shed light on the making and implementation of immigration policy, the demographic characteristics of immigrants, and the impact of immigration on the Canadian economy and on issues related to integration and assimilation. Often connected to major research institutes and highly statistical in their approach, sociologists have produced impressive aggregate analyses of occupational ranking, income, and household structure. While their studies reveal much about the stratification of

Canadian society, and the generally disadvantaged position of immigrant groups, they nonetheless draw North American evaluations
of immigrant behaviour. In short, they do not take sufficient account
of the immigrants' own standards of success.[12]

In recent years, there has been a growing awareness among social
historians of the need to know something about the social and cultural background of immigrant workers, and to be sensitive to the
ways in which the demands of family life affected the work careers
of its male and female wage-earners. There has also been a growing
interest in immigrant women, and an emerging awareness of how
ethnicity and gender mediate the class experience. The literature on
Italian immigrants who entered North America before 1930 has figured prominently in this process, and the work of its most prominent
practitioners – among them Rudolph Vecoli, Virginia Yans-Mc-
Laughlin, and Robert Harney – has led to sophisticated theoretical
advances in the field. Together, these historians have argued for a
deeper understanding of the connection between the immigrants'
past and present, for the need to see the family not merely as a static
arrangement but as a flexible institution capable of adjusting to a
new environment, and they have probed the intimate connections
between immigrant culture and radical protest. In keeping with the
aims of the new social history, the new immigration history of the
past two decades has rescued the immigrant from being understood
merely as the object of host society observers or as a victim of economic forces. Immigrants have come to be seen as actors in the
process of transformation in which they were involved.[13]

In seeking to capture the early immigrant experience of Toronto's
postwar Italians, this book addresses four major themes. The first
relates to the issue of class and ethnicity, and concerns, in particular,
the transition southern Italians made from a peasant to an urban
industrial society and the concomitant patterns of continuity and
discontinuity. For two decades now, scholars have been challenging
the once popular model of immigrants as dispossessed and uprooted
peoples who, after being washed up on the shores of North America,
eventually embraced American conformity. The view had been most
forcefully put by Oscar Handlin, whose pioneering work on the
movement of European peasants to American cities emphasized the
break between the close-knit rural society of the Old World and the
alienation of the New; it depicted the initial immigrant experience
as one that involved serious social dislocation and individual an-
omy.[14]

This study joins the work of scholars who reject the view that
North America has historically received Europe's most destitute

classes, or that there is a sharp dichotomy between pre-industrial and industrial societies. In earlier works, there was a tendency to posit a linear model of immigration according to which the immigrants moved inexorably from a pre-modern or traditional rural society to a modern and atomistic society. Such terms, however, are too static to describe the changes that were often occurring both in the sending and the receiving society on the eve of immigration. Recent studies indicate that European immigrants came largely from the middling stratum of the peasantry, and that even when recently dislocated peasants or agricultural labourers joined the emigration stream they possessed significantly more resources than the poorest residents they left behind. Also, their decision to emigrate reflected not so much a desire to sever their connections with the past as a flight from the changes threatening their customary way of earning a livelihood. In their examination of immigrant life, these studies also emphasize the innovative ways in which immigrants met the challenges of their new environment and how they recreated their culture and community life by transplanting the associations, political groups, cultural rituals, and other customs of their homeland.[15]

These themes have been reinforced by the interest among labour historians in working-class culture. Herbert Gutman's seminal work on the waves of American farmers and European peasants who entered the factories of early industrial America, and the patterns of conflict and resistance that accompanied the process, led a generation of social historians to view the phenomenon of proletarianization as immensely complex. The plethora of studies on Italian immigrants reflect an ongoing interest in how the immigrants made use of non-industrial culture and work habits to resist the imposition of industrial discipline and how ethnicity mediated the new class experience.[16]

This study is also concerned with these issues. It argues that the process whereby former peasants were transformed into industrial workers was a complex phenomenon characterized by patterns of continuity and change. These were not uprooted peasants who abandoned their value systems, cultural rituals, and institutions on arrival in Canada. Neither did the Italians preserve their traditional ways completely intact amid the new material circumstances. Instead, the encounter between the immigrants' pre-migration traditions and the realities of the new society gave rise to a pattern of adjustment that incorporated elements from the immigrants' past and present.

Immigration historians have sometimes fallen into the trap of ascribing all immigrant behaviour as necessarily reflecting some set of culturally predetermined norms and customs. But such a perspective is insufficient; in the case of Italians, for example, it fails to account for the differing work and housing patterns that Italian immigrants have exhibited in various locales. Clearly, the opportunities and limitations posed by the local economy, and not solely the immigrants' resources or traditions, deeply affected the choices they made. The behaviour of Toronto's postwar Italian immigrants did not merely represent the cultural transplantation of peasant values, but also the attempts of newly arrived working-class families to survive amid conditions of scarcity. While the immigrants proved resilient in withstanding the new economic demands and cultural pressures, largely by drawing on the traditional supports of family, kin, and paesani, they also found new ways, such as striking and joining unions, to defend their interests. By stressing the dialectical nature of this adjustment process, this study allows for the possibility that the experience of immigration itself might have changed the newcomers in some way.

Ethnicity, or culture, was not the only variable that mediated the class experience for, as feminist historians have observed, men and women experienced their class position in gender-specific ways. While much of this study considers southern Italians as working people with heavy family responsibilities and as immigrants who brought with them certain cherished traditions, it also points to the differing experiences of men and women. Moreover, the cooperative ethos that underscored the Italian family did not mean that gender relations within the household were rooted in egalitarian principles. [17]

Drawing on the work of historians of the family, immigration historians in recent years have contributed much to our understanding of immigrant family life. However, like the family historians whose models and insights they borrowed, immigration scholars have largely ignored the issue of gender relations within the household, depicting the family as an indistinguishable unit, as a nongendered and reified collective that acts in a self-interested manner. At the same time, the lack of a gendered perspective has not precluded most historians from highlighting, and thus prioritizing, the experiences of men. A recognition of the central importance of the family need not lead us to assume that the larger collectively, rather than the members who compose it, should be the primary subject of analysis. In tackling the issue of gender – the book's second major theme – this study, then, provides a separate treatment of the roles and perceptions of the men and women who belonged to the Italian immigrant households of postwar Toronto.

More specifically, however, the study also seeks to redress a major gender imbalance in the historical literature on immigrants by devoting considerable attention to women. The neglect of women in the literature on immigration has characterized the study of Italians in particular. For Canada, this lacuna reflects in part the preoccupation with the sojourning men who dominated the pre-1930 migration phase, though studies of prewar communities have largely ignored women.

The recent flowering of works in women's history, especially the literature on women workers and radicals, has contributed significantly towards rescuing immigrant women, including Italians, from obscurity.[18] Moreover, the appearance in recent years of several valuable historical studies of immigrants in Canada and the United States suggests that the field, though still in its infancy, will continue to be an arena of innovative and lively scholarship.[19] Even with these recent accomplishments, there nevertheless remains a tendency among feminist scholars to perceive of immigrant women as victims. Nowhere is this bias more evident than in contemporary works on postwar immigrant women. By dealing almost exclusively with the structural determinants of immigrant women's oppression – on the racial and gender inequities of the labour force of advanced industrial economies – these studies focus on the ghettoization of immigrant women in dead-end jobs, on their lack of access to language and retraining programs, and on the triple oppression that they, as immigrants, women, and workers, must endure. Few people will doubt that these are formidable obstacles and that they ought to be eliminated, but by isolating only the structural factors we learn little about how the women themselves learned to cope under these conditions and, moreover, how they have given meaning to their lives.[20]

A third theme of this book concerns the relations between immigrants and the host society, and includes both a consideration of the attitudes of Anglo-Canadians towards the Italians and the relations between the immigrants and the caring professionals and volunteers they encountered. For decades, the study of nativism has been most closely identified with John Higham's pioneering work, but many scholars, both in Canada and the United States, have recorded the racist backlash that each new wave of immigration seems to evoke. Many studies have focused on the institutionalized forms of racism to which racial minorites, namely the Chinese, Japanese, and Jews, have been subjected.[21] In tackling the topic of racism, the present study does two things: it examines the views and actions of government officials and recruitment officers involved in the process of Italian immigration, and it explores a variety of host society responses to the newcomers. The research demonstrates that during the years immediatly following the Second World War, policy makers and inspectional officers operated with stereotypical views of Italians, particularly southern Italians. Cultural chauvinism also characterized the early reactions of Torontonians to the large Italian presence in their midst.

The fourth theme of this study concerns the issue of immigrant militancy. Once again we are drawn to works on pre-World War II immigrants, since the literature on postwar immigrants and the labour movement remains scanty. During the 1970s, radical historians had sought an explanation for the relatively weak tradition of labour radicalism in North America in the persistence of ethnic rivalries among workers and in the presence of European sojourners who expressed little interest in union activity.[22] In recent years, however, ethnic and labour historians have uncovered a rich history of immigrant militancy and radicalism. These studies have stressed both the highly politicized culture of radical ethnic leaders and the fact that the brute working conditions of the factory or frontier contributed to the radicalization of many ordinary workers.[23] Earlier stereotypes of Italian immigrants as backward peasants easily duped by employers into strikebreaking have been superseded by more complex portraits of workers who at times engaged in dramatic confrontations at the workplace. Research on the pre-1930 period has revealed plenty of instances of grassroots militancy among Italian immigrants and the leadership roles of radical northern Italian artisans and intellectuals.[24]

In an effort to enhance our understanding of ethnic militancy and of the conflicts that characterized the relations between immigrants and the trade-union movement, this study offers a detailed look at a set of explosive strikes that were spearheaded by Italian immigrant construction workers in Toronto's house and apartment field in 1960 and 1961. These strikes were important for several reasons. Although they resemble other strikes involving immigrant workers in some respects, they also represent a significant contrast in that they involved a group that had made a permanent commitment to Canada and an industry that was dominated by Italian newcomers. The strikes also revealed some of the internal divisions within the Italian community during the early postwar years. Finally, my treatment of these historical events suggests that the men's sense of themselves as hardworking immigrants and as family breadwinners was an important element in the organizing drives.

This book has certain limitations. It focuses on the working-class experience of post-war Italian immigrants, particularly the relations between newly arrived immigrant workers and their families. Little space is devoted to immigrant entrepreneurs or to the community's elite structures. More specifically, the book deals with the early waves of southern Italians who came to Toronto before 1965. To be sure, many Italians continued to arrive during the later years, but a study of the period immediately after the war offers an opportunity to discuss the origins of postwar migration and to examine how this pioneer generation survived the most difficult years of adjustment. After 1965 the composition of Italian immigration changed somewhat as more skilled and more highly educated people began to join the stream. Their migration to Toronto tended to be easier not only because they possessed marketable skills, but also because their predecessors had paved the way. Furthermore, after 1965 the exodus to the suburbs and economic advancement marked a new phase in the experience of many Italians. In these years, other issues also came to the fore, among them the streaming of Italian and other immigrant students into vocational high schools and the health problems associated with an aging construction work force.

With more than 400,000 residents claiming an Italian heritage, Toronto today ranks behind only New York City, São Paulo, and Buenos Aires as the city with the largest Italian population outside of Italy. Moreover, as John Zucchi noted, the 160,000 Italian-born immigrants in Toronto match their counterparts in number in those other cities.[25] The overwhelming majority of Toronto's Italians came during the heyday of postwar immigration; close to three-quarters of them had entered the country by 1965. Unless otherwise specified and with the exception of chapter 1, I have used the term Italian to refer to the Italian-born immigrants who arrived in Canada after 1945. My focus is on the adults; when referring to their children, I consider them the children of immigrants whether they are Italian- or Canadian-born. When data refers to the Italians as an ethnic group (including the total number of Italian-born and Canadian-born Italians), I have indicated this fact in the text, table, or endnote. In recounting the story of the first great wave of southern Italians who arrived in Toronto in these years, this study draws on a wide range of sources, including the government records of the Immigration Branch, the Department of Citizenship and Immigration and the Department of Labour, English- and Italian-language newspapers, the archival collections of immigrant aid societies and social agencies, parish records, census material, and more than seventy interviews.

Such Hardworking People

Southern Italy and
Its Emigrants

[handwritten: HISTORY Italy + reason Emigration]

In 1950 Nino and Laura Donato were landed peasants who found themselves in increasingly difficult financial circumstances. Before the war they had been relatively comfortable, owing some property and holding several long-term leases on land in their home town in southern Calabria. Like most peasants, they had proved eminently resourceful, maintaining themselves by growing their own food and by combining incomes from various sources. During the fruit harvest, Laura and their three children had picked figs and almonds on nearby farms; Nino had found seasonal work on local railway construction projects, and he had responded to Mussolini's offer of jobs in North Africa. Despite the money sent home, depression and war wreaked havoc on his family. Hit with a crop failure in the winter of 1943, Laura was forced to spend much of the family savings on food. By then, Nino was a prisoner of war. In 1946 he returned home to find it ravished by bombs and his family facing mounting debts. Seeing little chance of acquiring more property or otherwise substantially improving their lot, the couple agreed that Nino should emigrate to Canada. By the end of the decade the entire family had successfully resettled in Toronto.[1]

In making the decision to emigrate, the Donatos and others like them were drawing on tradition. For decades emigration had been a popular response to economic problems in Italy. During the period 1880–1929, commonly referred to as the era of mass migration, millions of Italians migrated, temporarily or permanently, to work opportunities in other countries, including Canada and the United States.[2] This flow of Italian emigrants was abruptly cut off by the onset of the Great Depression, which prompted national governments across the world to close their doors to immigrants. The Depression, along with Italy's fascist policies and the Second World

[handwritten: key]

War, ensured that most doors to Italians remained shut for nearly two decades.[3] In the late 1940s, however, the exodus resumed, especially from the Italian south. Why was it so many Italians left their homeland? What had their way of life and culture been like in the long-troubled south?

STRUCTURAL UNDERDEVELOPMENT AND EMIGRATION

The postwar exodus was in part the result of long-standing economic problems in the Italian south that had also given rise to earlier waves of emigration. Far from resolving these problems, depression, fascism, and war had exacerbated them.

Italy's southern problem had deep, historic roots.[4] Unfavourable natural conditions had long placed the south's agricultural sector in a considerably inferior position in relation to the north. Severe swings in climate – arid summers and wet winters – combined with a mountainous terrain and inferior soil, produced extensive erosion and deforestation and precluded farm mechanization, while generations of surface ploughing and intensive cultivation exhausted the soil's limited nutrients. The agricultural sector was characterized by labour-intensive farming that relied on an ox or cow, rudimentary implements, and brute strength. Apart from some wheat, oil, wool, and citrus fruit exports, agricultural production was tied to local markets. So, too, was regional industry, which consisted primarily of handicraft shops and small workplaces employing only a few workers.

The features of southern poverty were evident even before the country's unification in 1870 – semi-feudal land tenure, low productivity, and overcultivation. But the southern problem was also the result of a strategy of underdevelopment adopted by a succession of national governments committed to modernizing agriculture in the north and centre and to promoting northern industrial development. Harsh fiscal policies that transferred northern debts to the south, and industrial policies involving massive deforestation and exploitation of southern mineral resources, reduced southern Italy to a rural hinterland. Southern towns were adversely affected by late-nineteenth-century industrialization, which upset the close interdependence of peasant agriculture and household production on the one hand and domestic, artisanal, and small-scale industry on the other. This dislocation was exacerbated by state policies that permitted northern goods and foreign grain imports to penetrate the south and by decades of political neglect. Huge disparities in government spending on commercial infrastructures and other services intensified the gap between the two regions. In turn, the sharp contrasts between a flourishing north and a stagnant south confirmed the prejudices of northern middle-class observers, who invariably blamed southern poverty on the absence of entrepreneurial talent and the cultural inferiority of the residents.[5]

Eric Wolf defines peasants as "rural cultivators whose surpluses are transferred to a dominant group of rulers."[6] Exhorbitant rents, insecure tenancies, and highly fragmented landholdings continued to reduce the fruits of peasant labour in the postwar Italian south. The weakness of southern agriculture was largely due to the persistence of a land tenure system that had been forged in the post-unification period and to the mentality of the local rural bourgeoisie that had emerged in these years. The massive expropriation and sale of ecclesiastical estates that had occurred at the time had not benefited the land-hungry peasants, who had been unable to compete in the scramble for land. Rather, the process had accelerated the formation of a petty rural borgeoisie (*galantuomini*) interested in amassing property as a means for gaining social status and securing rent revenue.

In the late 1940s, huge tracts of land still remained in the hands of absentee landords. While wealthy landowners ran their large estates as commercial enterprises and relied on wage labour, most of the region's landlords owned middle-sized properties that, in turn, were subdivided into parcels and leased to peasants. In their constant struggle to acquire land, peasant families entered into many unfavourable contract arrangements, simultaneously renting, share-cropping, and perhaps owning several unconnected plots of land. Moreover, while the extensive acreage devoted to commercial farms predominated in more fertile locations, the areas marked by multiple small holdings generally lay in barren mountainous and isolated regions. In Sicily, the system had given birth to a class of ruthless entrepreneurs (*gabelloti*) who oversaw the estates of absentee landlords and charged outrageous rents and surcharges. The mafia had, in turn, evolved out of this class.[7]

The problems created by the sharp competition for land and the limited job opportunities available outside agriculture had been partially alleviated in the period before 1930 by emigration and by immigrant remittances. That emigration did not entirely resolve the situation is evident in the emergence during these years of movements of peasants and agricultural workers and in the peasant riots and socialist movements that flourished briefly before being brutally repressed by the state.[8] Nevertheless, the cash that sojourners earned overseas did enable many families to break out of the cycle of debt and insecurity. The mass exodus of men also created a crisis in labour power, from which agriculture workers, including women, benefited in the form of higher wages. As Bruno Ramirez observes, the profoundly unsettling effect that the newly found independence of peasant-owners had on the landowning class suggests that North American wages had indeed permitted many peasant households to improve their lot. These changes had not been revolutionary; the south's continuing subsistence-oriented agrarian economy and its underdeveloped commercial infrastructure prevented returning peasants (*ritournati*) from doing anything more dramatic than transforming themselves from labourers or tenants into independent smallholders. But given the unfavourable conditions and the class structure of the south, such advancement represented a significant leap for the peasants involved.[9]

As nearly as the 1920s, emigration was already becoming an elusive option, thanks to the restrictionist policies of popular receiving countries such as the United States. (In 1924, Italian entries had been restricted to just 4000.) The rise of fascism in Italy compounded the problem. Beginning in 1926, Mussolini, determined to build an empire, introduced incentives to encourage procreation and imposed severe penalties for birth control and abortion. He later outlawed trade unions, destroyed the peasant leagues, and rescinded the land concessions made to peasants and agricultural workers in the aftermath of the First World War. By 1928 emigration was illegal and restrictions existed on internal migration from rural areas to northern cities. Soon, even had Italians managed to escape, they would not have found any country willing to accept them. International economic collapse and another world war curtailed the emigration of Italians beyond the North African colonies.[10]

Such a long-standing ban on emigration caused a build-up of pressure on the south's ill-developed resources and land. Although migration to the north and the failure of fascist procreation policies alleviated the situation somewhat, even the modest population increases of the 1930s adversely affected productivity and landholding in a region plagued by serious demographic pressures. Conditions were worsened by the absence of immigrant remittances and by the state's failure to create alternative job opportunities in the region. The war wreaked further havoc on southern Italy, which bore the brunt of the wartime damage. Immediately after the war, Italy's economy was in a shambles; internal commerce had broken down, export markets were virtually nonexistent, and postwar unemployment soared. By 1947, 2.5 million Italians were officially unemployed. Millions more were underemployed, especially peasants and workers in the south's agricultural sector. [11]

As early as 1950, the north showed remarkable signs of recovery as foreign aid revived industrial output. Italy's decision to join the European Common Market in 1958 created new markets for northern exports and stimulated the expansion of various industries, including chemicals, iron and steel, electrical goods, and especially automobiles. With the benefit of Marshall Plan dollars and state support, Fiat turned to the mass production of cars in 1953; by 1960 the Turin-based firm contributed almost half of the national income.

Italy's "economic miracle" did not extend to the south, however. Postwar recovery policies benefited industrial centres, nearly all of them in the north. The traditional disequilibrium in the distribution of industry between north and south increased steadily in these years, and southern producers lost valuable export markets to northern interests. In 1951 the region contained 38 per cent of Italy's total population (46 million), but produced only 20 per cent of the national income. The mean per capita income was less than half that of the rest of the nation, and by 1960 it had dropped even further.

Fundamental to the southern problem was the failure of agriculture to keep pace with population growth. After the war, the birth rate began to increase at a pace faster than the national average. Slow economic recovery and a low level of industrial growth meant a continuing shortage of alternative employment opportunities for the growing rural population. Excluding the industrial province of Naples, over 60 per cent of the working population of the south was still engaged in agriculture in 1950. In the poorer, mountainous regions such as Molise, the proportion stood at over 80 per cent. Manufacturing enterprises employed only 8 per cent of working persons, compared with 21 per cent for the north. Apart from a few large industries located in Naples and Bari, southern industry still consisted primarily of artisan shops and small plants producing furniture, clothing, shoes, and foodstuffs for domestic markets. [12]

The results of postwar economic stagnation were obvious – further pulverization of land holdings and the cultivation of vastly inferior land. By 1951 many peasant holdings had been reduced to less than 2 hectares; over half of them were on steep slopes and lacked irrigation. Peasants desperate to increase their holdings resorted to cutting terraces out of rocky mountain sides so poor in soil quality that earth had to be brought to the plots. As a result, the accumulation of more holdings failed to improve agricultural productivity significantly. Low output meant miserable living standards, though peasants were still better off than agricultural labourers (*braccianti*), many of whom could not find work for more than 100 to 150 days of the year.[13]

When southern Italian immigrants in Toronto are asked why they left their home, they invariably respond with one word: "la miseria." It is a word that suggests how poverty can be a brutalizing experience. For the emigrants, it was the fear of descending into the poverty all around them that prompted them to leave. Statistics taken from the 1951 Italian census reveal something of the intensity of the misery experienced in the postwar south. While only 1.5 per cent of northern Italians were found to be living in poverty as defined by government standards, the figure for the south stood at over 25 per cent. Approximately 40 per cent of all southern dwellings lacked sanitary arrangements; over half were without on-site drinking water. Almost 53 per cent of southerners were living in overcrowded conditions, a sharp contrast to the 19 per cent in the north. Nearly 900,000 of them did not occupy proper dwellings; they inhabited the shells of bombed houses and buildings or, as the exiled poet Carlo Levi found (in Matera, Basilicata), dark, dank caves. Depressed conditions were evident in the high numbers of children suffering from malnutrition and dysentry, and in the unhealthfulness of people's diets, consisting of bread and pasta occasionally supplemented with potatoes, a few vegetables, or sardines. Rudimentary health services, low levels of education, and high rates of illiteracy filled out the portrait. In 1951, one-quarter of the southern population over six years of age was illiterate, compared with onesixteenth in the north. In some areas, including parts of Basilicata and Sicily, illiteracy reached staggering proportions, exceeding 40 per cent.[14]

The particular severity of the postwar economic dislocation triggered, among other responses, a wave of peasant uprisings and land occupations throughout Italy, including the south. The Communist party, riding on the crest of popularity because of its role in the resistance movement, lent critical support to the revolts. As the rioting spread, federal authorities in 1950 introduced reforms involving the expropriation of 1.6 million acres of land for distribution to smallholders and landless peasants.[15]

Another tried and true response, and one now openly encouraged by Italian authorities, was emigration. As the barriers to immigration were dismantled throughout Europe and overseas, Italians left in the hundreds of thousands. A majority of the Italians who chose to immigrate to Canada – fully 60 per cent – hailed from the predominantly agricultural regions of the south. As in the case of earlier waves of overseas emigrants, the poorest residents of the Mezzogiorno – landless agricultural labourers and the unemployed poor – did not figure prominently in the exodus. The agricultural labourers who toiled on the large commercial estates of Crotone, Calabria, for instance, could not have raised sufficient funds to pay for ocean travel, which in 1950 stood at approximately 110,000 lira ($180 Canadian). Rather, emigration served to offset the dwindling opportunities of young, comparatively better-off peasant families like Nino and Laura Donato's. Peasants and, to a lesser extent, rural artisans and shopkeepers from regions characterized by extensive landholding arrangements were most likely to emigrate. Whether small landholders, tenant farmers, sharecroppers, or artisans, they saw emigration as a way of avoiding what appeared to be an inevitable descent into poverty and as a means of obtaining a better standard of living elsewhere.[16]

SOCIAL BACKGROUND

The peasants who arrived in postwar Toronto brought with them values and habits forged in the rural peasant economy of southern Italy. They did not come from a background of isolated, closed villages, nor were they completely self-sufficient farmers isolated from a market economy and ignorant of the world beyond their town. Typically, they resided in agro-towns (*paese*) perched on a hilltop or nestled into a mountain-side. Daily, the town's peasants and agricultural labourers walked long distances to the scattered fields and the commercial estates below. In some cases, people also resided in houses scattered outside the town, thereby creating a less distinct break between urban centre and countryside. The towns themselves consisted of clusters of simple houses that formed neighbourhoods surrounding a *piazza* at the town centre, where the church, municipal offices, a few shops, a doctor's or midwife's office, and a café were to be found.

With populations that numbered in the thousands, even tens of thousands, many southern towns had complex social structures and class divisions separating the gentry, landowners' managers and middlemen, professionals and civil servants, and artisans, peasants, workers, and the poor. They maintained a few retail services – a blacksmith, a tailor or seamstress shop – and a train station. Artisan shops employed only one or two apprentices. Some towns boasted slightly larger workplaces, such as a sawmill or food-processing

plant, which seasonally employed small groups of industrial workers. Mining towns had moderately sized establishments, while textile mills hired significant numbers of women as well as men.[17]

Peasants were also part of a larger market economy; they had
economic connections to the surrounding regions and urban centres,
where they made exchanges. Families regularly sold small surpluses
of wheat, eggs, and vegetables to co-villagers. Those people from
hamlets too small to sustain artisans or retail activity had access to
larger urban centres. Major trade fairs drew people from surrounding towns; farmers came to sell crops and purchase tools, artisans
to peddle their wares, and gypsies to tell fortunes. Economic ties to
neighbouring towns were bolstered by social connections. Marriages
between families from different towns were common, and many
peasants had kinfolk residing in several villages in their area. Given
the prevailing pattern of patrilocal residence, such links usually operated through the woman and her family. Entire families periodically travelled long distances to attend religious feasts and
pilgrimages. While men were more likely to travel unescorted to
neighboring towns, women went on group tours to historic and
religious sites.[18]

The very poverty of the south, which made total reliance on sub-
sistence farming impossible for peasants, compelled families to pursue strategies directed at earning supplementary incomes; family
members, usually men, would embark on temporary sojourns of
varying lengths and distances. Hiring themselves out as day labourers to the managers of commercial farms or to prosperous peasants, many men found seasonal work in the local or regional
economy. Others took jobs in seasonal logging operations, on public
works projects, or in small factories located in neighbouring towns.
During the sowing or harvest periods, some migrated to more distant
regions in search of cheap share-tenant contracts. Still others sought
jobs in agriculture, railway construction, and in the building trades
in Europe or overseas.

Patterns of sojourning were so common among peasant families
that scholars have described them as members of a "part-culture,"
belonging simultaneously to their village and to a host of outside
regions to which they migrated as wage earners. Many of Toronto's
immigrants came from families in which fathers or grandfathers had
once been sojourners in Europe, North America, or Italy's North
African colonies. Others had kin who had settled in the United States
or Canada before the Second World War.[19]

Southern peasants subscribed to a family culture of work. Though
scholars debate definitions of nuclear and extended family, they

agree that the peasant household was the primary form of economic and social organization. The peasant household was the site of production, and each family relied on the maximum labour power of every member of that household. In turn, each person was expected to sacrifice individual needs and aspirations and contribute to the family's survival. Parents trained children at an early age to work on the farm. Given the scattered nature of holdings, the family economy did not operate in one space but involved members' working several plots located at some distance from each other. Any wages earned by members doing outside work belonged to the family.[20]

The literature on southern peasants is marred by efforts on the part of scholars to apply modernization theory, thereby depicting peasants either as members of a traditional self-sufficient society or as individualists imbued with essentially modern notions of capitalist accumulation.[21] This dichotomy fails to take into account that peasant economies rarely demonstrated absolute levels of self-sufficiency and that peasants historically participated in the market economy, if only on a local scale and to a limited extent. Italy's postwar peasants remained small-scale agricultural producers who relied on simple tools and worked the land as a family productive unit. Their main aim, though they could not always meet it, was to achieve some level of self-sufficiency. They possessed the means of production, for even if they did not own the land they managed it. Peasants were not simply petty capitalists: their primary commitment was to secure for the needs of the family rather than to make a profit.[22]

As peasants, they found themselves in an exploitative relationship vis-à-vis absentee landowners, who now came mainly from an urban bourgeoisie. Many peasant families were indebted to more than one landowner. To each they owed rent or a portion of their produce, including cash crops such as olives and almonds. Though peasants usually lacked the resources to invest much money in farm improvements, such contracts nevertheless benefited absentee landowners by shifting the risks involved in production to the peasantry.[23]

The rhythm of work and leisure in southern society was largely determined by the agricultural cycles of the region. The heavy demands of spring planting and of autumn fruit and grain harvesting and preserving contrasted sharply with the winter slack period.[24] The work rhythms of local artisans and small producers were similarly shaped by seasonal demands. During downswings in the trade, apprentices and journeymen who belonged to peasant families would return home to work on the family farm.

Artisans in southern towns were mainly tailors or seamstresses, barbers, shoemakers, carpenters, and bricklayers. Many ran small family shops. The low level of demand and stiff competition from mass-produced goods from outside the region meant that artisans were typically underemployed. They were compelled to take on work that undercut their craft pride, such as repairing rather than making shoes. Some artisans were the descendants of long-standing artisan families and enjoyed more prestige than the neighbouring peasants. In the past, many of these craftspeople had joined radical movements. After the Second World War, the south's "red towns," such as Sambucca, Sicily, reflected in part the ongoing importance of this small but influential class. Nevertheless, in most towns such artisans represented a tiny minority of the population, and the class distinctions between artisans and peasants were blurred by the presence of the sons and daughters of better-off peasants who apprenticed with a master tailor, shoemaker, or seamstress. Many of these apprentices remained as part-time or seasonal members of the work force of their own peasant families and they did not belong to trade unions. They were also more likely to emigrate than the children of artisanal families.[25]

In the southern Italian town, the peasant household was the focus of economic production and social relations. Individual households usually consisted of a nuclear family – a married couple and children – though in some cases a family might also support elderly parents. Here, mutual obligation between individuals was most clearly defined. The nuclear family was the fundamental social institution. Outside the household, varying degrees of intimacy and social contact marked relations between married children and their parents, and among married siblings. In some towns, entire neighbourhoods might consist of related families; in other places, families might be dispersed in different neighbourhoods or neighbouring towns. Married couples usually lived near the husband's family, which, typically, had given the couple a house and some land.

Theoretically, parents stopped making demands on their children once they were married, though scholars have documented many cases where married daughters or sons offered financial help or emotional support to ailing parents. Intimacy was often linked to the proximity of parents to married children, and cases have been cited where fathers intervened to protect a daughter against an abusive husband or, conversely, to scold a "disobedient" daughter. Married brothers and sisters also had varying degrees of involvement. Where patrilocal residence traditions predominated, brothers might be in frequent contact with each other after marriage, while sisters, scattered across various towns, might see much less of each other. In other cases, siblings might have little to do with each other, though they could still be called on for help at harvest-time or in the event of a problem.[26]

Beyond the privileged sphere of the close family were the members of the extended *familiari* – cousins, aunts, uncles, and in-laws. Relations among kin were more limited, yet they were also bound by mutual rights and reciprocal obligations, when such possibilities did not interfere with the priorities of the nuclear family. In times of crisis, households expected and usually received help from relatives. At harvest-time, male kin might help with field duties. Women would prepare food and take care of housecleaning tasks when a family member became ill. Status was also conferred to *i compari*, non-relatives who gained admittance to the family circle through the ritual kinship of godparenthood (*comparaggio*). Many people called on their childhood friends or neighbours to act as their child's godparents or confirmation sponsors.[27]

Earlier studies of southern towns either ignored or downplayed the importance of friendships to peasants. This was especially true of Edward Banfield, who developed the concept of southern peasants as "amoral familists." He argued that peasants acted only to maximize the material, short-run advantage of the nuclear family and that they viewed all other relationships, including those with more distant kin, with deep suspicion and distrust. They extended assistance to others only because they expected the favour to be returned at a later date. Recent studies have challenged these prevailing stereotypes. Without denying competition and conflict within villages, they show that peasants relied on the help of harvest work parties consisting of neighbours and friends as well as relatives, and that women valued the friendships they forged with female neighbours. While families might gossip about others' misfortunes, they also shared a spirit of loyalty to their native village and its residents (*campanilismo*).[28]

Did a family culture of work exclude participation in wider institutions? In fact, mutual-benefit societies (*mutuo soccorso*) proliferated throughout southern Italy after 1870 as a response to the economic changes unsettling village life. Rather than directly challenging the family, these societies, composed of associations of artisans, peasants, or braccianti, drew family members and neighbours into wider exchanges of mutual assistance. The associations of agricultural workers, such as the Sicilian *fasci*, and peasant leagues resembled labour unions, challenging landlords who ignored traditional grazing privileges and defending members' interests in contract and tax disputes. Mutual benefit clubs provided sick and death benefits for their members; they set up local savings and credit banks, producer cooperatives, and reading classes. Women were not members but they could receive benefits, and some joined demonstrations.[29]

For Toronto's postwar Italians, however, the experience with collective organization had been pre-empted by fascist policies that destroyed older voluntary associations. Although a significant minority hailed from regions such as southwestern Sicily, which was marked by rich traditions of protest, the majority came from rural areas where neither labour unions nor socialism or communism had enjoyed widespread support before the onset of fascism. While organized workers suffered under fascist reversals of working-class gains, such as the eight-hour factory day and checks on eviction and rack-renting in the countryside, state fasci usurped the role filled by the rural mutuo soccorso. They controlled farm and credit supplies as well as large tracts of land that were leased out in small parcels to members. Apart from those who joined outlawed organizations, most people's contact with genuine, non-fascist voluntary organizations did not extend beyond the committees that organized the town's religious feasts. This created a situation in which political patronage rather than the collective strategies of self-help groups became the most effective tool for improving one's lot.[30]

Scholars such as Banfield have overplayed the parochialism of southern peasants, seeing it as synonomous with backwardness. A sense of loyalty to the village, campanilismo, was however, an important aspect of town life. It took various forms, including local folklore and special celebrations commemorating the history of a town's patron stains. It was expressed in the social activity of the piazza, where chaperoned couples, families, and men gathered for an evening stroll or drink and after mass on Sundays. It also fed rivalries between neighbouring towns and encouraged the practice of applying humorous derogatory stereotypes to describe the villagers of another town. Anthropologist Rudolph Bell found that the residents of a Sicilian town took much delight in referring to those of five surrounding towns as, respectively, "struck by evil spirits," "mentally backward," "cuckolded husbands," "perfumed," and "gangsters." Interviews with immigrants in Toronto revealed similar stereotypes, among them "lazy fools" and "witches." A Calabrian woman recalled how as a girl she had been warned against the oversexed men who were said to live in a neighbouring town.[31]

Though the relations between peasants and landowners were the central class relationship, southern society was actually stratified along many lines. In a society in which status continued to be rooted in land ownership, even small gradations of wealth took on special meaning. Landowning peasants who possessed sufficient savings to offer loans to poorer tenant farmers and sharecroppers enjoyed an enhanced social status. One such man, Nicola Ceresa, recalled that among his network of kin and neighbours he was considered to be "the man with the money." While peasants were most acutely conscious of their disadvantaged position in relation to absentee landlords and to the local elite, they were equally keen to distinguish themselves from landless labourers and the poor. In interviews, immigrants described their family in these terms, saying that though they had little, they had been far better off than the braccianti and unemployed poor who lived in their village. They recalled how they gave small scraps of food to women who came begging, or how, on occasion, they hired an unemployed man to work a few weeks on the farm in exchange for food. One woman told how she would give the water in which she had boiled her beans to women who, though having recently given birth, were too malnourished to produce sufficient milk for their babies.[32]

As scholars have noted, a central feature of life in rural Italy was the system of patron-client relations or *clientelismo* that characterized the interactions between the popular classes and the middle class. As a people who, historically, have been victimized by unfavourable government policies, ruthless absentee landlords, galantuomini, and sundry intermediaries, southern Italian peasants understandably harboured a resentment and distrust of local government officials, many of them also landlords, and professional elites. Yet their lack of formal education and the heavily bureaucratized nature of Italian government meant that in almost all their dealings with government they found themselves at the mercy of local dignitaries – civil servants, notaries, the town mayor or village doctor, and perhaps even the teacher or cleric. Because they could not afford to alienate important political intermediaries who might one day have to help them cut through bureaucratic tape, they invariably showered them with deferential respect.[33] Canadian officials, though condescending in their tone, captured the essence of this class relationship. A 1964 memorandum on relations between local dignitaries acting as travel agents and potential emigrant clients stated: "the poor uneducated peasant gets exploited; he knows it and willingly does it with the belief that the 'favour' which he is doing the person rendering him a service will bring upon him some benefit, first of all because the person is 'important,' can read and is educated therefore knows how to 'get things done' and secondly, one never knows, 'he could have influence.' Of course the person rendering the service makes free with his important connections, his knowledge and assurances that he can fix everything."[34]

In their recollections of the past, some of the immigrants who settled in Toronto after 1945 remembered the resentment they and their kin and neighbours had felt towards the local *prominenti* (middle-class notables). As one man remarked: "Those few rich people went around calling all the shots, did what they liked. Their purpose was to keep the town ignorant, in slavery. The mayor was one of them too, a landowner."[35] Such resentment harked back several centuries, when mighty landlords exercised their right to recruit private armies from their estates and otherwise flaunted the power they enjoyed over the peasantry. But while the old aristocrats had long been replaced by the land-owning urban bourgeoisie and while legal reforms had outlawed other practices, peasant men and women could nevertheless remember the exactions paid to land-owners, or their agents, and tax collectors. Such payments made it difficult for even the most resourceful peasant families to enjoy fully the fruits of their labour. Moreover, the age-old view that people of influence pulled the strings of government was, for many, confirmed in the fascist era when loyal fascists were appointed to previously elected positions of mayor and town councillor. Although appointments generally went to those who were already part of the town's elite, fascism nevertheless destroyed any pretext to democratic traditions. Even for labouring jobs, candidates had had to proclaim their loyalty before a local dignitary would give them a recommendation. It confirmed the view that access to prominenti was an indispensible tool.[36]

Village loyalties and clientelismo also informed southern Catholicism, a complex amalgam of church dogma and pagan rituals steeped in an ancient belief in the efficacy of magic and devotions to the saints.[37] It was a folk religion, writes Rudolph Vecoli, a fusion of pre-Christian and Christian beliefs, of animism, polytheism, and sorcery with the Holy Sacraments. It was evoked by a sense of awe, fear, and reverence for the supernatural, and some of its practices did not conform to formal church doctrine. Nevertheless, clerics had long accepted such rituals as an integral aspect of the people's culture. While acknowledging the religious superiority of the church, the popular classes of southern Italy, including the peasantry, did not necessarily feel a special affinity for the official church as an institution – not surprising, perhaps, given its historical ties to Italy's landowning classes. Naturally, local clerics were viewed by all as an integral part of the community, yet there was a social distance between the priest and the common folk. Popular jokes and folksongs that poked fun at the supposed sexual philandering of village priests are an indication of that social distance, as is the casual attitude that some adopted towards regular attendance at mass.

As in the case of other rural, peasant-based European societies, southern Italian peasants generally perceived of God as a remote authority figure, who, though just, generally dispensed only punishment. By contrast, they viewed the local saints as real personages who could act as a person's patron before God, using influence to obtain benefits for devotees. Each village had its own set of madonnas, saints, and witches; every event was attributed to either the benevolence or the malevolence of these supernatural beings. Individuals and families bargained shrewdly with them, making promises and sacrifices, and offering praise and gifts, such as human hair, in exchange for a favour. If the saint failed to grant the request, its statue was likely to be cast out. A Sicilian peasant interviewed by anthropologist Charlotte Chapman in 1928 summed up the patron-client relations central to this religious system:

Of course all benefits come from God, but the saints are the friends of God, and they can help us. It is as if I should go to see the American Consul in Palermo to ask him a favour. I give my name to the young lady at the door, and she tells me to wait ... At noon she tells me that the Signor Consul has gone for lunch and will be back at two-thirty. I go back in the afternoon, and maybe five o'clock comes, and she tells me that the Signor Consul is going home now and that I should come back in the morning. No one knows how long it will be before I can see him. If, on the other hand, I go carrying a note from you, Signorina, who are a friend of the Consul, what happens? She takes the note to the Consul, and in two minutes the door opens. "Come in Signor Carminu! What can I do for you?" It's the same with God. If we pray to the saints and get their favour, they can more easily obtain grace from God than we can. It is only logical.[38]

The annual celebrations held in honour of a town's patron saint(s) marked the high point of social life in the hometown. They included a special mass, elaborate processions through the town, brass bands, festive meals, and fireworks. Rituals reflected Italians' perceptions of saints in human terms and their preoccupation with outward signs of respectability. Because they believed it admirable to *fare a bella figura* (to cut a fine figure), they honoured their saint by draping its statue in fine robes and jewels. In some places, such as Rocella Ionica, Calabria, a coastal town, the annual feast was accompanied by a week-long fair. On the final Sunday, the procession began at dusk after the retrieval of the statue, which had been carefully put

out to sea in commemoration of its discovery near the coast generations earlier. Having spent the day visiting and eating with kinfolk and neighbours, the townfolk accompanied the procession and
attended the outdoor mass. At night the fireworks began, and people
visited until dawn.[39]

Not all peasants were cynical about the church, however, and
many, particularly women, regularly attended Sunday mass. Even
so, their piety did not preclude their subscribing to beliefs that the
church did not officially condone. One such belief was *mal'occhio* –
the evil eye. It was an impersonal force that brought misfortune to
whomever it struck. Allowing for local variations, most agreed that
the evil eye could strike a victim at any time, producing consequences that ranged from severe stomach cramps to crop failure and
death. Social action of any kind might unleash it. It might occur at
the prompting of a rival, who either knowingly or unwittingly
caused an evil spell to be cast by thinking ill thoughts of the intended
victim. Certain persons or locations in the village might be considered to be foci of the force and were thus avoided. Peasants believed
also that the lavish praise of a neighbour might trigger mal'occhio
because the giver of the praise was not genuine or the subject not
wholly worthy of it.[40]

To rid themselves of the curse, peasants turned to midwives, witch
doctors, and female kin. In order to break the spell, healers resorted
to various amulets, potions, and magical rites. As a means of coping
with the supernatural, explains Vecoli, these practices carried as
much weight as the sacraments. Despite the vociferous protests of
church leaders, peasants did not attempt to reconcile these two sides
of their religion. Rather, they invoked religious symbols and rituals
to rid victims of evil spirits, combining potions with prayers and
placing a statue of the Virgin Mary in their homes next to a red horn,
a pagan symbol meant to keep the evil spirits at bay. Baptism was
as much a ceremony that helped to ward off evil spirits from an
unsuspecting infant as the cleansing of the infant's soul. Such beliefs
would continue to be a distinguishing feature of the culture of Toronto's Italian immigrants.

Many of Toronto's Italians had lived through the fascist era and
the war as young adults, and the hardships they endured helped
convince them to leave. Notwithstanding the important pockets of
resistance in the south, many peasants, including those who later
settled in Toronto, considered Mussolini a potentially great states-
men whose fatal error had been to pair up with Hitler. Many of
them had also benefited from the state's social welfare policies. By
the same token, they were not strongly opposed to the postwar

outbreak of peasant protests because they identified with the aspirations of those involved.[41]

In terms of actual votes, however, the postwar south supported
the Christian Democrats (DC), the Catholic liberal party. Sydney
Tarrow argues that whereas in the north, liberation largely restored
the organized parties that predated fascism, the fall of fascism in
the south gave the church and its political ally, the DC, a political
importance they had previously lacked. In the north and centre,
early postwar elections indicated growing support for Italy's historic
left parties despite the long exile between 1921 and 1946. Of great
concern to Canada and her Western allies was the fact that the
Communists and their Socialist allies, despite their expulsion from
Italy's governing coalition in 1947, captured more than eight million
votes in the first "free" elections of 1948. Most of this support came
from central and northern Italy. By contrast, the south registered a
moderate rise on the left and far greater support for the Catholic
and far-right parties. In 1946, southern voters showed their con-
servatism by solidly backing the restoration of the monarchy, while
the rest of the country called for a republican democracy. Two years
later, southerners supported Alcide De Gasperi, and in 1958 they
gave the DC a solid majority, with over 44 per cent of the popular
vote.[42]

Despite these overall patterns, electoral results within southern
towns reflected the prevailing personalism and localism of southern
politics. In most towns, local notables, including the clergy, helped
to secure DC victories. But many towns also displayed a complex
pattern of political allegiances. Dramatic voting shifts within one
town were common, often leading to a situation in which Christian
Democrats, Communists, and Socialists practically rotated their positions on town council. These shifts reflected the continuing importance of clientele politics among southerners; electoral results
were strongly linked to the personal prestige of local leaders and to
the amount of patronage given to local residents.[43] In short, southern Italy had its own distinctive brand of politics, and, like its culture,
work traditions, and family life, they were rooted in the region's
peasant society.

CHAPTER TWO

Getting There

The extensive migration that linked villages and towns in Italy to postwar Toronto was based on networks of family and kinship. Angela and Giuseppe Izzo, for example, young peasants from southern Molise, were eager to make their futures in Canada because of their poor prospects at home. They turned for help to relatives in the United States. In the fall of 1950 Giuseppe's uncle travelled to Montreal and hired a travel agent to arrange for his nephew's arrival in Canada. Taking advantage of Canada's new admission requirements permitting the entry of individuals sponsored by employers, the agent located a Quebec farmer who recruited Giuseppe as a farm worker. Soon after arriving at his post, however, Giuseppe was laid off and he joined the growing stream of Italian men entering Toronto's construction trades. One year later, he applied for the admission of his wife and two sons under Canada's family sponsorship program. They came in 1953. Over the next few years, the couple sponsored twenty relatives. As each of the families, in turn, sponsored more kin, the Izzos were ultimately responsible for the arrival of more than forty Italians, all of whom hailed from the same cluster of towns in the southern Molisan province of Campobasso.[1]

As government officials at the time remarked with begrudging admiration but increasingly with considerable anxiety, Italians were immigrants *par excellence*, readily pursuing every available option for gaining entry into Canada. Italians on either side of the Atlantic kept each other informed of changes in Canadian policy and adjusted their strategies accordingly. Many candidates pursued several options before finally gaining their exit visas for Canada. Particularly during the early postwar years, before the movement of sponsored immigration got fully underway, Italians entered the country through one of several routes. Canadian immigration policy was largely linked to work opportunities available to Italian men, and it ascribed women an inferior status as the legal dependants of their husbands or fathers. Thus, most of the early postwar arrivals were men, many of whom preceded their families to Canada. Large numbers came to Toronto, though many did so via a circuitous route, often beginning their stay in Canada as contract workers in the country's agricultural or resource regions. The growing Little Italies of Toronto acted as a magnet drawing still more kin and paesani to the city. As the process of Italian migration gained enormous momentum, however, the Canadian authorities increasingly sought ways to manipulate the volume and character of the Italian flow.

Few immigration historians have explored in detail the relations between immigrants and immigration policy. Written largely by immigration historians influenced by the new social history, working-class history, and family history, many of the recent valuable studies documenting the lives of immigrants who entered the rising industrial cities of the United States before 1930 ignore policy. At the other end of the spectrum, studies of Canada's postwar immigrants are dominated by policy experts, economists, and scholars of mobility, who pay only perfunctory attention to the actual experiences of the immigrant generation.[2] Yet an analysis that explores the intersection between policy making and its implementation, on the one hand, and the immigrant perspective, on the other, can yield fruitful results. Such a view allows for the possibility that the immigrants themselves influenced the formulation or, more likely, the actual implementation of immigration policy.

OPENING THE DOOR TO ITALY

In the postwar period, Canada initially hesitated to admit large numbers of Italians. Several factors account for this policy, not least of them the decided lack of enthusiasm for immigration that prevailed throughout Canada immediately following the war. Fearful that recession might follow wartime prosperity, federal officials were reluctant to return to the more open-door policy of the pre-Depression era. They busied themselves with pressing reconstruction matters, such as the reestablishment of veterans. Quebec premier Maurice Duplessis's adoption of an anti-immigration platform reflected the views of many Quebeckers, while English Canadians were almost as reticent. A Gallup Poll released in April 1946 showed that 61 per cent of Canadians and 71 per cent of Quebeckers opposed mass immigration from Europe. Some 45 per cent of Canadians were even hostile to British immigration; in Quebec 73 per cent were opposed. When asked who they most wanted to keep out – the subject of another poll – most said the Japanese and Jews, though 25 per cent said the Italians.[3]

At the time, Italy was still an enemy state. Moreover, there were long-standing prejudices regarding Italians. As southern Europeans, Italians had long been considered far less desirable than the British, white Americans, and northwestern Europeans who traditionally were Canada's preferred immigrants. Nevertheless, many non-preferred immigrants, such as Italians, had gained entry into Canada before the Depression precisely because they performed critical but unappealing work, such as laying track across remote regions or building the infrastructure of growing urban centres. Ottawa had even turned a blind eye to companies that recruited Italians for industrial jobs, thus violating the official immigration policy designed to settle the rural west. With the coming of the Depression in 1930, however, Canada had firmly closed the door to Italian immigration.[4]

After the Second World War, nativist opposition to Italians, based on assumptions equating hot climates with darker populations and cultural backwardness, resurfaced. Anticipating the large postwar influx of immigrants, an Anglican church report applauded the sturdy character and assimilability of northern Europeans and portrayed them as far more adaptable to Canada's "northern latitudes" and political institutions than were the Italians. The latter were depicted as "amenable to the fallacies of dictatorship," "less versed" in democratic traditions, and thus better suited for the hot climate and "fragile" political structures of Latin American nations. Calling Canada "a country suitable for white settlement," the report advised restricting entry "to those people who have the 'Anglo-Saxon idea' if not the Anglo-Saxon blood."[5]

Echoing Italy's traditional prejudices, Canadians showed a particular antipathy towards southern Italians. Such views were steeped in centuries-old racialist assumptions about the "Germanic" roots of northern Italians and the Mediterranean customs of the southerners. Federal officials commented repeatedly on the backwardness of southerners and worried they might outnumber the "more industrious" northerners. "The Italian South peasant," wrote Laval Fortier, commissioner for overseas immigration, "is not the type we are looking for in Canada. His standard of living, his way of life, even his civilization seem so different that I doubt if he could ever become an asset to our country." Others, already steeped in the politics of the emerging Cold War, developed new prejudices. While the British

Dominions Emigration Society agreed that northern Italians were culturally superior to the southerners, its manager warned Ottawa that since "communism is so widespread in the Northern cities … great care in selection must be exercised."[6]

Certain interested parties, including the Italian government, early on pressed Ottawa to admit Italians. If Canada accepted numerous Italians, came the pleas from Italian officials, Italy would be relieved of her overcrowded population and Canada would obtain large numbers of "zealous workers and worthy citizens." Noting that labour shortages were already being felt at home, domestic employers such as the Canadian Manufacturers' Association suggested recruiting "husky unmarried men" from Italy to "fill the gap." Other companies included the Canadian National Railways, the Canadian Pacific Railway, and the R.F. Welch Company, a contracting firm founded in 1905 by Vincenzo and Giovanni Veltri, Calabrian immigrants who became *padroni* agents for the railways. By 1945 Giovanni, his brother now dead, had returned to Consenza, and his eldest son, Raffaele, ran the firm's operations in Port Arthur (Thunder Bay).[7] Italians on both sides of the ocean exerted their own forms of pressure. As hundreds of discharged Italian soldiers who had served the Allied forces in the last stages of the war applied to emigrate to Canada with their families, Italian-Canadian groups lobbied Ottawa on the men's behalf. They had the help of a few politicians from ethnic ridings, including Toronto Liberals Lawrence Sky (Trinity) and David Croll (Spadina), and Douglas Fisher, CCF member for Port Arthur.[8]

When rejecting the early requests, officials usually cited Italy's enemy alien status, but other reasons were also given. Officials claimed that "a good many" of the Italian soldiers seeking entry were now communists. In response to employers willing to recruit Italian workers, officials pointed to the current prohibitions on contract labour, though in fact they had already introduced special exemptions for groups of British tradesmen.[9] As one official succinctly put it, Canadians "are not now anxious to receive an influx of Italians whom they do not regard as the most desirable type of immigrant."[10]

Within a short span of time, however, the situation changed markedly. Canada's shift towards a more open-door immigration policy coincided with the mobilization of a disparate array of immigration forces in the country. Although their political views and motives differed substantially, these groups agreed that Canada's current prosperity could not be maintained unless acute labour shortages in leading industries such as mining and agriculture were filled. Outspoken advocates of an ethnically selective, open-door immigration cluded employers keen to increase the labour supply and consumer demand. Pro-refugee groups desperate to find relatives displaced by the war and prominent liberals such as Senator Cairine Wilson joined the rising chorus of pro-immigration voices. Canada, they argued, could provide opportunities for people, and the country was morally obliged to accept wartorn Europe's surplus population. Together, these voices defeated the dissenting views of organized labour, fearful that immigration would mean a loss of jobs, and of nationalists opposed to disrupting the country's racial make-up.[11]

"Immigration policy," Robert Harney wrote, "has always reflected a dialectic between the desired population increase and the impact of immigration on Canadian ways or on the racial and ethnocultural composition of the country." Historically, the central aim of Canada's immigration policy has been national growth through the importation of foreign labour and talent. The policy of using immigrants as part of a strategy of national development has fostered among Canadian authorities a continuing preoccupation with the country's "absorptive capacity." It has also encouraged the view that the migration phenomenon exists to serve the host country, not the migrants, and that the national sources and character of immigration can and should be manipulated. In his oft-quoted 1947 statement, Prime Minister Mackenzie King not only advised that the volume of postwar immigration be related to Canada's absorptive capacity but insisted that Canadians "do not wish to make a fundamental alteration in the character of their population through mass immigration." The list of preferred immigrants – which included American, British, French, Dutch, Swiss, German, and Scandinavian peoples – had remained consistent for decades. It was rooted in the basic premise that northern Europeans had a greater proclivity to orderly society and free parliamentary institutions, or at least shared the same complexion, mores, and religion as English Canadians, and thus were the most easily assimilated.[12]

As initial fears about the possibility of postwar recession gave way to growing optimism regarding the economy, and in an effort to attract immigrants to fill a variety of jobs in the country's expanding economy, King's Liberal government moved cautiously to open the doors to Europeans. In May 1946 the classes of admissable immigrants were still restricted (by the draconian 1930 order-in-council) to British subjects, US citizens, the spouse, unmarried children under eighteen or fiancé(e)s of legal residents of Canada, and "agriculturalists" with sufficient means to farm in Canada. Over the next year, the admission requirements were liberalized. In November 1946 cab-

inet agreed on emergency measures to admit refugees with Canadian sponsors. In light of the urgent need for labour in domestic industry, in January 1947 the category of admissible occupational classes was enlarged to include persons experienced in mining, farming, or logging and entering Canada to engage in assured employment. In April all prohibitions on contract labour were dropped. By May the range of close relatives eligible for sponsorship had been expanded. [13]

None of these changes were aimed at dismantling Canada's ethnic preference ladder. The priority which Canadian officials had always placed on attracting British and American settlers, for example, was reflected in the minimal requirements regarding their admission. British subjects and citizens of the United States could gain entry as long as they were healthy and could support themselves until employed. Largely as a symbolic gesture, this privilege was also extended to French nationals. At the other end of the spectrum, government officials, bowing to the anti-Asian voices in western Canada and elsewhere, continued to impose strict quotas on the admission of immigrants from Asia and the Far East.

In the aftermath of the war, there were available pools of prospective European immigrants who could fill Canada's labour needs while at the same time not seriously antagonize the nativist constituencies in Canada. International and pro-refugee pressures, as well as the demands of the domestic economy, led Ottawa to turn first to the displaced persons' camps for their supplies of immigrant workers. Among these refugees, Canadian immigration teams selected men to fill the thousands of vacancies in agriculture and primary industry. Women were recruited for work as domestics and as hospital workers. The first recruits were a group of 4000 Polish war veterans, former allies refusing repatriation to Soviet-occupied Poland. They signed contracts that required them to work as farm labourers, mostly within the sugar-beet industry, for two years before they could enter the general labour market. These terms of admission led to a period of what amounted to virtual indenture in those industries suffering acute labour shortages. The subsequent recruitment of larger numbers of displaced persons was modelled on the Polish "bulk movement," with the term of the contract reduced to one year. By 1952 over 165,000 displaced persons, mostly Balts and other eastern Europeans, had arrived under this scheme of recruitment. Similar schemes would also be used to recruit other foreign nationals, including the highly desirable Dutch as well as such non-preferred groups as southern Europeans and, later, women of colour from the Caribbean. [14]

The more liberal immigration laws introduced in 1947 made possible the early postwar Italian influx into Canada. (Italy was taken off the enemy alien list in January 1947.) The response from Italy soon swelled. In the spring of 1947 J.R. Robillard, officer-in-charge in Rome, reported that 12,000 applications had been received. Most were from first-degree relatives (that is, immediate relatives of Canadian residents), though candidates sponsored by Canadian employers were also included.[15] In 1948 3203 Italians came, and thereafter the requests for Italian admissions snowballed. Canada's growing importance as a target of destination among prospective Italian emigrants was linked in part to the expansion in shipping facilities and to the disappointments of Italians who earlier had gone to Latin America and Australia. High unemployment and political troubles in Argentina in the early 1950s, for instance, had prompted thousands to return home and discouraged others from going there. The recession of 1952 led the Australian government to tighten its sponsorship laws, while the United States' national quota system prevented many Italians from emigrating. Booming postwar Canada increasingly became an attractive alternative.[16]

As labour shortages in major industries persisted and the supplies of so-called "quality" displaced persons were said to be dwindling, more and more Canadians came to view Italy, long an exporter of migrants, as a potential supplier of low-skilled workers for Canada. Quebec farmers keen on importing farm workers expressed a preference for Italian peasants accustomed to hard work and to securing a livelihood from unfavourable agricultural conditions. It was hoped that Italians might also participate in future colonization schemes to settle northern lands. Calling Italy a "great reservoir of manpower," David Croll urged Ottawa to recruit Italians to fill jobs in primary industry and the building trades.[17] Government advisers reached similar conclusions. An Ontario report stated emphatically: "We ... need more labour – much more ... [and] only by increased immigration can it be obtained in time for the emergencies that are upon us." It recommended that Ontario recruit 15 per cent of its immigrant labour force from Italy. An External Affairs report advised Ottawa to follow the example set by other countries and to take advantage of Italy's current crisis and its aggressive emigration policy. The report, however, favoured the selective recruitment of farmers and industrial workers from the more prosperous northern and central regions. As immigrants with a permanent commitment to Canada, these men, it stated, could "contribute much to the life of a nation which welcomes them."[18]

Pragmatic considerations were paramount in this shift of attitude towards Italy, but international pressures also counted. Canadian officials were acutely aware that to maintain Canada's new status as a middle power and peacekeeper, the country had to be seen to be playing a positive role in Western Europe's reconstruction. Such a view had earlier helped to prompt the decision to play a role in the relocation of displaced persons and former allies. In addition to the economic benefits, Canada's participation in the Marshall Plan involved new commitments to Italy. America's endorsation of Italy's recovery policy placed pressures on Canada to accept a portion of Italy's surplus population. So, too, did the United Nations' claim that emigration from Italy would aid Europe's economic recovery. Such pressures intensified with the signing of the NATO alliance in the spring of 1949 and the formal arrival of the Cold War era. An expansive country of twelve million people, Canada was expected to aid an ally plagued by an acute population and unemployment problem. Canada's interest in seeking European allies to act as a "counterweight" to the United States could also be partially met by forging favourable links with Italy.[19]

Certainly, fears of communism spreading through Western nations like Italy helped the entry of Italians into Canada. Canadian officials linked the increased popularity that the Communist party in Italy was enjoying after the war to the country's economic collapse and argued that full recovery would eliminate the communists' support. If Canadian officials acted quickly, the country could have its pick of quality immigrants while also enhancing its own international status. One report voiced these motives succinctly: "Any increase in emigration to Canada would be of practical help to Italy in tackling her gravest problem. It would also be a small, but distinctly Canadian, contribution to strengthening the present democratic 'Western' government and in making less likely its replacement by Communists or by extremists of the right."[20]

Thus, it was in response to both international and domestic pressures that Canada agreed to encourage large-scale immigration from Italy. In the fall of 1949 Fortier, soon to replace Hugh Keenleyside as deputy minister of immigration, toured Italy. He returned home convinced that plans could be made to recruit quality immigrants from Italy. The Italian government, he noted, was so anxious to arrange a movement of workers and to improve the reputation of the Italian immigrant that Canada could practically dictate the conditions, including quotas on the numbers of southerners. "Around Rome and in the North," he wrote, "we could certainly select a much better type of migrant who would fit in our way of living, our way of thinking and our way of working."[21]

In the fall of 1950, as Canada established overseas immigration posts throughout Europe, Ottawa entered into a bilateral agreement with Italy to foster and process large-scale immigration to Canada. This led to significant increases in the volume of Italian immigration to Canada. In 1951, a year that saw an unprecedented postwar influx of 200,000 immigrants enter Canada, over 24,000 Italians arrived, three times the 1949 figure. For the next three years the annual Italian flow hovered around 24,000; in no year between 1951 and 1960 did it drop below 20,000 (see appendix, table 2).

The 1950 agreement was expected to improve matters in two ways. It authorized the Italian Ministry of Labour to carry out the pre-examination of candidates applying for admission under family sponsorship terms, with the exception of spouses and minors. This was expected to help the Rome office process cases at a faster rate. It also formalized a system for importing contract labour, one based on the displaced persons model. Under that model, immigrants would enter Canada under contract to fill a specific labour demand, but once the contract had been completed the worker could choose to reside permanently in Canada and seek to fulfil normal citizenship requirements. Officials referred to such immigration as "bulk orders."[22]

ORDERING IN BULK

The bulk-order schemes involving Italians reveal how during the years immediately following the Second World War labour priorities underlay Canada's approach to immigration generally and to Italian immigrants in particular. They reinforced a long-standing association between Italian immigration and the importation of a foreign proletariate. The recruits would be sent only to those industries suffering serious labour shortages – agriculture, mining, domestic service, and, to a lesser extent, the metal trades and logging. It was assumed that, as in the past, the Italians would tolerate irregular employment, low wages, and physically demanding work. Expressing this view, Arthur MacNamara, deputy minister of labour, wrote: "Italians have done a great deal to develop this country. They have handled heavy jobs on [the] railway ... highway building, municipal sewer and water systems [and] have been splendid workers."[23] From the perspective of the immigrants themselves, the schemes also permitted prospective immigrants who did not have first-degree relatives residing in Canada to gain entry into the country. They, in turn, would be responsible for the admission of many more Italians. Moreover, an examination of the schemes reveals how completely the southern Italians defeated the efforts of Canadian officialdom to keep their numbers to a minimum.

Of all the immigrant procedures, the bulk orders entailed the greatest amount of state involvement, most of it during the period 1950–3. The initial pre-selection of candidates took place in the many local offices of the Italian Ministry of Labour. Applicants submitted to standard medical tests, including lung x-rays, and were required to present documents, such as a military record, or a "family certificate" signed by a local priest or official testifying to their marital status and moral character. Once past the pre-selection procedures, candidates were assembled at emigration stations in Naples, Rome, and elsewhere, where they underwent final selection and processing by Canadian teams.

While Canadian officials preferred young, single men, married men willing to precede their families were also picked. Selected candidates signed an "undertaking" obliging them to stay in their placement for one year. After that period they were free to take any job and, after five years, to apply for citizenship. Owing to the scarcity of overnight facilities for immigrants in Halifax, the arrivals were usually divided into groups according to destination and placed on trains headed either to their final placement or to hostels at St-Paul-l'Hermite, Quebec, or Ajax, Ontario. They were required to repay their employer for the cost of inland transportation through monthly deductions from their wages. An Immigration-Labour Committee consisting of representatives from Immigration, Labour, External Affairs, and Health and Welfare oversaw the movements, though, as committee chairman, MacNamara enjoyed considerable authority. Finally, the bias against southerners was reflected in the imposition of a quota on the composition of each order: 70 per cent were to be northern Italians (including north-central Italians) and 30 per cent from the south.

The first bulk orders involved farm workers. Provincial authorities in Quebec won approval for an order of 500 Italian farm labourers in the spring of 1950. Employers were obliged to offer conditions and wages that were equivalent to local standards and rates. For farm workers, this meant $40 per month plus board. The first group of 237 men to arrive as part of this order set sail in June 1950. Given the urgency of getting the workers to Canada before the end of the harvest, the final processing had been hurried through on board ship. Since the Canadian team was generally pleased with the early recruits, a second order for 500 men for Quebec won quick approval.

So, too, did a series of requests from Ontario, Nova Scotia, and elsewhere, so that in the spring of 1951, a movement involving 1500 farm workers was underway.[24]

Conflicts nevertheless emerged over the handling of the first orders and these set the tone for subsequent relations between Italians and Canadians. Canadian overseas officials blamed costly delays encountered in the selection process on Italian bureaucratic incompetence. What annoyed them most, however, was the blatant attempt by Italian officials to stack the orders with southern Italians. At one point during final selection of men destined for Quebec, Italian officials had suggested to the Canadian team that most of the openings should go to southern candidates since they were the most keen to depart. This had so incensed the Canadians that once the southern quota had been filled, they stopped inspecting southern candidates. In the end, they recruited only 117 northerners, yet turned back "a large number" from the south standing by at their regional labour offices.[25]

The man responsible for supervising the final selection of these and many other workers was John Sharrer, a senior Labour official who had been involved in recruiting displaced persons in Germany. In selecting Italians, Sharrer resolutely weeded out candidates he considered unsuitable for physically demanding work, but he was generous in his estimation of the men he did pick. In March 1951 he described those selected for farming as "genuine farmers, hardworking men, used to tilling the soil." There are, he added with satisfaction, "no lawyers, philosophers or other such professions among them."[26]

Still, the nature of the selection process could create hardships for prospective emigrants. Since the numbers of pre-selected men always greatly outnumbered the available positions, the centres overflowed with prospective candidates who were kept waiting for days at a time. Hundreds of men who had come long distances and could not afford accommodation slept outside the centres, awaiting inspection and the final selection. When the Canadian teams arrived, the men were subjected to a battery of questions, though they quickly learned to supply the appropriate answers. Each man's hands were also checked for callouses – leaving no doubt as to the type of jobs they were expected to fill in Canada.

The orders for railway workers and miners followed closely on the heels of those for farm workers. During the summer of 1950 and 1951, ships carrying 300–500 workers picked for various categories of work were leaving from Naples, Milan, and Genoa every few weeks. On 28 June 1951, for example, the ss *Vulcania* carried

337 track workers, 267 farm workers, 15 miners, and 12 woodswork-
ers, as well as hundreds of sponsored Italians. As shipping rolls
indicate, the contract workers were young men between the ages
of nineteen and thirty-nine, many of them accompanied by kin and
paesani from the same or a neighbouring town.[27]

Responding to requests from the CNR and Welch Company, Ottawa approved the first order of 500 track workers in November
1950. The men began arriving in early spring, in time to weed the
tracks and repair the damage caused by the spring thaw. The terms
of employment were $30–$35 per month for the extra-gang labourers
working a sixty-hour week, and $40–$45 for section men. The Welch
Company attained a favourable arrangement with Ottawa, winning
permission to carry out pre-selection in Italy. It also provided ca-
tering and commissary services to the Italian work gangs. In return
for each man supplied to the railways, the company also earned a
bonus.[28] Ottawa approved a joint CPR-CNR order for 600 workers,
the first of whom began arriving in May 1951. The CPR and CNR
made further requests for men, as did the Welch Company, which
also supplied employers such as the Algoma Central Railway in
northern Ontario. Periodic movements of Italian trackmen, as well
as other workers, occurred throughout the decade.[29]

Trouble concerning the north-south quota had resurfaced over the
handling of the track workers' movements. It stemmed from the
actions of the Welch representatives, who filled their pool of pre-
selected candidates with southerners. Many of them were Calabrians
from the Veltris' hometown region of Cosenza who had paid a sti-
pend for the privilege of being picked. A confrontation occurred in
the winter of 1951, when the Canadian team, charging the company
with profiteering, rejected many of the candidates presented to
them. In retaliation, Ottawa also suspended the movement and
turned to Finland and Norway in an effort to fill the orders on time.
But when it proved impossible to do so, officials shifted their attention back to available supplies in Italy.[30]

The early flows of men on mining contracts were actually experienced miners who came from the surplus crews of Italian mining
firms. Italian employers, legally compelled to provide social security
benefits to laid-off employees, opted for the cheaper alternative of
helping to finance immigration to Canada. In the summer of 1950 a
Rome-based association of mining companies, La Societa Finanziaria
Siderurgica (Finsider), approached the Canadian Metals Mining Association (CMMA) with a proposal to transfer 500 experienced miners
to Canada. The CMMA leapt at the offer and, with Ottawa's approval,
accepted an initial order of 100 men. The stipulated wages ranged

from $45 to $60 per month plus board. The men, who were assembled for final selection at Perugia in central Italy, were expected to accept other posts if mining placements proved unsuitable or unavailable. By September the order was filled.[31]

Other orders followed, including one involving 500 men destined for construction and underground work in British Columbia's aluminum industry. In each case, Sharrer was instructed to reject men who were underweight or suffered from respiratory problems. Since employers had stated a preference for northern Italian miners who, they argued, were more likely to be of an appropriate build and genuinely experienced, he was also told to stick closely to the north/south quota. Sharrer soon sent home favourable reports of the northern recruits, describing one group as "men of good type for mining: all Northern Italians, none less than 135 lb., experienced and none exposed to dust."[32]

Further tensions emerged, however. In the fall of 1951 the movement of miners was temporarily suspended following complaints from employers that Italians were abandoning their jobs. Officials were also annoyed with the Italian authorities for protesting the placement of a group of miners in Whitehorse, Yukon. It was charged that the extremely high rail costs involved, and the remoteness of the area, made the men highly vulnerable to running up debts with the company and prevented them from saving enough money to leave the town when they so desired. The Italian officials demanded that, in future, married miners be sent only to locations where they could later bring their families. W.W. Dawson, head of the Labour department's National Employment Service (NES), curtly replied that while he himself preferred to send single men to remote areas, men were placed in jobs as they came up; they could not expect to be placed only in "ideal locations."[33] As labour shortages persisted, the orders for miners resumed.

All this activity could not mask the fact that increasingly the mining orders were being filled by men who were not experienced miners. Many of them were also southerners. Canada's strict medical standards resulted in high rejection rates among the more experienced miners. Even those with minor respiratory problems could not pass the medical tests. Although Ottawa soon relaxed these standards, there continued to be many rejections of bona fide miners.[34] Many of the empty spaces were taken up by the southern candidates who dominated the crowds gathered at the emigration centres.

The battle over the north-south quota had become a characteristic feature of the selection process for all of the bulk orders. During the selection of men at Trieste, Friuli, in 1951, Sharrer informed his superiors in Ottawa that the Italian government had been up to its "old tricks": "[It] consistently throws men from the south of Italy at me." In retaliation, he rejected many of them, including a group of Sicilians whom he had condescendingly described as "small in stature and less clean and hygienic." Canada's ambassador to Italy, Jean Desy, also expressed his disapproval of Italy's actions. In the end, however, many of the men selected had come from the south. Sharrer himself reported that to fill the Canadian orders on time, he had felt compelled to select large numbers of southern candidates. Significantly, he also noted that no one could doubt southern Italians had legitimate reasons for wanting to emigrate. [35]

By dominating the pools of pre-selected men, the southern Italians had successfully circumvented the discriminatory quotas designed to keep their numbers to a minimum. Frequently, aided by Italian officials or simpathetic priests who understood well the men's desire to escape deteriorating conditions at home and to pursue work opportunities abroad, many southerners benefitted from the overcrowding and confusion prevailing at the final selection centres and got themselves recruited. For their part, Canadian selection officers, burdened with heavy workloads and urgent deadlines and exhausted from travelling on a moment's notice to locales throughout Italy, increasingly had found they could only complete the orders by letting in large numbers from the south. [36]

Although the bulk orders involved mostly low-skilled workers, a significant exception was a scheme to recruit metal-trades workers during 1951–2. The workers' former employers helped to finance their movement, and the candidates were subjected to trade tests. Most of the pre-selection was handled by the Societa per L'Industria e L'Elettricita, one of Italy's largest manufacturing corporations. Confident about the market value of such highly skilled men, MacNamara actually approved the movements without having received any direct requests from Canadian employers. [37]

The first order involved fifty tradesmen, most of whom arrived in the spring of 1951. However, NES officers could find few companies willing to hire immigrants unfamiliar with the British measurement system, while employers in the defence industry opposed hiring former enemy aliens. Further troubles erupted when those men who had been placed complained they were not receiving the promised wage rate of $1.00 per hour. Employers countered by insisting the men were not worth that wage until they became "adjusted." Just as news of this conflict reached Italy, MacNamara received a curt letter from the International Labour Office (ILO) criticizing Canada for having given these mechanics a false impression of conditions in Canadian factories.[38]

Despite opposition from Fortier, MacNamara had Sharrer select another 300 men through Finsider. Aware of his intentions, the ILO sent a message cautioning him against treating these skilled men as a casual labour force. Arrangements were also made to secure the ILO's assistance in devising trade tests.[39] The first arrivals came during the summer of 1951. The selection process was soon stalled, however, when Finsider presented workers from the company's southern plant. Finsider officials had donated the space in their Naples plant for the trade tests, charged an angry Sharrer, in an attempt "to throw a number of Neapolitans or South Italians on me, hoping that I would accept them on their say-so." But being especially keen to prevent southerners from dominating this movement, Sharrer strictly enforced the southern quota. In order to secure more northern candidates, he also travelled to Terni, Umbria, in north-central Italy, where Finsider was based.[40]

The reluctance of Canadian employers to hire Italian tradesmen soon undermined MacNamara's pet project. The first seventy-one men to arrive in December 1951 had included toolmakers, welders, and machinists. Unable to place the men, NES officers had left them to celebrate Christmas in the Ajax hostel. By spring, all but one of the men were employed, but not before Finsider, kept abreast of events by some of the disgruntled men involved, submitted to the ILO a scathing report indicting Canadian policies that encouraged skilled workers to leave jobs in Italy and wait weeks in a hostel where conditions were comparable to "the poorest districts of Naples near the port," only to be placed in inferior jobs. Meantime, rumours (which later proved unfounded) were circulating to the effect that some Italian machinists placed in Kingston were communists. Organized labour's rising protests about nonunion immigrant competition also discouraged MacNamara. Admitting defeat in the early winter of 1952, he cancelled further orders.[41]

The major exception to the emphasis Canada placed on recruiting men was the 1951–2 scheme to recruit domestic servants. Italian women were recruited for the most heavily ghettoized type of female labour, and one frequently performed by immigrant women. The decision to recruit Italians arose as a result of concerns that insufficient numbers of domestics were arriving from preferred countries such as Britain, Germany, and Holland, and from the DP camps. A preference for northern Italians was again made explicit. Ethnic biases worked in tandem with paternalism; because "girls" were involved, Canadian officials, with Italy's approval, appointed female chaperones and introduced special precautions such as housing the women in convents in Montreal. As immigrants from a nonpreferred country, however, they were offered lower wages than domestics from preferred countries.

Discussion regarding the scheme actually began in the spring of 1949, when Ottawa asked the ILO to make discreet enquiries regarding "the possibility of Italian girls going to work in Canadian households." The ILO report, which stressed the scarcity in Italy of trained "city" domestics in hotels and other institutions, was dismissed by Canadian Labour officials interested in inexperienced farm women. (Presumably they could also be paid less than trained, experienced domestics.) The Canadian ILO director, V.C. Phelan, agreed with the idea of recruiting young women from the coutryside. "My view," he informed MacNamara, "is that in the country and small villages the appeal of coming to Canada would be strong."[42] Although MacNamara concurred, Canada did not act on the matter for a year, mainly, it appears, for two reasons. The first concerned travel costs. Even though Italian funding had not been requested for other orders, Canadian officials had tried to pursuade the Italian authorities to advance the ocean fares. Second, senior Immigration bureaucrats, including Fortier, were not prepared to accept Italian domestics until "better" alternatives had been exhausted. As MacNamara observed, "We could do with some Italian girls as domestics [but] there is a very definite view amongst Immigration officials that immigration from Italy is not desirable."[43]

While the Italian matter was dropped, Canada embarked in the spring of 1950 on an upgraded publicity campaign to attract domestics from Britain and northwestern Europe.[44] Applicants were to be eighteen to forty years of age, single, divorced, or widowed, women with no children. Terms of employment included monthly wages ranging from $45 to $75 plus room and board, and vague promises about free evenings. The response proved disappointing, and so, in November 1951, Ottawa approved an order for 500 Italian domestics. Officials provided assurances that social and religious organizations "would undertake to give spiritual and moral assistance" to the women. Italian women were offered lower wages – $35 minimum – and, initially, denied assisted-passage privileges.[45] Early results were not promising, which surprised officials such as J.L. Anfossi, second-in-command at Rome, who had expected a flood of applicants. "It is an odd fact," he wrote, "that of the thousands of persons in [Italy] desirous of emigrating we receive no requests from unattached women." He attributed this fact to women's lack of freedom and the high proportion of young women who were married or engaged. Even poor parents were not letting their daughters apply, it seemed, because "of the reluctance of religious orders who do not approve of their leaving families for reasons other than marriage."[46]

What Anfossi failed to see was that the high travel costs, combined with the low wages advertised, made the Canadian offer unattractive. After all, young single women were entering Canada as nominated cases and finding jobs as domestics. While some of the sponsoring Canadian employers were relatives, most were strangers contacted through travel agents. As an Italian Ministry of Labour report argued, without assisted passage, candidates might have to take out high-interest loans with Italian agencies and would have to devote most of their monthly wages towards repaying the loans, leaving only "a paltry" sum that could be sent home each month. An additional reason for the women's reluctance is that they wrongly assumed they would be placed in rural homes.[47]

After considerable debate, during which Canada rejected proposals to permit the wives of men already in Canada to qualify, Ottawa agreed in August to extend assisted passage to Italians and to increase the minimum wage level to $35–$45. Selection officers were told to inform the women where they were likely to be placed. This willingness to make concessions partially reflected the fears of officials who were sensitive to criticism that might be voiced by religious and political leaders should anything "untoward" happen to the "girls" involved. Overdramatizing matters, Anfossi advised NES officers to endeavour "to place these girls as promised since I foresee that the Italian authorities and the girls' families will follow their destinations closely as will the Communist Party whose war cry of 'white slavery' will be heard as soon as a girl goes astray or shows dissatisfaction."[48]

Canada's decision regarding assisted passage gave the movement the boost it needed. By late August, 240 women had been processed at Rome and another 300 were being presented for selection in early fall. The first sailing to include domestics – the ss *Fair Sea*, which sailed on 24 November 1951 – carried three trained nurses from Agnano, near Naples, bound for Toronto hospitals.[49] The first large group of 100 domestics arrived in Montreal in December 1951. Edith Cornell, the NES officer overseeing their placement, described them as "primitive villagers" who "have never been away from home before" and "express concern over the money owed at home for their passage."[50] Her unfavourable response proved typical of the reception the women received at the hands of employers, who complained about their ignorance of Canadian housekeeping methods and standards of cleanliness. By January 1952, 200 women had arrived. The rash of complaints voiced by employers and NES officers, combined with a decline in the demand for domestics in winter, prompted officials to postpone the order until the following spring. When its resumption evoked similar responses, the order was cancelled in April 1952 even though dozens of approved women were awaiting sailing departure times in Italy.[51] Thus, the only attempt to recruit Italian women through a government scheme ended dismally.

OUTSIDE THE CITY

While no precise figures are available, it seems clear that as many as seven thousand immigrants, mostly men, arrived with the Italian bulk-order movements. Like Guiseppe of our opening story, thousands more arrived as contract workers under nominated terms (see appendix, table 10). These contract workers usually received help from North American relatives who contacted travel agents to find employers willing to sponsor them. Because agents received a bonus for every steamship ticket sold, they were highly motivated to match a prospective client with a sponsor. Like so many of the bulk-order immigrants, many of these newcomers also ended up in Toronto, where they acted as a magnet drawing still more Italians to the city. Montreal and Vancouver, though falling a second and a distant third, also emerged as popular destinations. But regardless of where they eventually settled, the male contract workers, many of whom had been peasants or semi-skilled village artisans from southern Italy, had their first Canadian experience as proletarians, or wage workers, in the country's hinterland regions. In the countryside or on the frontier, they underwent a transition from peasants to immigrant wage-earners. What did their jobs entail? How did they respond to the working and living conditions they confronted?

Most Italian farm workers were employed on single-family farms in Ontario and Quebec, often as the family's only hired hand. For them, the nature of the work was familiar, though as newly arrived immigrant wage-earners there were new strains. As Fiore Carulli, a peasant from northern Molise who took a farm posting in southern Ontario in 1949, recalled, newcomers felt frustrated by the language barrier and by their unfamiliarity with mechanized farming. Driving a diesel tractor, for instance, might pose an altogether new challenge. Isolated on these farms, workers were subject to the goodwill or capriciousness of their employers. Many were put up in sheds or barns; few slept in the main house or shared their meals with the family.[52]

Unlike farm hands, most Italian contract workers, including track-men, worked alongside other Italians. As a single man of nineteen, Carlo Sanella, a native of Abruzzi, was recruited by the Welch Company in 1957 and placed with a CPR workgang repairing sections of track in British Columbia, Saskatchewan, and Alberta.[53] Trackmen usually enjoyed plentiful food, but harsh frontier conditions characterized the camps. As the crews cleared railway lines and replaced damaged ties, they did the back-breaking tasks. In summer, men endured soaring temperatures and pesky mosquitoes. Cold weather hampered them in the fall and made sleeping in their crowded bunkhouses – usually coverted railway boxcars – barely tolerable. Deductions for food and board, the repayment of travel costs, and stiff company fines for lateness and other reasons kept many from accumulating savings. Card games, drinking, and an occasional visit to a red-light district could drain the rest.

Underground miners were better paid than farm workers but, like loggers, they performed dangerous jobs. In the mines, the rhythm of work evolved around two work shifts and the endless routine of mucking, drilling, planting dynamite, blasting, and mucking out the debris once again. Greenhorns were put on tramming operations; shovelling the broken rock into carts, they pushed or drove the loaded wagons to a dumping point. While doing so, they faced the risk of being crushed by falling rock. At Noranda, Quebec, Cesare Caruso, a native of Campagnia who had worked as a miner in northern Europe for several years before coming to Canada, watched a close friend die in just this fashion shortly after the man's arrival in Canada. "Millions of dollars were in those mines," he recalls, "[but] what did we get for the backs we broke ... the heads literally split open? Peanuts."[54] Drilling teams, consisting of more experienced men, were enticed by piecework and bonus systems to work fast. They, too, faced serious risks in the form of cave-ins. Italians sent to Ontario logging camps took on equally arduous and risky jobs such as felling trees and clearing and building roads through the bush so that in winter the logs could be drawn out.

There was usually plenty of food in the logging and mining camps. Where company officials had introduced camp improvements, the crude bunkhouses of the prewar are were replaced by modern low-rise wooden buildings offering separate beds and showers. While some mines were located in very remote locales, many Italian miners actually resided in mining towns and were thus more likely than other contract workers to arrange to have their wives join them during the time of their placement. Women, however, found few job opportunities in such communities, although some earned money in the informal economy by taking in laundry or babysitting.[55]

Italians had been recruited to fill unattractive jobs that Canadian workers had shunned, and they were expected to be docile workers who accepted, without protest, long hours, dangerous jobs, and back-breaking work. Yet almost immediately employers encountered some resistance. It took several forms. Disgruntled workers angry about long hours or low pay participated in deliberate slowdowns and extended lunches. Others enraged company officials by engaging in weekend drinking binges and then reporting on Monday unable to work. One group of Italian miners at Silverton, BC, defied company rules by taking a company jeep "for a joy ride to the neighboring town, without driver's license, knowledge of traffic regulation, etc."[56]

Still others obviously feared the unsafe nature of their jobs. In seeking to protect themselves they inevitably came into conflict with company owners and government bureaucrats. For example, some Italians sent to mining posts, especially those who had never set foot in a mine, tried to avoid "going underground" by conjuring up diseases and disabilities that had not appeared on their immigration papers. They preferred to work on construction projects about ground. A company manager with the Van Roi mines at Nelson, BC, reported having fired an Italian employee – a Sicilian man whose wife and children were still overseas – for repeatedly refusing to go underground on account of a weak knee he claimed to have injured while in a Siberian war camp.[57]

Similar complaints at a Van Roi mine in neighbouring Silverton led to an investigation in the fall of 1951. The subsequent report, written by regional NES officer George Wallach, passed harsh judgment on the men involved. All of the married men had eagerly pressed the firm to sponsor the arrival of their families. They had also strongly objected to "going underground," saying they preferred to find work on farms or in cities. Those who had been on tramming operations complained that the work was back-breaking and that the bonus system, based on the volume of material hauled, was deliberately set beyond reach. Their complaints drew unsympathetic criticism from Wallach, who wrote: "They expect miracles to happen." Although Wallach admitted that the men in question had been saving their money or sending remittances home, he responsed to the men's complaints that too many mandatory deductions were made from their monthly paycheque by calling them "adolescent, willful, irresponsible youngsters." After meeting with the proprietor of the hotel where they were staying, he also confirmed complaints that they were "a rowdy lot." Their sins amounted to sitting in the hotel tavern in their undershirts, playing the accordion, and singing in a "loud" and "obnoxious" manner. On several occasions their presence had resulted in fights with Canadian patrons. Wallach concluded that the Italians had failed to live up to their contract despite generous treatment by the company.[58]

Italians did more than complain; on occasion they also downed their shovels. To be sure, ethnic antipathies between immigrant and Canadian workers, and between immigrants from different backgrounds, combined with the highly seasonal nature of these jobs, prevented the development of a strong class solidarity in these resource-industry jobs. Moreover, at least some employers sought to prevent workers from joining forces against them by segregating their work gangs according to nationality and heading up each gang with a trusted foreman. Others threatened immigrants with deportation. Neverthless, some cross-ethnic class solidarities were evident in the spontaneous work stoppages and strikes that occurred. When, for example, loggers employed by the CNR stopped work in the winter of 1951 to protest against infested meat supplies at their northern Ontario camp, the Italian work gangs joined the fray. The strike ended when company managers agreed to ship in new food supplies. In November 1957 CPR extra-gang workers employed at Skeena, BC, spontaneously left their jobs following news that the company had refused to comply with a previously negotiated wage increase. Carlo Sanella, a participant, recalled how men began ripping up railway ties to prevent trains from passing through. The walkout lasted only a few hours, however, because company threats of dismissals and deportations persuaded the Italians to return to work. Though treated to a free lunch that day, they did not receive their expected wage increase.[59] Some Italian miners also participated in strikes, including one that erupted at Noranda in 1961 when a veteran worker was fired and then rehired at starting wages. The strike resulted in a victory and the worker was reinstated at his previous wage rate and union seniority level.[60]

Although it is impossible to generalize about Italian militancy from so few examples, it seems clear that Italian workers were not entirely docile. The limited nature of their commitment to workers' struggles in the interior was largely determined by the brevity of their encounter with the frontier. Moreover, as highly dispensable workers operating in a constantly replenished labour market, the most effective way to protest exploitative conditions very often was to escape them. With growing regularity, Italian workers, whether they arrived as part of the bulk orders or as nominated immigrants, took this route. They jumped their posts or ignored their contracts altogether.

The practice of jumping among Italian contract workers drew the ire of employers and government officials. Farm workers, who made up the largest group of contract workers, came under heaviest criticism. Indeed, no sooner had the first bulk order of Quebec-bound farm labourers arrived in Canada in the spring of 1951 than complaints began to surface. Significantly, Dawson suggested that such men might well have been misled by inspectional officials who "might have gotten a little bit enthusiastic about employment opportunities ... other than on the farm." His colleagues, however, were not as generous.[61] The officials who staffed the Immigration-Labour Committee insisted that Canada had always had "little success" with Italians as farm workers because they, particularly the southerners who usually filled these jobs, were too easily "enticed by the prospects of a comparatively high income and city living conditions."[62] The committee also authorized Professor Sandro Antonietti of the University of Bologna to undertake a tour of Canada during the fall of 1951 with a view to ascertaining Italian farming prospects in Canada. Anxious to bolster Italy's reputation as an exporter of quality immigrants, Antonietti, ironically, used the occasion to recommend emigration from central and northern Italy. He attributed the failure of farm workers to honour their contracts and to exhibit a desire to settle on the land as major reasons for Canada's antipathy to Italian immigrants. The publicity also damaged Italy's international reputation, he insisted.[63]

Antonietti's preoccupation with finding ways to improve Italy's reputation as a source of immigrants and his anti-southern bias led him to dismiss the motives propelling southern peasants to migrate. For their part, Canadian officials felt vindicated by the report because it provided justification for their hostility towards southerners. As Anfossi put it, "It is good to find an Italian not only willing to admit the errors of their ways but downright disgusted with the past policy practised by the Italian authorities in sending forward such a poor type of Italian immigrant."[64]

By the fall of 1951 complaints about workers jumping their mining and railway contracts also grew sharp. The CMMA reported that companies on the west coast were "having trouble" with Italian miners, and in Salmo, BC, the Western Exploration Company requested help in tracking down Italian "skippers." Since many of the workers owed the firm credit for transportation, company owners tried to force the government to track down skippers by refusing to reimburse the railways until the culprits had been caught and made to pay the travel loans out of their own pockets. Officials sympathized with employers, but they refused to act on company proposals that the government issue threatening communiqués implying that troublemakers might be deported. Predictably, few of the skippers were ever caught.[65]

Anticipating cries of protest from organized labour, some government officials expressed concern that Italian skippers were flocking to the cities and becoming "unnecessary competitors of Canadians for existing jobs."[66] These fears were reinforced by various reports detailing the large number of Italian contract workers who were arriving under nominated terms but never reporting to their Canadian sponsors. A 1950 investigation of farm workers destined for Quebec, for example, revealed that dozens of Canadian farmers had been enticed by profit-hungry agents offering "awards" ranging from $25 to $100 for agreeing to sponsor particular Italian candidates. Some of the farmers had sponsored several Italians, usually working through the local agent of a travel agency based in Montreal or Toronto. Evidently, they had no intentions of actually employing the candidate. Upon his arrival in Canada, the newcomer, having spent as much as $300 to grease the palms of various intermediaries, usually went directly to Toronto or some other city.[67]

DEFIANT DOMESTICS?

The Italian domestics who arrived under the 1951–2 scheme came under similar criticism. Labour officials invariably blamed the problems that Canadian mistresses were having with their Italian maids on the fact that southerners made poor housekeepers. Reiterating the ethnocentric and class biases of the Canadian employers, they viewed Italian domestics as poor country girls ignorant of North American standards of personal hygiene and cleanliness. As one overseas selection officer bluntly put it, southerners were "generally speaking, very poor material. Their standard of education is very low, coming from farm homes where they claimed to have worked only in the fields (most of them look it!)." She even suggested that they be placed as cooks and maids on farms and in public institutions where, she claimed, "less demanding attention" was paid to the quality of cleaning and food.[68]

In accounting for the obstacles encountered in placing the women, NES officers also noted that Canadian employers had become "more choosy" in their applications and usually specified that domestics should come from northern Europe. The limited appeal of Italians was compounded by the women's own insistence on being placed in Catholic homes. On occasion, disgruntled employers had shown up at local labour offices wanting to "trade in" their Italian maid for a "DP" or "Scandinavian."[69] An Ottawa report discussed an Italian domestic who, according to her employer, "was not clean about her person and has several men friends who call, against Mrs. [L's] wishes, each time she goes out." The maid was put in her place. Along with her sister, who had been transferred out of a private home for "impertinent behaviour," she was relocated as a cook with the Sisters of St Marie convent in Ottawa.[70]

Such women were said to suffer from their impoverished backgrounds and their lack of education. As one placement officer observed, "I do not consider the Italian girls have the requisite basic knowledge or qualifications for training in the average Canadian home," and, she added, "their lack of English, together with their only experience in comparatively primitive conditions in Italy, would not justify their placement as domestics." Others considered Italians less adept than other foreigners at learning English; one report noted uncritically that "employers state they find the Italian language a greater barrier than German."[71] What most irritated employers and officers alike, however, were the acts of defiance committed by domestics who complained about their placements, demanded job transfers, or abandoned their posts for more appealing prospects. Their apparently cavalier approach offended the sensibilities of Canadian employers and officials who had expected young Italian women to act submissively.

VICTIMS OR AGENTS?

Why did Italians apparently not live up to their labour contracts? Were they malicious manipulaters of the system? Certainly not. They were neither as cunning nor as malicious as their critics assumed. To be sure, many of the Italian men who accepted jobs in agriculture and primary industry saw the contract as a means to an end – gaining entry into Canada. Not all of them, however, immediately defected to the cities. This was particularly true of the earliest arrivals who came prepared to meet the conditions of their entry. Eager to create a favourable impression and loath to jeopardize the chances of paesani (co-villagers) keen to gain admission, they reported to their posts. Fiore Carulli, the farm worker who went to a southern Ontario farm in 1949, was one of them. Although eager to join relatives living in Toronto, he reported to his employer out of a sense of duty. Moreover, significant numbers of men who had been placed in resource jobs remained in the same line of work for several years. Cesare Caruso, for example, worked in Noranda mines for six years before settling in Toronto. Another man, Ruggero Carboni, spent three winter seasons in the bush before joining the pick-and-shovel gangs in Toronto's construction industry.[72]

What is especially ironic about the self-righteous indignation with which some government and company officials reacted to the actions of Italian skippers is that these men had been recruited for highly seasonal jobs. Put simply, they were not jobs at which workers could be expected to be employed for an entire year. For decades, employers had responded to the fluctuating labour demand in the resource industries by recruiting large numbers of immigrant greenhorns to fill low-paying jobs during the peak work periods. As the months of feverish activity came to an end, these same employers quickly disposed of their excess workers. Throughout the postwar years many immigrant contract workers, including Italians, "prematurely" abandoned their labour contracts through no fault of their own. In effect, it was the employers who defaulted on the contract. Immigrant arrivals employed on railway and mining jobs found themselves stranded with the arrival of winter. While the peak season within the logging industry differed – for here the winter months witnessed the most intense activity – employers operated on the same principle. As the slack season approached, the immigrant recruits were the first let go.[73]

Farm workers were equally dispensable. Most of those who arrived during slack times were usually dismissed immediately. This is what happened to Giuseppe Izzo of our opening story. He reported to the Quebec farmer who had sponsored him in November 1951. After travelling two days by train, he arrived at his post late one night, was given some bread, and sent to bed in a small shed. He soon discovered there was little work for him to do; two days later the farm couple admitted they could not afford to keep him on and suggested he try to find work in Montreal. When that failed, he wrote to his wife's cousin, who was employed with a construction firm in Toronto. At his encouragement, Izzo ended up in Toronto just months after arriving in Canada.[74]

A host of negative factors prompted other men to abandon their posts before the work season ended, namely low wages, abusive employers, and the isolation of farming or frontier jobs. Upon arrival, resource workers discovered that through fines and other means, company officials found ways of undercutting their wages, while farm workers were denied time off. Concomitantly, they were pulled by the prospect of better-paying jobs and/or the presence of relatives and paesani in cities such as Toronto. Often feeling legally helpless to defend their rights, men who felt cheated out of their pay or disliked their employer found it easier to abandon their job. This was especially true for farm workers, who tolerated low wages and the most isolated conditions. Nor were Italians the only immigrants caught in this predicament. Commenting on the high rate of jumping among recent immigrants "masquarading as farm labourers to gain entry into this country," S.E. Lewis, the provincial director of immigration in Nova Scotia, noted: "Our experience with all nationalities is about the same: Dutch, Italians, Poles, D.P's etc."[75] Indeed, the unappealing wages and poor working conditions that pushed Italian and many other postwar workers off the farms had for many decades accounted for rural depopulation in Canada. At the annual federal-provincial farm-labour conference held in December 1951, government representatives and farmers openly admitted that Canadian farmers could not expect their European recruits to remain in their posts unless wages and conditions were upscaled.[76]

The danger of the jobs, the remoteness of the camps, and seasonal layoffs were factors that help explain why immigrant miners, track workers, and loggers similarly did not complete their posting. The decision to jump might be prompted by a serious accident, as it was in the case of Attilio Sanci, a former peasant who spent a few years employed in coal mines in Belgium before arriving in Canada in the early 1950s. He worked for several months on a road gang repairing track lines in eastern Canada before barely escaping injury in an accident that killed a co-worker. As he recalled, he did not come to Canada "to die on a railroad."[77]

The increasing regularity with which Italians, and many other immigrants, abandoned or did not report to their placements reflected the disappointing experiences of earlier workers who had initially taken their placements seriously. As the contract workers of the later waves learned of the problems that had plagued the earlier arrivals, some obviously chose not to repeat the experience. The pattern also reflected a growing awareness among the bulk-order immigrants – Italians and others – that their labour contracts were not being legally enforced. Indeed, as in the past, government officials did not take action against either the defaulting employers or the immigrant recruits. In addition, many of the men who came under the employer-sponsored or nominated scheme also arrived knowing full well that their contract was a mere formality and that their employers neither expected nor wanted them to report to work.

Moreover, in spite of the indignation of certain officials, the Canadian government tolerated the defection of Italians to major cities such as Toronto precisely because, in most years, the men were filling equally serious job shortages there, particularly in the building trades.[78]

When female domestics skipped, they did so for some of the same reasons as men. Like male farmhands, the women disliked isolated workplaces and long work days, and they preferred the greater freedom and higher wages of factory work. They also preferred living among their own kin. Many of the domestics, who had been recruited along with sisters or cousins, had relatives or co-villagers already residing in Canada whom they were eager to join. In escaping their posts, some enlisted the help of male and female kin or sympathetic priests, who helped them secure a factory job, usually in a garment shop or laundry.[79]

From the perspective of some Canadian employers and officials, the Italian bulk orders, as well as the system of nominated immigrants, were something of a disappointment. For the immigrants, however, the schemes served a useful purpose. Both the bulk orders and the nomination system permitted those men and women who did not have close relatives living in Canada to gain entry into the country. By far the largest number of placements was in agriculture; between 1948 and 1961, 34,859 Italian men stated farm work as their intended occupation (see appendix, table 10). In circumventing the objectives of Canadian officials who sought deliberately to keep the proportion of southerners to a minimum, southern Italians revealed the depth of their desire to escape the deteriorating conditions of their homeland. In the end, southern Italians succeeded in dominating movements of contract workers, just as they would the flow of immigrants arriving under family sponsorship. The unfavourable conditions of those contract jobs and the immigrants' perception of better employment and living opportunities in urban centres like Toronto prompted many of them, in turn, to migrate to that city.

SPONSORSHIP AND CHAIN MIGRATION TO TORONTO

As many Italian male contract workers found their way to Toronto, they joined the newly arrived Italians whose admission had been sponsored by first-degree relatives living in Canada. Despite the breakdown in communication occasioned by the war or by years of separation, many Italians had managed to keep in touch with their Canadian relatives overseas and others quickly resumed their relationships after the war. When Canada's family sponsorship categories were expanded in 1947, these Canadian relatives acted as sponsors. For example, in 1949 Anna and Eugenio Scalise, peasants from the Abruzzi, were sponsored by Anna's sister and her husband who had settled in Toronto in the mid-1920s. More typically, however, the first sponsored kin to arrive was a man – usually the male head of the household or an elder son.[80] Together, the family-sponsored arrivals and the newcomers who arrived on labour contracts played a critical role in the process of Italian immigration. These early postwar arrivals initiated countless migration chains that drew hundreds of thousands of Italians from their hometowns to Toronto.

While few case studies of postwar Italian immigrants in major Canadian cities exist, the evidence suggests that family- and kin-linked chain migration operated in similar fashion in directing newcomers from Italy to Montreal, the second most popular destination among Canada's postwar Italian arrivals. Moreover, general statistics attest to the fact that the family character of Italian immigration to Canada was evident early on as women and children joined men who had preceded them. Of the 7230 Italians who arrived in the year following the spring of 1949, one-third consisted of "dependants," that is, wives and children. In 1953 they accounted for half of the Italian total; thereafter they represented between 40 per cent and 54 per cent of the annual Italian volume (see appendix, table 11). As kin and paesani followed the lead taken by others, chain migration transformed certain provinces into major sources of immigrants for Canada. Close to 60 per cent of the more than 240,000 Italians who came during the period 1946–61 were southerners. Together, the regions of Abruzzi, Molise, and Calabria accounted for 75 per cent of this volume. The most significant out-migration was from the provinces of Campobasso, Molise; l'Aquila, Abruzzi; and the Calabrian provinces of Cosenza and Catanzaro. Other major sources included Potenza province, Basilicata, and Bari and Foggia provinces in Apulia. Caserta and Avellino were the major provincial origins of those from Campagnia; Sicilians accounted for most of the Italian islanders.[81]

Given the early concentration of Italians in Toronto, it was not surprising to find thousands of sponsored newcomers flocking to the city. The role of sponsor was usually filled by men, and it was men who dominated the early flows of Italians into Canada. Fully 60 per cent of the more than 42,000 Italians who arrived in Toronto between 1946 and 1955 were men; thereafter, the gender gap was insignificant (see appendix, table 6). Within a few years of their arrival, some Italian men had acted as the sponsor for several relatives, including their wives and children, parents, and their married siblings (as well as the spouses and children of those siblings). As more newcomers gained entry into the country, the process was repeated. By mid-decade, with so many of these family chains set into motion, it became increasingly common not only for married couples to arrive together, but for entire families to sail for Canada. Extensive boarding arrangements among kin enabled people to provide housing and support to incoming relatives.

More than 90 per cent of Canada's postwar Italians were sponsored by relatives. By contrast, the average for all nations was 47 per cent, and for certain groups, such as the Germans, it dropped to below 40 per cent. Sponsored immigration operated in such a way as to link particular clusters of villages and towns in the sending society to specific locales in the host society. In some cases, nearly the entire population of a town or hamlet gradually resettled itself in Toronto. The large crowds of kinfolk and paesani who gathered to attend the weddings or funerals held in Toronto thus represented a nearly complete reconstruction of the hamlet. In the cases of other hometowns, a significant minority of the village folk emigrated to Toronto. For example, many towns with a population in the tens of thousands also produced a large number of immigrants to Toronto, but, in each case, many of the townfolk also remained. The families in Toronto still had close relatives in the village, including parents and siblings, and thus were more likely to maintain links with the town and the kin who still lived there.[82] In still other cases, a split could be found between the younger people who emigrated from a town or village and the older generation they left behind.

Italian chain migration reflected both the elasticity of kinship bonds among Italians and the set of reciprocal obligations that characterized them.[83] The exigencies of immigration led to a significant widening of kin relations to include a host of distant relatives and co-villagers who might never have formed part of an individual's support network in Italy. Many young men, for instance, were sponsored by uncles or other kinfolk whom they had never met. For their part, the Canadian relative may have been acting out of some sense of duty to the young man's parents or been returning a favour the man's parents had once extended to the relative's own family.

The chain migration so characteristic of Italian immigration to postwar Toronto unfolded in stages. For the earliest immigrants, the decision to emigrate involved serious sacrifices, including the sale of their home to finance the trip and the temporary break-up of the family. But as entire villages became affected by the momentum of migration, it became easier for Italians to reconcile themselves to the idea of leaving home. For many young couples, it was expected that marriage would soon be followed by emigration. Other couples arrived in Halifax carrying infants or small children. Those who made the voyage as single adults soon joined up with paesani and married in Toronto. The general youthfulness of the Italians who entered Canada in these years is indicated by the fact that the average age of immigrants during the 1950s was 22.7 years. In the later years, however, elderly Italians also arrived, many of them reversing their earlier decision not to emigrate, to join their married children.

TRYING TO STEM THE TIDE

In the fall of 1950 Italy's director of immigration reported on the success with which Italians in Canada were bringing their relatives forward. By then, however, the growing backlog of sponsorship cases that had developed in Rome was already causing Canadian officials great concern. By the spring of 1951 the number of backlog cases stood at over 20,000, and the consequent delays in processing cases led to growing complaints from sponsors and prospective emigrants alike. Overseas officials complained about the enormous workloads, and their inability to pay sufficient attention to other applicants, including those seeking admission on the basis of their marketable skills (open placement). What made matters worse was that most family-sponsored candidates were women, children, and the elderly – in short, immigrants not expected to seek employment in Canada – or men who quickly became part of the stream of unskilled and possibly unemployed workers in the cities.[84]

A related problem was the growing incidence of fraudulent practices perpetuated by travel and steamship agents on both sides of the Atlantic. These agents, some officials charged, initiated lucrative migrations from Italy by securing the entry of men who otherwise might not have gained access to Canada. At times, they falsified documents or found other illicit ways to satisfy their clients. Canadian officials were deeply suspicious of the agents and subagents scattered throughout the Italian countryside. "[They] pollute all across Italy," read one report. "Every small town and village in Italy has a travel agent who does this work on the side." Officials also expressed misgivings about the apparent willingness of the immigrants to allow themselves to be exploited or to engage in fraudulent activities.[85] That some did so indicates, of course, the depths of their desire to escape a war-ravaged country and depressed economic conditions at home. But their apparent complicity also gave officials a sense of moral justification for seeking to stem the tide of immigrants from southern Italy.

In the spring of 1952 immigration authorities attempted to alleviate matters by increasing staff in Rome and by agreeing to allow Italian state clinics to conduct the medical testing of non-accompanying dependants (wife and children) of men preceding their families to Canada.[86] More significantly, they imposed an informal annual quota of 25,000 and began to introduce bureaucratic controls on Italian immigration. On several occasions between 1952 and 1962, officials in Ottawa ordered their overseas officers either to slow down or to suspend temporarily the processing of applications for certain relatives. First priority was always given to the spouse, unmarried children, or fiancé(e) of Canadian sponsors; next came parents and unmarried children, orphaned nieces and nephews. Married children and their families fell third in the hierarchy. The controls most affected the fourth category – Canadian sponsors' married siblings and their families. While the quota remained in place until 1962, each year the numbers from Italy surpassed it by several thousand. Similarly, efforts made to counteract the flood of sponsored immigrants from the south by encouraging the emigration of skilled workers from northern Italy produced only modest results.[87]

When the Conservatives came to power in 1957, the whole issue of immigration came to a head against a backdrop of economic recession and a climate increasingly hostile to mass immigration. The new minister of immigration, Ellen Fairclough, embarked on an ambitious review program. The Italian backlog, now surpassing 50,000 cases, received much attention. Cabinet ministers and senior immigration officials alike recommended ways of reducing the volume of Italian sponsorship admissions. Officials keen to break the chain-migration pattern advised restricting the number of "port-of-arrival" applications for sponsorship. These referred to arriving immigrants' submission of sponsorship applications for family members. The advantage for an applicant, usually a man, was that by the time his relatives finally appeared on the processing lists in Rome some two or three years later, he would actually be in a position to sponsor at least some of them. Little more had been required of these sponsors than proof of a job and the ability to provide housing to the newcomer. Now, officials advised imposing more stringent criteria of eligibility as a way of restricting the number of prospective sponsors. Other suggestions included "downgrading" the status of those unmarried children who were not financially dependent on their parents from their currently privileged position within the sponsorship scheme.[88]

In the end, on Fairclough's recommendation, the cabinet passed an order-in-council in March 1959 restricting the admission of sponsorship cases to the immediate family – the wives, unmarried children, and parents of Canadian sponsors. J.W. Pickersgill led the Liberal offensive against the order, ignoring his own role in imposing bureaucratic restrictions when he was minister of immigration between 1954 and 1957. Nonetheless, the Liberals mobilized enormous support around the issue and, within months, Fairclough rescinded the order. She was subsequently demoted to the Post Office portfolio, and in the 1963 election that witnessed the defeat of her party, Fairclough lost in her own riding, Hamilton West. It went to an Italian-Canadian Liberal, Joseph Macaluso.[89]

In formulating the ill-fated order-in-council, Fairclough and her colleagues had not been exclusively concerned with curtailing the Italian movement. Indeed, cabinet had begun to explore ways of eliminating the racial bias that had long underscored Canadian admission requirements. The Conservative initiatives on this front during the early 1960s foreshadowed the policy adopted by the Liberals in 1967. Commonly referred to as the "point system," this policy was officially declared to be nondiscriminatory, though it did favour educated and professional immigrants. Nor did the new selection criteria, in practice, eliminate completely the racialist basis of previous policies. Nevertheless, the 1967 policy did dismantle some of the formal barriers that for decades had blocked, or severely restricted, the entry of Asian immigrants and the peoples of developing countries.[90]

Since the recession years of the late 1950s, Canadian authorities had hoped to stem the tide of immigrants from Italy, but their efforts to do so by tinkering with bureaucratic controls had not been very successful. The introduction of the new policy regulations, however, coincided with the decline of immigration from Italy after 1969, a pattern that reflected the changing nature of conditions in Italy. The massive exodus of millions of people from the country, coupled with major reforms of the land tenure system and the introduction of a wide array of social and welfare services, had eliminated the need for large numbers of additional people to emigrate. In recognition of this fact, the Italian government moved its focus away from encouraging emigration towards securing better social security benefits for Italians abroad. The volume of Italian immigration to Canada never again reached the heights of the peak years of migration before 1966. By 1971 the flow shrank to a mere trickle (see appendix, table 2).

CHAPTER THREE

Men, Work, and the Family Economy

In March 1960 the Italians of Toronto and the city itself were shaken by the Hogg's Hollow tunnel disaster and the subsequent revelations about unsafe conditions on construction projects. The tragic drama had begun at 6 PM on St Patrick's Day, when fire suddenly swept through the main shaft that provided air and access to a crew of six "sandhogs" or underground tunnel workers installing a watermain beneath the Don River at Hogg's Hollow, on the northern limits of the city. Five Italians and their Belgian supervisor were trapped inside. Unequipped with fire extinguishers, they could do nothing to douse the fire. The smoke was overwhelming, and, worse still, the fire had stopped the air pumps, leaving the men to face a rising wall of mud and water. Although firemen and emergency crews responded quickly, their rescue attempts were hampered by inadequate on-site equipment, including ill-fitting emergency air pumps. Moreover, they could not clear the smoke from the tunnel without first reducing the air pressure inside, and depression was likely to increase the seepage of water and silt. The trapped men were in danger of drowning or suffocating from the smoke and cave-ins.

News of the disaster spread rapidly through the Italian community, and dozens of relatives, paesani (co-villagers), and friends of the workers were soon gathering at the site. Experienced tunnellers also came, offering their services in the rescue mission. Spirits soared when rescuers pulled from the tunnel a stunned but breathing Walter Andrushuk, the Belgian supervisor. But as the evening wore on, hope gave way to pessimism. From his hospital bed, Celestino Valentini, a co-worker who had made several rescue attempts, told reporters: "I could see them lying there. I tried to lift one ... But there wasn't any room to get a grip and pull him ... The smoke was killing me ... I had to get back." A reporter on the scene wrote: "The gay laughter symbolic of the Italian race was missing ... it had turned to weeping as women and relatives braced against the cold wind to pierce into the abyss which marked the possible tomb of their loved ones."[1]

Finally, remaining rescuers confirmed the worst reports. At 1:45 AM the dead body of Pasquale Allegrezza was pulled from the tunnel and waiting priests hurried to administer last rites. As dawn broke, rescuers dragged John Corriglie's body from the tunnel. "Red-eyed relatives stunned with shock and disbelief ... women, dressed in black, gaze mutely at the steel pithead," wrote one journalist, as the vigil continued. Hours later the remaining bodies of John Fusillo and Guido and Alexandro Mantella were recovered. Concluding his story about the day's tragedy, the reporter added: "The gusty March winds racing down the hills, whistling through the trees and whirling powder of snow into the strong beam of the overhead lights sing a silent requiem to the men who came to Canada from wartorn Europe to seek a better life."[2]

While most men would not suffer so horrible a fate, the Hogg's Hollow tragedy highlighted several features central to the Italian male immigrant experience in postwar Toronto. The image of the Italian "sandhogs" – of young greenhorns working deep beneath the surface of the earth, fulfilling the promises of politicians and developers to extend services to the fast-growing suburbs – vividly captures the labouring role that immigrants from every region in Italy played in Toronto's booming postwar economy. The workers who died in the tunnel collapse were typical of the Italian men who arrived in Toronto in another respect: although they had come alone, they had upheld their familial obligations, channelling their wages overseas to help support the wives, children, and parents they had temporarily left behind and to finance their sponsorship to Canada. A native of Carpino, Apulia, John Fusille, twenty-seven, had been boarding with his four brothers while awaiting the arrival of his wife and eight-month-old child. Like many Italian men who preceded their families to Toronto, he had cut costs by boarding in over-crowded flats so he could send remittances home to his wife and his elderly parents. At twenty-three and twenty-five years of age, respectively, Alexandro and Guido Mantella were the youngest of the group. Their earnings, and those of another brother also working in construction, had been supporting a family still residing in Tuffo di Minturo, Latina. Pasquale Allegrezza, twenty-seven, had been doing the same for his parents in Italy. The tragic difference between these men and the majority of Italians is that they never realized their plans. At forty-six, John Corriglie was the eldest member of the group and the only one who had reunited with his family. He had also realized another goal to which many of Toronto's Italians aspired – home ownership.[3]

The collective portrait of the Italians who died at Hogg's Hollow demonstrates more than the role men played in the process of chain migration. These men laboured to support their families. As heads of households, they enjoyed a certain power and prestige within their own families, but this position also carried with it heavy responsibilities and pressures, both at the workplace and beyond. The family economy of southern Italians, as Judith Smith has astutely observed, combined an assumption of patriarchal authority with a commitment to economic collectivity and cooperation. The male head of the household often determined how and when the others would contribute, through paid work or otherwise.[4] It was the men who were expected to secure the major chunk of the family's income and to act as the family's protector from the outside society. Their degree of success or failure on this front was a critical factor in shaping the self-identity of Italian immigrant men, including the tens of thousands of southerners who came to Toronto during the two decades following the Second World War. Moreover, during the years immediately following their arrival in the city, the relations of men with their families, especially with their wives, were forged in a particular context – the transition that many Italians underwent from peasants to proletarians.

ENTERING TORONTO

Men dominated the early waves of Italian immigrant arrivals into Metro Toronto. They accounted for 70 per cent of the 5000 immigrants who arrived in Toronto by 1950; over the next decade, they represented some 60 per cent of the 36,000 Italian newcomers. Thereafter, the gap between men and women is insignificant (see appendix, table 6). Like so many of the immigrant males who entered postwar Canada, Italian men who arrived in Toronto were typically young fellows who were still single or who had recently married and started families. Though arriving alone or with other men, Italian men emigrated as members of families, and familial obligations figured prominently in their plans. They came with the purpose of making money for the family, and the urgency of this task was heightened by the need to pay back debts to sponsors, relatives back home, employers, or the Canadian government. Money was also sent home to help support wives and children or parents until such time as families could be reunited in Toronto.

Consequently, on entering Toronto, Italian men sought the cheapest ways of feeding and housing themselves. Typically, they benefited from networking among kinfolk and paesani. Some newly arrived immigrants joined the households of relatives who had already established themselves in the city. More commonly, however, temporarily unattached male newcomers saved on housing costs by boarding with other greenhorns. This alternative could take various forms. Frequently, men gravitated to boarding houses run either by immigrant or Canadian families in the immigrant sections of the city. Among Toronto's boarding-house keepers were enterprising Italians who had settled in the city during the prewar period, or their Canadian-born children. Many such houses were owned by a family that occupied the main floor and rented space upstairs to male boarders, each of whom shared a room with several other men. Kitchens often consisted of a hotplate and a table located in a small back room. Often, the men shared the cooking and laundry chores. They cut eating costs by relying on a pasta-heavy diet that was only occasionally supplemented with meat. Commenting on the monotonous menu, Paolo Donato, a young Calabrian man who, in May 1951, joined his construction worker father in a west-end Toronto boarding house run by an Italian-Canadian couple, recalled: "The cooking, this was terrible, mostly spaghetti. You had no time to prepare the sauce ... we used to fry everything fast. I used to get stomach aches all the time."[5] In larger boarding houses, the rooms were filled with beds that were shared between men on day and night shifts.

Boarding houses were also run by employers, usually construction contractors who housed their immigrant recruits. While small contractors rented rooms in their own homes, some of the more prosperous employers ran boarding houses where sometimes dozens of men shared accommodation. This arrangement greatly benefited the employer who had direct access to a cheap labour supply to hire and lay off at will. He could also deduct living costs directly from his employees' paycheques, a practice that, as later events revealed, led to cases of deceitful deduction, exhorbitant rental costs, and severe overcrowding.[6]

Male boarding arrangements were also established among small groups of relatives, paesani, and co-workers. Often, one, two, or three men with sufficient savings purchased a house and then rented space to the others. Additional boarders might also be brought in to share the expenses. This set-up provided boarders with cheap rents and homeowners with savings to put towards mortgage payments. Such ethnic-based boarding arrangments proved psychologically more satisfying, permitting men to engage in what Robert Harney called "fellow-feelingness." "It was better being with your own," recalled one man. "You had somebody to talk with at night. We talked about Italy, and about the jobs – what else?"[7]

The predominance of male households among Italian immigrant arrivals in Toronto in the immediate postwar years was an obvious product of the Italian migration process and the high rates of family fragmentation that characterized the early waves of immigration from Italy. A similar pattern of settlement, for instance, emerged in Montreal, where a large concentration of postwar Italians also developed.[8] As it became increasingly common for couples and whole families to arrive together, especially after 1951, the male-boarding arrangments gave way to mixed-gender households composed of entire families and additional male boarders. Even in the case of the male households, however, familial priorities were evident and they help explain the constantly shifting composition of these households as well as the turnover in owners. Men who put their money down on houses were invariably preparing for the eventual arrival of their wives and children, fiancées, or parents. In some cases, the original owners remained, and as their families arrived some male boarders were let go to make room for women and children and perhaps other first-degree relatives who had recently arrived. In other cases, the ownership of the house shifted as some men left to set up a separate household with their newly arrived wife or to join close relatives who arrived at a later date. Others then took their place as part-owners of the original house. Such a scenario might replay itself several times as growing numbers of families became reunited in Toronto.

The movement between households occurred within a fairly narrow geographical area, since Italians generally gravitated to specific locales in the city. The early male-boarding arrangements and the reliance among male newcomers on family and kin for support laid the basis for the development of Toronto's postwar Italian neighbourhoods, a pattern that was reinforced as greater numbers of Italians settled in the same areas. As James Lemon has observed, Toronto's postwar immigrants actually exhibited a more dispersed residential settlement pattern than had been the case in the past.[9] The Italians, however, were the most concentrated of the ethnic groups in 1961. Over half of them lived in the city itself, where they accounted for 12 per cent of the total population. The highest concentration was in the old College Street Little Italy, the centre of which was Grace and College streets. There, more than 16,000 lived close to the Italian-run shops and clubs, with Catholic churches staffed by Italian-speaking priests. Rents and house prices were comparatively cheap in this long-standing immigrant receiving district, though it was by no means a slum.

Other newcomers were similarly drawn to the other established but smaller prewar colonies, some of which maintained their regional identities. In the Junction colony near Dupont Street and Old Weston Road, people from Apulia, Abruzzi, and Molise predominated. In the east end, near Danforth and Coxwell avenues, most members of the small Italian colony hailed from Apulia and Sicily. Near Dufferin Street and Brandon Avenue could be found many from Abruzzi and Friuli. The fastest growing area of the 1950s developed in the vicinity of St Clair Avenue West and Dufferin Street. By 1961 the St Clair Little Italy, with its many thriving businesses, was twice as big as the older College Street colony. Significant numbers of Italians began to build houses in the suburbs during the late 1950s. The axis along which they moved north was Dufferin Street; when they reached Lawrence Avenue they generally moved westward. Although the pattern would soon change, in 1961 no area north of Highway 401 was more than 15 per cent Italian (see map 2).

AN OCCUPATIONAL PROFILE

While the process of chain migration had steered tens of thousands of southern Italians to Toronto, this process had been strongly reinforced by the city's postwar prosperity, its diversified economy, and, most importantly, the availability of unskilled and semi-skilled jobs. The city's boom conditions created a great demand for workers of all types, and the new recruits came from diverse locales within and outside the country. Among the many migrant Canadians drawn to the city were rural Maritimers who, facing grim prospects at home, headed "down the road" to Toronto. Another major source of labour power was the postwar refugees and immigrants, including the Italians, who by the early 1960s emerged as the single largest non-British ethnic group in the labour force.

The number of working Italian men in 1961 was 42,971, a figure representing 8 per cent of Metro Toronto's total male labour force. As immigrants with little formal education – many possessed an elementary school certificate – and few industrial skills, Italians in this period also occupied the lower levels of the occupational ladder. While many had had some previous experience with waged labour, most, including southern peasants, arrived in the city without the specialized skills to secure immediately a more stable position within the labour market.

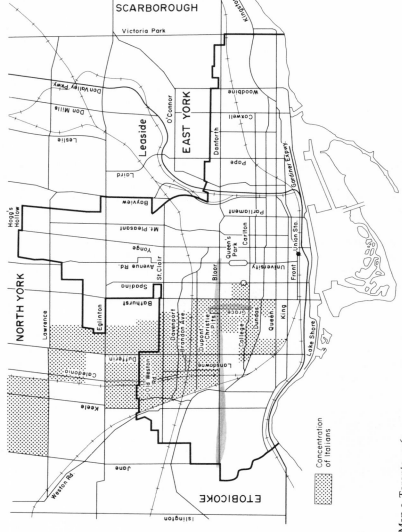

Map 2 Toronto, 1961

Even the most general male labour-force
dominantly working-class character of the It.
the early postwar era. Using John Porter's c.
mosaic," sociologist Anthony Richmond and
documented in detail the ethnic make-up of Torc
structure. Their studies reveal that the influx of .
to modify the predominantly British character of p
yet the city's class structure remained largely intact
nificant exception of the Jews, who had broken into th
managerial and professional class, the British ethnic s   .omi-
nated the most prestigious jobs, but were under-represer .ed within
blue-collar occupations. The Italians, by contrast, accounted for only
2 per cent of the professionals and highly skilled technicians, and
only 6 per cent of the city's managers. But they made up fully one-
third of the men who fell into the category of general labourer.[10]
They also earned the lowest incomes in the city. While the average
male income stood at $5080 in 1961, the average income earned by
Italian men was $3016 (see appendix, table 10).

Notwithstanding this working-class profile, there were some important gradations of class, status, and wealth among the Italians.
In the middle-class elite composed mostly of businessmen, builders,
and professionals, most belonged to the prewar Italian colony and
had come to Canada as young children before 1930 or had been born
here. Of the majority of Italian immigrants who took on blue-collar
jobs, close to one-third of them were in manufacturing. Here, the
largest numbers found jobs in the food and beverage sector, which
included slaughterhouses and meat-processing plants, dairies, fruit
and vegetable canneries, and distilleries. The next largest category
was furniture and fixture-making; then came the clothing industry,
where 8 per cent of the men worked. Italians employed in the leather
industries – tanneries, shoe, glove, luggage, and handbag shops –
represented 20 per cent of the total number of male workers in that
sector. Over half of them worked in shoe factories (see appendix,
table 12).

Official statistics reveal little about the gradations of skill among
these workers. A small core of immigrant tradesmen, including machinists, lathe operators, and bench fitters, enjoyed the more prestigious positions. Typically they had worked at lower skilled jobs,
often as assistants in their trade, until they obtained Canadian licences or gained the trust of their employers. Vittorio Iacobucci, an
experienced plumber who arrived in Toronto in 1957 after an earlier
sojourn to Argentina, worked in construction for a short while before
landing a job as a licensed welder. In another case, however, an

...anic spent more than five years employed as a car washer
...se he could not learn sufficient English to pass his licence test.
...s the economic recession set in after 1956, it became more difficult
even for skilled tradesmen to find work in their trade, but a considerable number of them did succeed in transferring their skills.[11]

Among the skilled Italian factory workers were men who were
employed in the leather and clothing industry. Working in shoe-
making and clothing shops, or as upholsterers in automotive and
furniture shops, some of them had been artisans in Italy and they
brought with them a sense of craft pride. In the Jewish-dominated
leather and garment shops, Italians provided a small but important
new source of male skilled cutters and sewing-machine operators.
Back home, many of them had still relied on a few simple tools,
such as a foot-pedalled sewing machine. In Toronto, village shoemakers and tailors, as well as former blacksmiths and butchers,
became machine operatives within more mechanized and hierar-
chically structured workplaces. They faced new industrial rhythms
and the impersonal relations between employer and employee.
Some, however, avoided the transition by working in very small
shops. Paolo Donato, the young Calabrian man who came to Toronto
in 1951, was the son of peasant farmers and had himself become a
journeyman tailor in his hometown. In Toronto he became a tailor's
assistant in a men's custom-made clothing shop. He was able to
practise his trade much as he had as a village tailor in Italy. But the
insecurity was greater, and he quit after only a year because he had
grown frustrated by repeated layoffs. An example of resistance to
the new regime was evident in the defiant stand taken by Enio
Garibaldi, described by his employer as an "excellent tailor," who
repeatedly refused to take orders from his foreman and demanded
more wages so he could support his family and also pay back his
debts. In another case, an experienced mechanic was fired from
an automobile factory when he did not return on time from his
holiday.[12]

Most of Toronto's postwar southern Italians, however, did not
come from an artisanal background and, as peasants, they had had
relatively little contact with a strict factory regime or with trade
unions. Keen to maximize their earnings and contribute to the welfare of their families, many of the newly arrived Italians who took
factory jobs responded to piece-rate systems and speed-ups in the
shop by working as hard and as fast as possible. This could spark
controversy between newcomers and the experienced Canadian
workers who had adopted strategies for resisting such pressures.
As a sewing-machine operative who worked in several leather
shops, one man recalled how employers promoted competition

among workers by the use of piecework and incentive bonuses: "They would put one against the other. If you want a raise you had to show you can make more than the next guy." Employed for a few years in a machine shop, another man remembered how he had been the object of his co-workers' resentment because he worked faster than the accepted rate. For this, he was also rewarded when he was one of the few men kept on during the winter slack period. As he explained, his decision to accelerate his pace of work did not stem from a desire to beat his co-workers but, rather, to increase his income and to help support his family.[13]

Many more Italian men found jobs in the unskilled and semi-skilled ranks of various firms, working on assembly lines in plastic novelty-making factories or food-processing plants, and as bakery helpers operating dough-cutting machines. Some toiled as helpers and assembly-line workers in metal and steel-making shops or in foundries and automotive plants. Others served as shipping and receiving clerks or as stock handlers in warehouses and grocery stores. Still others joined the cleaning staffs of hotels, offices, and department stores.

While employers encouraged concentrations of greenhorns out of self-interest, the immigrants had their own reasons for working with their compatriots. The concentration of paesani in the workplace acted as a buffer against the alienating features of factory life and played a major role in job-information networks among newcomers. Such concentrations could be found in large industrial concerns such as Christie's Bread Company and Bomarc Steel, in smaller plants such as Beverley Bedding, and among the cleaning staff of the large Royal York Hotel,[14] but they did not preclude the development of relationships with other workers on the job. Italian newcomers appreciated Canadian co-workers who helped them to learn English and with whom they shared their lunch hour. However, few of these friendships penetrated the sacred world of *la familiari*.[15]

While the insides of a factory became the new workplace for some men, the challenge of heavy, outdoor jobs made up the experience of most immigrant men.[16] In 1961 more than one-third of them were employed in the construction trades, where they performed physically arduous jobs as general labourers or tradesmen on building projects and as pick-and-shovel workers and tunnellers on sewage and hydro sites. Another 10 per cent were employed in the public service sector, working as street sweepers, gardeners, and snow-cleaners (see appendix, table 12).

Several reasons account for the strong presence of Italians in outdoor occupations, especially construction. There were many such jobs in the rapidly expanding city, and the seasonality of outdoor work meant that new openings periodically appeared. Most jobs required neither skills nor Canadian experience, which suited the newcomers well. What the jobs did require was physical strength and stamina and a willingness to risk dangerous working conditions. Healthy young immigrant men could answer these demands. As chapter 7 details, the building trades also offered newcomers an opportunity to learn a trade and thus earn comparatively high wages, or to enter into the ranks of the self-employed by becoming subcontractors. [17] Two other factors, both related to the immigrants' past work traditions, reinforced this pattern.

First, in comparison with factories where jobs were closely supervised, and the tasks boring and repetitive, outdoor work offered a measure of autonomy and some variety. Rather than being distressed by the seasonal fluctuations of outdoor work, former peasants accustomed to the peak and slack periods of agricultural cycles were familiar with such work rhythms. Italians were experienced in maximizing food and cash resources in the summer and stretching them to last throughout the lean winter months. It was not unusual, for instance, to find an unemployed construction worker spending the winter earning money in the informal economy – shovelling driveways, doing house repairs, or building fireplaces. Nor was it concidental that the annual butchering of the pig occurred at that time. Such resourcefulness had been perfected from years on the farm. [18]

Second, the kin and paesani networks that were so highly developed among southern Italians tended to increase the concentrations of men working at outdoor jobs. Take the case of Salvatore Pucci, who came to Toronto in the spring of 1957. Within days of his arrival, the brother-in-law with whom he and his wife were living took him to a gas company, where he landed a job digging tunnels on gas installation sites. He was soon laid off on account of "lack of work." With the help of a cousin, he was hired shortly afterwards as a landscaper at a cemetery, where he worked with two other relatives. At Christmas he was again unemployed. He was then hired as a labourer by a contractor who had obtained a contract from the Toronto Transit Commission to perform concrete and finishing work on a subway station being built on Danforth Avenue. Once hired, he himself brought in several kinsmen. Following the completion of the station, Pucci became one of many Italian subway workers who entered the TTC's maintenance department. No longer a newcomer, he had found a secure job at last. By the 1960s, the TTC maintenance department had several kin networks operating; the foremen and supervisors who headed them enjoyed a privileged status at the workplace and among their familiari. [19]

One of the few alternatives to the harsh realities of wage labour available to Italian immigrants was to make a living in the neighbourhood by setting up a shop that catered to their own compatriots. Toronto's postwar Little Italies boasted numerous fruit and vegetable stores, bakeries, barber and beauty shops, clothing stores, butcher shops, shoe-repair stalls, and cafés and restaurants. While they did confront some competition from the Italian oldtimers, many of whom owned the larger or more secure establishments on the block, these immigrant shopkeepers made their own impact on the city's Italian districts and significantly increased the foods and services available to a rapidly growing Italian population.

Among the Italians who joined the ranks of small-scale entrepreneurs were men who had been artisans in Italy, namely tailors, shoemakers, and butchers. Some of them chose to maintain a sense of independence by becoming self-employed in their trade, though typically they had first to endure a few years as workers as they saved money to set up a business. Dominic Colallo, a shoemaker, spent five years working on pick-and-shovel gangs before opening up his shoe-repair shop in the Junction colony. Although he says he would have preferred to have made shoes, he knew he could not compete against mass-produced shoes. It took Giancarlo Ferri, a Sicilian barber, much longer to reach this stage, but his was a less circuitous route. For ten years he worked in various Italian barbershops before finally establishing his own in the early 1960s. Others apprenticed with relatives or borrowed money from them.[20]

Self-employment was an equally attractive alternative to wage labour for many men who had been peasants in Italy. Without a trade, they tended to turn to the food industry, establishing groceries, butcher shops, or fish stores that catered to the Italians in their neighbourhoods. Sicilians, for example, owned many of the fruit and vegetable stores in the city's east-end colony. Kin networks also helped to steer enterprising immigrants into businesses in which their relatives or paesani were already engaged.

Though small businesses were typically associated with men, these enterprises were usually run by families and drew on the labour power of wives and other family members. Despite the important distinctions between petty proprietorship and blue-collar work, families who ran small ethnic businesses might straddle both worlds, at least temporarily. Often, the female or male head of the household ran the family store or business while the other partner continued to earn money in the paid labour force. This practice provided much-needed funds and acted as a buffer against the insecurity of newly established retail businesses. A few years after their arrival in Toronto, Maria and Eugenio Rossi pursued this strategy when they opened up a grocery store in the College Street Little Italy. Maria ran the store and took charge of inventory while Eugenio earned wages as a janitor and then as a construction worker. Their teenage daughter and Eugenio's mother helped out at the store, and on the weekends Eugenio delivered groceries. In other families, the reverse situation prevailed, with the woman earning wages outside the family enterprise.[21]

The local market was an exciting and integral part of the social life of an ethnic neighbourhood, and, as one historian has put it, bargaining was the lifeblood of the immigrant marketplace.[22] Shopkeepers were caught between rigid wholesale prices, the need for a profit, and the bargaining skills of their customers. People, especially women, familiar with the extended, elaborate bargaining in the paese, continued this valued practice in shops run by Europeans in Toronto. By doing so, they recreated a vibrant Old World ambiance that distinguished the shops of Little Italy and Kensington market from other shopping districts.

While shopkeepers escaped the pressures of paid work, they did not escape the reality of hard work. Maintaining a store or restaurant was exhausting work, and storeowners constantly faced the threat of business failure. Extending credit to financially hard-pressed clients could easily lead to financial ruin. And yet, for many small shopkeepers, including those men who had never been merchants back home, business still offered a far more attractive option than blue-collar work. As Bruno Ramirez notes, the entry into small business reveals the tensions and contrast between the proprietorial aspirations of Italian peasants and the reality they encountered in the host society as wage-earners. The move from labourer to small ethnic businessperson represented an important step for immigrants who had little opportunity to advance up the class ladder. The entry into the petty bourgeoisie represented one of the few qualitative leaps available to them, and it gave the successful ones a genuine sense of having escaped the wage-labour economy.[23]

WORK RHYTHMS AND RISKY JOBS

Many Italian male workers dealt an a daily basis with problems of job security and with physically exhausting, undesirable, and often dangerous work. The problem of seasonal work rhythms was not confined to construction workers, since many garment workers and other factory operatives were affected by seasonal layoffs, but it was true that among the most vulnerable workers were the thousands of men who earned their livelihood working out of doors. When winter approached, layoffs on housing, excavation, roadbuilding, and landscaping sites quickly followed. For these men, urban industrial life meant frequent job searches, employment mobility, and crisis periods of unemployment.

Given their circumstances, it is hardly surprising that Italian men talked endlessly about work opportunities and how to acquire them. Together kin and paesani developed information networks, sharing news of openings and lobbying on behalf of their kinsmen with their employers. They congregated at intersections known as pick-up depots for construction workers, each man hoping to be the one chosen out of the crowd by the foreman or contractor who came with his truck "to load up a crew." Others frequented the cafés, billiard halls, and parks of Little Italy in the hope of meeting men who knew about or could offer jobs. Still others turned to employment agencies operated by the National Employment Service, the Immigration Branch, the International Institute of Metropolitan Toronto, a publicly funded agency, or the Italian Immigrant Aid Society (IIAS), which in this period operated out of the rectory basement of the Italian parish of Our Lady of Mount Carmel.

Between 1952 and 1964 the IIAS placed some 7400 Toronto Italians, mostly in unskilled or semi-skilled positions in seasonal industries that did not pay good wages. With few alternatives, clients usually took what was offered, at least until something better came along.[24] Some did refuse to take work they considered too poorly paid or demeaning, and occasionally a client returned to complain about a placement and demand help in securing a new job. Most, however, accepted these jobs because, like the men who died at Hogg's Hollow, they needed the money to support their families.[25]

The seasonality of most outdoor jobs left Italian immigrants and others scrambling to compete for a limited number of winter positions. Many, including Bruno Cara, adjusted to the problem of winter unemployment by securing temporary indoor work. A former shoemaker from southern Italy who arrived in Toronto in 1954, he spent several years alternating between excavation work and winter jobs as an office maintenance worker, deliveryman, or shoe-factory operative.[26]

Individual work histories offer graphic illustrations of occupational mobility. For example, Pietro Minno, a twenty-five-year-old married man, spent six years after his arrival in Toronto in 1954 juggling numerous unskilled jobs. Starting as a labourer with a small construction firm, he was laid off the first winter. He found a position as a janitor in an office building before returning to work as a common labourer with a house-building subcontractor a year later. When the project was completed, he was again unemployed and sought work as a janitor at a school where a peasano was employed. Similarly, Silvio Lucca, a former peasant who had run a truck farm in Italy, held the following jobs during the 1950s: machine operator, truck driver, general labourer in a paper-making factory, construction labourer, moulder in a steel-products factory, and machine assembler in a car-parts shop. Like many others, Lucca had proved remarkably resilient in Toronto's fluctuating labour market; he had managed to keep finding work in spite of a lack of marketable skills. To do so, he had often turned to relatively low-skilled jobs characterized by high turnover rates. [27]

Another feature of the work worlds of many Italian immigrant men in early postwar Toronto was their association with physically arduous or dangerous jobs. Whether working in foundries, boring tunnels, or building houses, they took on back-breaking and risky tasks – digging on excavation sites that sometimes caved in, slipping off scaffolds or the ledges of incompleted buildings, losing a limb to a machine, or getting burned by gaseous fumes or chemicals. Serious back or spinal-cord injuries caused by heavy lifting and carrying were common afflictions among injured Italian workers. By far the most vulnerable workers were the Italians employed in the construction trades, an industry that in these years consistently registered the fourth highest rate of fatalities in Ontario – after mining, logging, and fishing. In their submission to the Royal Commission on Industrial Safety in 1961, the Ontario Workmen's Compensation Board (WCB) noted that, with respect to the number of settled claims recorded for the period 1955–9, construction had the fourth highest accident frequency rates. The WCB statistics for these years also revealed a marked increase in the number of compensable accidents. [28]

The Hogg's Hollow tragedy revealed how inattention to safety precautions could be disastrous. Apart from the sheer exhaustion that comes from hours of digging, hauling, and crawling underground, tunnellers faced the prospect of suffocation or bruises suffered in cave-ins, diseases related to air decompression – "the bends" or necrosis (a rotting of the bones) – and exposure to gas leaks, electrical shocks, and fires. In the aftermath of Hogg's Hollow, a reluctant provincial minister of labour, Charles Daly, admitted that as many as two hundred men who had worked on sewer projects suffered from the bends and that two of them had died from the disease. Also alarming was the news that the provincial regulations regarding air-compression work were inappropriate and had to be revised. The prevalence of these abuses was confirmed by the 1961

Royal Commission on Industrial Safety, which led the commissioners to insist on stricter enforcement of safety regulations and greater
efforts to inform workers of the on-site risks involved in any job. [29]
As late as 1975, experienced Italian construction workers pointed to
speed-up conditions as a major cause of job-site accidents. Their
concern about speed-ups is evident in the vocabulary they adopted:
"il pusciare" or "il push" are terms that connote speed-ups and the
foreman is often referred to as "the push man." [30]

A small sample of the accidents reported in Toronto's Italian newspaper, *Corriere Canadese*, illustrates the risky nature of the immigrants' jobs. In September 1954 Raffaele Lucchetta, twenty-six, was
digging a trench for the installation of a gas main when he was
buried by a landslide. Having narrowly escaped the debris, his co-
workers dug him out and found he was still breathing. Less fortunate
was Donato D'Erano, twenty-two, a native of Abruzzi, who was
killed the same month when a trench he had been digging caved
in, burying him under a pile of mud. His two brothers and other
crew members barely escaped the same fate. In the fall of 1956 three
Italian municipal workers suffered serious injuries in a violent explosion and fire while they were underground installing a gas main
in Scarborough. Sam Minardi, eighteen, and Giovanni Caruso,
thirty, suffered third-degree burns to the body, and the third man,
Sam's cousin Vincenzo Minardi, lost his sight in one eye. [31] Another
trench collapse on a sewage installation site in Etobicoke resulted
in the February 1959 death of an older man, Carmine Morra, forty-
seven, and serious injury to thirty-year-old Vito Martino. Still another cave-in, this one in June 1958, led to charges of criminal neglect
against the company when Mario Perizini, twenty-six, was buried
under six tons of rubble in a landslide on a sewage site in a Toronto
suburb. [32]

Accidents also occurred on building and road sites. Death struck
Giuseppe Radeschi, a young and recent immigrant from l'Aquila,
Abruzzi, in May 1958 after the explosion of a can of gasoline on a
road-paving project in the west end. According to friends, Radeschi
had been enthusiastic about Toronto. The irony of the words he had
used to describe Canada in a letter he wrote to his parents just before
his death was not lost on the reporters. "Canada," it read, "is a big
nation where the poor can succeed and create their own success." [33]
Finally, traffic accidents occurred as workers were herded into
overcrowded trucks and transported from site to site. In the summer
of 1957 one worker died when the truck in which he and his co-
workers were riding ran into on-coming traffic. In response, the
Toronto and District Labour Council publicly denounced the mis-

treatment of Italian workers who "were loaded up in trucks like beasts ... piled up on top of each other, like so many animals for the slaughter."[34]

Italian workers hardly needed these news reports to remind them of the dangerous jobs they performed. The harsh reality of their daily work lives was made painfully evident every time they watched a co-worker get hurt. Indeed, the collective memory of Italian immigrant men is filled with painful testimonies of having witnessed the death or injury of co-workers and kinsmen who became impaled on pipes, fell from scaffolds, or were buried at excavation sites. One man recalled how he watched four co-workers fall to their death when an elevator shaft in an apartment building collapsed. He had narrowly escaped death only because he had gone off to collect more nails. Speaking to the issue, he said: "It was very hard for us, we had to do those jobs and we did them, but the danger its always there. We could slip and fall – just like that!"[35]

Unlike their predecessors of a half century before, postwar immigrants benefited from various state-funded social services that cushioned the impact of injury or unemployment. Still, these schemes did not offer full protection to immigrant workers. Complications and costly delays frequently arose when injured workers applied for provincial compensation awards. They had to confront their employers who, anxious to prevent a record of injuries, tried to avoid filling out the requisite reports. Badgered by WCB caseworkers, who could not process an application without these papers, Italian workers might return several times before the employer was finally persuaded to comply with the regulations. Compensation awards, when granted, rarely sufficed, leaving families to find their own ways of earning additional income. Receiving an award also meant repeated intrusions by caseworkers and doctors, who made the decision about returning to work.[36]

Consider the case of Gianni Avellino, a father of five who in 1958 suffered a serious arm injury while operating a heavy industrial machine at work. He received emergency relief for a few weeks and seven months' compensation. The award, however, proved inadequate for his family, all of whom were dependent on his paycheque. Having given birth twice in the last three years, his wife did not work outside the home, and they had recently purchased a house. To lessen the economic burden, the couple took in several male boarders. They also sent their eldest, eighteen-year old child to work. Avellino himself eventually found a less physically demanding job in an upholstery shop.[37]

In some cases, injuries plagued worl
ferred not to hire former WCB cases for
further injuries, a situation that led so
and to work in fear of being found o
jected the advice to undergo operation
out of commission for long periods of
to obey doctors was equally worrison
compensation because they had failed t
their condition. While the permanently
future, the partially disabled tried to su
securing light jobs such as nightwatch
vantage of the retraining programs offere   .... WCB and the
Department of Labour. However, major strides in the rehabilitation
of Italian workers did not occur until after the creation in 1962 of
COSTI (Centro Organizativo Scuole Tecniche Italiane), a rehabilitation and retraining centre for injured Italian workers.[38]

WORKING MEN AND FAMILY ECONOMIES

The highly seasonal work rhythms and the risky nature of men's
jobs had particular implications for the other members of the men's
family, especially their wives. Italian women lived daily with the
fear that their husband, and the family's chief breadwinner, might
one day come home too mangled to return to work. Like the victims
of Hogg's Hollow, Italian men tolerated undesirable and even dangerous jobs because they took seriously their position as the family's
chief, if not sole, provider. Nor were they strangers to performing
gruelling work.

Labour and feminist historians generally agree that men and
women experienced class in gender-specific ways, but few scholars
have examined the relations between male workers and their families.[39] Many men defined themselves first and foremost in familial
terms. This was particularly true of Italian immigrants, who brought
with them a family-centred work culture. While Italian men prided
themselves on their role as the family's primary breadwinner and
as the family's official representative to the wider community, they
also felt the pressures that accompanied this status and they shared
the fear that they might not be able to meet the challenge. One man
captured the feelings of many when he said: "For us, everything is
for the family. You make sacrifices, get up at 5 o'clock in the morning
and wait for the truck to take you to sometimes you don't know

what? To clean out the mud and mix cement for
amily can make a better life."[40]

cerns were underscored by the fact that many Italian men
her recently married or male heads of young families. Like
immigrant populations, the postwar Italians were a youthful
oup with a high percentage of young married adults and children.
In 1961 more than three-quarters of Toronto's adult Italians were
married, compared with 62 per cent of the general population.[41] In
contrast to other ethnic groups, whose married population was more
evenly distributed across the various age categories, the married
Italians were predominantly young men and women in their twen-
ties and thirties. Many of these couples were in the process of forming families in these years; in 1971 more than three-quarters of the
Italians were children under ten years of age.[42]

Familial priorities loomed large in the lives of Italian men from
the start, even as the first groups of men who preceded their families
to Canada entered Toronto. The economic needs of Italian families
were compounded by the strong desire among the immigrants for
homeownership. To this end, Italian families continued, sometimes
for years, to "double up" and to take in extra boarders. In a survey
conducted in 1962 of immigrant households in the city's west end,
veteran social worker Edith Ferguson observed, with some disapproval, how Italian immigrants endured heavy financial burdens
and crowded households in order to one day afford their own home.
"One family," she noted, "with seven children and an eighth expected, live in two, dark and crowded upper rooms at the top of a
long dirty staircase and share the bath with 13 other people." She
nevertheless conceded that the strategy generally worked.[43]

Many families would indeed be successful. By 1971 approximately
77 per cent of Canada's Italians owned their homes, compared with
55 per cent for the general population. For Toronto, Italians recorded
the highest proportion, with over 83 per cent of Italians owning their
own homes.[44] As Ferguson herself understood, the desire for homeownership among Italians reflected in part the continuing influence
of a peasant background. "They bend every effort," she wrote of
the immigrants, "toward saving for a home, which gives them security, some roots and some status in the community." Having come
from a society in which wealth was predicated on landed property
and where their own impoverished position was linked to the inequities of the landholding system, Italian immigrants placed enormous value on the purchase of a house and property. But homeownership also represented a rational and effective working-class
strategy to minimize the financial insecurity suffered by families

operating in conditions of scarcity.[45] It reveals the patterns of continuity and discontinuity that characterized the immigrant experience. In order eventually to own their own homes, men helped initiate a strategy of living in multiple family dwellings, which had not been a common housing arrangment back home where single family households predominated. At the same time, the traditional support networks of kin and paesani made it a viable strategy. The system of mutual obligation and reciprocity that had permitted the process of chain migration to develop in the first place continued to operate in Toronto, enabling the Italians not only to find jobs but also to purchase homes. Moreover, for men, the possession of a house carried a special significance: it represented a tangible sign of their success as a family provider.

MALE BREADWINNERS AND SECONDARY WAGE-EARNERS

Despite the resourcefulness Italian immigrant men showed in a fluctuating and sometimes oversupplied labour market of the 1950s and early 1960s, many men did not in these years actually earn an income sufficient to support the entire family. In 1961, for instance, the average annual male income for Italian immigrants could barely keep a family of three living above the poverty line, let alone cover such additional costs as monthly mortgage payments.[46] Furthermore, the highly seasonal and unsafe nature of men's work meant there was always the possibility that a man's wages might suddenly stop because of layoffs or injury. Since most men earned the major chunk of the family income – among Italians women earned on average half what men did – male unemployment or underemployment profoundly affected other members of the family.

Where there were no additional income earners, the temporary or permanent withdrawal from the work force of the chief male breadwinner could precipitate a major crisis unless the family could secure outside help. Consider, for instance, the case of Mauro Agusto, a former peasant and construction worker, who settled in Toronto with his wife and four children in the late 1950s. For several years he worked as an operative in a machine shop while his wife was employed in a leather factory. None of the children were old enough to work. Then, Augusto's wife became ill, suffering major complications that required a lengthy hospital stay. Medical bills exacerbated the family's already difficult situation. They had been renting a tiny flat with rooms that were not heated even in the cold February weather. After contacting the International Institute of Metropolitan Toronto (IIMT), the family received outside help. The Department of Health sent a doctor to examine the children, who were suspected of suffering from TB, and arranged regular visits from a public health nurse. The family was given immediate assistance in the form of food vouchers, clothes, and an emergency welfare cheque, and applications were filed with the Toronto Housing Authority for a government-sponsored low-rental housing unit. Agusto later suffered a neck injury at work, and the family were dependent on state benefits for more than a year.[47]

In Agusto's case, government assistance was crucial to a family in crisis. Still, even in this era of the welfare state, most forms of government aid were temporary and the funds allotted for unemployment insurance benefits or compensation were usually insufficient to cover a family's economic needs. A far more effective strategy for meeting the economic constraints in their lives, and for preventing a descent into enormous indebtedness, was to draw on the labour power of additional wage earners. This was the most common way in which Italian immigrant families dealt with the reality of economic insecurity. The example of Paolo Principe, who became permanently injured in a workplace accident in 1957, illustrates how the presence of one or more secondary wage earners helped matters when a crisis arose. When Principe injured his leg on the job, his wife was fully employed and his teenage son worked part-time after school. Their wages supplemented the unemployment benefits and compensation award Principe received. Yet even he tried to persuade the WCB authorities to award him the permanent disability pension in one lump sum rather than in regular monthly payments, on the grounds that he could not otherwise cover his mortgage payments and the debts the family had incurred.[48]

Owing to the high proportion of young children among Italian immigrant families in Toronto, strict anti-child labour laws, compulsory schooling, and a greatly improved welfare system, postwar Italian families relied less on the wage-earning capacity of their children than did their early twentieth-century counterparts. However, in families where children turned sixteen and were old enough to work, many were encouraged by parents to do so. This happened to Agostino Nucci, a high school student in the late 1950s. Insisting that "he was now old enough to start to earn some money," his parents disregarded the advice of their IIMT caseworker to keep the boy in school on account of his good academic record. By contrast, Natalia Scoleri, who arrived in Toronto as a teenager in the late 1950s and disliked school, was only too happy to take a job at a local laundry when her father took ill. Many children who did stay in high school earned part-time wages in weekend or summer jobs.[49]

The statistics on education suggest that many sons and daughters closed off advanced educational opportunities and career options to contribute to the family's welfare. This pattern also reflects the streaming process in the schools, which discouraged immigrant children from pursuing a post-secondary education. By 1976 only 3 per cent of Toronto's Italians had a university education, compared with 15 per cent of Torontonians whose mother tongue was English. Only 10 per cent of the Italians had completed grade 12, and only 7 per cent had finished grade 13.[50]

The kinds of sacrifices made are illustrated by the case history of Angelo Cinchello, a regular client of the IIMT after 1955. At the age of nineteenth, Cinchello's aspirations for the priesthood were dashed when he and his mother left Italy to join his father, a former tailor who had recently lost his shop. Angelo spent the next decade juggling many jobs – a locker boy at various golf clubs, a clerk with three different department stores, a hot-dog vendor, and a dishwasher at several restaurants. Meantime, working adversely affected his studies. In 1958 he repeated night classes in high school English after failing an exam, and, a year later, the seminary to which he had applied rejected him. He worked for several years as a maintenance worker, completed high school in 1962, and finally went on to college.[51]

In most cases, working-age sons followed their fathers into blue-collar jobs. As they themselves prepared for marriage, they held little expectation of pursuing long-term career goals. Like Cinchello, many had come fully expecting to work, but unlike him, they never returned to school or opted for major career changes. Some, however, were torn between their familial obligations to their parents and their own plans to marry and establish a separate household. One man recalled how for four years he worked alongside his father in construction, always handing over his paycheque to his parents for use towards mortgage payments. When he turned twenty-three he told his father he hoped to save some of his wages to help him prepare for marriage and, after some debate, his father consented.[52]

Most typically, however, it was the wife who assumed the role of secondary wage-earner, and chapter 4 chronicles the work worlds of Italian immigrant women. By the 1950s the term "family wage" was not in popular usage, but, like the more intensely studied craftsmen of an earlier era, Italian immigrant men faced a dilemma whether to approve of their wives working. In reconciling themselves to the situation, they drew upon their own cultural tradition.[53] In southern Italy, men had prided themselves on their role as the family's primary breadwinner and official representative to the wider community. Once in Toronto, the capacity to bring home the "real" wages – the family's highest and most secure wages – continued to be a source of male pride. Typically, immigrant men stated that "it was the man's job to support the family," and they stressed the hardships endured in the early days – the long work days, the deprivations, the frugality – all for the sake of the family's well-being. Yet, they were also acutely aware of the economic pressures their families faced and their own relatively disadvantaged position within the occupational world. Despite the chauvinistic character of southern Italian culture, Italian men brought with them a cooperative work ethos and they were certainly accustomed relying on the labour power of their wives. As a result, many not only accepted the reality of "having to send my wife to work," as one man put it, but they stressed the contribution their wives made to the family's well-being.[54]

This is not to suggest that all Italian men openly encouraged their wives to work. Certainly, some refused on the grounds that a wife's place was in the home, raising children and keeping house, while others would not allow their wives to mingle with mixed company in the workplace. Nor did men who lived with working wives take on a more equitable sharing of domestic chores. On the contrary, though many men were regularly laid off, especially in winter, few took over the housekeeping, even when wives went out to work. Given the double standard that informed the sexual mores of southern Italy, it is not surprising that some were relieved their wives were employed in largely female workplaces and often worked alongside their own kinswomen. Yet even those men who admitted it damaged their male pride to have their wives working for wages emphasized other concerns, especially the hostility they felt about their wives having to perform menial and low-paying jobs. "I didn't come to this country," said one man, "so my wife could be the maid and make pennies to pick up the dirty clothes for some family. I didn't want that."[55]

Most men adopted a pragmatic response to the situation, however. A central theme to emerge from the oral testimonies of both Italian men and women is that a wife's wages "made a difference" to the family economy. The comments of Michelle D'Antonio, a construction worker who later became a subcontractor and helped support a daughter and his parents, captured the meaning of this phrase from the male perspective when he said: "In those days, there were a lot of bills to pay, the children were coming too. If my wife could do a little bit, make money, it makes a big difference; we have money coming in winter, she can buy groceries, things like that, and then it's not so hard, you worry less."[56] For Italian immigrant men like D'Antonio, coming to terms with a wife's working for wages was an essential, gendered component in their transition from peasants to workers. In many Italian households, men and women who had formerly toiled together on the farm become immigrant wage-earners, each of whom left for a separate workplace to earn an income.

EXPLOITED WORKERS AND IMMIGRANT MASCULINITY

The Italian male workers' sense of masculinity was most seriously threatened by long-term unemployment and by the unappealing nature of their jobs. A serious injury, for example, had deep emotional and psychological repercussions for Italian men, who feared being defined a failure as a husband and father and as an immigrant. An illustration of such a crisis in male pride is evident in the case file of Fluvio Pisticci, who arrived in Canada with his wife and children in 1955. A few years later he developed a sinus problem while working in an upholstery shop. Unable to qualify for compensation or disability benefits, the family spent three years on public welfare, a time when they lost their house and the wife became ill. As a result, Pisticci suffered from an acute sense of failure, which he expressed to his IIMT caseworker: "He seems to have had his share of bad luck and was very discouraged. He is on welfare and feels ashamed of it. He has been in hospital ... [and] therefore could not perform a very hard labourers work. He has lost his house due to his illness and is still very upset about it."[57]

A father of three who came to Toronto in 1958 responded similarly after his WCB doctor advised him against ever returning to construction work. According to his caseworker, he "broke down in tears when he said that one of his sons asked him why he could not go to work yet. He explained to the child that his doctor would not allow him." Oral testimonies are also full of references to the *vergogna* (shame) accompanying a loss of job. As one informant put it, "you came here to make a better life, and when you can't, you feel ashamed, you want to do for the family."[58] Fortunately, however, most Italian men even during the difficult early years before 1965 were more likely to face seasonal or occasional periods of unemployment than to find themselves altogether unmarketable.

Another important aspect of the male culture of Italian immigrant workers was their resentment at the disparity between the official portrayal of Canada as a land of opportunity and their own experience of performing "dirty," disagreeable, and risky jobs that Canadians shunned. Men recalled, with some bitterness, how they had laboured as "beasts of burden" and how the city's tremendous growth had been predicated on their labours. At the time of the Hogg's Hollow disaster, an editorial in the *Corriere Canadese* charged that the Italians were being made "sacrificial lambs at the altar of Canadian progress." Dominic Collalo also spoke for many when he remembered the humiliation he felt at performing low-status jobs, such as retrieving coins from fountains, sweeping streets, and digging sewers, before he could save enough to start his shoe-repair shop. "Those kinds of jobs," he said, "they give only to the immigrants."[59]

Nevertheless, during the early difficult years of adjusting to life in Toronto, Italian men learned to cope with these strains, and they did so primarily by developing their own standards for success. Their work was made more palatable by viewing the weekly paycheque as proof of a capacity to endure tough working conditions and to meet the challenge of providing for a wife and children and perhaps additional family members. As scholars of masculinity have argued, to be the family's chief breadwinner confirmed a man's prowess.[60] This notion of male prowess also has its ethnic variations. Italian workers adjusted to the harsh reality of their working lives by viewing their work through a particularly immigrant, male frame of reference, seeing themselves as enduring jobs that Canadian workers would be incapable of doing, and, moreover, attributing to themselves the status of "nationbuilders." Italian men derived considerable pride from the contribution they believed they had made to Toronto's postwar progress – a sentiment most typically expressed in the phrase "the Italians, we built this country." The self-image of the honest, hardworking Italian immigrant worker – an image, incidently, with which sympathetic observers concurred – provided an important psychological defence against their low position on the city's occupational ladder.[61]

Ready to leave for Canada: grandmother would be left behind in Abruzzi. Author's collection

The voyage over, c. 1956. Multicultural History Society of Ontario (MHSO). Italian collection

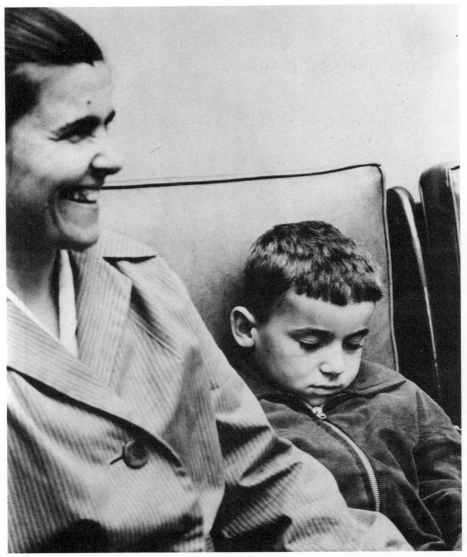

Mother and son arriving in Toronto, July 1960. York University Archives, *Toronto Telegram* collection

Italian railway-track workers
recruited by the Welch (Veltri)
Company, northern Ontario,
c. 1953. MHSO, Italian collection

Cooking for track workers,
northern Ontario, c. 1957.
MHSO, Italian collection

A track worker with the Canadian Pacific Railway in British Columbia, before migrating to Toronto, c. 1957. Author's collection

A young family reunited in Toronto in the late 1950s. Author's collection

Women's work at home: preparing tomato sauce. MHSO, Italian collection

After a hard day's work, c. 1958. Author's collection

At work in a sock factory, Spadina Avenue. Vincenzo Pietropaolo

A successful business. Vincenzo Pietropaolo

Cleaning up at the hall. MHSO, Italian collection

Proud gardener. Vincenzo Pietropaolo

CHAPTER FOUR

From Contadin
Woman Worker

One Thursday in mid November 1956 Maria Rossi and her daughter arrived in Toronto from their peasant farm in Italy. They were met at Union Station by Rossi's husband, who had left them a year previously for work in Toronto. After eating dinner with relatives, Rossi was ushered into her new home in a basement flat in the house of a Calabrian family who had settled in the city a few years earlier. Next day, the couple went shopping for household necessities, including an espresso coffee-maker and pots for cooking spaghetti, at Honest Ed's discount department store. (It was known as "la polizia" [the police] because of the uniformed security guards.) To Rossi's delight, the next morning the Santa Claus parade passed by their Dupont Street home. At seven o'clock Monday morning Rossi went directly to work at a nearby laundry where a sister-in-law had secured her work as a steampress operator at $37 a week. For twenty years Maria Rossi worked at many low-skilled jobs – sewing, cooking, tending a grocery store, and operating a cash register – when she finally withdrew from the work force to care for her dying husband. [1]

Performing demanding roles as immigrants, workers, wives, and mothers, women played a critical role in the immigration of southern Italian families to postwar Toronto. Their active commitment to the family helped bridge the move from Old World to New as women's labour, both paid and unpaid, contributed towards the material well-being of their families. The transition from *contadina* (peasant woman) to worker did not require a fundamental break in the values of women long accustomed to contributing many hours of labour to the family. As immigrant workers, however, they confronted new forms of economic exploitation and new rhythms of work and life. Women at home similarly performed valuable support roles and ed the alienating aspects of urban industrial life. Bolstered by works of kin and paesani, women not only endured these hardships but displayed a remarkable capacity to incorporate their new experiences as working-class women into traditionally rooted notions of familial and motherly responsibility.

Women and children, of course, figured prominently in the flow of Italian immigrants who entered postwar Canada. By the mid-1950s they made up half of the annual Italian volume. More than 81,000 Italian adult women came as part of the first major wave of immigrants who entered Canada during the decade of the 1950s, a figure representing over 30 per cent of the total volume of Italian immigration in this period. Young peasant women sponsored by their husbands or families predominated, although those from artisan and merchant backgrounds also came. Only a minority of women arrived as trained domestics, hairdressers, and seamstresses (see appendix, table 9), while even fewer entered the country under nominated terms – as immigrants sponsored by Canadian employers. After 1951, as the process of family reunification got underway, the number of female immigrants entering Toronto roughly equalled that of male arrivals. By 1961 almost 42,000 Italian women had entered Toronto; another 29,000 arrived during the subsequent decade (see appendix, tables 5 and 6).

During the years following the Second World War, Italian women, like men, fell victim to North American sentiments regarding the supposed inferiority of southern Italians. However, as women they confronted additional prejudices. This was particularly true of married peasant women. Because Canadian government officials did not expect such women to work and make a direct economic contribution to the country, they ignored them. In the rare descriptions of peasant women contained in the Immigration Branch files, Italian women emerge as helpmates and housekeepers but never as farmers in their own right. Following a lengthy discussion of the work routines of southern peasants, one official summarized women's contribution in a single sentence: "Where cattle were owned they were often tended by the women."[2] A 1950 agreement that removed customs duties on Italian bridal trousseaus entering Canada recognized women's role in setting up a home in the new society.[3] Yet it also reflected prevailing notions about married women's prescribed roles as wife and mother and reinforced the assumption that married southern Italian women, most of whom had obtained low levels of formal education and possessed few marketable skills for an industrial economy, were inferior immigrants. This position of inferiority was reinforced by the fact that most of them entered Canada under the family classification scheme – as dependants who, along with their children, were officially deemed to be the responsibility of their husbands. This status also rendered them ineligible to apply for government assistance or training programs.[4]

Contrary to contemporary assumptions that women were little more than part of the male newcomer's cultural baggage, southern Italian women, like their compatriots who came from Italy's other regions, were active agents in family migration. A consideration of their role must begin with life in rural Italy where, as chapter 1 detailed, peasants generally resided in simple households, each of which made up an agricultural work group. Also, each family drew on the labour power of every household member and combined incomes from a variety of sources – farming, agricultural or other forms of wage labour, and selling home-made goods such as cloth and produce.

The literature on southern Italy, which consists largely of the postwar ethnographic accounts of social anthropologists, emphasizes the segregation and subordination of women and virtually excludes consideration of how women's work contributed to family survival. In his study of a Calabrian village, anthropologist Jan Brogger stresses the predominance of "female exclusion" – a code of conduct that imposed severe restrictions on women's interaction with males outside of their own household. Whenever they found themselves in mixed company, including harvest time when two or more families joined forces, he notes, women were prohibited from engaging freely in conversation with men and were closely chaperoned by their parents or female kin. John Davis, who studied a postwar village in Basilicata, treats the entire issue of women's farm labour as a potentially dishonourable activity. Although he readily concedes that women regularly performed critical field duties, he posits the view that the presence of a women working in the fields called into question the husband's ability to support his family and, unless she was obviously working, cast doubt on the woman's chastity.[5]

While such extreme views must be rejected – indeed, a careful reading of the anthropological texts reveals that, as in most cultures, the actual practice of the villagers repeatedly contradicted the ideal types so carefully charted by academics – it is clear that, as in the past, the patriarchal organization of the southern family and the cultural mores of southern society significantly shaped gender relations inside and outside the family in the postwar south. Such factors imposed heavy restrictions on the choices and behaviour of women. The age-old concept of familial *onore* (honour) that pervaded the culture not only of southern Italians but of many European and rural societies rested in large part on the sexual purity of wives, daughters, and sisters, the men's successes in guarding the virtue of their women, and the men's ability as family breadwinners. While men were expected to provide for their wives and children through hard work and self-deprivation, women were to reciprocate by remaining sexually faithful. Linked to prevailing notions of male self-esteem and authority was the corollary – the fear that a woman might engage in pre- or extra-marital sex and thereby bring shame to her family. Supervision of women's public activities was the inevitable result. [6]

As in other European cultures, male privilege within Italian society was exercised widely within the public sphere. Within the towns and villages of southern Italy, men were freer to socialize outside the household, and they led the religious and social feasts celebrated in the paese. Considered the family's chief decision-maker, the male head acted as the family's representative in its dealings with the outside world – making annual rental payments to absentee landlords or their agents, journeying out of the region in search of work, or acting as the main marriage negotiator for children. One Calabrian woman, Vincenza Curtola, recalled, for instance, how her father spent two weeks consulting people, including the town cleric and doctor, before granting final approval to his daughter's prospective husband. [7]

A model of male-dominance/female-submission is ultimately too simplistic to account for peasant women's experiences in the Mezzogiorno. It ignores the complexity of gender relations in Italy and underestimates the importance of female labour to peasant family production. The dictates of the household economy regularly drew women outside of the home to participate in agricultural production. Though the supposed natural link between women and domestic labours persisted, women's work roles included domestic and farm duties. And both involved back-breaking efforts.

Domestic responsibilities included cooking, cleaning, and child-care, as well as weaving, sewing clothes, and, especially during the winter slack, producing embroidered linens and crocheted table-cloths for bridal trousseaus. Well into the years after the Second World War, such labours remained time consuming and arduous. As Guiseppina Mazoli, a Molisan woman recalled, doing laundry involved fetching water from the town well, boiling it, soaking the items for an hour, and then carrying them out to a nearby stream where they were rinsed and laid out on the rocks to dry. Cooking over open wood stoves was hot and dirty work, and the stoves required constant maintenance and cleaning.[8]

Women and girls also farmed – clearing the plots, sewing and planting, hoeing, and sharing in the overall work of the summer grain harvest, a project that drew on the help of kinfolk and neighbours. At home, women were responsible for the threshing and winnowing. During the autumn ploughing, women transported manure from the barn to the various plots. Though the task of breaking the ground was usually performed by men, women also did this exhausting work. And throughout the season, they travelled back and forth between town and the fields carrying food and supplies in baskets on their heads.[9]

Because the landholdings of a single peasant family were scattered, the family members worked at some distances from each other. In some parts of southern Italy, such as western Sicily, the gender division of labour was quite rigid: women were responsible for the upkeep of the nearby garden plots, while the men worked the fields farther away from town. But this was not the case for all regions. One woman, Elizabetta Marcone, explained how on her farm in southern Abruzzi the women and men of the family performed similar tasks, each on a different plot of land. Every morning, she said, each of her parents took a few children and set off for a field. They would return each night to the dinner that Marcone's grandmother had waiting for them. The relentless tasks of farming were made more enjoyable, she added, by the camaraderie of the family work group. "We worked very hard, get up at the crack of dawn to work in the *campagna* (fields), but we're singing, happy because we're together."[10]

Female members of the peasant household helped in other ways. They grew vegetable gardens, fed the animals, and herded them into grazing grounds. Women made cheese from the milk of goats and cows, and sold the surplus locally. Many of the women who later migrated to Toronto had also regularly sold wheat, eggs, and vegetables to people who came to the farm from nearby villages. During the harvest, they had threshed wheat and beat out the broad beans that had been insufficiently threshed on the treading floor. In southern regions, women and children also picked olives, nut and fruits growing on their land, or they picked for large landowners on neighbouring estates in exchange for a portion of the product. The women also husked and cracked the almonds. Girls and boys of coastal towns brought home smelts and other small fish. Women preserved vegetables, fruits, and meats, and they helped collect fuel wood from communal lands.[11] In the wintertime, women wove cloth, either for their personal use or for sale to the travelling merchants who passed through town. During the war they also earned money by sewing military uniforms.[12]

While there were few nonagricultural job opportunities in southern towns, some parents, including those who belonged to the peasantry, encouraged their daughters to learn one of the few artisanal trades available to women. Usually, the young women were sent to the local seamstress to learn pattern-making and sewing or to train as a hairdresser. This is what happened to Assunta Cerelli, who in the late 1930s apprenticed with a local seamstress in her hometown in Sicily and later set up her own business as a seamstress and embroiderer in her parents' home. After her husband was killed in the war, she set up shop in a house her parents gave her. She soon established a stable clientele among the local womenfolk.[13]

Other daughters were sent to work in domestic service or in the garment, textile, and silk factories of the region. While some of them lived in chaperoned boarding houses, others moved into the homes of their employers. They regularly sent home their wages. Teenage girls were also employed as live-in domestics in their own hometowns, while small numbers of married women found work as cleaning ladies, toiling on a daily basis in the village offices or in the homes of the local prominenti. Southern peasant women also joined the expanding reserve army of labour employed in the hidden economy of postwar Italy – earning their wages on a piece-rate basis at home by embroidering linens, weaving carpets, or cleaning fish. Predictably, the incomes earned from performing jobs that in Italy became known as *lavoro nero* (black work – that is, work that was performed without benefit of protective industrial legislation) were low, unstable, and even exploitative. But given the critical importance of alternative forms of income to peasant families, the money women earned in this informal economy was highly valued by their families.[14]

In the daily work and family worlds of southern peasants, the distinctions between the work roles of women and men were often blurred, especially during the Second World War. When large numbers of southern men were conscripted into the Italian army, women were left with the responsibility of operating the farm. As one woman put it, "Lots and lots of men went to war. There were only kids and old people in our town and the women. The women worked on the farms then, with their kids helping. They worked hard, like the men. They kept the farm going." Similarly, wives, sisters, and daughters compensated for the absence of men who were making seasonal sojourns. With perhaps a little assistance from their parents, women continued to run the family farm, and many of them were left to make major decisions affecting their children and the family as a whole.[15]

Like men's work, women's labours were specific to the agricultural season. It was during the slack winter months, for example, that women wove cloth from their looms or embroidered linens and patched clothes for the children. Very often, young women embroidered many of the tablecloths and sheets that went towards their dowry or were sold to raise extra cash. Similarly, wintertime was a busy season for making preserves. The nature and rhythm of women's labours were also linked to lifecycle and to the size and composition of households. When there were several women in one household, younger females were released from domestic chores to work in the fields or, as in the case of Christina Di'Angelo's younger sister, to apprentice in a dressmaking shop. When single, Maria Rossi often worked in the fields with her parents, grandfather, and brother because her grandmother had taken charge of the daily house chores. Other women, including Vincenza Curtola, noted that life after marriage actually became easier because they no longer divided their time between housework and field duties; they now stayed at home while their husbands and in-laws farmed. By contrast, Angela Izzo did not live with her in-laws and shared the field work with her husband.[16]

It cannot be assumed that under patriarchal structures women were simply passive and powerless victims. The emphasis that scholars have placed on the importance of Italian men's public role and of women's modest conduct in mixed company can be very misleading. For it is within the private sphere that women could wield influence over their families; here, some women made extremely effective use of informal means of persuasion, alternatively berating and coaxing a reluctant or disappointing husband. Other women exhibited an impressive capacity to argue, manipulate, disrupt normal routine, and generally make life miserable for men in order to achieve certain demands. By the same token, men who might publicly boast about their authority could act differently once beyond the purview of fellow men. In the privacy of the home, some husbands shared decison-making as a matter of course while others frequently gave in to the demands of a persistent wife. In her study of postwar southern women, Ann Cornelisen captures an element of the public/private dynamic in her description of a married women who supported her elderly parents. When asked who made the family's decisions, the woman claimed she consulted with her parents. But when Cornelisen confronted here with the fact that she did not usually confer with her parents, she responded: "The Commandments say Honour thy father and thy mother, don't they? No reason to let any one know what happens inside the family." Another woman Cornelisen describes endured months of verbal and physical assault from her husband as she tried to persuade him to work in Germany so they could pay for their son's operations. In the end, however, she emerged triumphant, having secured the necessary work permit and presenting it to her husband as a *fait accompli*. Shortly afterwards he left for Germany.[17]

Most Italian women had a say in the selection of a marriage partner, though in many cases the courtship was closely chaperoned and the man was known to the family. One woman, Elizabetta Marcone, explained how back home she had been unable to marry a man she loved because his family was wealthier than her own and his parents disapproved of the match. The recollection still stirs emotions in her: "He was a lovely singer, he would come by my house and sing beautiful love songs. I married a good man but I never forget my first love." Other women, however, proved more defiant, either marrying against their parents' wishes or carrying on covert relationships. Francesca Morelli, a seamstress-trained daughter of peasants from a large southern town, was prohibited from marrying a local man. Yet she continued to carry on a relationship until the man immigrated to Toronto. A few years later, he returned home to tend to a family problem, at which time they resumed their courtship. This time the parents abandoned hope of blocking the marriage. He returned to Toronto and shortly thereafter they were married by proxy.[18]

In her account of life in a Sicilian village, Charlotte Chapman similarly noted that there was a large gap between the assumption that women did not engage in the family's decision-making and the reality she observed. "My impression," she wrote, "is that most women know a great deal about the husband's business and social relations ... [and] they pride themselves on their ability to conceal information, sometimes hiding from their husbands their children's affairs and their own."[19] Oral testimonies suggest a similar pattern. Some women, for example, regularly hid from their husband the money they earned selling eggs, surplus produce, or embroidered linen. They would then purchase a few luxuries for themselves, such as nylons or shoes, buy some clothes for the children, or add to a daughter's trousseau. The rationale that one woman, Eva Arrigo, a Molisan peasant woman and mother of four children, offered to explain her actions – she hid the money made from selling eggs door-to-door to purchase dresses for her daughters – captured a scenario that likely occurred between wives and husbands in many households. As she bluntly put it: "If I give him the money he puts it away and that's the end of it. I can't spend it my way. But if I buy the girls something and he sees they have a nice dress or something, he just says, 'That's nice, they look nice.'"

Behind the public veneer, then, women exercised considerable power. As the family social convener responsible for arranging visits, gifts, and entertainment, women placed themselves at the centre of wide networks of family, kin, and paesani. Women also wielded great influence over their children; it has often been said that because fathers were the dispensers of corporal punishment, children confided in and felt more emotionally close to their mothers. Mothers would spare their children a spanking or beating by concealing the mischief they had done, or women would act as their children's mediators. According to Elizabetta Marcone, her mother sent instructions in 1955 to her husband in South America asking him to grant formal approval for their daughter's marriage. While the father's role as the family's chief decision maker was symbolically affirmed by the couple's having to await his approval, in fact the wedding preparations had been quietly underway for weeks before his reply arrived.[20]

Far from Ann Bravo's model of the lonely, isolated peasant woman with a truncated self-identity, women's close identification with their families did not preclude bonds of friendship with other women.[21] Peasant society offered numerous opportunities for women to establish friendships, and many did so. Within households, in-laws who worked together at domestic or field chores became close confidants, while tasks undertaken jointly by neighbours permitted women from different households to work together and, during breaks, to chat and gossip. While doing laundry, shelling beans, or making cheese outdoors, women talked endlessly and, very often, they forged close bonds. Of course, not all women were natural allies; rivals could be suspicious of, and cruel to, each other. In many instances, however, relations between female neighbours were more intimate than those between kin who lived at a distance from each other and thus could not maintain daily contact. A sign of the intensity of these female friendships is that many women chose long-time friends to be their children's godmothers.[22]

In their daily conversations women exchanged information about sex, marriage, and breast feeding. Assunta Cerilli's dress shop was a regular meeting place for the young women in her village. There they spent hours gossiping or dancing to the music of her record player. When asked what it was they talked about, she replied: "Everything! When someone is going to marry, who's going to leave, and those private things." Among the topics women discussed in hushed tones was abortion. News spread quickly among the townswomen whenever someone sought out the *lettrice* (midwife) to perform an abortion. It was not only single women who had abortions but often married women who did not want to have more children. Women were also brought together by their shared belief in mal'occhio and in their powers to cure those who were suffering from the evil eye. They compared remedies and results. So too did women believe in their capacity to predict the future; many an hour was passed as women shared their private confessions and predictions about their visionary dreams and premonitions.[23]

The numerous bonds that women formed with female kin and neighbours led inevitably to a women's culture. Women were constantly in the company of other women, as they baked bread, put out their laundry, threshed wheat, and shelled beans. As an old Sicilian proverb put it, "the women cannot stand being unable to talk, to work together."[24]

THE EXPERIENCE OF EMIGRATION

Women were generally denied a formal voice in the decision of the family to emigrate, but by making use of informal mechanisms of persuasion, they sought to influence the timing and target of migration. Desperate to get married and leave her wartorn hometown in northern Molise, Margherita Caravelle, the eldest of six children, convinced an initially uninterested fiancé that after marrying they should join her sister in Toronto. When she first raised the idea, her husband refused, telling her she was "crazy" even to consider abandoning the small bit of property they had recently inherited from her parents. However, several months later, with a loan from her parents in hand, their bags were packed for Toronto. More daring still was Maria Grande, an unmarried daughter in a large family who, despite her parents' disapproval, arranged her own voyage and joined two brothers who had previously migrated to Toronto. Christina Di'Angelo, however, recalled how her parents initially decided to send her, her two sisters, and a brother to Toronto to raise money for her father's medical bills and for the family butcher shop in Calabria. It was only after they had settled in the city and successfully found jobs that her parents decided to sell the shop and join the family overseas.[25]

Typically, the married women who dominated the flow of female immigrants from Italy shared with their husbands the desire to immigrate to Toronto. Although anxious about the prospect of leaving home, they believed in the "dream of America" and were convinced that several years of hard work would secure for them "a better life," as it was most commonly put. Several women recalled, for instance, how in the days before the Second World War they had always been impressed by the sojourners who had returned to the home town wealthier men, and they hoped they would be equally fortunate. Others felt firm in their conviction that immigrating to a booming industrial metropolis such as Toronto offered the best possibility of securing a comfortable future for themselves and their children. As Luisa Bacci, a Basilicatan woman who hailed from a town near Naples, put it, "We were full of worries, in those days, 'Am I doing the right thing?' But we knew too that we had to try, and we believed that we could make a better life in Canada, especially in a big city like Toronto. There were lots of jobs and we knew we could work hard. It was a chance to take."[26]

As an earlier chapter chronicled, Italian immigration occurred in a comparatively ragged fashion, and the process frequently involved the temporary fragmentation of families. Women in many instances bore the hardships caused by this fragmentation. Consider the case of Rosa Carpi, the twenty-five-year-old daughter of southern Italian peasants, who in the early 1950s married Liugi, a local man she had met during his periodic visits home while he was working for three years in Belgium coal mines. Soon after they married, he returned to Belgium, and two years later, Carpi, now pregnant, followed him there. When they received news that a relative had sponsored Luigi to Canada, the family returned home and Luigi left immediately for Toronto. In 1961, after her husband had sponsored his father and youngest sister, Carpi and her child finally arrived in Toronto.[27]

Significantly, women were familiar with economic strategies that involved the temporary departure of family members, for many had experienced the absence of fathers and brothers who had worked temporarily outside of Italy or served in the war. One woman, Elizabetta Marcone, explained that she had barely known her father because he had spent so many years away from the family – working at a variety of jobs in Albania from 1936 to 1938, in Germany from 1938 to 1939, and in Argentina for six years after the war. Even so, loneliness and hardship ensued, especially for women who were separated shortly after marriage, a situation that also led to a further blurring of gender-linked work roles. With only the occasional help from her father and brother, Angela Izzo ran the family farm in Molise for two years while rearing two children, including a son born just two days before her husband's 1951 departure for a Quebec farm. Immediately after their marriage in Calabria, Evalina Caputti's husband left for two years to work in agricultural and railway repair jobs in Switzerland. He made only two brief visits in as many years, though he respected his familial obligations by regularly sending money home. Eventually, he accompanied a brother to Toronto and, one year later, he called for his wife and child.[28]

In contrast to a previous era, when an earlier generation of immigrants had crossed the ocean in steerage, the postwar immigrants, including Italians, made the voyage in relative comfort, unless, of course, they suffered from seasickness. Women, however, did put up with the additional strain of having to care for their children on board ship. With the crowded conditions that prevailed, it was difficult, for instance, to keep children from wetting themselves before their turn for the washroom came up, and a mother suffering from seasickness found it hard to contend with a sick or otherwise disagreeable child. Still other women feared their children might fall overboard or disturb passengers by crying in the cabin at night. At Halifax, they worried about becoming separated from their children. When one woman arrived in Halifax on a cold day in November 1953, she was embarrassed by her lightly clad sons and feared the Canadian officials might consider her a bad mother. The train ride through eastern Canada evoked concern because the wood-frame houses resembled more the poverty of home than the expected wealth of the New World. As one woman put it, "When I saw all those little shacks I thought, my God, is that what Toronto is going to be like, living in a small crowded place just like in Italy?"[29]

But Toronto brought familiar faces and relief. In many cases, women's most vivid recollections are of the excitement that prevailed at the train station, as relatives and paesani were reunited, and of the comfort they felt at being together with their families.[30]

WOMEN AND IMMIGRANT HOUSEHOLDS

With the arrival of women in Toronto, the system of male boarding gave way to more complex, or blended, household arrangements. In many instances newly arrived or recently reunited families passed through an intermediate step, renting a small flat in a house owned by non-kin or non-Italians until such time as they could afford to enter the housing market. Despite the crowded nature of the extended family households, most Italian women preferred this set-up. Those who spent their early immigrant years living in a rental flat resented daily intrusions on their privacy. As a newly arrived immigrant with two children, one of them born just weeks after her arrival in Toronto in the spring of 1957, Evalina Caputti had been so distressed by the complaints of her landlady, who kept insisting that the children were too loud, that she wanted to return home. What with the family plot and furniture sold to finance the trip, even she knew this was not a likely possibility. Another woman, Elizabetta Marcone, so resented her landlord's complaints about excessive water and electricity bills and her child's ruining the hardwood floors that she made her husband move to other quarters within a month of her arrival in Toronto.[31]

For much the same reason as the men, Italian women preferred the the familiari arrangement. Confident that this strategy would enable them to one day own their own home, they tolerated the crowded conditions, the constant noise, and the long line-ups for the bathroom. However, at least in the short term, the crowded household also held particular advantages for women, especially for those whose arrival in early postwar Toronto coincided with the years of childbirth. Women passed on cribs, baby clothes, and advice on breast feeding, and during the labour-intensive projects in which all members of the household participated, such as wine-making and the annual butchering of the pig, expectant mothers could rely on the help of their female housemates. Extended households also let women collectivize housekeeping and exchange confidences. Women who were at home all day – one nursing a newborn, another sewing clothes, and another unemployed – frequently shared domestic chores. In their testimonies, women also commented on how rare serious outbursts were in a house containing up to twenty people. Fernanda Pisani, a Molisan woman who lived for a decade in such a household in the Junction colony, nostalgically recalls those early years as a special time when *parenti* (kin) united during hard times: "Sometimes, it seems, we cared more for each other then than now, when we have our big houses but not so much time for each other."[32]

Far from huddling indiscriminately, people living in these crowded households had a deep-seated sense of propriety and retained as much as possible their sense of nuclear family. At supper, for instance, families sharing a kitchen ate at different or overlapping times as each woman, who alone was responsible for her family's meals, awaited her husband's arrival from work before heating her pot of water for pasta. Individual families shared private quarters and, while several women might be entrusted to do the grocery shopping, each family paid for its share of the supplies.

WOMEN'S UNPAID LABOURS

Whatever the household structure, women at home performed crucial economic roles that contributed to the welfare of their families now struggling to survive in Toronto. Like other working-class women, they stretched limited resources and found ways to cut costs and earn extra cash. Women's labours daily replenished the male breadwinner, and they fed, clothed, and raised children. In extended households, they might take care of extra menfolk who were unmarried or had not yet called for their wives, elderly parents, and in-laws. Since some households lacked refrigerators, women daily purchased perishables such as milk and bread. Without washing machines and often with access only to hotplates located in otherwise unfinished basements, basic chores were time-consuming and arduous.

In an effort to cut living costs, Italian women drew on traditional and inexpensive ways of generating food, primarily by growing vegetable gardens and by preserving fruits, vegetables, and meat. With pride, one woman recalled how she had produced most of the family's food. "I did everything," declared this woman, "tomatoes for sauce, pickles, olives. I did pears, peaches, apricots, everything we eat. We bought the meat from the store and I make sausages and prosciutto." Another stay-at-home wife saved money by shopping at a large farmers' market near the city limits. Still others earned additional cash by taking in boarders or extra washing, and many babysat for working relatives. All of this increased the domestic chores.[33]

As in many working-class families, Italian housewives frequently acted as the family's financial manager, allocating funds for groceries, furniture, and clothing, paying bills, and depositing savings in the bank or putting them towards mortgage payments. Several described how at the end of each week the husband would hand over his paycheque. In one woman's words, "My husband would bring the money home and give it to me, and he say, 'You know what you're doing, take care of the money.' I tried to save money and I did. After three years we bought a house." Women considered financial management a task of utmost importance. Though men later usurped this role when finances and investments grew more complex, it appears that during the critical early years of adjustment women's control over the family budget was considerable. Certainly, when families were barely surviving, men relied on women's re-sourcefulness to help make ends meet.[34]

Although it is generally assumed that Italian women expressed little interest in the world beyond their home, in fact many immigrant housewives made friends with the other women of their neigh-bourhood, including the non-Italians. Margherita Caravelle and her sister, for example, befriended several Ukrainian and Jewish women living nearby. In the spring and summer they spent hours talking outside, and they made a point of celebrating each other's birthdays. At home with her own and her cousin's children, another woman spent afternoons with a neighbour who also babysat children. Each would take a turn working in her garden or her house while the other supervised the children.[35]

Whether at home or in the factory, urban industrial life could evoke anxiety and fear in women who no longer enjoyed the pro-tection of the paese. Several women recalled being afraid to go out alone at night and the mocking looks of native-born Torontonians. They also confronted prejudice. Caravelle remembered how one day in 1949 she cried all the way home after being laughed out of a department store where she could not make herself understood. Interestingly, this incident spurred her on to learn English. And Angela Izzo recalled being robbed one day while she was at home with her two children. The thief who came to the door armed with a knife got away with the week's grocery money – about $20.00 – though not before he sent the following warning: "Get lost wop, or I'll be back."[36]

The new context also engendered new strains with respect to motherhood. Throughout the early postwar years, many Italian mothers feared for their children's safety at school where outbursts regularly occurred between Canadian and Italian schoolmates. Al-though confident in their ability to raise their children, many women worried that they might not be considered adequate mothers by the social experts and professionals of the host society – doctors, school nurses, social workers, and teachers. In her 1962 report on the Ital-ians in west-end Toronto, the International Institute of Metropolitan Toronto social worker, Edith Ferguson, commented on how some of the women contacted were suspicious of even the Italian-speaking social worker who came to their door. No doubt such responses were linked to immigrant women's concerns that the priorities of the Canadian "experts" did not necessarily reflect their perceptions of what was best for their children. The distance that sometimes marked relations between the professionals and the newly arrived immigrants is well illustrated by an story involving Giuseppina Mazzoli, who found herself in labour and giving birth to a premature son the morning after she arrived in Toronto. Having delivered her child in a large, busy hospital and having been treated by a doctor with whom she could not communicate, she was afraid to leave her son in the hospital because she thought he might die in her absence. As she noted, the comfort traditionally provided by the village midwife, and by the female kin and neighbours who assisted a new mother, were missing.[37]

WOMEN'S PAID WORK

For thousands of Italian immigrant women who had settled in Toronto in this period, the tasks associated with domestic chores and reproduction swallowed up only a portion of each day. The rest of the time was spent inside the factory walls or at home, bent over a sewing machine or madly packaging novelty items or advertising flyers – all for a nominal wage. More than any other factor, economic need, and the insufficient incomes earned by their husbands, prompted many Italian women to contribute directly to their family's finances by entering the paid labour force. They were part of the dramatic postwar increase of women, including married women, in the Canadian work force.

The proportion of married women in the Canadian female work force increased from 12.7 per cent in 1941 to 30 per cent in 1951; by 1961 it had grown to almost 50 per cent. Immigrant women, including Italians, figured prominently in this movement. In 1961 almost 11 per cent of the million working women in Canada were European-born, of whom Italian-born women represented more than 17 per cent. They made up 15 per cent of the 100,100 or more European-born women workers in Ontario. Some 16,990 Italian women, most of them immigrants, made up 6.5 per cent of Toronto's 1961 female labour force. While working women accounted for more than one-third of the total Italian adult female population in Canada and Ontario in 1961,[38] for Toronto this figure was 41.5 per cent. And these statistics do not cover the numerous women who earned money informally by taking in children or laundry, or by cleaning homes.[39]

While Canadian-born women swelled the ranks of the white-collar work force in the decades following the Second World War, immigrant women, most of whom lacked English and possessed few marketable skills, provided low-paid, unskilled, and semi-skilled female labour in industry. With the approval of employers who considered them hard-working and docile, Toronto's Italian women figured prominently in the city's postwar female immigrant workplaces. Their jobs included garment homework, operating steampresses, sewing, and novelty-making machines, packaging, bottling and labelling, laundry work, and domestic service. And they earned among the lowest incomes in Toronto. In 1961 Italian women whose mother tongue was not English earned an annual average of $1456 – about 60 per cent of the average female income (see appendix, table 10).

Manufacturing and domestic service were the largest employers of European immigrant women in Canada. In 1961 almost 57 per cent of the more than 32,000 Italian women workers in Canada were in manufacturing, most of them in clothing, food and beverage, textiles, and leather-goods shops. In service, where 28 per cent were located, three-quarters were domestic servants.[40] Statistics for Toronto reveal similar patterns. The number of Italian women employed in the city grew from under 3000 in 1951 to almost 17,000 a decade later (see appendix, tables 13 and 14). By 1961 Italians represented 6.5 per cent of the total female work force of 260,633, and 21 per cent of working women who were of European origin. Almost half of the city's Italian women workers were employed in the manufacturing sector, especially in the clothing and leather, textile and knitting categories. Large numbers could also be found in the tobacco, food and beverage, and rubber industries, while the strong new Italian presence in the city's needle trades was most evident in the leather-making shops, where Italians represented fully 40 per cent of the women employed.

The other major employer of Toronto's Italian women in these years was the service sector. Here the Italians, who made up one-third of the female work force, were most concentrated in laundries and dry-cleaning shops. Indeed, by 1961 they represented 28 per cent of Metro Toronto's female laundry workers. Another 14 per cent could be found in personal service work. Most were cleaning ladies employed in private homes, offices, and public buildings. Only 2 per cent of the women employed in service appear to have worked as live-in domestic servants. While agriculture employed comparatively few women in Toronto, Italian women accounted for 15 per cent of those who were employed in temporary jobs picking fruit and vegetables on farms on the outskirts of the city (see appendix, table 14).

WOMEN'S WORK AND FAMILY ECONOMIES

Whether a woman worked outside the home depended on various factors such as a husband's attitude, childbearing, the availability of babysitters, and work opportunities. Women in search of work typically headed for the garment and light manufacturing areas of the city, where they went door-to-door asking for jobs. Some women turned to outside agencies for help in locating jobs, including the Italian Immigrant Aid Society, which not only served as an employment centre but also ran industrial sewing classes for women. According to its annual reports, most clients were placed in jobs as unskilled factory workers, machine operatives, and cleaning ladies. Only a tiny minority were directed towards white-collar positions as clerk-typists or saleswomen.[41] Like the Maria of our opening story, however, most Italian women in search of work benefited from networking among female kin.[42]

In examining the role of female kin networks, specialists of Italian immigration have stressed how these occupational enclaves eased men's concerns about women working outside the home by providing traditional checks on female behaviour. This argument was forcefully put by Virginia Yans-McLaughlin, one of the first social historians to give serious attention to the work experiences of Italian immigrant women in North America. In her study of Italian cannery workers in Buffalo, she argues that women's entry into the factory did not place undue stress on the families because women deliberately sought jobs that placed a minimum of strain on family relations and still maintained traditional female roles.[43] That women worked in occupational enclaves did help to ease men's concerns. However, Yans-McLaughlin's model is misleading in two significant ways. First, it assumes that women could exercise a wide range of choice in deciding where they might work. Yet, as Yans-McLaughlin herself points out, apart from the fruit canneries, Buffalo's economy offered immigrant women few job alternatives. In their oral testimonies, Italian women in Toronto emphasized the utility of their kin ties in getting them much-needed jobs, and the camaraderie of the workplace where groups of female kin and paesane were employed. Several women pointed out that they would have worked wherever they found suitable jobs, provided that the plant or shop was not exclusively male. And some noted that they had worked in ethnically mixed as well as gender-mixed workplaces.[44]

The second problem with Yans-McLaughlin's argument is that it focuses almost exclusively on patterns of continuity and thus ignores the impact that women's entry into paid labour may have had on the women themselves. This bias, like the first one, permeates the historical literature on Italian immigrant women in Canada. And yet, when questioned about their work lives, Italian women themselves declare that working outside the home for wages had been an empowering experience, that it had made them feel more confident about themselves. As one woman put it, "I feel proud that I did something. Maybe my English it's still not so good, but I did it. I got up each morning at 6 o'clock, take the subway when its dark, work all day. I could tell you all the streets in Toronto, I can find a job I need. I can say, I did it."[45]

In her 1974 study of the value systems of Italian immigrants, social psychologist Giuliana Colalillo found that the Italian women who had worked outside of the home during the 1950s and 1960s believed that experience had better prepared them for coping in the new society and for better understanding the more Canadianized values of their daughters. And in their report on the isolation suffered by immigrant housewives, Judith Ramirez and Roxanna Ng suggest that despite the problems associated with paid employment, working outside the home might help to ease the strains that immigrant women confront in the new society. Certainly, much of the self-pride that Italian women expressed in relation to their labours was linked to their commitment to their family and to their ability to contribute to the well-being of their husbands and children. But this should not discount the women's own beliefs that in at least subtle ways they had changed as a result of their long-term encounter with paid work.[46]

Italian women's paid labour was part of a well-articulated working-class family strategy of success, one most often measured in terms of homeownership. Female wages helped support families through periods of seasonal male unemployment. Women's earnings were also used for daily living expenses, such as groceries, clothing, and household necessities, while men's paycheques went into savings deposits and towards houses and other investments. Characterized by low wages and high turnover, women's work experience also reflected the gender inequities of the postwar occupational structure. Predictably, the desire of capital for cheap workers and of immigrant working-class families for additional earnings were inextricably linked.[47]

Like many unskilled male and female workers, Italian women worked long hours at either monotonous or hazardous jobs that were physically demanding. Women employed in drapery and clothing factories endured poor ventilation and high humidity, as well as speed-ups and close supervision. Women assembling items in plastics factories put up with dust and foul-smelling fumes. Laundry work required much lifting, and steampresses made the workplace almost unbearable in summer. Constant bending over a sewing machine led to sore backs.[48] Italian women in factories also confronted the new time and work discipline of industrial capitalism and the impersonal relations between employers and workers. At the same time, the daily experience of the workplace, where Italians learned to speak English from co-workers and sometimes forged friendships, may also have had a partially empowering impact on women hitherto confined to the household. By contrast, domestic workers who cleaned house for middle-class clients toiled in total isolation from their working sisters.[49]

During the 1950s, Italian women workers did not articulate a political response to their exploitation. This resulted in part from their low status as low-paid and unskilled workers and from the barriers of language and ethnicity erected in the workplace. Another important factor was the isolation of domestic workers. Household duties also kept women away from organizing meetings, and many were unsure about union organizers who visited their shops. Since joining a local might endanger their job, they truly feared compromising their main goal of helping the family's financial situation. Moreover, unionization was made more difficult by the fact that Italians were in industries characterized by high concentrations of unskilled female workers and high labour turnover rates.[50]

By the early 1960s the image of the working Italian immigrant woman was fully entrenched in the minds of social observers. They also recognized that familial priorities, especially the duties of newly married women to bear and raise children, helped shape the timing and rhythm of women's participation in the labour force. Some women, such as Carmelina Gallo, a trained seamstress from Abruzzi who worked for three years in a garment shop until she had her first child, never returned to work after they started families. Others, such as Vincenza Curtola, did not work until all their children reached school age. It was not until ten years after her arrival in Toronto in 1955 that she found work in a garment factory.[51] Large numbers of Italian women, however, regularly moved in and out of the labour force. They turned from one type of factory work to another, and from factory work to service jobs such as cafeteria and chambermaid work or to fruit and vegetable picking.

Frequently women left jobs as a protest against poor working conditions and pay. One woman quit work as a shirt packager after losing overtime hours; in only a few weeks she secured work as a bow-machine operator in a factory producing party accessories. A cleaning lady who had secured her job through the IIMT, Filomena Ianucci returned to the agency one month later to say she had quit because she found "the job was too tiring." She was promptly placed in another cleaning job. Husbands sometimes urged their wives to leave what they felt were disagreeable jobs. In 1963 Giuseppina Mazzoli quit her job as a hotel chambermaid to appease her husband, who disliked her cleaning up for strangers and working on Sundays, even though his father and sister also worked at the hotel. Several years earlier, however, Mazzoli on her own initiative quit her job in a department store cafeteria when management shifted her into a more stressful job in inventory. And Italian women's dislike of live-in domestic service is illustrated by the actions of a woman who was placed in a private home through a local immigration office in Toronto. Claiming that she hated the work and resented not being able to converse in her own language, she showed up at the IIMT wanting a factory job. She was placed in a shoe factory where she operated a shoe-stitching machine.[52]

Most often, however, women left work temporarily to fulfil family obligations – having children, tending to a family crisis, or resettling the family in a new home. Speaking about a group of sixty-seven Italian and Portuguese women who had been employed as sewing-machine operatives over the previous two years, Ferguson observed: "These women work irregularly and intermittently at times, when family duties permit it." "While a number are not working at present," she added, "in another six months or a year later, the ones now unemployed might be back at work, and a different group at home for family reasons."[53]

Oral testimonies and case studies reveal how women juggled their various familial responsibilities. Shortly after Lenora Fericci immigrated with her parents in 1958, for instance, she found work as a seamstress on Spadina Avenue and continued to work there for two years following her marriage in 1959. One year later, she left to have a child, and then returned in 1963 to similar work at a garment factory on College Street. Three years later she left to have her second child, and then returned to the same job two years later. Following the family's move to the suburbs, she secured work in a local plastics factory, which she left for a period of six months in 1971 to have her third child. Later still, a workplace injury would keep her out of the work force for a decade. Another woman had been employed in a garment shop for two years when she was compelled to quit in the winter of 1962 on account of her son's illness. Because her husband suffered a workplace injury shortly afterwards, the family was able to obtain a loan from the Public Welfare Department to cover their upcoming mortgage payments. One month later, with her son fully recovered and her husband receiving workmen's compensation, she returned to her old job. There were other ways in which women succeeded in adjusting their work schedules to meet the needs of their families. For example, when one woman's son developed serious sinus trouble, she switched from daytime to nighttime cleaning jobs so she could take her son to his weekly hospital visits.[54]

When babysitting could not be provided by female kin, many Italian women put off work until a sister, in-law, or cousin became available to watch the children. (These relatives might themselves be recent immigrants or new mothers earning a little extra cash.) Mothers who hired landladies or neighbours sometimes felt uneasy about leaving their children with strangers unconnected by links of kin or village. One woman recalled how each morning she hated leaving her crying son with the landlady downstairs. Suspecting that her child was being neglected by the babysitter, who had young children of her own, she stopped working for over a year until her mother's arrival in the city in 1959 gave her the opportunity to re-enter the work force. As Ferguson observed in 1962, at least women could take temporary jobs during the winter months when their husbands were unemployed and took over the childcare duties for a few hours in the afternoon.[55] Opting for a different solution, some women worked as daytime domestics and brought their pre-school children to their clients' homes. Women who turned to industrial homework often did so for the same reason: they could watch over their children while they earned some extra cash.[56]

Nor did outside work reduce the burden of housekeeping. While men did some tasks, such as stoking the coal furnace, shovelling snow, and perhaps watching children briefly while their wives shopped or cleaned, working women were almost wholly responsible for the household chores, even during periods of male unemployment. Indeed, other women often watched children while their mothers performed domestic tasks. This double burden hung heavily on the shoulders of Giuseppina Mazoli, who for over a year combined full-time work as a steampress operator with caring for a son, a husband, his father, and two brothers. "Oh poor me," she recalled, "fulltime work ... wash, clean, cook, I did all that! I was really just a girl, 19 years old and thin, thin like a stick. I had four men, a baby. I was with no washing machine. I would go down to the laundry tub to do it. Then I had to cook and I had to work. And it was not only me." Elizabetta Marcone likely voiced the frustration of many working women when she said of her husband: "Of course he should help in the house. My back, I hurt it at work. It hurts to wash the floor, pick up the clothes. But what you gonna do? Can't have a fight every day about it, so I do it.[57]

Assumptions about Italian women's alleged docility and their hostility to unions may be exaggerated. During the 1950s militancy in the workplace was hardly pronounced among women of any background. Nor is there any reason to assume that Italian women should have felt any sense of working-class solidarity with their Canadian sisters, especially those who were white-collar workers. Some women insisted that for years the topic of unionization had never come up at their workplace, while others noted that employers exploited ethnic divisions among new arrivals and played one group against another.[58]

In Italy some women were radicalized by their participation in the resistance movement, and in the early 1960s they spearheaded Italy's modern feminist movement. Few of them emigrated, however. The vast majority of the southern peasant women who settled in Toronto had little if any prior experience with industrial work and lacked traditions of worker protest.[59] Furthermore, their concerns as working women did not initially receive serious attention within the ethnic community. Some parish priests, for instance, attributed the declining attendance among women at Sunday mass to the high numbers of Italians who worked on the weekends. The Italian Toronto newspaper, *Corriere Canadese*, did not address women's issues in its advice columns to workers, while its women's page was decidedly middle-class in orientation. Far more likely to be of interest to an audience of women who belonged to the city's prewar and Canadian-born Italian community, it covered the volunteer work and social activities of various women's organizations and clubs, and offered household hints and recipes as well as a fashion and a horoscope column.[60]

Nevertheless, as peasants long resentful of the exploitation they had suffered at the hands of landowners and local elites, Italian women in Toronto perhaps understood instinctively the exploitative relations between employers and workers, and many were truly angered by the injustices they suffered as working immigrant women. Even an anti-unionist woman dismissed what she considered ruling-class rhetoric that portrayed Canada as a land of limitless opportunity. "Why feel grateful?" she said. "We really suffered for what we got. I have four back operations. I have to leave my kids alone and work ... And we don't live like Kings and Queens. I work hard for what I got." Moreover, increasing numbers of women grew to support unionization during the 1960s and later. According to oral informants, they favoured unionism not only because higher wages helped their families but because they identified improved working conditions, greater job security, and health benefits with a recognition of their labour and with self-respect. A unionized laundry worker since the mid-1960s, Angela Izzo, who had worked in various non-unionized garment shops and laundries before landing work in a unionized laundry, summed up these feelings when she said: "Sure we should get more money. We work hard for it: we leave our kids, come home tired, do the dirty jobs."[61]

The first concerted efforts to unionize women occurred during the early 1960s, at the same time that the Hogg's Hollow tunnel disaster and the construction strikes focused public attention on Italian workers in Toronto. At that time, union officials in the needle trades claimed that up to 85 per cent of the garment shops in the city were nonunion shops employing a high percentage of immigrants, mostly Italians. A representative with the United Garment Workers of America (UGWA) claimed that Canadian women were being squeezed out of the city's garment industry because employers relied heavily on the cheap labour power of immigrants, especially Italians. These New Canadians, he charged, were working up to eighty hours a week for forty cents per hour. The small subcontractors who predominated in the trades, he added, successfully skirted the female minimum wage law by "forcing immigrant girls to finish bundles of clothes at home or on weekends." Speaking specifically of the men's sportswear industry, he claimed that half of the 1200 workers in the field earned wages that were less than one-third of the rate in union shops.[62]

The lead in the organization campaigns was taken by unions in the needle trades, the boot and shoe industry, and laundries – precisely those sectors where many Italians were concentrated. In 1957 the "Italian local," Local 235, of the Amalgamated Clothing Workers of America (ACWA) boasted a membership of 1000, though most were men. It took over four weeks in the spring of 1960 for the Fur Workers Union to organize the 200 workers, many of them women, who were employed by the three Toronto firms who produced the bulk of the industry's synthetic fur fabrics. The first contract included a forty-hour week, overtime pay, and sick and pension benefits. By April 1960 the union was negotiating a third contract for the synthetic fur trade, where up to 95 per cent of the Italian women in the fur industry were concentrated. The contract included a thirty-five-hour week and an increase in hourly wages. The union had also recently succeeded in organizing leather workers at the Great Northern Fur and Leather Company. During the early 1960s efforts were made to organize women in the boot and shoe industry. In the fall of 1960 the International Laundry, Dry Cleaning and Dye House Workers' Union, Local 351, announced a first contract for 500 workers employed by five companies. It called for wage increases and vacation pay.[63]

In interviews, women who joined certification drives or entered already unionized shops in the needle trades said they preferred the union shop. Some added that it made them feel better able to protest mistreatment at the workplace. Assunta Cerilli, an experienced seamstress, recalled how one day in 1962 she had responded to her forewoman's orders that she sew an entire bundle of dresses again: she had simply walked off the shop floor. "I was so mad, fuming, when she started yelling at me, calling me an idiot. I thought, I don't have to take this, and I threw the whole bundle at her. I was shouting: 'You want me to redo them, okay. But don't treat me like a dog to spit at.' I was so mad, I yelled and then I got up and walked out. I walked straight to the union office. They weren't too happy with me but they got me another job." Most Italian women workers, however, were not protected by unions. Organizing campaigns remained sporadic and strikes were weakened by the employers' ability to hire other immigrants, including Italians, and replace the strikers. Few efforts to organize women in small shops and in domestic service were made before the 1980s.[64]

The entry of southern Italian peasant women into Toronto's postwar labour force reflected a pattern of continuity, for women had been important contributors to the peasant family economy in the Mezzogiorno. Since women's work was already justified in terms of peasant survival, no dramatic change in values was needed to allow these women to work outside the home. Given the scarcity of resources accessible to southern Italian immigrant families newly arrived in postwar Toronto, additional wages earned by women, including those at home, amounted to an effective familialist response.

Still, women's entry into an urban industrial work force did not occur without difficult adjustments, especially for married women. These strains reflected a dialectical process by which southern peasants became transformed into working-class families. Their familialist and collectivist behaviour was not simply the expression of traditional peasant culture; it also reflected their new economic position as members of working-class families coping with conditions of scarcity and restriction within industrial capitalism. This held particular significance for working Italian women, a fact ignored by scholars who view Italian immigrant women exclusively in terms of family and home. Scholars, too, have ignored the possibility that, even where wages and conditions are poor, paid employment could be an empowering experience for immigrant women who might otherwise have been isolated in their homes. Motivated by a commitment to family, women linked their self-identification as women and mothers to the paid and unpaid labours they performed for the benefit of parents, husbands, and children. In the process they developed a sense of feminine pride that was rooted both in their peasant and in their immigrant working-class experiences. They saw themselves as indispensable to their families. The nature of their labours had been largely transformed when they entered Toronto's industrial economy, but their paid and unpaid work remained critical to the daily survival of their newly arrived families in postwar Toronto.

CHAPTER FIVE

Ethnic Intruders and Hardworking Exotics

By the mid-1960s the Italian "invasion" of early postwar Toronto was nearly complete and several images of the Italian had become etched on the minds of the city's Anglo-Celtic residents. In 1964 Robert Allen, a writer for *Maclean's*, sought to capture Torontonians' contradictory views of Italians. Describing the College Street Little Italy, he wrote:

Here one finds people from Naples and Palermo looking at snails in grocery stores, listening to Italian records, and enjoying the novel life of a community of Italian movies, espresso bars, pizza parlours, pointed shoes, short jackets, Sicilian shawls and such vitality that going home to, say, North Toronto, is like entering a decadent suburb ... Many welcome this exotic tidal wave that has given texture to the city and suddenly made Toronto as self-consciously cosmopolitan as a teenager who has just discovered beer. Others look on these changes dourly, still call Italians "Eyetalians" and misuse the word "ethnic" to mean exactly what they used to mean when they said "foreigner." A few think vaguely of Little Italy as a cluster of grocery stores in an old part of town but many think of it as a tough neighborhood of ward heelers, underground societies, and Tammany hall politics, where Italian youths pinch girls' behinds, and more mature citizens, when they aren't eating spaghetti, are stealing jobs from Canadians. [1]

What best characterizes the early responses of Torontonians, and others, to the Italians who flocked to the city during the heyday of postwar immigration? There were positive images, though they were often expressed with a patronizing tone, but more often than not in this period of heavy immigration the Italians emerged as a target of scorn. In addition to enjoying a certain notoriety as Toronto's largest non-British ethnic group, the immigrants' propensity for clustering in distinct neighbourhoods, the darker skin colouring of many of the newcomers, particularly those who hailed from Italy's Deep South, and their concentration among the city's working class made the Italians all the more visible to nativists.

NATIVISM'S DEEP ROOTS

It is not surprising that many postwar Torontonians opposed the large-scale arrival of Italians and other continental Europeans, nor that familiar, negative stereotypes of Italians should resurface. As in the case of other major receiving countries, immigration to Canada has engendered a history of racial intolerance and nativism. With each new wave of immigrants, Canadians have reacted with anxiety or alarm; they have denounced the indiscriminate mixing of diverse peoples and the changing racial make-up of the country. Basic prejudices have informed even the more sympathetic views of middle-class reformers, many of whom welcomed the opportunity to remake the immigrants in their own image.

In any given place, the actual targets of people's scorn may change over time; this usually occurs as new waves of immigrants, whatever their ethnic origin, take up the undesirable jobs and unfashionable districts previously occupied by earlier immigrants. Even among these shifting currents, however, certain patterns of preference and prejudice have emerged. Canadian immigration historians have coined the term "ethnic preference ladder" to describe the fact that immigrants have always been accepted into Canada in descending order of preference. Their ordering, moreover, reflected prevailing notions regarding the superior civilization of northwestern Europe and its white, colonial offspring. While few historians have emphasized the point, the nativist response to immigrants has also been a gendered one. The popular stereotypes portrayed foreign-born men as potentially violent and as sexual threats to Canadian-born women, while immigrant women were depicted as the suffering wives of domineering husbands.

Far from being a product of the postwar era, these racialist judgments reflected centuries-old attitudes. They were deeply rooted in late-eighteenth-century social and scientific theories that relegated to the bottom of the social hierarchy the "coloured" peoples of Asia, Africa, and the Americas, Mediterranean nationals, and the Jews. In English Canada, as in the United States, the opposition to immigrants has been most profound in cases where the newcomers have not shared the same cultural or political inheritance as the country's dominant Anglo-Celtic population. In the past, racial minorities such as the Chinese have encountered state policies designed to prevent, or at least hamper, family reunification, while the Jews have endured anti-Semitic outbursts from both anglophone and francophone Canadians.[2]

Italian immigrants have rarely encountered the degree of systemic racism meted out to racial minorities, but they are no strangers to the indifference and bigotry of North Americans. When an earlier generation of Italians had come to Canada and the United States during the mass migration years of 1880–1930, their growing presence in the cities and towns of North America produced a nativist blacklash. Drawing on long-standing stereotypes regarding the inferiority of the Italian race and the alleged inability of Italians to practise the rules of democratic government or conform to middle-class standards of conduct, North Americans made their prejudices clear by depicting Italians as "hot blooded" and "culturally backward" peasants. As with most stereotypes, the popular images of Italian immigrants always contained contradictory strains. Patronizing portraits of Italian peanut vendors and barbers as child-like innocents happily performing their jobs contrasted sharply, for instance, with the hot-tempered, stiletto-wielding punk.

Above all, it was the southern Italian peasant who provided the source for most of these negative images. Portrayed as stocky, dark-skinned, and suffering from malnutrition and poor levels of education, southern Italians were considered to be among the least capable of adjusting to the industrial economies of North America. Burdened with large families and born of a deep-seated fatalism nurtured in an environment of grinding poverty, these immigrants, conventional wisdom had it, lacked both the resources and the resourcefulness to make the transition to urban life in North America. Southern Italians were also thought to be highly emotional, temperamental, and lacking inner discipline. Many of these stereotypes were concepts borrowed from Italy itself; the north-south dichotomy that marked Italy's uneven development and the ancient prejudices of northern Italian intellectuals, politicians, and others towards the southern peasants provided North Americans with a pat rationale for their own dislike of these newcomers.[3]

NEW CANADIANS

The resurgence in Italian immigration to Canada after the Second World War was accompanied by a resurgence in anti-Italian and, in particular, anti-southern-Italian sentiment. The rise of Italian fascism and the war had added the term "enemy alien" to the list of marks against Italians, though, as the Cold War era set in, many Canadians welcome Italy's newly regained status as a Western ally. Few, however, were willing to forget Mussolini's partnership with Hitler and the bitter war their country had just waged against Italy. This resentment towards Italy was evident in the 1946 national opinion poll in which one-quarter of those interviewed were opposed to Italian immigration. Ten years later, only 4.4 per cent of Canadians polled welcomed southern Europeans from any Mediterranean country, though 30 per cent favoured immigration from northwestern Europe.[4]

The resurgence of anti-Italian sentiment in early postwar Toronto occurred in the context of the massive entry of continental Europeans into the city in the years before 1965. Many Torontonians feared that the large foreign presence, coupled with the declining importance of British immigration, signalled disastrous and irrevocable changes in the city's social and racial make-up. For many, the growing Italian presence was a clear sign of the changing character of their city and a harbinger of worse things to come. While Toronto had long been a home to many immigrants and racial minorities, no population influx had so dramatically altered the city's Anglo-Celtic and Protestant character as did the postwar arrival of tens of thousands of Europeans. With a mixture of anxiety and alarm, Torontonians recognized that their city would continue to attract vast numbers of people from the world's non-preferred nations. Moreover, in the years before the arrival of a large number of immigrants of colour from Asia, Africa, and the Caribbean – a migration that would not reach significant proportions for another decade – the southern Italians, by virtue of their darker skin colouring, were at times virtually ascribed the status of a visible minority.

When, in 1954, a Toronto Orangeman wrote to the Ontario premier to complain about the recent infestation of "these ignorant, almost black people," his response was a particularly cruel one. F.J. Love went on to express his total distaste for the men and women whom he claimed hailed from "a Vatican controlled country" and brought with them contagious diseases. He saved his worst criticism for the young single men "armed with knives and ... continually holding up people and especially ladies near parks and dark alleys." And yet, beneath the extreme language, this letter expressed more generally held sentiments of the era. In sympathetic circles, Italians and other immigrants were described as "New Canadians" – a term that gained popularity in the postwar period and was intended to be stripped of any negative connotations. Yet, as the *Maclean's* writer observed, for many Canadians the old-fashioned term "foreigner" more accurately conveyed their resentment towards the postwar newcomers.[5]

As oral testimonies make abundantly clear, throughout the 1950s and early 1960s the newcomers themselves were acutely aware of their general unpopularity. In the city's streets, Italians felt the voyeuristic curiosity or hostility of Torontonians in the cold stares, bemused smiles, or insults they received. "It was a hard time for us," recalled an Italian construction worker who remembered the embarrassment he felt each day as he rode the streetcar home in his dirty work clothes and muddy boots, and with his cracked and calloused hands exposed to the disapproving eyes of the better-dressed passengers. He added: "In a strange country with a different language. We were the working people. Even riding the streetcar was not that simple. They would humiliate you with remarks and insults – you know, 'dirty wop' [or] 'go back to Italy.'" In these years, young single Italian men encountered prejudice at local dances where they regularly faced the rejections of Canadian-born women. The attention of the men also elicited jeers and insults from young Canadian men, and such incidents quickly escalated into back-alley fights.[6]

A persistent theme in oral testimonies is the resentment Italians felt at being indiscriminately referred to as "wops" and "DPs." That they came as bona fide immigrants was a source of pride to Italians, and many a skirmish resulted from young men defending their honour on this score. Youth fights were a familiar feature of the urban terrain of early postwar Toronto; indeed, by the mid-1950s law-enforcement officers were voicing concerns about rising incidences of "juvenile delinquency aimed at Italian youths." In one published case, a twenty-two-year-old Italian suffered a broken jaw after some youths attacked him in an east-end park following the Queen Victoria Day fireworks celebrations. The youth had been left lying unconscious until an alarmed passerby notified police. The culprits were never picked up. Another incident involved "six young deliquents" who, roaming the streets of the St Clair colony, came upon a young Italian man whom they beat and then damaged his car. They were caught and given stiff fines. Skirmishes frequently broke out at Christie Pits, a popular West-end park located near several Italian neighbourhoods, and at soccer games throughout town. In school yards young boys learned "to take a punch," while other children, including girls, "played hooky" out of fear of being ridiculed.[7]

Another instance of cultural conflict involved unlicensed Italian café and billard-hall owners who spiked their patron's coffee with liquor or moonshine supplied by local bootleggers. In 1957 a café owner in the St Clair Little Italy was fined for contravening provincial liquor licensing laws. In an effort to diffuse the outburst of criticism surrounding the incident, Italian community leaders insisted that the immigrants meant no real harm but were simply following familiar customs. The local authorities were not convinced. Toronto mayor Phil Givens called on the archbishop to advise against the practice, and a *Globe and Mail* editorial remarked, "these people must learn to respect the law."[8]

As the examples above suggest, much confusion, ambiguity, and ignorance lay behind the cold stares, harsh words, and even blows that Torontonians meted out to the Italian newcomers. Certainly, there was a huge disparity between the romanticized myths that Canadians held about Italy's rich cultural heritage, its sunny piazzas, architectural jewels, and contented peasants and the mud-covered trench diggers and haggard-looking female factory operatives they confronted in their own city. With the arrival of TV and cheaper transatlantic flights, many more Canadians than ever before were attracted to the tourist's romantic image of Italy. At least initially, some could not adjust this image to accommodate the overcrowded immigrant households and cluttered neighbourhoods that dotted their cityscape. Significantly, however, the few Italians who publicly responded to criticism, and who sought to defend the honour of their compatriots, also drew on the images of sunny Italy. As one indignant Italian worker put it: "Don't these people know we come from the country of Michelangelo and DaVinci, and we have the greatest opera singers and best architecture in the world?" It was precisely the gap between the romantic image of Italy and the unappealing reality of the immigrants in Toronto that helped produce some of the hostility.[9]

The familiar interplay between economic insecurity and nativism manifested itself in the complaints of Torontonians who argued that immigrants created unfair competition for Canadians. Shopkeepers came under attack from one woman who claimed they had an unfair advantage because they could tap a ready-made clientele. Attributing the proliferation of Italian food stores to the failure of Italians to learn English, she wrote: "Because Italians cannot read the labels on processed foods, let alone the directions, they continue to buy the foods they are used to. Thus a great many Italian food, grocery, and fish stores have opened up to the detriment of established Canadian stores." Furthermore, she complained, "some of these stores display smelly fish and other foods far out in front of their stores and quite large crowds gather blocking the sidewalks." She had tried to have the Health Department remove the offensive fish, but without success. [10]

It was the Italian worker, however, who was singled out for special attention. In the eyes of critics and supporters alike, the city's Italian districts were not only ethnic enclaves but also working-class areas and, for some, even urban ghettos. The Italians themselves were portrayed by their detractors as unskilled immigrants who were highly vulnerable to seasonal layoffs, which, in turn, meant that they threatened to drain social and welfare services. And yet, even with respect to this issue, contradictory arguments surfaced. To be sure, most critics agreed that by tolerating low wages and deplorable working conditions, Italian newcomers had stolen jobs that might otherwise have gone to Canadian workers. That many Italians had taken the jobs that many Canadians had expressly shunned and that government officals had expected them to fill was of little consequence. When one disgruntled man claimed that "many foreigners, including enemy aliens, are disrupting the labour market and disturbing our economy," he was expressing a popular view of the period. Many Torontonians feared that the massive influx of Italians as well as other European immigrants had helped to depress wages, lower workplace standards, and inflate the unemployment rolls. Among angry trade unionists were those who blamed the Italians for helping to weaken a labour movement already crippled by the politics of the Cold War. The fact the perpetrators were former enemy aliens only added to the bitterness. As one writer put it: "Not long ago a great many Canadians lost their lives fighting these people. Now they come here and take jobs under conditions that no Canadian would stand for." [11]

When unemployment rose in the late 1950s, nativist sentiment grew more harsh. Critics blamed the recession on the government's open-door immigration policy, and warned of thousands of unemployed and unemployable newcomers draining the public purse. As scholars have observed, anti-immigrant sentiments are most forcefully expressed during hard economic times and when immigrants themselves are engaged in strikes. The irony of the situation – that when exploited immigrant workers struggle to improve their lot, their actions are interpreted by conservative exponents as selfishness – has not been lost by different generations of immigrants. Often, the two events, recession and strikes, are intimately connected. Nowhere was this more true than in Toronto in 1960 and 1961. A period of continuing recession and unemployment, these years saw bitter strikes by thousands of Italian construction workers within the nonunionized house and apartment field. The strikes, which are detailed in chapter 7, engendered an angry outpouring of letters to the city's English-language press. Dozens of readers expressed their disapproval, even contempt, for what they dubbed the "selfish behaviour" of Italian workers.[12] Given the conservative politics of the leaders, few critics could accuse the Italian strikers of being radicals. Many did, however, accuse the strikers of being impressionable immigrants easily duped by power-hungry leaders offering false promises of fatter paycheques. Finally, the instances of violence that marked each campaign only served to confirm the suspicions of those who argued that "hot-blooded" Italians could not be trusted to respect the law. These skirmishes, claimed one angry critic, revealed the Italians for what they truly were: "nothing but a howling, screaming pack of unruly hooligans."[13]

The compelling image of the Italians as vulnerable workers who might resort to desperate acts of violence or be misled by demogogues stood alongside a contrary image of them as pampered immigrants who, thanks to the postwar welfare state, enjoyed a standard of living and a state-funded support system that had been denied an earlier generation of immigrants. The Italians, noted one observer, "soon have their own homes, cars, TVs, and many other good things they never had in Italy." Many of these critics were themselves elderly British immigrants who had struggled under adverse economic conditions in early twentieth-century Toronto. Their resentment was fuelled by the high levels of Italian homeownership.[14]

Home-ownership was a goal that Italian immigrant families throughout the postwar era pursued with dogged determination. To this end, family members, male and female alike, endured exhausting and risky jobs and found effective ways of reducing living costs. The apparent ease with which the immigrants purchased homes soon after their arrival in Toronto elicited bitter responses from some unsympathetic onlookers, who suggested the Italians were not as economically disadvantaged as they or their supporters would have people believe. At the same time, however, some of the means by which Italians achieved early home-ownership – the cost-sharing arrangements and multiple and crowded households – gave rise to cries from outsiders who had never stepped foot in these homes about immigrants wallowing in unhealthy conditions. As one man who claimed to be surrounded by these crowded Italian households put it, "it tends to create a low standard of living and is not Canadian in character." At least some government authorities of the period concurred. In a 1955 report, Immigration Branch officials voiced the concern that "the standards of sanitation, health and welfare which have been established openly throughout Canada will be undermined in some degree at least by the evident willingness of these immigrants to accept lower standards across the board on the basis that they are still better than Italy."[15]

The fear that ethnic clustering would lead to urban ghettoization was eloquently expressed by a Torontonian whose opinion piece appeared in *Maclean's* in 1956. According to Major-General Macklin, the recent influx of European immigrants had severely exacerbated the social problems accompanying rapid urbanization. These concerns included "a disturbing increase in public disrespect for law and authority," a "very marked growth in the incidence of revolting crimes of violence," and "juvenile deliquency." While admitting that the cause of these ills was complex, he insisted that they arose primarily from "the too-sudden herding of too much humanity, of diverse cultures and backgrounds, into overswollen communities that are consequently lacking in communal cohesion." "No country," he insisted, "has tried with good reason to absorb so large a proportion of totally alien human stock in so short a time." But all he could offer in response was an outdated lament for the loss of "the quiet integrated life of farm and village."[16]

On the question of residential concentration and integration, the reports of government officials and the observations of social scientists in this period echoed each other. Moreover, experts repeatedly singled out for special attention the sponsored movement which, they claimed, had permitted hundreds of thousands of the most poorly equipped Italians of all – southern peasant men and women – to gain entry into the country. In a study prepared for the Department of External Affairs in 1955, immigration officials commented on Italian residential patterns. The tendency of Italians to cluster together and to gravitate to the run-down, working-class districts of the cities was contrasted unfavourably with the dispersed urban patterns exhibited by more assimilable groups such as the Dutch, Scandinavians, and Germans. The report went on to claim that the spread of these "urban slums" might have been prevented had Ottawa more effectively stemmed the tide from the south and recruited larger numbers of immigrants, especially skilled trades people, from northern Italy. So long as Italians from poor backgrounds continue to dominate the influx, the report concluded sourly, "we shall continue to have the formation of 'Little Italies' with the overcrowded housing conditions, etc., which go with this situation."[17]

Not surprisingly, the large presence of newly arrived immigrants and the expanding ethnic neighbourhoods of the city attracted the attention of contemporary social scientists and other social experts. While their evaluations were often more carefully couched in the language of their respective discipline, they, too, operated with the assumption that "ethnic neighbourhoods," if useful to immigrants in the short-term, nevertheless retarded their absorption into the mainstream society. Thus, social scientists viewed the tendency of Italians to congregate in neighbourhoods, and their continuing attachment to large, extended kin and paesani networks of support and community, as obstacles preventing the immigrants' desired integration into Canadian society.

In an era before questions of ethnic and racial identity and of the rights of immigrants not only to preserve but also to celebrate their cultural heritage gained a serious audience, such views reflected, at least in part, the more widely held assumptions among Canadians of the period that the best measure of success with respect to immigrants was to ensure that their culture, habits, and traditions were Canadianized. Thus, even sympathetic observers, among them social researcher Martin Greenwood, who in 1961 conducted a study of Toronto's Italians, operated with the assumption that "ethnic clustering," as well as the predominance of extended-family and multiple-family households – rather than the prefered nuclear family unit – were patterns in need of reforming. In his study, Greenwood attributed what he claimed to be the low degree of integration among the city's Italian immigrants to the strength of their family and kinship bonds and to the variety of community and social supports available in Toronto's Italian neighbourhoods. Within the Italian districts, he observed, even the enterprises that were not owned by Italians hired Italian-speaking clerks and salespeople to serve the Italian clients. Consequently, he claimed, there was little incentive for the Italians to learn English or to form contacts with persons outside the Italian community. Friendships formed at work, he added, rarely penetrated the immigrant household. The image of Italians that emerges in the report is one of chronically underemployed immigrants suffering under the weight of their families and their insular communities. According to Greenwood, the root of the problem lay in the fact that Italian immigrants came to Canada primarily out of economic need and did not fully comprehend what it meant to take up citizenship in an adopted country. This problem was exacerbated by the city's growing cosmopolitanism and the failure of the host society to indicate clearly whom the newcomers should emulate. As a result, "the newcomer is a part of two social structures – the Canadian, to which he is united by economic necessity, and the Italian (really his village), to which he is joined by sentiment."[18]

While sociologists struggled with questions of integration, the seeming irreverence of Italians for Canadian customs and middle-class mores infuriated the less scientific but more self-righteous and intolerant residents of Toronto. If Italians were genuinely concerned with fitting in, they insisted in their letters to the editors of Toronto dailies, more of the newcomers would learn English, secure better jobs "outside their own small circle," and consciously adopt a Canadian lifestyle.[19] "My observation," wrote one woman, "is that a lot of them aren't at all interested in learning English but are quite content to stay Italian and keep to their own group." The efforts of newcomers to improve their homes were not always welcomed. Others complained of Italian neighbours causing a racket with their hammers and saws as they renovated their homes and disturbed the Sabbath. "Do these Italian immigrants earn respect?" asked one woman who wrote to recount her frustration at returning home from church one Sunday to find "the sidewalk ... blocked by a huge van unloading furniture for one of them." "I can find no excuse," proclaimed another, "for these people to come to our country to earn their living and ... attain a better life ... when they have no intention of accepting our ways and customs. They belligerently refuse to learn our language and constantly speak their own Italian in public places even after having been here for long enough to converse in English if they wanted to." She found this to be "extremely annoying and rude, almost like whispering in company." By way of consolation, this observer, like many others, placed her faith in the assimilative powers of the school system and looked forward to a time when the immigrants' children would be reared as proper Canadians.[20]

Images of Italians shouting in high-pitched, foreign voices, of men slapping each other on the back or, worse still, embracing, flew in the face of a Protestant sense of propriety. "They are rather annoying," wrote one person, "the way they congregate in groups and the number of children they have running around." Other conflicts emerged over the habit Italians had of congregating outside church on Sundays or socializing out of doors. These, of course, were customs imported from home, where villagers socialized in the town piazza. In Toronto, however, the police were sent to disperse them. When the Italians refused to move, police officers retaliated with threats of vagrancy charges or insults and shoves. As one man recalled: "We would be doing no harm ... talking, telling jokes ... standing up on the sidewalk or the grass. They would tell us to move. If we don't, then they start pushing us ... saying, 'Com'on move. Move it, you wop.'"[22]

Torontonians anxious about these public forms of socializing became all the more enraged when the crowds in question were composed entirely of men. Images of dark swarthy men lurking about ready to prey on Canadian "girls" fed the popular mythology of Italians as hot-tempered Latins. Contemporary critics charged that the young Italian men who stood in front of stores and cafés, in parks, and on street corners were members of street gangs and ready to prey on unsuspecting passersby, especially Canadian women. The police appeared to share this view, for they routinely picked up Italian men congregating on corners and charged them with "curb-cruising."[23] The profoundly complex gendered dimension of the question whether "foreign" men wittingly or unwittingly threatened Canadian women could be overshadowed by the harsh responses of the host society. In 1965, for example, when an Italian man was arrested for allegedly harrassing a Canadian women, he seems to have become the victim of police abuse. According to the Italian consul general who protested matters to the Ontario attorney-general, the accused had been slapped and punched by two officers, and then told to lick his blood off the floor, before being detained in jail for the night.[24]

When discussing the potential threat posed by Italian men, people generally referred to two types of crime: the spontaneous act committed out of extreme passion or anger, and the illicit activities of Mafia hoodlums who ran drugs across the border or carried out vendettas. No one, of course, would deny that certain individual Italians night have committed serious crimes, though it should be stressed that the official data indicate that throughout the postwar era the Italians as an ethnic group registered among the lowest rates of criminality in Canada.[25] Predictably, however, the exceptional instances of sensational cases attracted much publicity. In October 1954, for example, an Italian worker shot to death a Greek co-worker at a Toronto bread factory during one of many heated arguments that had transpired between them. More frightening still to observers were cases involving violence against women. On 4 August 1960, a young Italian man tried, unsuccessfully, to shoot to death a sixteen-year-old Canadian woman and himself after she broke off their relationship. In 1960 a married man whose wife had not yet joined him murdered his Italian neighbour after she repeatedly spurned his advances. And a German immigrant woman recently separated from her husband met her death on 26 July 1955 on the veranda of her west-end rooming house at the hands of her Italian ex-lover. Following a night of heavy drinking at a nearby bar, the man, knifed the woman repeatedly, cutting her jugular vein.[26]

The instances of Italian-related crime and murder covered by the press in these years proved a source of immense embarrassment to most Italians. The front-page coverage of such events, moreover, likely fuelled erroneous but prejudicial assumptions that it was the foreign-born man who was more likely to perform the deranged act. Such pat stereotypes obscure the reality that violence against women is a crime that, historically, has never been confined to a particular class or race.[27]

Perhaps even more threatening than the Latin temperament, at least in the minds of Canadian officials amid the Cold War, was the possibility of an influx into Canada of Italian communists. Government authorities were keen to prevent all communists from entering Canada, and Italy was given close attention because it was the seat of the largest Communist party in western Europe. When in 1957 pro-immigration lobbyists and lawyers charged immigration authorities with abusing their wide discretionary powers to reject or deport immigrants, officials cited the large number of communists in Italy as a case in point. It was essential, they said, to be able to select out those suspected of being political subversives without jeopardizing informants. In response to cries that informants were often anonymous people relaying unsubstantiated gossip, officials offered a stock response, saving it was in the interest of national security to deny these "undesirables" information, particularly the reasons for their rejection.[28]

In fact, Canadian security personnel suspected that Italian officials were so keen to rid themselves of their surplus population that they did not provide full security reports on suspected communists. On occasion this led to strained relations between the two countries. In April 1952, for example, overseas officials informed Ottawa that one of the farm workers who had sailed overseas as part of a bulk order had subsequently shown up on their security listings as a suspected party activist. After sending a terse cable to officials in Rome, Ottawa ordered the Royal Canadian Mounted Police to monitor the man's activities, though officials observed that unless he committed a crime he could not be arrested. An attempt to begin deportation proceedings was dropped when Italy proved uncooperative. The knowledge of this sort of incident likely would have enraged an avowed anti-communist like Fred Bodsworth, a *Maclean's* writer who insisted that federal immigration agents were being too lenient in screening Italian candidates. Canadian selection teams, he pointed out, "approved twenty thousand immigrants in 1951 from Italy, where more than one-third of the citizens voted Communist in the last election." He concluded by urging officials to be more stringent in their screening procedures.[29]

Canadian immigration officials, and others, were equally preoccupied with preventing what they labelled the "gangster element" from getting into Canada. They and their supporters employed the same arguments used with respect to suspected communists whenever they were asked to explain why rejected candidates or deported immigrants were denied legal recourse in the form of a trial or a hearing. In contrast to sensational news reports, however, neither the government nor the RCMP in this period believed that organized crime in Canada was extensive. In 1955 an officer in the RCMP Narcotics Division told immigration officials that, contrary to a recent Toronto *Telegram* article, "the mafia is not flourishing in Canada." While he claimed that there was an "active" criminal element of Canadian-born gangsters of Italian origin, some of whom "find it convenient to use the terrorist threat of the Mafia to silence our own simple-minded Italian immigrants," he concluded that, like older "ethnic" criminals, Italian criminals were mostly involved in the "narcotics racket."[30]

Still, there was no more compelling stereotype than that of the Mafia mobster. As Greenwood's 1961 report observed, this familiar image had been further popularized during the 1950s by the television series "The Untouchables," in which every criminal possessed an Italian name. One of the Greenwood's Italian informants sarcastically suggested that the show ought to be renamed "Cops and Wops." Greenwood himself added that the detective series confirmed a stereotype of Italians "as short, dark, particularly prone to criminal behaviour and complicity through 'the mafia' and other mysterious agencies." By 1961 the series' sponsor had responded to public pressure from Italian-American groups and ordered the producers to assign non-Italian names to some of their criminals.[31]

By the early 1960s newspaper and magazine writers in Canada began to chronicle what they claimed was the infiltration by American Mafia "dons" of gambling and legitimate business and of political and trade-union activities in various Canadian cities. They indicated that this was done in large part through Canadian-born petty criminals and narcotics dealers. They also insisted that new criminals were slipping through Canada's security net and joining these networks. Canadian press coverage of a 1961 crackdown on a major heroin drug ring operating out of Sicily, Ontario, and New York state devoted much attention to the role played by two Sicilian brothers temporarily residing in Toronto. Through contacts in Italy, it was reported, they had helped to bring drugs into Canada on ships carrying immigrants, and then smuggled them across the border by car, usually with the aid of a woman posing as a tourist. According to reporters, the men had a long list of petty and drug-related charges, and they had connections with leading American crime figures who had been caught.[32]

To be sure, journalists who portrayed the Mafia as an unbeatable new force in Canada usually included a disclaimer exonerating the majority of Italian immigrants who were praised for being law-abiding people. In a five-part series in *Maclean's* in 1964, Allen Philips, for example, noted that only a tiny minority of Italians had been drawn into the Mafia's web, though he added that he wished more would provide police information concerning criminals in their community. In his words, "The Italian community, 99 per cent honest, is too frightened or too ashamed to speak up. As a result the public gives the police little support and most policemen do not know whom they are fighting." Despite such disclaimers, reporters like Philips helped to keep alive in the minds of their Canadian readers the association between Italians and organized crime. Such stories were easy to sensationalize, and they sparked the imaginations of many.[33]

If some Italian men were said to pose a potential social problem, Italian women were depicted as submissive creatures closely guarded by possessive men and rarely roaming beyond the confines of their neighborhood – except, perhaps, to make their way to the local factory to earn their petty wages. In the descriptions of even sympathetic observers, Italian women emerge as plump, black-shawled women pushing "equally plump" babies in their carriages or shouting inelegantly at local shopkeepers in the hopes of getting a bargain. An indication of the depths of intolerance, if not absurdity, to which some Torontonians of the era could slip is indicated by the written comments of one angry woman, who deplored the "fact" that Italian women were not prepared to raise their children as Canadians. "When they have their children," she boldly noted as proof, "born in Canada, delivered by Canadian doctors, in Canadian hospitals, they accept these privileges and give thanks by giving the baby a difficult Italian name, [and] sticking rings through its ears [so that] it may as well be back in Italy." While they used less explosive language, others observers nevertheless shared the view that the influence of the "tradition-bound" mothers and grand-mothers would need to be broken for efforts aimed at Canadianizing the children to be successful.[35]

In the case of the younger, unmarried women, contemporary observers, including the sympathetic Robert Allen, could only express their bemusement at this chauvinistic streak in Italian culture. "Italian girls," Allen wrote, "are strictly brought up and strictly chaperoned. They're not allowed to go out with boys in cars. Drive-ins are so unthinkable that when I asked one girl if she'd ever been to one she appeared to turn a bit pale at the very thought of it. If a girl sits up with her boyfriend to watch a late show on TV, one of the family, probably a brother, sits up with her – and it doesn't make any difference if she's engaged." He then quoted an office manager he had interviewed who, pointing to a young employee, said: "Her mother belted her right in the office last week. She'd seen her talking to a boy in the coffee room." Rather than seriously explore the dilemma of young Italian women compelled to straddle two worlds, Allen merely joked, saying: "The behaviour of Italian daughters would wring an envious groan from most Canadian mothers." He cited another office employer who explained how Italian "girls" made wonderful employees because they were accustomed to taking orders without protest, did not smoke, and were "always willing to work late because when they go home they have to start working around the house anyway."[36]

HARDWORKING PEOPLE

While cultural chauvinism most typically characterized the early responses of Torontonians to Italians, the response was not entirely negative. Throughout the late 1950s and early 1960s, positive portraits of Italians emerged as writers and other observers praised hardworking, family-oriented Italians. Journalists such as Pierre Berton, Peter Newman, and the *Telegram*'s Frank Drea, the editors of Toronto's English-language dailies, as well as ordinary citizens argued that within a short period of time the Italians had proven themselves to be diligent, thrifty, and resourceful, and dutiful parents as well – in short, to share the same values as Canadians. As civic boosters, they also saw the Italians and their colourful and lively Little Italies as an increasingly important part of Toronto's new cosmopolitan image.

By no means did the more complimentary images of the Italian merely replace the negative ones. On the contrary, many of these sympathetic stories were written specifically to counter the nativist backlash that the construction strikes of 1960 and 1961 had engendered. Typically, their stories focused attention on the resourcefulness of Italian families. Take, for instance, Frank Drea's description of a striker, Dominic Moscone, a construction worker who lived with his wife and two children in a household in which ten other people also resided. Drea went to some lengths to describe how the Moscones and their housemates cleverly minimized living costs by "turning their backyard into a vegetable garden" and relying on a pasta-heavy diet. He also chronicled Moscone's struggles as an unskilled construction worker, rising at 4 AM to walk fifteen miles to his pick-up depot and not returning home until after dark – "all for the princely sum of $1.00 an hour." At the time of the interview, Moscone was recovering from a severely sprained hand, a job-related injury for which he did not receive compensation. He had taken a variety of odd jobs.[37]

A similar portrait of another striker, Angelo De Castro, was published by the *Star*. The column gave a voice to De Castro and his father-in-law, both of whom explained they had come to support the union organizing campaigns because greater job security, higher wages, and improved working conditions offered some compensation to workers who regularly faced underemployment. Seasonal layoffs had forced their family to stretch their resources over the winter months. The column described the warmth of the De Castro family, and how parents spent their few leisure hours in the park with their children or visiting relatives. Like Drea's portrait of Moscone, the column concluded that most of the strikers were hardworking family men making legitimate demands.[38]

Sympathetic editorials reflected the views of liberal journalists who were clearly outraged by the injustices from which immigrant workers were suffering in the city. They supported the construction strikes precisely because they believed the immigrants, by demanding the same rights as Canadian workers, were becoming citizens and integrating into Canadian society. As one *Star* editorial put it: "Native Canadians would be shortsighted if they sought to base their prosperity on the exploitation of newcomers ... Such a concept is immoral." Other reporters, including *Telegram* columnist Rosemary Boxer, openly chastized the critics. "If I hadn't seen and talked with these people," she wrote of the Italians, "I wouldn't have believed it possible that in this free country where racial hatreds and antagonisms are supposed to be abhored, a minority group, ignorant of our language and our ways, could be so shabbily treated, so disgracefully exploited." In an attempt to address this problem, her column provided glimpses of the difficulties the strikers' families confronted.[39]

Among the letters to the press were those written by ordinary Torontonians who expressed their admiration of the Italians for having surmounted enormous barriers in their quest to create a better life for themselves and their children. These people, wrote one reader, "deserve commendation for proving what can be achieved by hard work toward a definite goal. Native-born Canadians have a better chance to succeed in Canada than immigrants. If some are too indolent to grab it, let them blame themselves and let the better man succeed." Similar sentiments propelled another to ask: "How many Canadians who complain about immigrants would do some of the dirty jobs they undertake, support their parents ... [and] go out of their way to find a job?"[40]

Italians had earned the respect of some of their English-speaking neighbours, a few of whom wrote in an attempt to convert their less generous compatriots. As one Irish-Canadian woman magnanimously put it: "Only someone raised in an Italian neighborhood ... can appreciate the milk of human kindness flowing from these people." The same motives prompted another woman to write a lengthy letter to the *Telegram* in 1961. "About five years ago," she said, "when Italians and other immigrants began arriving in my neighborhood a lot of people moved away [and] said these foreigners were dirty, noisy, etc., and would depress the district." Nothing that "the two noisiest families" on her street happened to be Canadians, she praised the Italians for their sense of house pride, saying, "the Italians may have more people living in one house but they keep the house spotless and they improve the appearance. I can take you to streets ... that had become completely rundown and show you how the Italian has improved it with alterations, paint, gardens, etc." Like others, she also approved of their work ethic and strong family values: "I have watched the men go out with their lunch boxes in the morning ... [and] come home at dark, bone tired and weary but always with a smile and a laugh to quiet their children. I have talked to shopkeepers who cash their pay cheques and who marvel they don't starve on the wages they are getting, but they always bring out what they have when you visit." Putting it more simply, one man praised his Italian neighbours for being a "thrifty, honest, and sociable people."[41]

As Italian workers became associated with Toronto's phenomenal economic progress after the war and its growing cosmopolitanism, they increasingly received credit for having helped to build the expansive, modern city. The sights and sounds of Little Italy also received considerable press. *Star* writer Jean Belliveau emphasized the vibrancy of Toronto's Little Italies, the wonderful smells and colourful sights, and the Italians' strong sense of community.[42] During the 1960 and 1961 construction strikes, several writers asked readers to reflect on the fact that they owed Italian workers many thanks for the luxuries they enjoyed – more electricity lines and phones, new highways, and modern highrises and homes. One *Star* editorial sought to assure the Italians that their critics were in a minority and that "the true worth" of Toronto's Italians "is widely recognized and warmly appreciated." "The Italians," it added, "are vital, active, interesting people, and they have helped to make Toronto a dynamic, progressive metropolis in these times." By the end of the decade, the growing political importance of the Italian community in Toronto, and Canada, was evident in the declarations of politicians who began to praise the Italians openly. In May 1957 J.W. Pickersgill, the minister of immigration, delivered a speech at the Canadian Italian Business and Professional Men's Association, in which he stressed the "indispensible contribution" that Italians had made to Canada's postwar growth.[43]

While it is impossible to determine the impact that the Italians' public supporters had on their audience, it is worth noting that the values and assumptions lying behind some of the positive portraits of Italians reflected a certain degree of chauvinism in so far as the Italian newcomers were being judged in terms of the degree to which they appeared to share the same values as Canadians.

In a paternalistic fashion, these writers congratulated the newcomers on their progress or observed that, despite the marked differences in culture, customs, and physical appearance, Italians proved to be reliable and diligent. Yet their comments also emphasized the differences between Torontonians and immigrants. This tendency was reinforced by the curious voyeurism of some of the writings. An example was the decision of Andrew Thompson, a Liberal MPP, to spend a week living with a "typical" Italian working-class family. His observations were recorded in Berton's column in the *Star*. Although both men were clearly well-intentioned in their objectives, the very title given to the series, "A Strange Interlude," underlined the assumption that Thompson was entering an exotic and foreign world. The experiment was designed both the highlight the difficulty of the immigrants' lives and to illustrate that they were adaptive and hard-working. Thus, Berton referred to the fact that the family lived in a crowded household, that the men and women got up very early for work each morning, and that they proved remarkably adroit at stretching their limited resources. "Every square foot on the tiny backyard was devoted to a garden," he observed. "The men thought nothing of walking half a mile to buy cracked cans for a few cents cheaper, the women of waiting two hours in line at Honest Ed's for clothing bargains. Nothing was thrown out; nothing wasted. Worn out shirts were resewn into hankerchiefs or towels." Yet he also paid considerable attention to what he evidently considered the strangeness of the Italian immigrants' world, which he referred to as a "vast city-within-a-city ... this barren dormitory existence." And his conclusions reveal some of the same biases that prompted the critics to place their faith in the Canadianizing impact of the school system. Unless the parents improved their standard of living, Berton argued, their children would not receive a proper education and thus a wonderful opportunity to transform the children into productive Canadians would be lost. Berton supported the construction strikes not simply because he believed that Italian workers deserved better wages and working conditions; he also felt that by improving their material conditions, the immigrant generation would be in a better position to allow their children to get a decent education. The children, in turn, would be spared from living the same wretched lives as their parents, and they would become useful and productive Canadian citizens.[44]

Rather than lamenting the decline of "Toronto the Good," writers such as Pierre Berton took delight in the city's growing cosmopolitanism. Others, including Peter C. Newman, were more critical of Torontonians, claiming that by treating the Italians with indifference or hostility the city's Anglo-Saxon residents forced the immigrants to withdraw further into their own community, thereby destroying the opportunity for real communication and cultural exchange between the two groups. Only by aiding the newcomers to adjust to Canadian life and by exhibiting more open-mindedness about the immigrants, he concluded, could social relations between natives and newcomers improve. Taking up a similar theme, Hugh Garner, another *Maclean's* reporter, wrote: "Too many of us still cling to the crazy belief that we are better than the New Canadians because our parents come from the British Isles and English is our native tongue." Such narrowmindedness, he claimed, was "preventing Canadians from seeing the contributions which immigrants could make to Canada." But he also maintained that progress was being made, that postwar Canadians were becoming increasingly more tolerant towards the non-British immigrants – a fact that indicated that "we are growing as a nation and British jingoism and xenophobia are dying out."[45]

Not all Torontonians, then, took exception to the Italian foreigners in their midst, but they could nevertheless be patronizing in their praise. Even Robert Allen, a keen supporter of the Italians, took heart from the fact that many of Toronto's prewar Italians, including Joseph Piccininni, alderman for Ward 5 and the Canadian-raised son of Italian parents who arrived in Toronto at the turn of the century, spoke unaccented English and had become thoroughly Canadianized in dress and behaviour. Speaking of an Italian-Canadian Lions Club meeting he attended, Allen wrote: "I listened to 35 Italians, many of whom looked like Scotsmen and Englishmen, sing God Save the Queen [and] yell 'skibbydibbydoo' when guests were introduced"[46]

From the perspective of the 1990s, the prejudice that Italian immigrants encountered in early postwar Toronto seems part of a remote past. Most Canadians now look upon the Italians as one of the oldest and most established ethnic groups, while the media promotes the image of the Italian "super-rich" – the developers and other businessmen who have become wealthy and influential.[47] Furthermore, as many new immigrants have arrived, controversy has surrounded the racial and religious minorities from Developing countries. In short, Torontonians have found new scapegoats.[48] But for the Italian immigrants who entered early postwar Toronto, the city was a cold and unfriendly place. Particularly during the recession years of the late 1950s and early 1960s, they encountered considerable prejudice and discrimination. In the absence of large numbers of blacks and other visible minorities, the Italians, especially the southern Italians, emerged as a popular target of people's scorn.

CHAPTER SIX

Community Life

During the 1950s and early 1960s, contemporary observers routinely commented that the newly arrived Italian immigrants were too preoccupied with work and family life to show much interest in the world beyond their home and workplace. Certainly, during the early years, many immigrants, anxious to get themselves established and strangers to the language and customs of English Canadians, exhibited a guarded interest in the wider Toronto society. Having grown up under fascism and war, many of them also lacked prior experience with voluntary associations. Within the ethnic colony, the newcomers, at least initially, took a back seat to the pre-1930 Italian immigrants and their Canadian-born or raised children who initiated many of the community's earliest postwar organizations.

But like most immigrants, southern Italians were keen to nurture their treasured cultural and religious beliefs and belong to a community. In Toronto, they showed a continuing attachment to their own brand of peasant Catholicism and successfully transplanted cherished rituals and traditions. In times of need, they also turned to outside social agencies for assistance, though they rarely proved receptive to the idea of completely abandoning their own cultural ways and fully adopting Canadian habits. And while the Italian oldtimers dominated the formal organizations of the early postwar colony, the immigrants eventually developed their own institutions or otherwise participated in the colony's associational life. They resisted outside pressures to conform and found their own ways to maintain their culture and recreate a sense of community.

SEEKING SUPPORT

Unlike their predecessors a half-century before, Canada's postwar immigrants had access to plenty of government-funded social services associated with the burgeoning welfare state. The Italians benefited from a new federal system of unemployment insurance and from improvements in the Ontario Workman's Compensation Act and better health and welfare schemes. They also had recourse to other forms of temporary aid. Families could secure at least a modicum of help from local volunteer agencies, many of which had long served immigrant and working-class families in the city. Women's groups organized clothing and food donations, provided child-rearing lectures, and dispatched volunteers to meet new arrivals at Union Station. Settlement houses and other agencies acted as job placement centres and offered English classes and recreational activities, as did various Catholic organizations. Italians could also tap support systems within their own ethnic colony, the most important being the Italian Immigrant Aid Society, created in 1952 by a group of prominent Italian oldtimers. By 1957 the Metro Social Planning Council, a brainchild of the Toronto Welfare Council, had opened an Immigration Section and offered numerous community services to immigrants.[1]

From the perspective of the caring professionals and volunteers who staffed these agencies, Italian immigrants failed to make sufficient use of the social resources at their disposal, and they were overdependent on their families and kin. The fact that those Italians who did seek help usually arrived at an agency escorted by a relative, these social workers noted, was symptomatic of a much larger problem regarding the immigrants' failure to integrate into the wider society.[2] This concern was particularly evident in the discussions of women. Staff workers typically experienced great frustration in reaching married women, recruiting them into their classes and lectures, and convincing them to leave their children in nursery and daycare centres.[3]

While heavy domestic duties and cultural differences partially explain why Italian mothers did not attend classes or leave their children with strangers, the behaviour of these women, and of Italian families generally, more accurately reflected the selective ways in which they made use of the available services. Even those who returned again and again to the offices of a local charity or welfare office had only a temporary, even fleeting, relationship with the city's caretakers. Still, in seeking aid, many families suffered the indignity of opening up their lives and homes to outsiders – a situation that sometimes exposed them to the biases of intolerant investigators. In one case, a social worker employed with a public agency barred a particular Italian mother from receiving any more clothing handouts because she had become too "fussy" about what she would take. Another caseworker griped about an Italian mother of four who complained about the canned food she was being offered and requested food vouchers to purchase her own Italian food. Even though the home visitor confirmed the woman's story about her family living in a cramped flat and her husband's insufficient unemployment insurance earnings, she was not recommended for Christmas benefits.[4]

Notwithstanding the more sympathetic rhetoric of the postwar era and the formal adoption of a model of cultural pluralism, the city's caring professionals and volunteers still saw their agencies primarily as humane instruments of Canadianization. In the short term, they were genuinely concerned to provide immediate relief and assistance to newcomers. In the long-term, however, they sought to transform the immigrants into culturally assimilated Canadians – a process that they assumed could be pushed along by keeping immigrants steadily employed, and by offering them classes in English, citizenship, Canadian customs, and the law. According to the constitution of the International Institute of Metropolitan Toronto, a large immigrant aid agency, a major objective was "to assist immigrants in establishing themselves … and to hasten their integration into the Canadian way of life." The Italian oldtimers who ran the Italian Immigrant Aid Society shared the same goal, in part because they believed that by encouraging the immigrants to adopt Canadian ways, the public image of the Italian community would be enhanced in the eyes of Canadians. "We are a non-profit organization," their constitution read, "working exclusively toward fitting Italian immigrants into a Canadian way of life."[5]

The considerable interest these professionals and volunteer caregivers showed in Italian women, especially housewives, was linked to the larger commitment to Canadianizing the immigrants. Their agencies sponsored programs designed to teach Italian women Canadian techniques in everything from cooking to parenting. St Christopher's House, a west-end settlement house, for example, offered nutrition classes and regularly staged children's events that provided opportunities for mingling with Canadian children. Other agencies offered tours through middle-class households as a way of introducing Italian women to modern appliances and to the layout and decor of Canadian homes. Other volunteer groups offered classes in English, nutrition, and Canadian cooking, while in their public lectures on child-rearing, public health nurses encouraged immigrant women to adopt North American conventions. In providing these services, the women and men who staffed the city's various agencies drew a connection between providing material aid and their larger goal. They saw their baby clinics, home visits, and state handouts as tools for improving the immigrants' material lives.

By offering such help, they also hoped to make the women more receptive to the lectures and educational courses aimed at converting them, and their children, to Canadian ways.[6]

Their efforts, however, were often thwarted by the immigrants themselves, many of whom adopted a pragmatic and selective approach towards the agencies. This complex dynamic lay behind the angry words of a public health nurse who supervised a baby clinic in the basement of St Thomas Aquinas Church, an Italian parish in the city. She criticized the Italian mothers for making use of the available facilities and services – which included medical examinations, vaccinations, and pasteurized milk – while not remaining long enough to attend the nurses' lectures on Canadian childrearing techniques. In her exasperation, she attributed the problem to the narrow-minded and suspicious qualities of the southern Italian character. "One of the concomitants we hope to put over to these immigrants," she wrote, "is the North American concept of unpaid, volunteer aid to others." She continued:

Public Health nurse

They are completely mystified at the idea of "doing anything for nothing," and have had rather an unsettling effect on some of our volunteers, when their remarks have been translated. (I do wish the foreign-language press was given a good briefing by someone, re this old and much-respected pioneer virtue, of "neighbourly aid," and not the rather patronizing attentions often given in Europe by the wealthy towards the poor, called charity, nor the cold impersonality of bureaucracy and State Aid that they have left behind, and must forget.) It is an essential part of their integration into the Canadian way of life, and the sooner it is explained to them, the better. Their old ideas must not infect our people; so some missionary work is quickly needed to be done re this angle."[7]

If Italians were not receptive to mimicking Canadian customs, they were quick to tap existing support services. Italian housewives, for example, attended Christmas parties to collect the food baskets and presents for the children, picked up baby layettes and clothes from various depots, or hosted public health nurses' inspection visits in their homes. While some of the clients were destitute, more typically they were families suffering through a hard time. Often, they had been directed to an agency by relatives and paesani who had themselves benefited from the services the agency offered. In short, this aid was not a substitute for support from kin; rather, it was an additional form of assistance.

A sample of the case histories of southern Italian families who made use of two immigrant aid agencies – one outside the ethnic colony and the other within – illustrates the role such agencies played in family survival strategies. The International Institute of Metro-politan Toronto was a multifaceted immigrant aid agency created in 1956 when St Andrew's Memorial House, one of the city's oldest settlement houses, amalgamated with the New Canadians Service Association, a postwar friendly society established by several Toronto philanthropists. The institute, which received considerable funds through the United Appeal, employed its own staff of professionals and volunteers. It cooperated with various ethnic organizations, including the Italian Immigrant Aid Society (IIAS), the second agency under discussion.

As the case files of these two agencies indicate, the immigrants' most common problems were financial and were usually linked to unemployment or illness. For instance, matters became difficult for one family when the wife broke her leg at work and her garage mechanic husband, who was also recovering from injuries, was laid off without compensation benefits. For several months, she collected food and clothing donations from the institute. In 1955 a women with four children approached the IIAS stating that her husband had been inexplicably ill for some time. They had exhausted their savings by paying doctors who had been unable to diagnose the problem. At the IIAS's request, another doctor conducted tests and found the man was suffering from a liver problem. The woman was referred to the welfare department and given emergency benefits until her husband recovered. A family of seven sought help from the International Institute in the fall of 1959 when both the husband and son were laid off. The wife was at home with children and a sick, elderly father. This left a teenage daughter, earning $25 a week in a knitting factory, as the sole breadwinner. The mother secured food and clothes from the institute and received an emergency welfare cheque. Apparently, she came to see the agency as a useful vehicle for getting through tight situations, for she returned there several winters in a row. By the third winter, when the case history ends, the daughter had married and the mother was seeking paid work.[8]

Mental illness could strike a family, leaving a spouse and children ill-prepared to cope with the financial and emotional burdens. Since landed immigrants diagnosed as mentally ill could be deported, there was further cause for alarm. One woman spent months coping with her husband's apparently peculiar behaviour before approaching the IIAS. Public health nurses conducted a home visit, decided he was suffering from severe depression, and recommended him to the Ontario Mental Hospital. IIAS workers then found "suitable lodging" for the woman, who was expecting a third child, and helped her to move in. Years of juggling the pressures of work and home took a mental toll on some women. Their illnesses, in turn, affected their families. One working mother of four suffered a nervous breakdown several years after she and her husband had immigrated. During her hospitalization, the husband could not care for the children, who had also begun to cause trouble at school. He agreed to place the children in a Catholic orphanage until their mother had recovered.[9]

Family breakdown among Italians was rare on both sides of the Atlantic but exceptions did occur, and women bore the brunt of the problem. One case of wife desertion that came before International Institute workers involved a construction worker who had suffered a history of "emotional troubles." He abandoned his wife of eleven years in the summer of 1960, a few years after they had arrived in Canada. The agency arranged for Italian-speaking volunteers to visit the woman, who lived with her five children in a multiple household, and referred her to family and welfare services. Wife desertion was frequently preceded by domestic violence. One woman who was reported to have endured "years of physical and emotional abuse" was deserted by her husband of twenty years shortly after she suffered a work-related injury in the fall of 1962. She could not bring herself to seek a legal separation, even though this would have qualified her for long-term welfare assistance. As a result, two of her sons dropped out of high school to support her. The records document only one woman who left an abusive marriage. She frankly admitted to her caseworker that "she might never have married her husband had it not been for the social and religious pressure in her home country."[10]

The loss of a husband created serious problems for a woman. The 1962 death of a husband ten years after he immigrated left a forty-nine-year-old woman with a small widow's pension, mortgage payments, and serious mental problems. The caseworker's report read: "[She] has trouble with nerves, being very unhappy since husband died. Affected her stomach, brains and nerves in general. Takes injections, has private medical care, but no improvement. Spends a lot of money on drugs. Married daughters do not help, one just recently married (one month ago), the other married to a good-for-nothing. Very clean house, well looked after. Sad case, as wife cannot improve health." Far from falling into the abyss of self-despair, however, this woman eventually recovered her health, overcame a painful shyness, and began attending English classes. By 1965, when the case history ends, she was described as successfully caring for her youngest child and elderly mother.[11]

By the early 1960s the case files of both agencies begin to identify Italians who were refused assistance because they no longer qualified as recent arrivals or needy cases. This reflected the fact that as the first wave of postwar Italians had become more settled, the short-term aid such agencies offered had grown less relevant. As the social workers themselves recognized, many Italian families had survived the early difficult years of adjustment. Now, however, there were long-term needs to address – among them the provision of retraining facilities for the growing number of injured construction workers hoping to re-enter the labour force, and the upgrading of unskilled and semi-skilled workers. A related concern involved improving facilities to help tradesworkers applying for Canadian certificates. The major impetus for these programs would come first from within the Italian community.[12]

CHURCH, CLERGY, AND POPULAR PIETY

Conflict and accommodation aptly describe the relations between priests and Italian immigrants in early postwar Toronto. While the predominantly Anglo-Celtic leadership night have hoped to weld diverse ethnic and regional groups into a homogenous community of Canadian Catholics, the immigrants from southern Italy arrived with their own imported brand of rural Catholicism, with its mixture of pre-Christian and Christian beliefs, and its strong attachment to religious feasts. The growing resentment of the Italians – both the immigrant parishioners and the newly recruited Italian-speaking priests – over their perceived inferior status within the church created additional levels of conflict. The large Italian presence also severely taxed the city's existing Italian churches and eventually compelled the archbishop to expand the parish system.[13]

The Catholic clergy took delight in the fact that the arrival of large numbers of Italian immigrants posed a challenge to the Protestant majority in Toronto. In a 1957 radio broadcast authorized by the Chancery Office, the Reverend A. Carmignani observed with satisfaction that Toronto's population was "becoming increasingly more Catholic especially due to the important fact of [Italian] immigration." The comments of the archbishop, Cardinal James MacGuigan, reveal the extent to which the clergy believed the church could act as a vehicle for Canadianizing the Italian newcomers, particularly by ensuring that the immigrants' preoccupation with economic matters did not lead them to ignore their religious duties. During a mass commemorating the arrival of a new priest in 1954, MacGuigan said he understood that most of the Italians in the congregation had migrated for economic motives and not to "seek out the faith," but they were nevertheless obliged to guard against the temptation of neglecting their spiritual development. "This would be a fatal mistake," he explained, "because the loss of faith brings with it an infinity of disaster in this life and in the afterlife." As Catholics, he told them, they must attend mass regularly, "keep the Catholic faith in your workplaces and ... homes," "educate your young," and "contribute to an active Christian life."[14]

The priests saw their role among the newcomers as missionaries ministering to people in foreign lands. In an effort to encourage the Italians to "live better their Christian lives" and to "integrate into Canadian society," as one parish bulletin put it, the clergy offered a variety of programs, including catechism instruction for children attending public schools, and marriage, English, and citizenship classes. They also checked on any rival groups that might entice the newcomers away. These included the small groups of leftists within the ethnic colony and the outspoken liberals who were not adverse to criticizing the church. The priests also viewed the Protestant churches as religious rivals. This was particularly true of the United Church, which had enjoyed some success among the prewar Italians of Toronto and which now offered a variety of social services through its home missions. In large part these fears were based on the past exploits of the former Methodist Missionary Church, which had cultivated a small Italian following.[15]

Notwithstanding such concerns, neither Protestantism nor anti-clericalism posed a serious threat to the Catholic church. By 1961 over 95 per cent of Toronto's Italians called themselves Roman Catholics, and only a handful of Italians belonged to St Paul's United Church, the Protestant church that was usually described as the Catholics' major rival. By contrast, the 1961 membership figures for St Agnes and St Mary of the Angels – the two churches that, along with Our Lady of Mount Carmel, had been established as Italian national parishes in the prewar period – stood at 4000 and 2500, respectively. St Agnes was located on Grace Street, in the College Street Little Italy, and St Mary could be found on Dufferin Street, near Davenport Road, in the old Italian district that had evolved into the St Clair colony. Since the 1930s both parishes had been staffed by the Franciscan brothers from New York. Only Mount Carmel showed a marked decline in the number of Italian parishioners – a situation that reflected the fact that the Ward district, where it was located, was no longer an area of Italian settlement.[16]

It was the postwar influx of Italians that compelled the archdiocese to embark on a major expansion program. In the prewar era, church fathers had adopted a system of national parishes as a way of ministering to an immigrant population that was heavily concentrated in certain locales yet also dispersed throughout the city. As national rather than territorial parishes, these churches had been free to attract Italians from anywhere in the city. In the 1950s Archbishop MacGuigan and, later, Philip F. Pocock faced a similar situation, only this time the sheer volume of the influx required more than a few additional national parishes. Hence, the church went another route. In areas of heavy Italian settlement it turned the older, predominantly Irish territorial parishes into bilingual churches by introducing Italian masses.[17] It also subdivided the more expansive, suburban parishes and created new bilingual territorial parishes.

An obvious part of the expansion program was the recruitment of Italian-speaking priests to serve the Italians. The male religious orders from Italy and the United States – Franciscans, Redemptorists, Oblates, Servites, and Scalibrinians – assumed administrative control of some of Toronto's parishes. The remaining parishes were staffed with young secular priests who responded to the calls of the archdiocese, after clerics such as Toronto's Italian-speaking bishop, the Canadian-born Rev. Francesco Marrocco, went on lecture tours to Italy's seminaries. The archibishop also turned to the Ufficio Centrale per l'Emigrazione (UCEI), a training centre in Rome, to recruit secular priests interested in working among immigrants abroad. Still others came to join family members in Toronto. The city also attracted new recruits from the female religious orders, especially the Carmelite nuns, an order with considerable experience among Toronto's Italians.[18]

For the southern Italians who represented a preponderant proportion of the congregation of many, though not all, of the city's Italian and bilingual parishes, the regional composition of the Italian clergy was particularly significant. Overwhelmingly, these priests hailed from the north and central regions of Italy. As a church survey revealed, almost 80 per cent of Toronto's postwar Italian priests were born in Italy, while 12.5 per cent came from the United States and 3 per cent from other countries, principally Hungary and Croatia. Of the Italian-born, 32 per cent hailed from the north, 31 per cent from central Italy, and only 14 per cent from the south. This regional gap between clergy and the predominantly southern congregations they served likely intensified the age-old suspicions that Italian clerics and parishioners had of each other.[19]

The expansion program undertaken by the archdiocese was truly impressive. By 1974, when the process was virtually complete, Toronto had thirty-one parishes serving Italian congregations and sixty-five Italian-speaking priests. By that time, Metro's Italians represented a third of the 800,000 Catholics in the city. However, much of this expansion did not begin to take off until the mid-1960s. There was thus a decided lag between the arrival of the first major wave of Italians into Toronto and the efforts of church leaders to accommodate the growing Italian population. As a result, throughout the early postwar years, the parishes serving the immigrants suffered from insufficient space and inadequate clerical staff. Some of the newly created parishes carried on for years without the benefit of proper facilities. Although created as a parish in 1955 and located in an area of heavy Italian settlement just northwest of the city limits, the Church of the Immaculate Conception operated for six years in a bungalow and a small makeshift rectory before the main church was built. St Pascal Baylon began life in 1957 in a North York farm house and then rented space in a local Veterans' Hall for more than a decade before its church was completed. [20]

A far worse situation prevailed in the parishes, both national and bilingual, located within the city's major Italian districts. By 1962 St Agnes had enlarged its facilities and trippled the number of Sunday masses, but the overcrowding problems persisted as more newcomers arrived. Even the creation of children's masses had failed to prevent hundreds of children from overcrowding the adult masses. At St Mary of the Angels, Father Basetti began offering Italian masses on Sunday evenings in the church auditorium. In his case, he was equally concerned to encourage a greater attendance among working families. "We often find," he wrote, that "wives cannot leave the house to attend Mass on Sunday morning because husbands are out at work as watchman, bakers, railroad men and the like." Generally, however, such measures failed because few Italians were willing to spend an evening in church after working all day. Nor could many be convinced to attend early morning Sunday masses. As one priest explained, "since very few have to work on Sunday they crowd the Masses around eleven and twelve ... It often happens that they are out in the vestibule and standing on the steps leading into the main body of the church." [21]

In an effort to alleviate matters, parish priests held as many Sunday masses as they could, spreading out into the church basement, auditorium, rectory, and any other space that could accommodate worshippers. Within the bilingual parishes, however, it was the Italians who were invariably relegated to these basement or annex churches, while their English-speaking counterparts attended mass in the sanctuary proper. A distinct hierarchy emerged between the English-speaking Catholics, most of whom were of Irish origin, and the immigrants, who were expected to go downstairs or elsewhere to makeshift quarters. These events mirrored those of a previous era, when, as Rudolph Vecoli has shown, an earlier generation of Italian immigrants in North American cities found themselves confined to a system of annex churches. But even the proliferation of these basement churches in early postwar Toronto did not solve the problem of overcrowding, and on Sunday each church turned away dozens of Italians.[22]

These conditions were not conducive to instilling a greater sense of religious duty in the Italians, and the local clergy repeatedly called on the archbishop to provide funds for construction or expansion. When, for example, the Rev. M.J. Smith, pastor of Holy Angels parish in Etobicoke, requested approval for the construction of an auditorium, he declared that only by enlarging the facilities for Italian masses and offering them more social activities could the immigrants "be brought closer to parish life." The situation also gave rise to serious tensions between the immigrants, who resented what they believed to be a second-class status within the church, and the Canadian parishioners. In recalling these days, one man declared: "It was a disgrace, the way we were herded into the basement, and the English get to have a real church, to worship with dignity."[23]

As overcrowding persisted, the resentment of the Italians grew sharper. It culminated in the late 1960s, with the cries of protest coming from those who had been tolerating the situation for years. In their letters and petitions they demanded recognition for their right to "a proper church," as one female parishioner put it.[24] The petitions reveal the anger and frustration of the Italians, many of whom felt that the clergy had taken undue advantage of their patience. One petition from St Thomas Aquinas Church located near Eglinton Avenue West and Dufferin Street read: "We ... have been attending Holy Masses in the basement for several years; and now we have reached such a point that the Ushers must pack the people like canned sardines, being unable to let everybody in." "This basement," it continued, "could be a convenient place for anything else, but it is certainly not ... a decent place for worship, and much less for the celebration of Holy Mass." It ended with a plea that Archbishop Pocock "grant us a decent place which we could really call the house of God." In their petition, the Italians at St Charles Borromeo, a parish located at Lawrence Avenue West and Dufferin Street, pointed out that when they first joined the new parish in 1954, they made up only 20 per cent of the congregation and accepted their relegation to the basement church. More than ten years later, however, they represented 75 per cent of the congregation, but still the situation had not changed. They demanded equal access to the "upper church" on the grounds that they now commanded a majority of the congregation.[25]

The problems at St Charles Borromeo had prompted a nun, who was also the daughter of immigrant parents, to write to the archbishop. "On Sundays," she wrote, "the Italian people celebrate their two Masses down in the basement of the Church where there aren't as many conveniences as upstairs, like light, organ and enough seats for them especially at the 10:00 o'clock Mass." If the scheduling of the masses could be revised in order to accommodate the jItalians, she added, "it will ... give them a sense of equality with our Canadian brothers." When a top-ranking church official informed the pastor of St Charles about the nun's letter, he also openly acknowledged that the resentment was widespread. "The mentality which resents being considered 'second-class,'" he wrote, "has made itself known in various areas of Metro. Italians especially seem to feel the need of the warmth of a church atmosphere."[26]

With time, church leaders did concede the need to build new, larger churches and to approve additions on existing churches. In doing so, however, they had to balance the Italian immigrants' demands with the protests of the older Canadian constituents who felt the newcomers were being given too much. A typical complaint came from an Irish-Canadian man and a veteran parishioner with the St Clare parish on St Clair Avenue West near Dufferin Street. He strenuously disapproved of the rising number of Italian masses being offered there. With four other parishes in the general vicinity of the St Clair Little Italy also offering Italian services, the action, he erroneously charged, could only be construed as "the first step in changing St. Clare's into an all Italian parish." Rejecting the argument that the extra Italian masses were even needed, he claimed that he usually found "the same number of people downstairs as upstairs or maybe fewer downstairs on some occasions." "The Italian people," he concluded, "knew that Canada was an English speaking nation before they came ... why should'nt they adjust to our way of life. It is not unusual in the business world to be eased out. Who would ever dream of being eased out of the Catholic Church?"[27]

Tensions between Irish and Italian intensified after the recommendation of Vatican II in 1962 that churches replace the traditional Latin with the vernacular during mass. This practice, along with that of turning the altar to face the congregation, was adopted unevenly in Toronto, and it was in those bilingual parishes that did not immediately adopt the new system where controversy boiled. Canadian Catholics blamed the failure of their parish to implement reforms on the Italians, who opposed them, and they chastised their clergy for conceding to the immigrants' outmoded views. A veteran Sunday school teacher at St Clare's was especially vocal. After attending a mass at St Thomas, she wrote a letter accusing the Italian priest of having conducted the mass "in exactly fifteen minutes and naturally in Latin, with his back to us." "If he had been saying mass privately at a side altar with no one present," she added, "it couldn't have been more private." Apparently, the clerics at St Clare's were no better. She too claimed that as the Canadians outnumbered the Italians at most Sunday masses, there was no reason to continue celebrating the mass in Latin.[28]

Italian parishioners opposed the liturgical reforms, but for pragmatic reasons. They feared that by replacing the Latin mass with masses in English and Italian, the two-tiered system would never disappear and the Italians would never be invited upstairs. It was just this kind of short-sightedness, argued one pious Italian male parishioner of St Clare's, that was responsible for the failure of Toronto's parishes to attract young Italian men, most of whom, he claimed, prefer "the billiard halls and bars." Noting the irony of the problem – that reforms meant to improve relations between clergy and parishioners were having the opposite effect in Toronto – he continued: "Being forced to have midnight mass in the basement while the English upstairs don't even fill up the room and are allowed to save seats for each other while we descend downstairs, is far from an expression of fraternity, equality and charity." The Italians, he concluded, "want to integrate with the English but without suffering suffocation."[29]

Significantly, church leaders occasionally intervened in this conflict on the side of the Italians. Canadian parishioners were advised to show more charity towards the newcomers and the problems their clergy faced. When, for instance, the Chancery Office received a letter from a parishioner at St Thomas Aquinas who insisted that since her church was "a normal English speaking Canadian parish," the priests should be obliged to deliver mass only in English and not in Latin, Archbishop Pocock curtly informed her that the parish was a bilingual one in which the vast majority of the adults were Italian-speaking. "So true is this," he added, "that it is necessary for Father McGuinn [the pastor] to have three Italian-speaking assistants to provide spiritual care for his parishioners." This show of tolerance no doubt reflected the concern of church leaders that the immigrants be given some sign they were welcome within the church.[30]

A major source of anxiety for the Italian clerics in the early postwar era was the failure of their immigrant parishioners to provide strong financial support to their churches. During these years, Italian clerics regularly commented on the poverty of their "immigrant parish." The pastor of Holy Angels attributed the failure of his parish to raise sufficient funds for a main church to the fact that three-quarters of his congregation were relatively recent Italian immigrants. Eschewing both the pledge forms and the envelopes set aside for recorded contributions, many of the newcomers instead preferred to drop their modest contributions in the collection basket.[31]

Both economic and cultural factors accounted for this situation. As recent immigrants, many Italians had little extra money to spare for the church. Also, they did not have strong traditions of religious voluntarism; the church in Italy enjoyed considerable state support. This was understood by the Italian-speaking clerics, including the pastor of St Catherine of Siena, an east-end parish serving thirty-five English-speaking families and 500 Italian families. In his 1963 annual report he recorded a disappointing total of $700 for Sunday donations. By way of explanation, he wrote: "Many people are convinced that the Church has been already paid for by the pope ... or by the bishop ... Of course people are people and too many excuses they bring to avoid to support the church. But this is the situation." The Chancery Office made suggestions for raising collections, such as having priests collect money at the door after mass, but at least during the years of heavy immigration these stratagems failed to improve matters.[32]

The comparative poverty of the Italian parishes in these years helps explain the relatively inferior position of Italian clerics within the church during the early postwar period. Italian priests evidently harboured a growing resentment towards their Canadian confreres and their superiors in the archdiocese. It would reach crisis proportions in the early 1970s, prompting concerned church authorities to address the problem. An immigration and religion specialist with the Center for Migration Studies in New York, Lydio Tomasi, was commissioned to explore the dimensions of the situation. He attributed many of the church's internal troubles to the long-standing hostile relations between "English" and "Italian." His interviews with fifty-six Italian priests revealed that for years they had resented their inferior status and their absence from the church's decision-making structures. When asked to evaluate the pastoral care the church had given to immigrants, almost 65 per cent of these priests said it had been less than adequate – 47 per cent rated the church's record as "poor" and 18 per cent as "non-existent." They offered several explanations, among them that church leaders had not been adequately prepared to serve such a huge influx of newcomers and that their own ghettoized position was linked to the immigrants' inferior status within the Catholic community; despite the city's cosmopolitan character, the chancery was still composed almost entirely of English, Scottish, and especially Irish Canadians; that no "ethnic priests" sat on the priests' synod; and no Italian priest had ever been offered a pastorship in a non-Italian parish. The Italians, they said, had been given their own churches "as a result of much pressure," and the Italian clerics who came to serve them were "made to feel like servants of Canadian pastors who refuse[d] to share or cooperate."[33]

Tomasi's report also alluded to the unwillingness of the predominately English-speaking leadership to integrate the Italians fully into their church. For support, he noted that a recent church-commissioned study on Catholics in Toronto had deliberately excluded foreign-born members "on the unwarranted assumption of the transitory nature of their values." He also noted the continuing "low levels of religious practise" among the Italians, an observation that suggests that two decades after the first postwar newcomers had arrived, the Italian immigrants had not get become fully fledged members at the Canadian Catholic church. Other evidence supports this view, including the immigrants' low rate of participation in the various devotional groups – among them the Holy Name Society, Sodality of Mary, and League of the Sacred Heart – and other formal organizations of the church. In part this pattern reflected the fact that many of these societies were unfamiliar, North American inventions. But it was also a strong reflection of the immigrants' continuing attachment to their own brand of Catholicism and its attendant rituals and traditions.[34]

In the towns and villages of the Italian south there had never been a clear separation between the official teachings of the church and the people's more personal world of saints and madonnas, of good and evil spirits. Whereas the church offered them the promise of salvation in the afterlife, their own belief in the possibility of coveting the favours of the divine spirits offered them a potential defence against misfortune or disaster in this life. These age-old beliefs made their way across the ocean. It was thus not merely nostalgia, but also a concern for their spiritual enhancement that led the Italians to adorn their homes with the cheaply made icons and trinkets that had once graced their peasant households, and to christen their cars by hanging the trustworthy *cornu* (red plastic horn) on the rear-view mirror. Tucked in the corners of a living room or front hall of many an Italian immigrant home in Toronto in the 1950s and early 1960s were the modest shrines of families who had assembled plastic statues of Jesus, the Virgin Mary, or some popular saint, a few religious postcards, and perhaps a candle to be lit on holy days. In some cases, the only pictures to grace the sparse walls were the religious portraits purchased in bargain basement sales. Going to church was not only a sign of dutiful worship, for attendance at mass could also raise one's status with the saints and madonnas. Even religious cynics still found compelling their beliefs in the magical powers of saints and madonnas, and they took some comfort in the view that the good spirits watched over them. As one man put it, "Me, I'm not much for the church, but yes, we believe that the spirits can protect us, even help us. Even if you think maybe its not true, maybe just the ideas from home, well, what if you're wrong?"[35]

The complex character of this worldview is clearly revealed in the dual role women played in religious life. As in most cultures, Italian women attended church more regularly than men and they were considered to be more pious members of their family. On any given Sunday, hundreds of women could be seen inside a local Toronto parish, donning black veils and diligently working their way through the rosary. But even this intense attachment to the church did not preclude their active, indeed passionate, involvement in the officially unsanctioned aspects of southern Italian piety. It was the women, for instance, who were still thought to possess the powers required to cure relatives suffering the discomforts brought on by mal'occhio or the evil eye. To protect their new-born babies against the evil spirits and the malicious intentions of others, women pinned gold ornaments on the infant's clothes, provided gold necklaces and bracelets, and sewed traditional good luck charms into the underclothes. When misfortune did strike – when a child suddenly became ill or bad-tempered or another family member developed headaches or became melancholic – the family could in many instances turn to the same woman who had performed the healing rituals in their hometown. She, in turn, made use of familiar spells, incantations, and, on occasion, certain folk potions. Such women continued to demand the respect they had enjoyed in their paese. A sure sign of cultural adaptiveness, some of them also insisted they had learned to transfer their healing powers over the telephone![36]

In tackling problems, Italians also sought out the talents of a host of miracle workers and psychics who peddled their magic in Little Italy. Palm readers, witches, sorcerers, and medicine folk all vied for the business of immigrant families. Their popularity both reflected the immigrants' traditonal distrust of medical doctors and offered them yet another line of defence. If in times of need or distress Italian women tapped the city's social agencies, so too did they seek out the homes or storefronts of traditional folk healers. These healers handled a wide assortment of clients – distressed parents seeking help in improving a son's school performance, a young widow suffering depression, or a mother distraught over the news that her child's engagement would not end in marriage. When, for instance, one woman discovered that her son and future daughter-in-law had broken off their engagement, both she and the prospective mother-in-law sought the aid of a sorcerer who, having requested that each mother bring him a piece of clothing belonging to her child, performed a series of incantations and cast a spell on the two lovers. To help matters along, the mothers applied considerable familial pressure on the young couple. In the end, the children were married, and the mothers, downplaying their own role in the process, expressed delight in the fact that their wishes had been answered by the saints.[37]

One of the most graphic illustrations of the immigrants' continuing attachment to the cherished religious and cultural traditions of their homeland was the festa celebration. Throughout Toronto's Italian and bilingual parishes, the immigrants engaged in elaborate festivities in honour of their favourite patron saints. Very often, the only parish club that drew a significant number of immigrants was the predominantly male festa organizing committee, though here the newcomers often shared leadership with the Italian oldtimers of the same parish. The choice of feasts usually reflected the regional composition of a specific parish. For instance, at St Francis of Assisi, located on Mansfield Avenue in the College Street Little Italy, where the Italian congregation was primarily southern, with numerous Calabrians, the parish celebrated the festa of the Madonna della Pietra, the patron saint for Chiaravalle Centrale and its surrounding towns in Catanzaro, Calabria. As with other patron saints, the Madonna della Pietra was assumed to have miraculous powers; she was attributed with having saved the villagers of Chiaravalle from a disastrous flood in 1905. She was also the patron saint of work.[38]

As in Italy, the festa involved a religious procession in which men and women, dressed in their Sunday finest, rushed excitedly towards an elaborately robed statue to pin to its robes money and holy pictures. At times, the procession was led by men who belonged to the colony's older organizations, such as the Knights of Columbus, and paraded in their traditional regalia. Other times, newcomers took the lead, including the men of the *Azzione Cattolica* (Catholic Action League) associated with St Mary of the Angels. Women took the most active part in public worship, and they did so in a dramatic fashion. As the procession wound its way into the church, the women could be seen clasping their rosaries to their breasts and clinging to the statue, wailing their prayers to the madonna. A great deal of merry-making accompanied the procession and mass and the banquet and games that followed. While most of the games were designed for the children, the largest attractions were the highly competitive events that tested the muscle-power and stamina of the men. This included *la cumana*, a game in which men were challenged to climb a heavily greased pole and take possession of the various prizes – cheeses, salamis, and the expensive *prosciutto* (cured ham) attached to a ring at the top of the pole.

The festa was one of the most enduring features of Italian im-migrant life, and these celebrations revealed the way in which the immigrants nurtured and recreated their own sense of culture and community in the New World. The overlapping networks of family and community were evident on these occasions, which drew not only Italians from the local area but relatives and paesani who lived outside the parish boundaries as well. The daily struggles of life and work were temporarily lost in the day's festivities, and in the circus-like atmosphere that was highlighted by the elaborate show of fire-works at the end of the evening. With time, these events also became increasingly more elaborate as orchestras, dance floors, and lotteries were added to the customary games and foodstands.

During the turbulent years of the early postwar era, these annual events exacerbated tensions between Canadian Catholics and new-comers, compelling members of the church hierarchy at times to act as mediators between the two groups. Some Canadians, for instance, found this display of "showy Catholicism" offensive, and felt that it fed popular Protestant stereotypes of Roman Catholics as idolaters. The protests of Canadian parishioners at St Pascal Baylon, for ex-ample, compelled the festa committee in 1962 to discontinue a pop-ular game in which teams of men competed to catch a pig. In July 1965 the archbishop received an angry letter from a woman who had witnessed a religious procession in front of St Mary of the Angels. What disturbed her was the obviously exuberant and festive character of the occasion, and the sight of Italians crowding around the statue of Mary and trying to kiss and adorn it with money and trinkets. "While I appreciate that such events are meant to be joy-ous," she wrote, "surely they should possess a certain dignity, and it is my opinion that a balloon vendor is uncalled for. Coupled with such practices, admittedly discontinued, as placing the name of the Church in neon lights ... one wonders if the worthy monks are deliberately trying to give the Church a circus atmosphere." "After over hearing the comments of other[s]," she added, "I fear that such displays are detrimental to the dignity of the Catholic Church."[39]

While some Italian priests similarly disapproved of the processions and their carnival atmosphere, they also recognized that the festa, and its accompanying celebrations, represented an important aspect of the piety of the immigrants. This is made clear in a letter from a group of Italian-Canadian youth at St Mary of the Angels to the archbishop. According to the young people, who dubbed the procession "an embarrassing spectacle," their parish priest shared their sentiment but had nevertheless bowed to pressure from the festa committee to hold the planned festivities.[40] Church leaders also chastised Canadian parishioners who criticized the annual festa. Archbishop Pocock admonished one woman for not being more generous in her view of the Italians and for failing to appreciate the importance Italians attached to such customs. In so far as he encouraged the woman to tolerate rather than embrace such unorthodox practices, the response strongly suggests that the church had grown to accept the central role of the festa in the immigrants' religious life.[41]

Catholic leaders, then, gradually reached some degree of accommodation with the newcomers. Although initially reluctant, they expanded their facilities at considerable expense to the episcopate. While the clergy, including the Italian-speaking clergy, considered their Italian congregations to be unsophisticated on the question of formal religion, they nevertheless understood they could gain little by alienating their flock. The clergy permitted the Italians to celebrate their feasts and generally tolerated the merry-making that accompanied them. This tolerance reflected a recognition of the importance the festa and other customs played in the lives of the immigrants, and a desire to encourage the immigrants to keep the faith.

BUILDING INSTITUTIONS

In July 1954 the first issue of the Toronto newspaper *Corriere Canadese* declared on its front page that the new immigrants showed little interest in joining the formal organizations of the Italian community. "The 50,000 Italians in Toronto," it read, "have the opportunity to belong to one of thirty-eight organizations. However, only 3,250 persons or 6.5 per cent of them participate in an Italian association or group." Noting that most of the community activists were old-timers, the editors concluded by encouraging the newcomers "to get involved." Arturo Scotti, a native of Milan and a respected intellectual who acted as the paper's editor until his death in 1959, and coeditor Gianni Grohovas, a self-educated northerner from Friuli and an energetic community activist, were among the few newcomers to gain a public profile in this period – no doubt because they wrote for a newspaper that enjoyed a virtually unrivalled position within the colony. By contrast, the majority of the immigrants in the years before 1965 were largely removed from the colony's formal community life.[42]

In detailing the diverse associations among ethnic communities, historians have focused on the first generation of immigrants who settled in North American centres before 1930.[43] In postwar Canadian cities such as Montreal and Toronto, however, the Italian immigrants encountered an existing community of prewar Italians and their Canadian-raised or Canadian-born children, some of whom were eager to resurrect associations that had been largely dismantled during the war. In Toronto, the newcomers, at least initially, took a back seat to the Italian oldtimers.

John Zucchi has documented the process of institution-building in Toronto's Italian community before the Second World War. At the turn of the century, as a group of successful entrepreneurs and professionals gained ascendancy, several regionally based mutual aid societies and cultural associations were formed. Meantime, a smaller group of radicals and artisans established their own self-help clubs. By the 1920s, a group of young, upwardly mobile immigrants wrestled for the leadership in some of the old organizations, established new ones, and in the process succeeded in dominating the institutional and political life of the community. With the rise of fascism in Italy, many of the colony's organizations came under the influence of the fascist Italian vice-consul, who implemented locally Mussolini's program of "exporting fascism" to Italian communities abroad. Few Italian immigrants had ever been genuine fascists, but, drawn by a nostalgic nationalism for their homeland and troubled by their sense of inferiority in the New World, many North American Italians had joined newly created fascist organizations or those which, like the Sons of Italy, came under the sway of fascist leaders. Fascism did not go unchallenged in the Toronto colony, however. Radicals on the left and labour activists such as Louis Palermo, a CCF sympathizer and an organizer for the Amalgamated Clothing Workers of America (ACWA), fought back. They were joined by members of the old elite who, according to Zucchi, resented the ascendancy of their younger rivals and now regrouped into their own anti-fascist organization, the Società Italo-Canadese.

All these battles came to an end shortly after Canada declared war on Italy. Throughout the 1930s, the centre of fascist activity had been the Casa d'Italia, a mansion located on the corner of Beverley and

Dundas streets, southeast of the College Street Little Italy. The house had been purchased with community subscriptions and donated to the Italian government. In June 1940, Zucchi says, the RCMP brought an end to this association when it seized the Casa and interned 200 men. This act, coupled with continuing RCMP surveillance of the community and the hostilities of Torontonians, forced many Italians to maintain a low profile. Some stopped speaking Italian and anglicized their names. After 1945 the Italian community, composed as it was of a diverse collection of prewar Italian-Canadians and an ever-growing number of postwar newcomers from every region of Italy, faced the task of rebuilding formal institutional structures or creating an altogether new associational life.[44]

As in most ethnic communities, the campaigns designed to create formal, public arenas of political and social discourse and organization were dominated by men rather than women. Not surprisingly, the earliest efforts to build formal institutions within Toronto's post-1945 Italian community were initiated by Italian-Canadian oldtimers, many of them successful businessmen and professionals or political activists anxious to rid the older Italian colony of its prewar association with fascism. As Gianni Grohovaz has explained, they also wanted to establish a political and social infrastructure for incorporating the new arrivals.[45] While efforts at building a community-wide associational life would eventually bear fruit, in the period immediately following the Second World War such efforts were hampered by the old, prewar rivalries among groups that, on occasion, resurfaced, and by the tensions that in these early years characterized relations between the prewar Italian-Canadians and the postwar newcomers. As scholars have observed, such rivalries and tensions were characteristic of many different ethnic groups in cities across Canada. Jeremy Boisevain has documented the case for Montreal's Italians. Contemporary sources, including social researcher Martin Greenwood's 1961 study of Toronto's Italians and Samuel Sidlofsky's 1968 dissertation on Italian construction workers, as well as oral interviews, detail the Toronto case.[46]

As some of Toronto's Italian-Canadian oldtimers embarked on their plans to resume their organizations, they naturally viewed he newly arrived immigrants as potential new recruits. While some of the more regionally based groups tended to restrict their recruitment efforts to newcomers from their own regions, the larger groups appeared willing to accept anyone. In the spring of 1954, for example, the Vittorio Emanuelle Society hosted a banquet with the stated aim of "meeting new arrivals" and "help[ing] them to gain confidence in the new society, where they can hear the expressed voices of old Italians."[47] When newcomers joined the prewar organizations, tensions sometimes developed in situations where old-timers sought to consolidate their control over the executive positions. In an interview with Sidlofsky, one newcomer, for example, recalled that when in 1957 he was elected to the position of secretary of a regional organization, the president, who was the son of one of the club's founders, objected so strenuously that the newcomer left the group. Because the meetings of these societies were frequently conducted in English, some newcomers also felt excluded from the preceedings and soon abandoned these organizations. Many of the older societies, though they continued to draw on oldtimers, evidently did not regain their prewar status.[48] As Robert Harney observed, the once popular prewar associations – including the Sons of Italy, which by 1948 had resumed its meetings in the parish hall of St Mary of the Angels – did not succeed in these years in shaking their prewar association with fascism. Even the chief anti-fascist group, the Società Italo-Canadese (later renamed the Order of Italo-Canadians) similarly failed to attract large numbers of newcomers in the immediate postwar era.[49]

The oldtimers' domination of the immediate postwar period of institution building is well illustrated by the 1947 campaign to establish the Italian Canadian Recreation Club or Brandon Hall, which was located on Brandon Avenue near the Dufferin Street and Davenport Road intersection. The campaign was initiated by a disparate array of prewar groups – among them the Sons of Italy, various regionally based mutual benefit societies, several leftist groups, some devotional societies, and the ACWA's Italian local, Local 235, headed by Louis Palermo. All of the participants considered it important that a community centre be established that could be home to the city's diverse Italian clubs and socials and eventually help foster a wider sense of community. In this spirit, the various factions involved agreed to put aside their differences and to work as a united front. Still, in the course of the campaign, conflicts inevitably surfaced, particularly between the more conservative groups and the anti-clericals. A crisis erupted, for example, when the Catholic church donated a large gilt cross for the front entrance of the building. Some participants welcomed an association with the church while others rejected the gift, seeing it as a betrayal of the campaign's expressed non-partisan character. In the end, Grohovaz recalled, they reached a compromise: there were no celebrations commemorating the acceptance of the gift and the cross was placed in a seldom used library room. Nevertheless, time proved the campaign organizers correct and, by the early 1960s, Brandon Hall was attracting a wide variety of community organizations and had become a regular meeting place for business groups and trade-union locals.[50]

By far the most concerted drive initiated by the Italian-Canadian oldtimers in their efforts to re-establish community institutions (and overcome their association with fascism) was the protracted battle to retrieve Casa d'Italia from the Canadian government and return it to Toronto's Italians. As Nick Forte has observed, and correspondence from the early years of the campaign reveals, the initial strategists were largely Italian-Canadian professionals and businessmen who saw their actions as part of a larger concern to improve the public profile of the Italian community and begin the process of rebuilding a strong associational life. One of the participants wrote to Prime Minister Louis St Laurent in 1953 requesting his assistance in the matter, saying they hoped "that the last memories of the war years may be forever forgotten by the return of the Casa to the 30,000 Italo-Canadians comprising the Italian colony in the city of Toronto."[51]

The author of this letter, Joseph D. Carrier, an Italian-Canadian businessman, was one of the initial strategists and he remained committed to the campaign throughout its decade-long history. A prewar immigrant who had come to Toronto as a young man, Carrier had been a union organizer in the boot and shoe industry during the 1930s; by the 1950s he was a successful shoe manufacturer. Other key players included Silvio Venchiarutti, an architect, Donald Di Giulio, a businessman who had grown up in Toronto during the 1920s and had helped found the Order of Italo-Canadians, and Sam Sorbaro, a native of Calabria who arrived as a young man in the 1920s, sold insurance, and later established a successful insurance business. In 1951 some of these same men would help launch the Italian Canadian Business and Professional Men's Association (ICBPA), initially as part of an effort to raise funds for the victims of the Po Valley floods. Apart from the support it threw behind the Casa campaign, the ICBPA also went on to help finance several community organizations, including the Italian Immigrant Aid Society, and to establish academic scholarships for Italian students.[52]

The campaign to regain the Casa d'Italia was, as Robert Harney once observed, "fraught with many ironies." To complicate matters from the start, the Canadian wartime custodian who had seized the property from the Italian government had since sold the building to the Canadian government, and the RCMP, which had been using the premises (and had paid for some renovations), did not want to leave. And while the Canadian officials at first insisted that any negotiations surrounding the reacquisition of the building had to involve the Italian government, since it had been the official owner of the property at the time of its confiscation, Italian government officials initially appeared to show no interest in the affair.

By 1951 those interested in regaining the Casa struck a committee to lobby Ottawa. With the help of local politicians, including David Croll, then a Liberal member of parliament, the committee campaigned for a few years but with no concrete results. In the meantime, efforts were being made to broaden the community base of the committee by encouraging more individuals and organizations to join the campaign. Such a strategy could also aid the campaign strategists in their efforts to convince Ottawa that their organization genuinely represented the wishes of the entire community. By the sprint of 1953 the committee scored a victory when, at a March meeting attended by the delegates of several dozen organizations, the Federation of Italo-Canadian Organizations (FACI) was created as a cross-community umbrella organization designed to represent the interests of the entire colony. It also assumed the leadership of the Casa campaign. Most of the affiliates were the older organizations that had been resurrected: regional associations such as the Famee Furlane (a Friulan group), Circolo Calabrese, Società Trinacria (a Sicilian benevolent society), and Marchegiano Club, and several paesi or village-based clubs. Other participants included the Italian CCF club, the ACW's Local 235, and the ICBPA. With time, and as a result of effective lobbying, other organizations, including the newly formed immigrant clubs, were also brought into the campaign. Indeed, in considering these events, one scholar has suggested that, notwithstanding the conflicts and difficulties that accompanied the campaign, the protracted battle to win back the Casa created an important precedent that interest groups with different politics and constituencies could join together in a fruitful alliance.[53]

In the short-term, however, the campaign dragged on. By 1954, one year after the founding of FACI, Ottawa finally agreed to transfer the ownership of the property to the FACI Board of Trustees, where it was to be held in trust until such time as the requisite monies could be raised for its purchase. For another six years, legal complications, internal problems, and financial snags kept trustees from gaining outright ownership of the house. Although considerable funds had been raised from various constituencies within the community, these did not cover the substantial, outstanding mortgages and debts on the house. By early 1960 the house was empty – ostensibly the property of the community – but in need of extensive renovations. The whole matter was not finally resolved until later that year when the Italian government agreed to assume responsibility for the house. It then became the official property of Italy and the site of the Italian consulate. The consular officials also stuck to their promise to offer space in the building to several voluntary organizations and to devote space for such community needs as a library and a daycare centre for working mothers.

Earlier, we discussed the Italian Immigrant Aid Society that was officially established in 1952 as a social agency dispensing valuable services to the city's needy immigrants. In the context of the early postwar period, it can also be seen as an elite ethnic organization in so far as its founders and executive directors were closely associated with the middle-class Italian-Canadians who were assuming an increasingly higher public profile in these years. To be sure, during the period before 1965, the agency regularly employed an immigrant administrator. One such administrator was Frank Colantonio, who exhibited a tireless devotion to improving the economic position of his compatriots. Other able administrators included Isa Scotti and John Pedoni. Nevertheless, the IIAS executive itself was drawn largely from the same group of successful men associated with the ICBPA and their wives.[54]

In many respects, the creation of the IIAS was a successful attempt on the part of the more socially conscious middle-class members of the prewar colony to provide some system of support for the immigrant newcomers. Before its inception, many of them had already been responding to distress calls involving immigrants, donating money for basic necessities and calling on friends and associates to do likewise. The decision to create a formal agency, observes Enrico Cumbo, occurred as a result of such an incident. In the winter of 1950 Father Jeremiah Hayes, pastor of Mount Carmel, received a phonecall from the stationmaster at Union Station who reported on a group of Italian men sleeping in the station. Hayes contacted several people, including Carrier, Sorbaro, and Nicoletta Nuti, wife of the Italian consul general, and together they collected mattresses, food, and clothes, and put the men up for a few nights in Mount Carmel's rectory. Soon after, they and others formed a permanent organization, which, during the next ten years, depended mainly on the ICBPA for funds. Other sources of income included the annual teas hosted by the Ladies Auxiliary and the picnics held each summer at the Italian Gardens, a stretch of parkland located on the city's outskirts near Finch and Islington avenues. The association received support from the church and from the Italian consul general, Piere Nuti. Along with several other women, Nicoletta Nuti founded the Ladies Auxiliary. In addition to the clerics who sat on the IIAS Board of Directors, throughout this early period the executive directors were drawn largely from the ICBPA. The Ladies Auxiliary volunteers drew mainly (though not exclusively) on the wives and other female relatives of these men. The women proved to be especially energetic members of the agency, acting as court interpreters, distributing clothing, translating documents, and fund-raising.[55]

Surviving records show that as well-to-do members of the community, the prewar Italian-Canadians who sat on the IIAS board genuinely believed they had a social responsibility to lend a helping hand to the less fortunate. They were even prepared to assume some of the costs that such an enterprise entailed. At the same time, they were also trying to project a more postive image of the Italian community to the wider society. Perhaps some of the well-established leaders were embarrassed by the onrush of newly arriving rural folk from Italy. In any event they worked to ensure that the newcomers, whose presence on the unemployment rolls was sure to be cause for many a caustic comment from outsiders, were settled with a minimum of disruption. Such concerns are evident in the priority the agency gave to job placements and, to a lesser extent, English classes. For their part, the immigrants were expected to fulfil their role in this scenario by quickly learning English and eventually abandoning menial labouring jobs for skilled trades and perhaps even entrepreneurial pursuits.

Historians of immigrant communities across North America have observed that the rising elites within ethnic colonies have sought to enhance their position as community leaders. Zucchi documented such patterns for the elite of Toronto's prewar Italian community. In the immediate postwar era, the available evidence suggests that the IIAS directors, as well as the others who launched the colony's community associations, appeared interested in consolidating their position as leaders of the fast-growing postwar Italian community and in projecting this image to the wider Anglo-Celtic society of Toronto. One special event that provided the IIAS directors with just such an opportunity in this period occurred in June 1960 – a time when the recent Hogg's Hollow tunnel tragedy had helped unleash a torrent of stories regarding the blatant exploitation of Italian immigrants in the city's construction trades. The occasion was the visit to Toronto of Gina Lollabrigida, the popular Italian movie star. In response to the request of the IIAS executive, Lollabrigida agreed to act as special guest at an elaborate fund-raising banquet held on 8 June in the Canadian Room of the Royal York Hotel. At the head table with Lollabrigida sat the members of the IIAS board as well as Toronto dignitaries Mayor Phil Givens and

Gina Lollobrigida

Metro Chairman Fred Gardiner. In an era when movie stars seldom visited Toronto, reporters fawned over "Gina," giving her and the gala plenty of coverage. The IIAS executive succeeded, temporarily, in gaining the spotlight.[56]

From its inception, the IIAS, understandably, had been committed primarily to providing newcomers with short-term aid and job placements. This aim, moreover, was very much in keeping with the needs of the newly arrived immigrants who, on entering the city, were most concerned to land a job and tend to the immediate needs of their family members. By the early 1960s, however, some made the argument that the time had come to explore new directions and to meet head on the new challenges of the day – the growing number of injured construction workers who required retraining before they could hope to re-enter the workforce and the many labourers eager to up-date their skills. Italian tradesworkers also needed support in their efforts to learn English and acquire their Canadian trade certificates.

The initiatives in this regard came from some of the immigrants who had joined the IIAS board, in particular, Joseph Carraro and Charles Caccia, whose efforts would give birth to COSTI (Centro Organizzativo Scuole Tecniche Italiane). In 1960 Carraro, who had left his home in Treviso (near Venice) a few years previously, was a young, energetic, socially conscious priest at St Helen's parish. Caccia, a university-educated Italian from Milan, launched his career in Toronto by running a small consulting and publishing company, but he also quickly became involved with efforts to improve the lot of Italian workers. *Industrial English,* a booklet he had written and printed at his own expense in 1955, was widely distributed in the city's Italian neighbourhoods. In 1962 Caccia would enter municipal politics and, later, become a member of parliament.

Along with others, Carraro and Caccia had by 1960 become committed to the notion of setting up a trade school to train Italian immigrants in the skills of a trade and, at the same time, provide them with a working command of English. They hoped that already certified tradesmen of Italian descent would provide the necessary instruction to enable men to gain Canadian certificates in a trade. In 1961 night classes began in the basement of St Helen's parish, and the following year COSTI was founded. The program began operating in the industrial arts rooms of some of the schools within the Toronto School Board. Initially, the plan to employ bilingual tradesworkers created some consternation from the Toronto Board of Education because the Italian instructors, though bonafide tradesmen, did not meet the provincial standards for teaching English.

Owing to the help of certain sympathetic educational officials, however, the program eventually received approval and the classes were
held in cooperation with the Provincial Institute of Trades and the
technical schools of the City of Toronto. COSTI also joined FACI, and
later moved its offices into the basement of the newly refurbished
Italian consulate. The program received some funds from the Italian
government, as well as grants from the Canadian and Ontario governments. Later still, facilities would be open to women as well as
men. More than a decade later, COSTI and the IIAS would be united
and, since the 1980s, COSTI-IIAS has provided crucial social services
to the Italian and other immigrant communities in the city.[57]

Notwithstanding some of the important gains made by the Italian
community by the 1960s, it is clear that throughout the early years
prior to 1965 the daily demands of work and family that impinged
on the lives of recently arrived immigrants precluded their active
involvement in the more formal institutions of the colony. It is not
surprising to find that the postwar institution building was launched
by men who possessed the requisite language skills and could afford
the time and energy to carry it out. Indeed, the initial efforts to
regain the Casa d'Italia and the other campaigns waged by the colony's more established members in the late 1940s and the 1950s
likely did not directly affect the majority of the Italian immigrants
who had recently arrived in the city. As late as 1968, when sociologist
Clifford Jansen conducted a survey on the topic, he found that few
of the postwar immigrants showed an active interest in the procla-
mations and activities of those who had emerged as the community's
leaders and spokespeople.[58]

But this is not to suggest that in the years before 1965 the immigrants did not find ways to enjoy their limited leisure time or that
they did not show an interest in recreating a sense of community.
As we have seen, the festa celebration marked an important date
on the cultural calendar of the immigrants, and the enthusiasm with
which they helped organize and attended such events suggests their
commitment to recreating familiar cultural mores – even at the risk
of attracting the disapproval of intolerant observers. So, too, did
their demands for better worship facilities reflect a deeply felt need
for culture and community that went well beyond the confines of
household and workplace. During the early postwar era, the extended family and kin networks, as well as those of paesani and
neighbourhood, often provided the newcomers with their main
source of entertainment and community. In these years, many
southern Italian immigrants, like those from other regions, spent
their precious moments of leisure time not in attending formal, com-

munity events, but in enjoying a summer evening with their children in Christie Pits or on their verandas and spending Sunday afternoons at the local swimming pool, the beach, or around the kitchen table eating and talking with friends. Family-centred celebrations remained the main source of recreation; holidays, weddings, baptisms, and a child's confirmation were occasions marked by parties that drew together relatives, distant kin, paesani, and neighbours. As in the case of the festa, the harsh realities of people's lives were momentarily forgotten amid the generous outlay of food and drink. Family events also offered a familiar forum for courtship, one closely supervised by relatives. Such celebrations were the most common way in which the immigrants in these years maintained their culture and recreated community.

This world of kin, family, and paesani would increasingly overlap with the wider world of parish, clubs, and other community activities. Social outings and formal meetings would form a greater part of the lives of many immigrants, in particular those of the men. By the early 1960s, for example, newcomers had begun to get more involved in public life. Most tended to do so at a local level, joining a regional club or a soccer team. Others supported newly created immigrant organizations, such as the Catholic Action League, which, during the 1950s, enjoyed a successful but brief life as a social club for men and women. But it was the regionally based clubs and neighbourhood cafés and clubs that grew rapidly in number in the next two decades. Among the paesani clubs that were either formed by or drew in the southern Italians was Club Sicilia, Club Consenza, the Pisticci Club (Basilicata), the San Giorgio Morgeto Club (Calabria), and the Montorio Nei Fretani Social Club (Molise). Other clubs, like the Amicizia Club, located along the Danforth, drew on several regional groups in the area. By 1971 there were approximately sixty Italian clubs in Toronto. The postwar welfare state had largely eliminated the need for immigrants to finance their own self-help schemes – a need that had prompted an earlier generation to create mutual benefit societies and credit-sharing ventures. The clubs were important gathering places, especially for men, while the annual dances and picnics they sponsored provided an opportunity for women and children to participate. As in the past, the clubs helped to cultivate an Italian male immigrant culture as members sought out friends, played cards, and enjoyed an espresso coffee.

The immigrant presence also grew stronger at Brandon Hall, which increasingly attracted a wider membership. Attendance at the centre's theatrical and musical concerts grew streadily by the late 1950s. The Piccolo Teatro Club, for example, a theatrical troupe composed mostly of newcomers and directed by Bruno Mesaglio, also an immigrant, drew large audiences. Increasingly, newcomers also joined soccer teams. While initially these teams had a strong regional identification, the largest organization, the Friuli Soccer Club, evolved into the Italian-Canadian Soccer League in 1957. Later still, the popular Team Italia was born. Brandon Hall also hosted the Fourth of November celebrations marking Italy's liberation in the First World War; these festivities were usually organized by various political groups in the community and the Italian consulate.[59]

The rise of more elaborate structures, such as Villa Colombo, a senior's home, Columbus Centre, the recreational complex located nextdoor to Villa Colombo, and various Italian-Canadian national organizations, would not emerge until the 1970s. In that decade, the Italian government also began to fund organizations such as ACLI (Association of Italian Catholic Workers) and FILEF (Federation of Italian Workers and Emigrants) that were designed to assist Italian workers and their families. By then, Toronto's Italian immigrant generation could boast a few of its own nationally prominent leaders, among them Liberal Senators Charles Caccia and Peter Bosa, a Friulan immigrant, successful businessman, and an active promoter of Italian soccer teams in the city. Others, including Tony Grande, a one-time member of the Ontario legislature, and Joe Pantalone, a city alderman, developed reputations as effective grass-roots organizers with the New Democratic Party.

Time for a party, basement flat, Toronto, c. 1960. Author's collection

An extended family celebrates Christmas, 1957. Author's collection

Celebrating the *festa* honouring San Francesco di Paola, St Francis of Assissi parish, Toronto. Vincenzo Pietropaolo

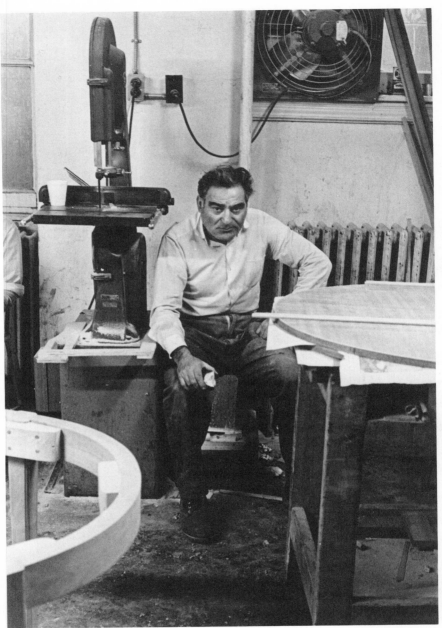

A tough assignment: learning a new skill at COSTI. Vincenzo Pietropaolo

Fundraising for the Italian Immigrant Aid Society, Ladies Auxiliary, c. 1964. MHSO, Italian collection

Resuming activities at the Casa d'Italia. MHSO, Italian collection

A dangerous job. York University Archives, *Toronto Telegram* collection

Outside the Lansdowne Theatre, where Italian construction workers met regularly during the 1960 and 1961 strikes. York University Archives, *Toronto Telegram* collection

Frank Colantonio, a young labour organizer. Author's collection

Injured striker at a picketed work site in North York, June 1961. York University Archives, *Toronto Telegram* collection

Police instructing Italian strikers, June 1961. York University Archives, *Toronto Telegram* collection

"Victory is ours." Strikers at the Landsdowne Theatre, July 1961. York University Archives, *Toronto Telegram* collection

Solidarity rally for striking construction workers, Grandstand, Canadian
National Exhibition, Toronto, 25 June 1961. York University Archives,
Toronto Telegram collection

CHAPTER SEVEN

The Immigrant Strikes

On 26 June 1961 more than 17,000 Italian immigrants, most of them young men with few years' experience as construction workers, and their supporters poured into Toronto's Canadian National Exhibition stadium to protest low wages, unsafe jobs, and employer abuses in the city's residential construction industry. It was the second illegal strike to hit the housing field within a year. The large crowd made an impressive show of strength as negotiators entered into talks in an attempt to end the month-old strike. In the spotlight were the two men who had called the rally – veteran organizer Charles Irvine and Bruno Zanini, an Italian-Canadian bricklayer who had led the first union drives among the immigrants. To thunderous approval, Irvine called for the release of Italians arrested for alleged picket-line violence. Cheers met Zanini's orders that no one break ranks until all the striking trades reached an agreement. As the rally ended, squads of picketers packed into trucks and descended on worksites throughout the city and its suburbs.[1]

In the summer of 1960 and again in the summer of 1961 Italian immigrant construction workers in Toronto's residential field engaged in a dramatic struggle for union recognition and better pay and working conditions. Both campaigns involved mass rallies, charismatic leaders, stiff employer opposition, and violence. Occurring within a sector of the industry that Italian immigrants had come to dominate, and set against a backdrop of recession and rising labour unrest, the strikes provide a graphic illustration of immigrant workers' militancy in postwar Canada – a topic that has not yet attracted the attention of historians.[2] At the centre of the campaigns stood 6000 of Toronto's relatively recent Italian immigrants. As we have seen, most of Toronto's postwar Italians, including many of those men who had previously been village artisans, had come from a peasant or rural background. Consequently, when they came to

Toronto, few possessed highly marketable industrial skills. Their peasant background also meant that few of these men had more than a limited, or even fleeting, union or radical experience before emigrating to Canada. Their decision to adopt a militant, even illegal, trade union strategy after years of toiling in Toronto's residential construction industry marked a major turning point in the transition of Italian immigrants from peasants to proletarians.

Drawing on both a common Old World and New World immigrant experience, southern Italians joined forces with Italians from other regions to engage in a class-conscious action to protect their rights and improve the quality of their working lives. For most of them, this was their first serious encounter with unionism. Once again, familial priorities and self-definitions of masculinity contributed significantly to the decision to walk out. By demanding concrete improvements in wages and safety codes, Italian workers, who had long equated their self-identity as men with their ability to act as the family's chief provider and protector, sought to bolster their role as male breadwinners and thereby improve the material and emotional lives of their families. Italian workers also saw the campaigns as a legitimate, indeed honourable, struggle on the part of immigrants who, having proven themselves to be hard-working and reliable workers, sought to earn the rights and protections enjoyed by organized Canadian workers. Their demands for "Canadian standards" reflected a genuine desire for recognition for the dangerous jobs they performed and for their role in building the postwar city. In short, the campaigns were a call for dignity by immigrant men who had been treated abysmally in their adopted country. They were also challenging the Labour Relations Act and demanding special legislation that would recognize the uniqueness of construction labour relations. The events surrounding the strikes of 1960 and 1961 exposed nativist elements within the Canadian organized labour movement of the immediate postwar era, though they also helped pave the way for an early alliance between Italian immigrants and Canadian workers in the Toronto construction trades and evoked varied responses from Torontonians. They also revealed some of the tensions within the city's growing Italian community, particularly between the Italian colony's established business and social elite and its newly arrived working-class constituents.

THE INDUSTRY AND ITS IMMIGRANT WORK FORCE

The two main branches of construction are building, which refers to residential, industrial, commercial, and institutional structures, and engineering construction, which includes roads and water and sewage systems. By 1960 the value of Canada's new construction and repair work was $6.9 billion or 19 per cent of the GNP. Booming postwar Ontario accounted for one-third of this total. Contributing almost two-thirds of the total value of construction work in most years, the building sector underwent the greatest expansion. Residential building led the way, often equalling in value the amount spent on all other types of building combined. In the period 1951–61, 460,000 units were added to Ontario's housing stock, an increase of 40 per cent. The rapidly expanding metropolis of Toronto accounted for more than one-third of this output. As developers eagerly exploited the rising demand in housing, new roads, sewer systems, and other services, as well as houses and apartments, were extended into the city's sprawling suburbs.[3]

This expansion created numerous job openings, many of them filled by Italian immigrants. In 1960, employment in the industry in Ontario stood at 418,000 persons – 7 per cent of the Canadian labour force – while thousands more worked in jobs generated by the industry. Between 1951 and 1961 the number of Italians employed in Toronto's construction industry grew over three times, from 3572 to 15,560. The latter figure represented not only one-third of Toronto's working Italian men but also one-third of the city's total construction work force. While Italians worked on construction sites of all types, the vast majority of them found jobs in the house and apartment field. Here, estimates of the Italian presence ran as high as 65 per cent for the sector as a whole, and 85 per cent for certain trades such as bricklaying.[4]

Various factors account for the Italian concentration in residential construction. As a rapidly expanding sector, it offered plenty of jobs to immigrants with few industrial skills and little formal education. Greenhorns quickly snapped up seasonal jobs digging foundations, carrying materials, pushing wheelbarrows, mixing cement, and helping more experienced tradesmen. Moreover, this sector provided immigrants with some opportunities for advancement – the acquisiton of a trade or access to the subcontracting field. These opportunities held some short-term advantages for immigrants, but they also led to serious long-term problems.

The construction industry is highly specialized; this is evident in the organization of firms by specialty trades and of the work force by crafts. For decades, the craft Internationals affiliated with the Building Trades Department of the American Federation of Labor (AFL) had maintained closed shops in large sections of the nonresidential building field. These locals were also affiliated to the Toronto

Building and Construction Trades Council, an umbrella organization that spoke for the AFL building trades unions in Toronto. The council bargained with employers belonging to the Toronto Builders Exchange. In road building and paving, a highly specialized field dominated by a few large firms, a council of unions representing the Operating Engineers, the Teamsters, and the Labourers, bargained with an association representing employers in the field. The same council also negotiated terms with sewer and watermain employers.[5]

Italians were not completely excluded from the membership of unions in the nonresidential field, but in the early postwar years they tended to be concentrated in the labourers' unions within these sectors. In 1961, for example, Local 183 of the International Hod Carriers Building and Common Labourers' Union of America, which enjoyed jurisdictional rights over labourers on tunnelling and excavation projects in the commercial field, claimed that 85 per cent of the 2000 members were Italians.[6] Altogether, however, the unionized Italians represented only a minority of Italians in the nonresidential fields. Even fewer Italians had joined the craft unions within the commercial and industrial field. The old-line or commercial unions, as they were called, consisted mostly of Canadian-born workers.

The absence of union dues, closed shops, and formal training programs facilitated the entry of Italians into the housing field. Informal methods of recruitment flourished, giving workers direct access to contractors or foremen and allowing them to build up extensive paesani occupational networks. In a highly competitive field marked by a continuing supply of newcomers, such methods, at least in the short-term, might prove more effective than hiring halls. At the same time, of course, these networks also benefited employers keen to recruit greenhorns and happy to hire relatives of hard-working employees.

During the immediate postwar period a small minority of Italians did arrive in Toronto as trained craftsmen, but they were more likely to seek work in the better-paid, organized trades, once they acquired provincial licences or served apprenticeships. In many residential trades, however, the newly arrived and thus inexperienced Italians, facing few prospects for job mobility, eagerly sought to gain an informal training in a trade while serving as apprentices or "helpers" to skilled tradesmen. Stealing time from lunch breaks or after work, many newcomers practised on their own, with little help from journeymen. Italian immigrant bricklayers who today are certified and experienced tradesmen recall how in those early days they received some of their first informal training at home in the basement or backyard by kin and paesani who had only recently acquired some experience in the trade. In this period a worker often achieved the status of tradesman simply by declaring to a prospective employer that he was one. Many employed "tradesmen" actually performed semi-skilled work normally done by apprentices or "improvers." Residential carpenters, for instance, spent hours simply hammering together precut pieces of wood to construct the frames of houses. That this sector did not require highly skilled workers largely accounts for this pattern. It also explains why Italians dominated carpentry and the trowel trades, including bricklaying and cement finishing, yet avoided the more technical, certified trades, such as plumbing and electrical work. Eventually, of course, Italian residential tradesmen did achieve acceptable levels of skill in their respective trades; many of them obtained the appropriate trade certificate and became respected and reliable skilled workers. But the preponderance in the 1950s and early 1960s of semi-skilled and newly arrived immigrant men in the housing field gave rise to negative stereotypes of Italian tradesmen as inferior pick-and-shovel men masquerading as craftsmen.[7]

Throughout this period mainstream union organizers appear to have largely neglected the immigrant-dominated housing sector. Certainly, the obstacles to unionization appeared formidable: the profusion of scattered sites and tiny subcontracting firms, highly seasonal and irregular employment patterns, and the ever-shifting work force dominated by low-skilled newcomers. The features that generally hampered certification drives in construction found their most extreme expression in the residential field, where the market was more volatile, employers far more numerous, work crews more scattered, and the competition for jobs more intense. As former peasants or village artisans whose experience with unions in Italy had been largely confined to fascist-imposed organizations, many of the postwar immigrants were unfamiliar with free unions and did not know their legal rights.[8]

When the economy faltered in the late 1950s, the rising rate of unemployment among organized Canadian workers, and the loss of members in their respective locals, meant that the old-line unionists showed even less interest in organizing the immigrant sector. In part, their response reflected the general view of the labour movement that, in times of recession and high unemployment, immigration posed a threat to domestic workers. But craft pride, bolstered by nativism, also played a role. In this period, many organized Canadian tradesmen considered the Italians to be inferior craftsmen who threatened to undercut their wages, and they opposed admitting the immigrants into their unions. A group of bricklayers expressed these views in a letter to the *Toronto Telegram*. "It seems," they wrote, "that anyone who dug a post-hole in Italy suddenly becomes a skilled tradesman in Canada merely by working for low wages." Predictably, they advised restricting immigration from Italy. A similar proposal was tabled by a Toronto delegate at a 1960 conference of the Ontario Building and Construction Trades Councils of Ontario. During the early immigrant organizing drives, this issue strained relations between the members of the established unions and those of the newly created residential locals. "The old-line guys used to say to me," recalled an Italian carpenter who participated in these campaigns, "'These Italians, they're not carpenters, just cheap hammer and nail men.'"[9]

On the employer side of the industry, Italian immigrants also had a strong presence, but on the lowest rungs of the ladder. In contrast to other sectors, where a few large firms predominated, it was easy to become a subcontractor in the residential field. Many Italians who in these turbulent years did become tradesmen were keen to make the leap from wage-worker to small ethnic businessman, and they were attracted by the possibility of increasing their earnings by becoming small employers. This desire to escape the wage labour market and to attain a modicum of independence was evident in the proliferation during the 1950s and early 1960s of small trade-specific subcontracting Italian firms in the house and apartment field. But this activity also played into the hands of the large builders and real estate developers who dominated the construction industry at its top echelons and benefited enormously from the increased competition among smaller contractors and subcontractors for contracts.

Indeed, as the royal commission headed by the prominent labour lawyer Carl Goldenberg would later reveal, builders and general contractors encouraged this pattern throughout this period by enticing tradesmen to go into business with offers to supply them with building materials and future contracts. Since setting up a firm required relatively little capital investment, many agreed. Often, all the tradesman had to do was supply the tools, which he already owned, and raise funds for a downpayment on a truck. This, he usually did by forming a partnership with a relative or paesane and taking out a loan from the bank or the builder. In assembling workcrews, Italian contractors drew on former co-workers, kin and paesani, and newcomers eager for work. By 1960 there were hundreds of Italian firms, most of them in the trowel trades and carpentry.[10]

Once in business, however, these small, often undercapitalized Italian employers faced a highly competitive market, and their own inexperience and unfamiliarity with the hidden costs involved in building led them to offer unrealistically low tenders. They were especially vulnerable to the cost-cutting tactics of builders who "shopped" the market and engaged in bid-peddling (prodding a contractor into lowering his price below his competitor's by revealing the latter's bid). They also had little legal recourse if builders, declaring that their work was substandard, simply withheld payment. Many small contractors suffered enormously under these conditions. The bidding wars and absurdly low tenders forced many of them to run their businesses on a shoestring. Feeling an obligation to their work crews, some contractors even forgave their own salary to pay their men. Still others fell victim to business failure. In the end, however, it was the workers who in these years paid the highest price. With neither the protection of unions nor a minimum wage, the thousands of immigrants desperate for work felt compelled to tolerate the attempts by hard-pressed employers to cut costs wherever possible.

In an effort to cover their losses on tenders for which they had underbid, and under pressure from their own "employers" – the builders and developers – to complete projects on time, numerous small subcontractors invariably were forced to subject their workers to speed-ups and long workdays, to ignore costly and time-consuming safety regulations, and to withhold wages from their workers. Caught in this position, many employers regularly violated the province's protective labour legislation that laid the basis for workers' legal rights in Ontario, including the Hours of Work Act, which set rates for overtime work, and the Vacations with Pay Act. A 1959 survey of Italian bricklayers conducted by the Italian Immigrant Aid Society (IIAS) revealed that half of the men had not received their vacation pay. (They were entitled to receive 2 per cent of their regular earnings.) Among those who had, most had not received the total amount.[11]

With growing regularity, Italian workers in the field complained of being "docked" hours on their paycheque. To hide this fact, some contractors kept a double set of books. In his private records, the employer noted the accurate number of hours worked and the actual rate paid per hour. However, on the official payroll record, which was subject to government audit, he divided the lawful rate per hour into the gross wages paid and entered a reduced number of hours. Other employers circumvented the Workman's Compensation Act by failing to keep an adequate work record for their workers, and the Unemployment Insurance Act by nonpayment of premiums or by contriving to set skilled workers up as subcontractors.[12]

When economic recession and rising unemployment hit the industry in the late 1950s, conditions worsened. Ironically, as com-

petition for jobs escalated, newly arri
desperate to find jobs in a tight labour i
position of older Italian workers in the fiei
same work at lower wages. Typically, they a
at a site and, discovering the going pay rates,
for less. Speaking in sympathetic terms of "t
unemployed people," IIAS administrator Johi
economic need had forced them to accept low v
ness to work," he later reported, "is mirrored
broken English: 'Me work cheap' ... For them a
keep their family from starving."[13]

To make matters worse, growing numbers of ily-by-night contractors, many though by no means all of them also Italian immigrants, entered the scene. Unable to cover costs on projects for which
they had grossly underbid, these men ruthlessly exploited their employees and then disappeared before the workers' paycheques
bounced at the bank. By the time workers discovered the fraud, the
firm had declared bankruptcy, obtained a new company incorporation, or otherwise disappeared. Typical was the experience of a
crew of eighteen men who completed a two-month housing project
in Richmond Hill in 1959 only to discover that their final and largest
paycheques were fraudulent. As the men could not identify their
employers, described only as two Italian brothers, police could not
lay charges.[14]

To compete in this cut-throat competition, legitimate small contractors increasingly found themselves forced to resort to similar
cost-cutting tactics, such as hiring two men for the price of one. The
payroll record showed appropriate hours and wage rates for one
worker, leaving the other without an employment record, which
disqualified him from unemployment insurance or compensation.
Among the most notorious schemes were the kickbacks, wherein a
worker returned or advanced a portion of his wages to the employer
as a condition of his employment. As the contractor was invariably
involved in a similar arrangement with the builder, developer, or
general contractor who had hired him, he was in effect transferring
his losses directly onto his workcrew. But it was an unequal exchange: the worker was not only deprived of his wages, but the
employer received the money tax free (in cash) while the worker
was taxed on the amount of his official wages.[15]

Significantly, Italian workers throughout this period distinguished
between the large numbers of honest contractors forced by circum-
stance to resort to illegal acts and a minority of unscrupulous men
who deliberately preyed on their competitors and workers. They
saved their most vociferous criticism for the well-established, large-

s and developers who profited most from the situation.
orker insisted, "People said we were exploited by our own
Exploited by whom? The builder hired peasants and made
em employers. He's getting rich, but the Italians, doing the work
cheap, are going under."[16] This sensitivity of Italian workers towards
their compatriots who ran the small contractor firms largely reflects
the ethnic, regional, and family bonds that cut across class divisions
within the industry. Indeed, Italian employers largely resembled
their work crews and some of them welcomed the efforts of workers
to organize the field, standardize rates and wages, and thus eliminate the excessive competition. While many of the small subcontractors were southerners, they hailed from every corner of Italy and
most of them had picked up their trade in Canada. Nevertheless,
as the decade wore on, fraudulent employer tactics grew more common, resulting in longer work days, speed-ups, and falling wages.

While abuses occurred across the industry, especially on sewer
and watermain, road, and landscaping sites where many Italians
also worked, exploitation was widespread in the housing field. By
the spring of 1960, many men were working a ten- to twelve-hour
work day and a six-day week, but rarely collecting the overtime pay
due them. A standing joke of the day noted that "on week-ends
only Italians work." Men working more than seventy hours a week
were being compelled to accept partial wages under threat of dismissal or deportation. Already trailing behind the commercial trades,
residential wages plummeted. In bricklaying and carpentry, hourly
rates dropped by half, from $2.50 to between $1.00–1.50. Labourers
earned as low as 80 cents. As employers ignored safety codes, accidents and injuries also increased. Recalling these events, Marco
Abate said: "The residential field was a jungle, a no man's land.
And Italian casualties were high. It was like our life was so cheap,
not worth anything. Like we could hear a builder saying, 'Some
Italians die today, got injured. Oh well, send us another load.'"[17]

PRELUDE TO THE STRIKES

Amid this brewing crisis, in March 1960, the five Italian workers
were killed in the Hogg's Hollow tunnel collapse. The subsequent
inquiry revealed that the project had violated numerous provincial
safety standards. Charles Daly, the provincial minister of labour who
had earlier claimed the project was safe, came under sustained attack
for his department's failure to enforce safety codes. Labour inspectors who had told on-site supervisors to bolster the faltering timber
supports at the project's various shafts and to clear up water leaking
into the tunnel admitted they had not followed up on their rec-

ommendations. Loath to delay production, foremen had cut corners on repairs, plugging up holes with caulking cement rather than rebuilding supports. Moreover, untrained men had worked long shifts underground under compressed air conditions and then been insufficiently "decompressed" by inexperienced co-workers put in charge of the taps controlling the air chambers. This practice made men highly vulnerable to the bone-crippling "bends" disease, which had led to the deaths of workers on other tunnelling jobs. When it was discovered that the regulations governing underground work were out of date, several critics, including Ontario CCF leader Donald MacDonald, called for Daly's resignation. [18]

In their testimonies, Italian workers admitted they could not read the safety regulations posted at the site and claimed that foremen had allowed drinking on the job and even smoking underground, where workers used blow torches to weld pipe fittings together. Finally, confusion prevailed over who was in charge of the site. A holding company had taken over the project in mid-stream after the initial contractor had gone bankrupt. But none of the project's various supervisors would accept responsibility – prompting John DeToro, an Italian oldtimer, a contractor, and the Italian representative on the jury, to berate the men for their "regretable performances." While it did not attach blame to any one individual, the jury's conclusions amounted to a wholesale indictment of the employers, supervisors, and officials involved, whose ineptness or callous attitude towards the workers had, in the jurists' eyes, made the tragedy inevitable. [19]

Public outrage over Hogg's Hollow reached such heights that the Conservative premier, Leslie Frost, established a cabinet committee to probe charges of immigrant exploitation, and announced the appointment of a provincial royal commission to investigate safety conditions in Ontario industry. [20] The tragedy also served to focus considerable public attention on immigrant exploitation in Toronto. For days, the English-language press carried stories of related abuse. One case involved two Italian dump-truck drivers who approached the Attorney-General's Office with claims showing they had paid a total of $150 in kickbacks to an excavation subcontractor on a subway project. The Marble, Tile and Terrazzo Workers Union, a commercial union, also exposed a "vicious kickback racket" said to have victimized over forty immigrants. To make matters worse, the company had recently claimed bankruptcy, leaving the union trying to recover thousands of dollars in unpaid wages. [21]

Although the tragedy had occurred outside the field, Hogg's Hollow also triggered a massive organizing campaign in the residential sector, where discontent was widespread and conditions ripe for a strike. That the eruption occurred here reflected the fact that residential workers had recently begun to organize. The two men who, for better or worse, would dominate the leadership of the immigrant campaigns – Zanini and Irvine – had already scored some important gains.

The first trade to organize had been the bricklayers, who became the militant core of the later campaigns. Their militancy did not reflect the presence of a radical artisan leadership, the group usually highlighted in historical accounts of immigrant strikes.[22] Indeed, no group of politicized craftsmen emerged in these campaigns. Rather, the bricklayers' militancy is attributable to structural factors. This trade had the highest concentration of Italians and thus it offered the best prospects for ethnic solidarity. Moreover, the bricklayers were in some respects the natural leaders of the movement since they represented the pivotal trade. A work stoppage by bricklayers usually halted work on the rest of a project.

Following various recruitment drives initiated by Zanini, by the spring of 1960 approximately 1300 bricklayers were organized. The first drives had occurred in 1955, following the death of Gerrada Trillo, the wife of an immigrant bricklayer arrested on charges of shoplifting. Convinced she was to be deported, Trillo had hanged herself in a police holding cell. In their coverage, the English-language press focused on the desperate fears of a mother for her children and for police mistreatment. (The police had ignored Trillo's hysterical cries and had not bothered to explain the situation to her husband, who sat in an adjoining cell.) For their part, Italian workers had stressed the meager wages Trillo's husband had earned, arguing that his inability to earn a sufficient wage to support his family had precipitated the crisis. *Corriere Canadese* also came under attack from outspoken workers for failing to express the sense of outrage with which Italians had responded to the affair. Several construction workers also called for the organization of the industry.[23]

The idea of a union drive had been forcefully put to Zanini by the Italian consul, Pierre Nuti, during a benefit concert held to raise funds for the Trillo family. Claiming the Building Trades Council would reject a plan to organize residential workers, Zanini formed a Canadian union. Within weeks, more than 1000 bricklayers signed. Responding to overtures from the AFL, the members later accepted a charter from the federation, becoming Local 35 of the Bricklayers, Cement Masons and Plasterers' International Union of America. However, the leadership of the union's long-standing Toronto local, Local 2, objected to the new residential local on the grounds that it was raiding the established local's potential membership. In response, the International liquidated Local 35, merged its membership with Local 2, and made Zanini a business agent. Italian members soon complained that Local 2 discriminated against them when handling placements and grievances. In 1959 they retaliated by forming another independent union. The Canadian Bricklayers Association was composed of men who had earlier joined Local 35.[24]

Charles Irvine, himself an old-line unionist and an International vice-president with the Operative Plasterers and Cement Masons' International Union, had enjoyed similar successes. An organizing drive launched among residential cement finishers in the summer of 1957 resulted in 400 men joining Local 117-C (Cement Masons) of the Plasterers and Cement Masons' Union. He then led a successful drive to recruit residential plasterers into Local 117 of the same union. In November 1957, 800 plasterers spearheaded a five-day strike, which brought a first contract with wage increases and a closed shop.[25] Influenced by these events, the executive of Toronto's established Carpenters' union hired Italian organizers to lead what proved to be an impressive drive among residential carpenters. Although the work stoppage they called failed to produce a contract, approximately 500 immigrant carpenters organized themselves into Local 1190 of the United Brotherhood of Carpenters and Joiners of America.[26]

In some respects, both Zanini, who had no organizing experience, and Irvine, a veteran AFL union official, were both odd choices for leaders of an Italian immigrant drive. An Italian-Canadian who had grown up in Toronto's small prewar Italian colony, the stockily-built Zanini could not, by the 1960s, really be considered an immigrant. Zanini was an experienced bricklayer and an amateur opera singer who performed at many community events. What many of the workers may not have known was that he also had a checkered past, including a record of petty gambling and theft convictions that years earlier had culminated in a brief stint in jail. In 1949 he left for Genoa in an attempt to launch a singing career; three years later he returned to Toronto and resumed his bricklaying trade. Union leadership and an organizing drive offered him a chance to return to the spotlight. His charisma and tough, aggressive style gained him a huge following, though his inattention to democratic procedures would draw the ire of critics.[27]

Equally tough was the tall and rangy Scottish-born Charles Irvine, whose aggressive style so impressed Zanini. At union meetings Irvine liked to brandish a two-by-four with a spike driven through it as a symbol of militancy. As the contemporary news suggests, Irvine no doubt realized that his own membership would be more secure if the Italian immigrants were organized. Yet it is also evident that he enjoyed being an unpredictable maverick, and had even initiated the 1957 drives without notifying his International headquarters in Washington. Like Zanini, he showed a keen interest in establishing himself as a champion of the Italian immigrants, and he was willing to employ unorthodox methods to do so.[28]

It is not difficult to understand why deeply embittered immigrant workers, utterly frustrated with their plight, responded eagerly to Zanini's and Irvine's appeals to end their exploitation and to reform the industry through unionization. Far from being duped by these charismatic personalities – as their critics charged – Italian workers recognized the leaders' talents. Both men were effective grass-roots organizers, especially Zanini, who, during the early drives, had spent hours talking with men at worksites and in billiard halls and cafés. Zanini shared with the Italian newcomers a resentment towards the old-line unions. As an Italian-Canadian who spoke both English and Italian, Zanini appeared to the workers as an effective intermediary between themselves and the host society. Even more than Zanini, Irvine met the need for dynamic leadership. "Charlie had such a way," recalled one worker. "Nobody knew English, but the way he talked, it made sense to everyone. He inspired so much confidence, a born leader."[29] While Italian workers were impressed with Irvine's interest in them, they also expected to benefit from his clout as an International vice-president.

With little support coming from the Internationals or the Trades and Labour Council, by the spring of 1960 the new locals were barely holding their own. Then Hogg's Hollow served as a catalyst for a union drive in the residential field, and Irvine and Zanini forged a partnership. At Irvine's encouragement, Zanini convinced his members to dissolve the independent union and rejoin the AFL. Italian bricklayers obtained a residential charter as Local 40 of the AFL's Bricklayers' International Union. Under Zanini's leadership, Italian labourers also obtained a charter as Local 811 of the AFL's Laborers Union.

Irvine and Zanini used their respective unions as a base from which to establish an umbrella organization that would operate as a separate council of residential building tradesmen. The five residential locals eagerly joined the new organization, subsequently known as the Brandon Union Group, the name being derived from Brandon Hall, where their early meetings were held. The core of the Brandon Group consisted of the five new residential locals: the Bricklayers, Laborers, Carpenters, Plasterers, and Cement Masons. These locals did not affiliate with the Toronto Building Trades Council. Zanini and Irvine hoped that the Brandon Group would act as a bargaining agent on behalf of its affiliates, but this never materialized. Initially, only a few of the commercial unions, namely the Laborers and the Painters locals, actively cooperated with the Brandon unions.[30]

The Brandon Union Group was a loosely structured organization dominated by Irvine and Zanini, but they were by no means the only organizers who could claim responsibility for launching a major union drive. A diverse collection of approximately twenty-five Canadian and immigrant organizers and business agents representing the various member locals comprised the Brandon executive. Several Italian-Canadians, most of them sharp and seasoned representatives of the International, were members of the executive, among them Anthony Mariano, an International vice-president with the Cement Masons. Some of the immigrant organizers who joined the executive, including Frank Colantonio and Marino Toppan, were by the early 1960s experienced tradesmen who had been in Canada for several years and had helped launch the early union drives within their respective trades in the period preceding the founding of the Brandon Group. An organizer with the Carpenters, the Molisanborn Colantonio had spent a decade in Toronto, had acquired a certificate in drafting, and had been an administrator with the Italian Immigrant Aid Society. Toppan was a native of Friuli who had arrived in Toronto in the mid-1950s as an experienced bricklayer and had later joined the union movement. By 1961 they and several other organizers had already demonstrated a commitment to improving the lot of their fellow workers. The remaining Italian members consisted largely of relatively recent immigrants who had responded enthusiastically to a campaign to end exploitation in the industry. They included Angelo Burigana, a northerner from Castelfranco, Treviso, who worked diligently on behalf of the Plasterers, and a former barber from Molise, George Petta, a popular agent for the Laborers who proved to be an extremely effective speaker at union meetings. Finally, a few non-Italian immigrants, most of them from Germany, also joined the executive.[31]

In the aftermath of Hogg's Hollow, the Brandon leaders launched a major union drive. The first mass meeting took place on 1 April at Brandon Hall. It drew hundreds of men, an impressive first showing. The membership presented the attorney-general with a list of forty firms "blacklisted" for their refusal to comply with regulations regarding vacation pay. A second rally held on 14 April drew 2000 men. The crowd greeted Irvine and Zanini's arrival on stage enthusiastically. Rising to the occasion, both men delivered the blistering speeches that became their trademark. In his written account of that first meeting, Colantonio recalls: "The louder the speakers, the louder the applause. The enthusiasm of the workers manifested that night indicated that they were ready to protest in any way for the sake of improving their lot." Zanini appealed to the men's sense of justice and family. Turning to the single men he said, "You work eighteen hours a day ... You can't expect to get married and raise a family under these conditions." When he asked for a show of hands from those who had been cheated out of vacation pay, hundreds went up. More followed when he asked how many had received threats of job dismissal from their employers should they attend the rally. Amid a roar of approval, Irvine then took the stage, delivering a fiery speech and congratulating the men on their commitment to the campaign. "Nothing can stop us now," he concluded.[32]

THE FIRST STRIKE

By late June the Brandon unions boasted 3000 members. As the leaders of a recently constituted strike committee, Irvine and Zanini called an organizational walkout for Monday, 1 August. The strike, which aimed at organizing 20,000 men and winning first contracts with wage increases and the closed shop, turned into a three-week struggle. As the only unionized trade covered by a collective agreement, Local 117 Plasterers were instructed to remain on the job. The strikers also called for new legislation in certification and collective bargaining rights. Like most building trades unions, they found existing certification procedures time-consuming and inappropriate to an industry where workers exhibited a high rate of shifting among firms on a job-to-job basis.

In calling the strike, Irvine and Zanini involved the workers in an illegal walkout and jumped the gun on the AFL Building Trades Department, which had recently endorsed an industry-wide certification drive to organize Toronto's immigrants. (The International's campaign appears to have reflected a concern that Irvine and Zanini would take full credit for organizing these men.) Speaking to reporters, Irvine justified the strategy on the grounds that the International, long complacent on this issue, could not be trusted to carry through with its campaign and that the delays involved in following the legal route could have a debilitating effect on the entire drive. This first strike, then, was plagued by a rift between old-line and Brandon unions.[33]

To maintain morale in a strike that had picketers scattered across many worksites, strike leaders staged morning rallies. For the Monday kick-off rally, one thousand men descended on the Lansdowne theatre, a movie house located in the west-end on Lansdowne Avenue at Bloor Street. In response to anxious calls about Italian men milling outside the theatre, police set up patrols. (Later, as the crowds grew, organizers rented a second theatre nearby and linked by wires and speakers.) Inside, the crowd was keyed up and eager to hear their leaders. Beginning on a ceremonial note, Irvine and Zanini led the men in a silent prayer. Then came unanimous support for a pledge requiring all workers to stay out until contracts had been reached with every trade.

These morning rallies became a notable and regular feature of both strikes. Taking place in the dark and smoke-filled rooms of Italian movie theatres, the rallies were boisterous events, complete with fiery speeches and spontaneous outbursts from the floor. In their speeches, Irvine and Zanini stressed the integrity of the immigrants' struggle and denounced the developers and builders who opposed them – themes close to the workers' heart. During the first rally, Zanini arrived on stage with his pockets stuffed with cheques stamped NSF. Waving them furiously about, he shouted: "This is the sort of exploitation that should be stopped. Canada is a free country and immigrants should be treated the same as Canadians!" As the crowd roared its approval, four men jumped onto the platform to produce their own NSF paycheques. Joining them, Toppan shouted out to the enthusiastic crowd: "An end to immigrant slavery – think of your families!" The meeting ended amid cheers, as men chanted one of the battle cries of the strikes: "Canadian wages, Canadian hours!"[34]

The leaders' reliance on aggressive rhetoric and symbols – which included Irvine's two-by-four "plank of action" – were obvious appeals to the strikers' masculinity and their sense of fair play. Workers were addressing a basic injustice; fed up with being treated like second-class citizens, they felt their years of hard work had earned them the right to be accorded the same respect as Canadian workers. As one worker put it to reporters, "We are tired of being too timid to step on someone else's shoes." He wanted Canada "to recognize him as a son, to respect him, and defend the honour of his work."[35] Precluded from entering alternative industries because of their own lack of skill and largely excluded from the established building trades, these men were prepared to make a permanent commitment to the residential sector. They also felt that unless they established a union base, they would continue to fall victim to the downward competitive pressures of the labour market and would feel compelled to accept unsafe and even degrading work without fair remuneration. The growing bitterness after a decade of exploitation translated into an open willingess to organize and strike. Commenting on these events some thirty years later, Abate described the campaign as "an Italian uprising ... We were saying 'Enough to this kind of exploitation.'"[36]

Zanini and Irvine also likely understood an equally compelling element of the Italian male ethos – the seriousness Italian men attached to their role as the family's chief and, in some cases, sole breadwinner. As worsening economic conditions and falling wages seriously challenged their capacity to ensure the financial well-being of their families, thousands of men decided to take action. Those who took the plunge did so as the family's representative.

The walkout was not 100 per cent. The campaign faced the same obstacles that had hampered earlier drives, among them scattered workcrews, employer intimidation, and workers' economic need. The reluctance of some workers to protest was linked to their all-consuming desire and need to secure a job – at virtually any price. Some men did not join the campaign because of the opposition of their wives, who insisted that the family could not afford to lose their income. For years many Italians had been too fearful to protest blatant violations of their rights, while others were ignorant of those rights. Some truly feared that government officials might use the occasion of an illegal strike to deport newcomers. No doubt, among the most fearful were former contract workers who had "skipped out" on their contracts, those who had paid handsomely for sponsorship letters from employers whom they had never met, and those who had lied on their immigration papers. Some employers and builders, it was claimed, had exploited such fears, threating job dismissal and deportation. In other cases, workers felt intensely loyal to their employer. This was particularly true of the new arrivals who had been sponsored by the same kin and paesani who now employed them.[37]

Still, 6000 immigrants did join the campaign. They did so not only in defiance of the industry's powerful builders and developers but also without much support from Italian community leaders, the church, and even, at this point, *Corriere Canadese* editor Gianni Grohovaz. While Grohovaz genuinely sympathized with the workers' plight, he initially opposed the drive largely because he distrusted the leaders, especially Zanini, whom he described in one editorial as being driven by "his own selfish desire to be *il capo* (the head) of all the Italian workers." Since Hogg's Hollow, Grohovaz had called for major government reforms but had not advocated unions. He had also laid some of the blame for the abuses on the workers themselves, saying that "the immigrants, by accepting work that was unsafe or paid less than the legal rate, were letting themselves be treated as if they were second-class citizens." And he was dismissive of the early union meetings, claiming that communists were "much in attendance" and that "gossip, profane language and political speeches had taken the place of a proper program."[38]

Opposition also came from some of the members of the colony's elite. To be sure, these men had shown a concern for the plight of Italian construction workers. The executive members of the Italian Immigrant Aid Society (IIAS), for example, had staged various events, including a benefit concert, to raise funds for the families of the Hogg's Hollow victims. They did not, however, come out initially in support of the strike, evidently for fear of the unfavourable publicity it might generate for the community. An early incident that attracted press courage involved Johnny Lombardi, an Italian-Canadian entertainment promoter who had acquired the unofficial title of Toronto's mayor of Little Italy. Insisting that "the majority of Italian immigrants are very very happy," he blamed "the recent noise" on "a small group of young rabblerousers." "The poolroom, coffee-counter hangers-on," he added, "have no right to speak for the Italian community ... The statements they are making about exploitation is hurting the well-meaning married immigrant – the one who needs a job and will work at anything to provide for his family." Lombardi's comments were echoed by the IIAS executive, and by the employers' Metro Toronto Home Builders Association (MTHBA). Some parish priests came to the defence of the Italian subcontractors, arguing that given their oven vulnerable position the men had shown some charity towards the recent arrivals by offering them work in these hard times.[39]

Infuriated by Lombardi's remarks, Italian workers responded with a rash of angry phone calls and pickets around Lombardi's store. An agent for the Laborers, Nick Gileno, told reporters: "We are hard-working people. Lombardi lives with us and should tell the truth." Representing the Bricklayers, Toppan also complained to the press, saying: "I am a good bricklayer and have worked myself up. I want Lombardi to know that I haven't time for poolrooms – I have worked every day since coming to Canada." And Colantonio added: "I know more about the construction industry than a fellow behind a salami counter. Our people – and other immigrants – are being cheated every day of the week." Other workers sent letters to the press. "Italians," wrote P. Palozzi, "did not come to Canada to steal jobs or to work at low rates, but to build a better, stronger Canada. We don't know where the race track is, or where Florida and California are in winter – but we know where our job is." In response,

Lombardi, who admitted he had not been aware of the extent of exploitation in the industry, issued a formal apology, and later he would publicly support striking Toronto construction workers.[40]

The strike did generate the nativist backlash that its Italian opponents had feared. Letters to the press depicted the strikers either as ungrateful foreigners or as the dupes of union dictators. In denying that Italian workers were truly exploited, and thus unjustified in their action, critics typically pointed to the fact that many of the immigrants were homeowners. One man wrote to say he "was highly amused" to read that "slave wages were being paid to New Canadians," since it appeared to him that Italians were better off than most working-class people.[41] By contrast, the newspapers themselves, at least initially, were sympathetic to the strikers, although some *Globe and Mail* editorials did express concern over union rivalries and the illegality of the strike. The *Star*, for example, welcomed the opportunity to eliminate immigrant exploitation in the construction industry, while columnist Martin Goodman expressed some hope that the "controversial" leaders would succeed in their efforts to improve the conditions of Italian construction workers. This early support was linked to the Hogg's Hollow revelations, which had truly outraged many journalists and prompted them to criticize the labour minister, call for major reforms, and urge stiff penalties for abusive employers. A *Telegram* editorial published at that time captured this sense of outrage. "Men who labor beneath the surface of a city," it read, "provide physical comforts and civic security for hundreds of thousands. What a lavish expenditure of energy and sacrifice to give city dwellers the most commonplace conveniences of modern life."[42]

The *Telegram*, traditionally a conservative newspaper, emerged as the most enthusistic supporter of the Italian strikers. Much of this support is attributed to its labour columnist, Frank Drea, then a young reporter determined to expose immigrant abuses in the city. Often appearing on the front page, Drea's stories detailed hardship cases and offered positive portrayals of the immigrants. Typical of his crusading style was his sympathetic portrait of struggling construction labourer Dominic Moscone and his family. Drea stressed it was precisely this sort of hard-working and family-oriented immigrant, and not radicals or subversives, who supported the Brandon drive.[43] For his efforts, Drea won a journalism award and was held in high regard among Italians.

On-site skirmishes did occur throughout the strike. Although workers considered builders and developers to be the real villains, much of the actual conflict was played out at the job sites. Here, Italian picketers confronted, and an occasion clashed with, Italian subcontractors and, at times, even the Italian workers whom they hoped to recruit into the union movement. Emotions ran high at the sites and skirmishes inevitably occurred. But while it is impossible to determine who initiated each outburst, media coverage invariably laid the blame on the picketers. Some employers took advantage of this bias, portraying picketers to police and reporters as "goon squads" of "ruffians" indiscriminately destroying property and machinery.[44] Several participants admitted that on occasion some strikers got carried away during the face-to-face heckling that took place between them and the men who were working. But what critics failed to mention, they insisted, was that countless nonstrikers responded positively to the arrival of picketers, that their presence gave men the encouragement they needed to join the campaign.[45]

Arrests began on the third day, which saw several outbursts and increased police patrols. It started with a morning incident in which police broke up battles between strikers and nonstrikers at a Markham housing subdivision. Two days later, strikers in North York were arrested after allegedly trying to prevent a police officer on a motorcycle from driving through the crowd of picketers in an effort to disperse them. A furious Brandon executive promptly issued a complaint claiming police were arbitrarily confiscating picket signs from workers, roughhandling them, and calling them Wops, DPs, and other derogatory names.[46]

Despite these problems, Brandon workers appeared strong during the early days of the strike. The morning rallies attracted more than 2000 men, and almost 5000 workers had signed union cards. Furthermore, several contractors and MTHBA president H.P. Hyatt admitted that the strike was adversely affecting projects across the city, though they were quick to add that the problem was temporary. The pivotal trade was the bricklayers, whose absence most seriously affected the completion of projects. Strikers received a real boost when Local 211 of the Teamsters voted in favour of a sympathy strike, which immediately interrupted truck deliveries of ready-mix cement and other materials to nonunion projects. Similar actions were taken by the Marble, Tile and Terrazzo Workers, and the commercial Bricklayers' Union, Local 183, whose support reflected the concerns of Italian workers in the local. The police arrest of an employer, a non-Italian, for waving a pistol at picketers, also gave credence to union charges of employer intimidation. Police denied the claims of a contractor who charged strikers with having incited the violence that erupted at his Don Mills site.[47]

Heartened by this chain of events, the strike committee called a meeting with interested contractors for Friday, 5 August. Of the 700 contractors invited, 400 came, though there was little agreement among them over strategy. Brandon leaders led off by stressing that unions would not only assist workers but also aid the small contractor by eliminating cut-throat competition for contracts. They also urged employers to form or expand their associations and appoint negotiating committees. While some of the subcontractors conceded that unions might help rationalize the field, others hinted that as small firms dependent on the large developers, they were compelled to oppose the strike. Any possibility of a fruitful exhange was dashed, however, when a vocal group of contractors took serious exception to the dramatics of the labour leaders, which included waving about NSF cheques. The meeting deteriorated into a barrage of name-calling and insults.[48]

Shortly afterwards, employers in Etobicoke and North York launched an offensive by calling a lockout on their projects. They also urged the Home Builders Association to advocate lockouts by member firms. This response could not hide the fact that the strike had brought a significant portion of the field to a halt. Indeed, no sooner had the lockout been announced than various contractors formed associations, struck negotiating committees, and agreed to a set of preliminary talks to be held during the upcoming weekend.

Negotiations between masonry contractors and Locals 40 (Bricklayers) and 811 (Laborers) took place at Brandon Hall. At the nearby Conroy Hotel on Dufferin Street, Locals 117-C (Cement Masons) and 1190 (Carpenters) faced concrete and drain and carpenter contractors. The sessions, however, were short-lived. When, on the second evening, talks broke off between masonry contractors and bricklayers, strike leaders began approaching contractors on an individual basis, encouraging them to agree to a master contract securing standardized rates for the industry. Then, two unexpected events took place. The first was the announcement that a tentative settlement had been reached between Local 1190 and the Carpenters' Association, which was said to cover 3000 workers. The second incident involved the decision of the residential Plasterers to walk off the job, a move which prompted more masonry contractors to join the Masonry Contractors Association. Another round of talks culminated in a tentative contract between 175 firms and 3500 bricklayers and labourers.[49]

The settlement, in turn, provided a basic formula for all of the trades. With the exception of the Laborers, who received a forty-five-hour week patterned after the helpers' rates in the commercial trades, the formula stipulated a forty-hour week and an across-the-board increase of forty to fifty cents per hour to be phased in by the next spring. This raised the official hourly rate of the highest paid

trade – bricklayers – from $2.60 to $3.05, and of the lowest paid –
labourers – from $1.55 to $2.00. Together, the contracts covered
approximately 7000 workers. Union leaders, however, could not
deny claims that there were still many holdouts among the contractors. At the same time, striking plasterers were seeking contracts
with nonunion employers, and the hoisting engineers, now facing
the expiry of their collective agreement, called a sympathy strike in
the commercial field.[50]

As the strike entered its third week and pickets began spreading
to downtown sites, picket-line skirmishes and police arrests
mounted as did strikers' protests about the increasingly aggressive
tactics employed by police departments. Two Italian strikers were
charged with malicious damage after allegedly running through
freshly laid cement sidewalks in the west end. Fifty others had fled
the site as police on motorcycles and horses arrived. A housing
project in Markham was the site of great excitement as 150 strikers
and workers engaged in a brick-throwing exchange, which resulted
in several serious injuries and put some of the duelling men in
hospital. As police officers attempted to place a handcuffed striker
in a cruiser, picketers grabbed hold of him and there ensued a "human tug-of-war." Failing to rescue the man, strikers surrounded the
cruiser and prevented police from moving for almost two hours.
Over the next few days, the police arrested several more men on
suburban housing sites.[51]

The rivalry between the Brandon and the old-guard unions resurfaced when, on 15 August, the Building Trades Council formally
launched its immigrant recruitment drive. The council's plan received the support of various mainstream labour organizations, including the Canadian Labour Congress (CLC), the Ottawa-based
central labour organization of Canada, whose official organ, *Canadian
Labour*, considered a campaign aimed to organize "New Canadians"
a timely move. No mention was made of the Brandon group. At the
local level, however, there had been signs throughout the strike that
indicated the ongoing tensions between old-line and Brandon unionists. For instance, Bill Jenovese, president of the commercial Bricklayers' Local 2 and a leading labour figure, had publicly said he did
not think the Italian workers could sustain a protracted struggle.
According to press reports, this had not only antagonized Brandon
workers but had also alienated some Italian members within Jenovese's own local. These men had sent a delegation to the Brandon
meetings. Some had even joined the pickets set up by residential
brickayers outside Jenovese's office to protest his actions. Brandon
organizers now refused to support the new AFL drive. Claiming his

group was being run on a shoestring, Irvine issued a statement that he would welcome any new unions to the Brandon campaign.[52]

As the strike entered its third week and many workers were feeling the pinch, Brandon negotiators became more determined than ever to bring about an end to the strike. Round-the-clock bargaining sessions over the next few days resulted in collective agreements being signed with hundreds of contractors. Although conceding the largest firms had not been signed, Irvine assured his members that since many of the firms signed were medium-sized companies, conditions were certain to improve. The workers, he added, must do their share by refusing nonunion work.[53]

Italian workers were thoroughly pleased by the project of winning a first contract: 6000 men had been organized; they had won a wage increase of $1.00 per hour, 4 per cent vacation pay, and safety provisions for the movement of workers in trucks. The press and city labour leaders stressed the strike's historic importance. Taking up a major theme of the strike, the *Star* observed that by eliminating "this sweated labour," Italian workers had taken a major step towards shedding their second-class status and attaining full Canadian citizenship. David Archer, president of the Ontario Federation of Labour, described the strike as a turning point in the history of Toronto's labour movement and the start of a meaningful partnership between Canadian and immigrant workers.[54] In his written account of events, Colantonio summed up the sentiments of the strikers at that time: "Now these people could finally feel for the first time since they came to Canada (some of them ten years earlier) that they too had a say in their jobs inasmuch as they and their employers had the union agreement to abide by."[55]

Although the mainstream labour press barely acknowledged their role in the campaign, Irvine and Zanini emerged from the strike as working-class heroes of Toronto's immigrant community. At a Sunday rally held on 20 August at Lansdowne Theatre to celebrate the victory, an estimated 3500 workers showed up to sing the praises of their leaders. They presented Irvine with a painting bordered with Stella Alpina flowers, which grow in the mountains of Italy, and gave flowers to Zanini's wife. A week later, some 7500 men marched, many for the first time, in the city's annual Labour Day parade. This was indeed a time for celebration. Italian immigrant workers had accomplished what many said could not be done. As one participant would later declare, "Nowhere in North American have more than 5,000 workers been organized in the short period of three months."[56] The Brandon unions now wielded some political clout, and the workers' actions had prompted the old-line unions to take notice. In the aftermath of the 1960 campaign, the Building Trades Council and the Brandon executive agreed to join forces. Former rivals thus forged an alliance. It remained to be seen, however, whether the gains made in the strike could be protected.

THE SECOND STRIKE

The euphoria that accompanied the conclusion of the 1960 organizing drive gave way to considerable anxiety during the course of the following year as contract violations and familiar abuses occured with increasing regularity. The root of the problem lay in the failure of the 1960 campaign to unionize a majority of the firms in the residential sector – a situation that benefited the developers and builders in the field. Since less than half of the approximately 600 carpentry and masonry contractors had signed collective agreements, a large group of firms in each trade remained unorganized and so naturally continued to operate with non-union employees and pay wages below union rates. As builders and general contractors continued to shop for the lowest bids, union firms simply could not compete with unorganized employers who paid below-union wage rates and could thus offer significantly lower tenders on project contracts. While some union contractors went bankrupt as a result of the deteriorating conditions, others sacrificed their modest profits to pay their work crews. When the situation dragged on into the new year, however, growing numbers of union contractors found themselves increasingly compelled to turn their backs on their contracts and resort to age-old cost-cutting tactics.[57]

By the spring of 1961 more than 1000 grievances had been filed with the courts or the Ontario Labour Relations Board (OLRB). Workers were unhappy with the cumbersome procedures and with the legal loopholes some companies found to avoid paying outstanding wages. In one case, a medium-sized plastering firm went bankrupt owing over $80,000 to former employees. After six months of expensive court proceedings, the unions collected only $39,000 to distribute to the workers. On the few occasions when, according to the collective agreements, wages were scheduled to rise, employers plainly admitted that, since they could not extract higher payments from the builders, they could not afford to grant the raises. In response to the growing crisis, some members of the Brandon executive, including a few immigrant organizers, began to sympathize with contractors who genuinely could not respect their union contracts. They feared that unless they agreed to renegotiate new contracts at reduced wage rates, the entire union structure would be dismantled. Zanini and Irvine, however, refused to consider rollbacks of any kind – a decision that some considered to be a tactical error. Nevertheless, as the situation went from bad to worse, the Brandon leadership faced the difficult decision of calling another strike in less than one year.[58]

In an effort to stop the fall in membership and to unionize a greater proportion of the field, Brandon leaders planned a second strike to begin on 29 May 1961. Two days before that date, a major collapse at a downtown subway station killed two men and seriously injured three others. It served as a strong reminder of Hogg's Hollow. It also triggered a spontaneous though short-lived walkout by commercial carpenters, who refused to work on subway projects until greater precautions were taken in the building of timber supports.[59]

Although similar to the first one, this strike differed in some significant respects. This time, workers faced a more determined opposition from employers and police. But they also had the explicit support of the Toronto Building Trades Council and the Internationals. The strike committee was composed of three members each from the Brandon Group and the council, with Irvine as chair. Essential aid now came from leading unionists, such as Jenovese, the recently retired and influential former president of the commercial Bricklayers and the council, and Gerry Gallagher, secretary-treasurer of the commercial Laborers' Local 183 and council secretary. An Irishman, the popular Gallagher had established a solid reputation within the labour movement by organizing Ontario Hydro workers. He was also one of the few old-line leaders who had favoured organizing residential workers from the start. Finally, this strike triggered a series of sympathy strikes that threatened to shut down the entire industry.

Although still reeling from a lengthy strike and winter layoffs, Italian workers responded eagerly to the call for another walkout. More than 4300 workers and sixty labour leaders crowded the Brandon Hall auditorium on the morning of 29 May. In his familiar oratorical style, Irvine addressed the animated crowd, warning them that failure this time would mean "you are through, you might just as well pack up and return to Italy." The Teamsters also lent their support and pledged to boycott deliveries to picketed sites. As the meeting ended, car and truck convoys transported picketers to worksites.[60]

Within days, the major apartment projects had shut down because of the presence of pickets or the lack of tradesmen. Flying squads of picketers also targeted pick-up depots where employers "loaded up" their crews. They hit the smaller and more scattered housing sites, ripping out hydro wires, overturning mortar boxes, and convincing the men who were working to join them. Police arrests of men on strike-related charges began on the second day. In Etobicoke, police picked up a group of strikers and the project contractor, who had waved a gun at the pickets. Another contractor, a non-Italian, was arrested on similar charges. Most of the arrests, however, involved strikers. Indeed, it soon became apparent that police had hoped to discourage mass picketing and raiding of sites by arresting large numbers of strikers. Among the first arrests were two young Italian men in their early thirties, charged with obstruction following a police crackdown on one hundred strikers picketing an Islington Avenue apartment site.[61]

As flying picket crews continued to target work sites across the city and its suburbs, arrests continued. On the third day, police descended upon a crowd of picketers at an Etobicoke housing project after the contractor phoned to announce a near riot situation. In Scarborough, seventy strikers who gained access to an apartment complex were dispersed by police and several were arrested. A housing project superintendent in North York told police he had been punched by a striker from one of twenty carloads of picketers who had arrived at his site. Six men were taken into custody. In Leaside, an east-end suburb, mounted police broke up a demonstration and arrested five Italian strikers in what some dubbed a "police raid." At a housing site located northwest of the city, twenty-year-old Giancarlo Stefanini, then a relatively recent immigrant from Rome who had quickly developed a reputation as an energetic organizer with the commercial Laborers, was arrested on obstruction charges. Thirty years later, Stefanini recalled the events surrounding his arrest to writer Kenneth Bagnell, noting that he had been terrified by the arrival of police cruisers at the worksite where he and his friend had been talking peacefully with working men. Finally, an episode in a Markham subdivision resulted in serious head injuries to two men. During the fighting, a nonstriker pushed his way through picketers by swinging an axe, while others battled with two-by-fours and hurled bricks. A total of twenty-two arrests were made.[62]

Following these events, police surveillance was increased and "special details" were ordered to keep a check on large sites. This sent a clear warning to the strike leaders, who once again countered with charges of police mistreatment and discrimination. The strikers themselves resented the excessive force that some, though not all, policemen were using in dispersing pickets. Some of the strikers had even suffered a beating at the hands of irate police constables.[63]

As in the first strike, Italian workers deeply resented what they considered to be the sensationalization of isolated incidents. In a letter to the *Telegram*, an exasperated participant wrote: "Your paper only mentions the violence ... but talks nothing of the orderly actions, where builder and police allow us a few minutes to ... talk to the men, who in the majority of cases pack up and join us." The workers' resentment was fueled by their recognition that in this strike they were facing a more determined opposition from Labour Minister Daly and law enforcement authorities. In response, Irvine and Zanini, who had earlier encouraged workers to use aggressive raiding techniques, now advised them to avoid attracting bad publicity.[64]

Signs of a possible general strike surfaced early on in the dispute when, at the end of the first week, it appeared likely that commercial projects might also be affected. The occasion was the firing of three Local 230 Teamster truck drivers for their refusal to deliver supplies to roadpaving, sidewalk, and subway excavation projects contracted to nonunion firms. Brandon organizers countered by calling mass walkouts at thirty city sewer and watermain projects controlled by nonunion firms.[65]

Daly took action at this point, openly expressing his disapproval of the strike, calling for greater police action, and encouraging contractors to file grievances with the Ontario Labour Relations Board. This was followed by an employer offensive spearheaded by MTHBA president H.P. Hyatt. On 7 June he raised the dreaded bogeyman when he asked Immigration Minister Ellen Fairclough to deport Italian immigrants convicted on strike-related charges of violent activities. Fairclough rejected the request, saying that the Immigration Act was not to be used as a weapon by either side in industrial disputes.[66]

Yet the request alone sparked tremendous controversy, pitting critics of the strikes against those who felt some sympathy for the strikers. In the nativist camp were both staunch conservatives and workers unprepared to welcome the immigrants into the labour movement. Typical of the first group were those who accused the Italians of instigating the violence. This included D. Allen, who said the strike had "shattered" her confidence in Canadian democracy by "permit[ing] a gang of union men to converge upon a construction development and intimidate the workers until naked fear makes them rush to protect their families." Another writer advised that as the strikers were preventing others from exercising their right to work, all of them should be deported. Working Torontonians opposed to the strike considered the Italians the authors of their own misfortune and warned they would not make trustworthy unionists. As one man bluntly put it: "They are disliked because they are willing to accept lower wages than the standard. Now faced with the problem of a strike, they want people to feel sorry for them." Finally, the deportation request received support from conservative ethnic organizations, including the German weekly, *Der Courier*, and the Czechoslovakian National Association.[67]

Newspaper editorials, however, lashed out at the builders. In the face of the growing violence, the papers had once again wavered in their support of the strikers, but now they switched gears and condemned the builders. A *Star* editorial expressed utter astonishment at such "unwarranted intimidation" of immigrants who, it argued, were addressing legitimate grievances. Another warned that "Canadian law should not be used as a club to scare men into docile acceptance of bad working conditions."[68] Even the *Globe and Mail* agreed. The request, read an editorial, "is so contrary to the principles of democracy that one is left wondering if the builders are aware that they live in a democracy." The incident also led journalists to criticize existing deportation laws. A *Telegram* columnist felt compelled to assure his readers it was unlikely that anyone would be deported. In fact, he added, federal officials had recently told police to "take it easy" on the strikers.[69]

Sympathetic Torontonians also wrote, condemning the deportation order and defending the strikers. Accusing Hyatt of "blackmail," H. Dust defended the Italians against charges of staging an illegal strike with claims that it was "equally abhorrent for some contractors to take unfair advantage of immigrant[s] ... to force them to accept substandard working conditions." And if unionists could be found among the strike's opponents, they also numbered among its most enthusiastic supporters. Several unionists, including D. Braithwaite, a rubber worker, applauded the Italians and welcomed the opportunity to create a more unified labour movement. The strike, he said, had revealed the deep-rooted grievances of immigrants and antiquated labour laws, and it had served to bring together major segments of the union movement. Reiterating this argument, another worker added, "the immigrants are fighting our fight along with their own."[70]

Daly and Hyatt's interventions also spurred the city's labour leaders to augment their support for the Italian strikers. They were beginning to view the strike as a test case for organizing immigrants across the province. As a gesture of their goodwill, a summit meeting of organized labour was held. It endorsed a harshly worded resolution condemning the Home Builders Association. "What should be deported," it said, "is long hours, low pay, deplorable and dangerous working conditions and the exploitation and cheating of immigrants who wish only to build for themselves and their families a better life in Canada." Various organizations pledged financial support to the strikers who still had no strike fund. The International at last came through with $20,000, donated by affiliated unions that conducted fund-raising campaigns in American cities with substantial Italian populations.[71]

THE STATE INTERVENES

As the atmosphere became more heated and criticism of Daly in the legislature grew more intense, Premier Frost made the first of several interventions, appointing an advisory "peace committee" composed of veteran conciliator Louis Fine and two government aides. When the employers were approached, however, Hyatt was dismissive, telling reporters he would not "be caught dead in the same room" with the Italian strikers or their leaders. He also reiterated his deportation request.[72] Frost's initiative was also undermined by the firing of more Local 230 Teamster truck drivers and of labourers who refused to work on subway projects supplied by boycotted ready-mix concrete firms. Gerry Gallagher issued an ominous warning that the commercial Laborers' Local 183 members employed on subway projects were "clamouring to walk out in sympathy strikes." The strike committee openly encouraged the commercial Laborers, who were now facing the expiry of their own collective agreement, to conduct information pickets and to turn back cement supplies at sites along the east-west subway line. More than one hundred labourers and carpenters soon walked off their jobs.[73]

A general strike loomed larger still on the following day when a group of commercial Carpenters, claiming that the employers had failed to bargain in good faith during recent contract renewal talks, triggered another sympathy walkout. Tunnel workers and other labourers followed suit, successfully halting all work on the east-west subway project, except near the Legislative Buildings, where, for safety reasons, work continued. As the old-line unions were in the midst of renewing their contracts and hoped to extract maximum concessions from their employers, their own interests converged with those of the Brandon group. Irvine and Zanini exploited the situation, threatening a shutdown of the entire industry unless ready-mix concrete firms agreed to stop supplying house and apartment sites and fired Teamsters were reinstated.[74]

At this point in the fourteen-day-old strike, Frost intervened again, announcing a formula for settling the affair. The "peace plan," as it came to be called, was a three-pronged program providing for more inspectors to investigate violations of labour standards legislation, a royal commission to investigate labour relations in the industry, and a special arbitration board to adjudicate the alleged violations of collective agreements that had occurred over the previous year. Both parties approved Frost's proposal in principle. The strike leaders publicly admitted that the plan, if accepted, might be an important first step towards a final resolution to the strike. Anthony Lisanti, chief spokesman for the small contractors, also conceded that the plan could lead to improved relations within the industry. However, neither side was willing to commit itself publicly to endorsing the plan.[75]

According to several sources, Frost had been given quiet assurances by Irvine and Zanini that they would advise their membership to return to work if such a plan were introduced. Frost had hosted private meetings with strike leaders, in the course of which Irvine and Zanini had agreed that in exchange for the peace plan they would call an end to the strike. However, they neither honoured the agreement nor informed the membership of it. Instead, they returned to the rank and file and declared the new plan signalled imminent victory, as long as the men stuck to their guns and stayed out on strike. Saying only that vague promises had been offered, Irvine and Zanini told the men that "to-day is a memorable day," for the strikers had succeeded in gaining the premier's attention. Urging the men to keep up the fight, Irvine ended the rally with the following call: "Our pickets tomorrow will be bigger and better and will continue that way until everyone in the housing field, from the hole in the ground to the shingle on the roof, is organized."[76]

Despite Frost's intervention, the strike gained momentum as walkouts spread throughout the commercial, industrial, and engineering sectors. On subway sites, dozens of Carpenters, Iron Workers, Bricklayers, Masons, and Laborers downed their tools and joined flying squads. By week four, more than 15,000 men were out. Meantime, negotiations with residential contractors remained stalled as employers still refused to accept the Frost plan's stipulation that contract violations committed over the previous year be subjected to a special arbitration board. The Toronto Builders Exchange rejected an offer by Local 183 (Laborers) to return to work in exchange for dropping lawsuits filed against Gallagher. Matters became still more heated as Irvine turned to the Teamsters' controversial American president, Jimmy Hoffa, who agreed to help by ordering Toronto's Local 230 truck drivers to boycott all the picketed projects. Next day, Teamsters truckers "roamed the suburbs," forcing back recalcitrant drivers delivering supplies to picketed sites.[77]

Government and law enforcement authorities now intervened. With Daly's support, on 20 June, Attorney-General Kelso Roberts ordered a major crackdown on the strike violence and placed provincial police at the disposal of municipal authorities. Police officers seemed determined to enforce the "get tough" policy as dozens of cruisers, motorcycles, and mounted police hit the streets. George Elliott, the deputy police chief for Toronto, told reporters that he had instructed his men to pick up strikers involved in disturbances of any kind, and similar directions were given in suburban police divisions. Putting it bluntly, Etobicoke chief Wilf McClelland publicly pledged: "We're going to take them up by the truckload and dump them in the Don [jail]." By late morning more than one hundred strikers had been arrested. As Drea observed, this was the largest number of strike-related arrests since the celebrated CIO strikes of the 1930s.[78]

The dispute spread still further as strikers picketed road-repair work on the Gardiner Expressway and projects at the city's airport and at a downtown hospital (Mount Sinai) to protest the contractors' use of ready-mix concrete materials from suppliers who had crossed picket lines. Squabbles between commercial subway workers and the Toronto Transit Commission (TTC) again broke out over the use of emergency crews to complete tunnelling sections beneath the Legislative Buildings. Members of the commercial Laborers' Local 183 were furious with the TTC for allowing the crews to continue working on the site well past the point of the emergency. By week five, the number of men on strike exceeded 15,000. Meantime, six firms with subway contracts launched lawsuits against Irvine, Gallagher, and the strike committee for damages incurred due to alleged interference with their businesses. They also sought injunctions against picketing certain contracts on the subway.[79]

Once again bypassing his labour minister, Premier Frost intervened in the twenty-two-day strike by calling for an emergency meeting of government representatives and strike leaders. The MTHB rejected the initiative and labelled Frost a Teamster sympathizer. Moreover, even as strike leaders agreed to meet with Frost, they forged ahead with plans to extend the strike onto various public utilities projects in the hopes of adding another 12,000 men to the campaign. Police chiefs continued to call out even more enforcements. "Arrests will be made," vowed Deputy Chief Elliott, "as long as groups of men roam the city and terrorize other workers, contractors, and citizens."[80]

Police authorities did suffer one embarrassing setback. A Metro police commissioner expressed concern about a group of strikers arrested in Etobicoke who spent the night in jail because they could not meet bail. The men had been asked to supply information about their nationality and length of residence in Canada. Anticipating cries of police discrimination, the Attorney-General's Office gave assurances that police officers would "show impartiality" in their handling of Italian strikers. But this did little to quell the anger of workers who, as one man put it, deeply resented being treated "like hooligans." Significantly, the issue also prompted Italian community leaders to come to the defence of the strikers. With the exception of Lombardi, who as a gesture of goodwill had attended the kick-off rally, most of the community's well-known public personalities had kept a low profile during this strike. Now, several of them, including city alderman Joseph Piccininni, publicly criticized the treatment of the men at the Toronto jail and demanded that the strikers be accorded the same treatment as Canadian citizens.[81]

Controversy then shifted to the courts as Stefanini, the business agent for Local 183 (Laborers) arrested on obstruction charges, received an unexpectedly harsh sentence of six months. Since his arrest, rumours had spread that the police had set out to arrest a high-profile figure in the strike. According to police testimony, he had led a group of strikers coercing workers on the job and had not dispersed the group when ordered to do so by police. When asked by Stefanini's lawyer how the arresting police officials would understand his client's alleged orders, since he had spoken in Italian, the officer in the witness stand said nothing. The crown counsel had requested a jail term on the grounds that a fine was insufficient punishment for a strike leader who had openly encouraged intimidation of nonstrikers. Magistrate W.F.B. Rogers agreed. In sentencing Stefanini to six months, he declared he was using him as an example to deter others. Evidently, even crown counsel was surprised by the length of sentence. It was, moreover, a definite blow to the strikers, who worried about the hundred men about to face trial during the next few weeks.[82]

The mounting violence and arrests, coupled with the threats of a general strike, translated into declining support from the mainstream English-language papers, which now began calling for an end to what the *Globe and Mail* dubbed the "growing anarchy of organized labour." By contrast, the left-wing press, including the *Tribune*, the organ of the Communist Party of Canada, and *Il Lavoratore*, a small Italian radical paper, consistently supported the strike.[83] The decline in support in the mainstream English press, however, was matched by more aggressive support in the mainstream Italian press. Since the deportation affair, the editors of *Corriere Canadese*, especially

Grohovaz, had taken an increasingly militant stance in favour of the strike. In response to Hyatt's call for deportation, Grohovaz had begun to speak about the necessity for unions to protect workers. Grohovaz was also responding to the concerns of his readers, many of whom were expressing fears that the strike was providing nativists with the opportunity to mount a smear campaign against Italians. Indeed, what most troubled Grohovaz and his colleague, Tino Baxa, was that it had taken so little to stir up nativist sentiments. A minor outburst at a local soccer game, they noted, had led to charges that Italians were "a revolutionary brigade whose aim is conquer the city with fire and iron." In response, the editors argued that it had become incumbent on all Italians to support the strikers. In an editorial that appeared in the *Telegram*, Grohovaz maintained: "The battle of the Italian workers has now become our battle. We must not give in, not even an inch, because now the strike is not only a labor dispute but involves us all in the defense of the inalienable rights of the Italian immigrants."[84]

As the morale of the Italian strikers began to flag, strike leaders planned the huge solidarity rally of 26 June. They hoped to draw building tradesmen from all sectors of the industry in a significant show of support for the striking workers. In the event of a successful rally, the committee was prepared to consider an industry-wide sympathy strike. The organizing committee launched an extensive publicity campaign and booked the CNE Grandstand for the event. They were not disappointed: estimates of attendance ran from 16,000 to 17,500, well over the anticipated numbers.

Familiar faces appeared on stage: Irvine, Zanini, Gallagher, Jenovese, Archer, William Sefton, president of the city's Trades and Labour Council, and other members of Toronto's labour establishment. Also present was a multi-denominational committee of religious leaders organized by Frost to investigate the strike. Among the supporters in attendance was a contingent of striking Royal York Hotel workers and hundreds of Italian construction workers employed outside the housing field. In booming voices, labour leaders addressed the huge crowd, congratulating the men on the turnout and predicting victory. Demands for Stefanini's release drew the largest response of all. (Though later released on bail, he would lose the appeal and serve the sentence.) The rally ended with Irvine's promise to forge ahead with negotiations scheduled for that afternoon. Drea described the event as "the greatest rank and file rally in the history of the Canadian labour movement."[85]

The talks involving masonry contractors and bricklayers were proceeding well, largely because of the conciliatory stance adopted by

Lawrence Eden, manager of the Canadian Masonry Association. A significant breakthrough occurred a few days later when both sides agreed to a tentative settlement. If accepted, it promised to provide the basis for other contracts. While there was as yet no clause regarding back pay, the agreement provided for a series of pay increases that would restore the rates incorporated in the previous year's contract. It also included the checkoff (employers' agreement to deduct union dues directly from their employees' paycheques and submit the funds to the union). The employers had accepted the authority of Frost's special arbitration board. Moved by this dramatic change of events, the strike committee was now convinced of a speedy end to the strike. As other trade negotiations began, various strikers in the commercial field voted to return to work. Members of the organizing committee abandoned the idea of a general strike. They anticipated a resolution to the disputes as soon as employers signed a master agreement covering all the trades in the field. By Thursday, 29 June, Brandon leaders were promising to have their men back at work on Monday.[86]

Then, suddenly, the atmosphere reverted to extreme animosity after meetings between employers and the striking subway Carpenters and Laborers. The emergency sessions had been organized by the Building Trades Council following the disturbing news that men were beginning to trickle back to work. These men believed that the council had not made sufficient effort to reach a settlement with employers in the commercial sector. The action came as a blow to strike leaders, especially Gallagher, who had spearheaded the subway workers' walkouts. As more workers followed, the council endorsed a general sympathy strike as the only means to save the situation.[87]

To show their contempt for this move, commercial employers with subway contracts applied for court injunctions against strike leaders on charges of counselling workers to engage in an illegal strike and creating a nuisance at the picketed projects. Included were Gallagher, Zanini, Colantonio, and Frank Scanlon, an organizer for the painters. Meantime, cracks in the rank-and-file forces of the commercial workers continued to widen as more of them buckled under employer pressure to return to work. This division was evident at a rally that drew 10,000 men, but few from the commercial sector.[88]

Soon, more of the unions in the commercial sector opted to go back to their jobs following assurances from employers that negotiations for contract renewals would start immediately on their return to work. With Frost's special arbitration tribunal now established, they were also convinced the machinery had been set in place for addressing past grievances. Workers returned to subway, telephone, and hydro sites; they resumed work on the Gardiner Expressway, the airport, and sewage projects. Only a militant core of Laborers employed on subway projects challenged this action, but in the end they too returned to work. As a token of their continuing support for the residential workers still on strike, each of the commercial locals donated funds.

Irvine and his colleagues did little to hide their annoyance with this turn of events. They also challenged those workers from the Brandon locals who had begun trickling back to work. At a rally, Irvine caustically described the latter as "mice – or rather rats," and the membership of the commercial unions as "fat and complacent." Those who believed that the special arbitration board or even the royal commission would operate in their favour were "misguided." In his view, such blind optimism betrayed an ignorance of the fact that the restrictive labour laws under attack had been legislated by the same Conservative administration. The only way to secure a real victory, he maintained, was to build strong unions to act as watch-dogs.[89]

Notwithstanding these comments, Brandon leaders worried that the workers, financially hard-pressed after twenty-three days on strike, could not endure much longer. Once again, the men had not earned regular strike pay. Occasional donations had come from the International headquarters of participating unions and from within the colony. Although the small groups of Italian radicals had never been formally involved with the strike – Irvine and Zanini had refused support from both the Communist party and the New Democratic Party – they contributed some funds. Efforts to solicit contributions from the Canadian Labour Congress and other unions produced disappointing results.[90]

The strike had placed heavy financial strains on the families of the striking men. Without the benefit of regular strike pay, workers relied heavily on their families and kin for support. The traditions of sharing and reciprocity among Italian immigrants enabled the casualties of the conflict – those who lost their homes by defaulting on mortgage payments or who could no longer afford to pay the rent – to seek aid from relatives and paesani. Kin networks of support flourished among striking families, as they aided each other by sharing resources and by taking in relatives who had been forced from their homes.

Most of this support work was done by women. Italian women did not play a public role in the strikes; they neither set up sympathy pickets nor attended rallies. Their absence reflected in part the logistics involved in waging a construction strike, for women could hardly be expected to bring supplies to men scattered across a large metropolitan area. It also reflected prevailing cultural norms among Italian men regarding women's proper place. Nevertheless, for many men, the decision to go on strike had been made in consultation with their wives. It was the women, moreover, who found ways to feed and clothe the family and pay bills on a much reduced income. One woman, the wife of a Brandon organizer who at that time had two children at home, summed up this fact in a few words: "It was a hard time, thinking for the children, worrying about the money. But I supported my husband, he was doing good things to help Italian workers, to help ourselves." Husbands also recognized the hardships their wives tolerated. "The women suffered a lot too," recalled Abate, "watching the kids, going for weeks without money or benefits." Nevertheless, they saw the strikes as their battle and the public streets as their battleground. The strikes were a male affair and the men, whether married or single, saw themselves as defenders of their families as well as fighters for justice.[91]

Many Italian women also actively supported their husbands and families by taking on extra paid work. The strike placed additional strains on wage-earning wives, some of whom put in long hours of overtime to increase the family paycheque. Still other wives were pushed into the work force as a result of the strike. Fortunately, for them, they could rely on kin to handle childcare and other arrangements. In her interviews with striking families, *Telegram* columnist Rosemary Boxer found that the wives' wages were supporting their families. Ironically, their desperate situation had forced them to tolerate substandard wages. One of Boxer's informants included a woman employed as a steampress operator in a laundry. She claimed she was not receiving the full wages owed her. "With her husband on strike and children to be fed," noted Boxer, "she just had to put up with it."[92]

Notwithstanding the efforts of wage-earning wives and, to a lesser extent, sisters and daughters, many families were in dire straits as the strike entered its sixth week. The urgency of the strikers' economic situation was made worse by reports that some of the commercial Bricklayers were completing a few of the residential projects that had been abandoned at the start of the strike. These matters prompted Marino Toppan to ask the Washington headquarters of the Bricklayers to order members of the commercial sector to stay away from picketed sites and to approve a substantial strike fund for the Italian strikers. "I am sure," he wrote, "that with the effort of all the men of good will and with the support of all the unions we are going to win but meantime we have hundreds of people begging for their hungry children. Please help these people that started the strike six weeks ago when still suffering the consequences of a long and frustrating winter."[93] The concern for the strikers' welfare may also partially explain why, at some risk to the reputation of his membership, Irvine again sought help from the powerful Teamsters' union. Irvine attended the Teamsters' annual conference in Miami Beach, Florida, where he formally requested financial aid. Union boss Jimmy Hoffa agreed to donate some funds, though the total was not revealed.[94]

THE FINAL STRETCH

If strikers were feeling the pinch, so, too, were the subcontractors. For days, the central obstacle to a settlement had continued to be the unwillingness of most contractors to accept the special arbitration board. Only the Masonry Contractors Association, which represented the trades in the bricklaying and masonry field, had agreed in principle to the board, and even within that organization there were dissenting voices. Now, however, other trade associations resumed negotiations. Shortly afterwards, tentative agreements were reached with all but three of the trade contractors' groups; the plaster, concrete and drain, and carpentry employers remained recalcitrant.[95]

In the midst of these developments, strikers had another setback when the special court set up under Frost to try strike-related cases convicted 51 out of 106 strikers; they received sentences ranging from small fines to jail terms of five to ten days. Convicted of causing property damage, for instance, were four Italian men who went before the judge in mid-July, each of whom received a five-day sentence. In his closing remarks, Judge James Butler did not comment on the compelling reasons that had prompted the men to strike. Rather, he declared: "The property of other people in this country is sacred and must be treated as such." Although workers were relieved that none of the men had received a sentence as stiff as Stefanini's, the high rate of convictions was still disturbing. This distressing news, however, was partially offset by Butler's conviction of four contractors for failing to give workers their vacation pay. They received fines totalling $350.[96]

As the court proceedings continued, another small but important breakthrough in talks occurred as the Bricklayers became the first trade to sign an agreement. It was expected that this contract, which included the checkoff, would provide a formula for the remaining trades. Almost immediately, however, several concrete and drain employers seriously affected by the Teamsters' refusal to deliver supplies broke off talks with the Plasterers. Lather contractors followed suit.[97]

Then, unexpectedly, on 15 July, the strike committee announced an end to the strike and instructed workers to report to a victory rally the next day before resuming work on Monday. Coming only two days after talks with hold-out employers had broken down, the announcement was a great surprise to rank-and-file workers. During emergency meetings held during the previous two days, recalcitrant contractors had accepted a compromise settlement based on a modified interpretation of the Frost plan. Union negotiators had been so keen to end the strike they compromised on what until then had been considered a noncompromise demand – checkoff. It was agreed that checkoff would be temporarily dropped from the agenda until contract negotiations reached the final stage of settlement. Amid the excitement generated by this news, little press attention was paid to the terms of contracts under negotiation, the rash of firings of Teamster truckers, or the walkout by a group of hoisting engineers at a major apartment project. Nor did reporters make much of the fact that the decision to end the strike had not been ratified by a vote of the membership; rather, Irvine and Zanini had simply announced that the strike had ended.[98]

On Sunday, 16 July, leaders staged the rally marking the conclusion of the fifty-one-day residential strike. Strike committee members applauded the efforts of workers, telling them to take pride in the fact they had crippled an industry worth millions of dollars, taken on powerful employers, and brought to the attention of everyone the plight of exploited Italian workers in Canada. "This is the day you can become men again and Canadian citizens," said Irvine. "You have a place in this country now and you can keep it. But remember that the next man that gets off the boat will not be treated as you are going to be treated now, so it's up to you to get new men into the union."

As he spoke, no cheers came from the crowd of 2000, only confused stares. No details of the contracts were divulged. In fact, firm settlements had not yet been reached with the three hold-out trades. Into the awkward silence, Zanini said vaguely, "We got everything we wanted plus the machinery to enforce it." Exasperated by the cool reception, he finally exclaimed: "Fellows, you don't realize the value of the good news you've just heard. Come on, what we won is great and I want you to be happy about it." It was only then that the workers broke into applause. The *Star* reported that the first embarrassing moments ended as the men "leapt to their feet, grinning, cheering, some with the hands clasped above their heads like boxing champions." At the conclusion of the meeting, the crowd surged forward and hoisted Zanini and other union officials head high in a march of triumph.[99]

The abrupt manner in which the strike ended, one could argue, betrayed the authoritarian character of Irvine and Zanini's leadership.[100] Irvine and Zanini had been able to maintain fairly tight control over both walkouts. As the events just covered suggest, they had not made it a priority to ask for direction from the rank and file. Yet, there is little doubt that during the turbulent events of 1960 and 1961 the two men had commanded tremendous respect and trust from immigrant workers who believed they possessed the aggressive leadership and other skills required to carry out the strikes. In the short term, at least, they successfully galvanized the growing militancy of Italian construction workers and gave it direction and organization. For their part, the striking Italian immigrant workers, despite their inexperience in labour disputes, had spearheaded two major organizing drives in the residential construction industry. So doing, they had exhibited enormous resourcefulness and fortitude, and had earned themselves respect from organized labour.

The 1961 strike produced some tangible and immediate gains, leading the CLC's chief organ, *Canadian Labour*, which had remained silent during the entire campaign, to herald the strike as a major victory for Toronto's construction workers. The collective agreements largely mirrored the contracts that had been signed at the end of the previous strike. They provided for a gradual increase in wages that ranged from $2.00 per hour for labourers to $3.05 for bricklayers. Rollbacks had been prevented. Only the bricklayers had secured the checkoff, however, and this second campaign, though more threatening than the first, had again failed to organize the majority of men employed by the large firms in the field. Approximately one-third of the residential firms had signed contracts, but most were small and medium-sized companies. Frost's own promises to encourage further unionization among employers carried little weight, especially with the announcement of his retirement shortly after the strike.[101]

THE AFTERMATH

What were the long-term consequences of these campaigns? The strikes spawned a royal commission, and its recommendations provided a basis for subsequent investigations and labour reform within the industry. In June 1961 Carl Goldenberg, a veteran labour mediator from Montreal, was appointed commissioner. He tabled his report one year later. Brandon workers welcomed it, for despite the cautious tone and the criticism of their illegal actions, it confirmed two of their major claims: the exploitation of immigrants in the housing field and the need for special legislative reforms. Overriding the claims of an unrepentant MTHBA, which blamed the strikes on union leaders, Goldenberg found that employer abuses had been an underlying factor in the strikes. In accounting for the abuses he also echoed the views of Brandon leaders, noting that "the surplus labour market offered ample opportunity to certain builders and contractors to take advantage of the needs, fears, and the limited experience in Canada of the immigrant labourer."[102]

Many of the commission's recommendations involved legislative reforms designed to meet the special needs of the industry, such as the provision for a special panel of construction experts to be added to the Labour Relations Board. Among the most important suggestions were those intended to expedite both certification and conciliation procedures. To speed up the former, Goldenberg proposed the appointment of hearing officers and suggested that the construction panel be authorized to grant interim certification without public hearing on the basis of field investigations conducted by the hearing officers. In order to avoid serious delays in the bargaining process, various changes were proposed, the most important of which would have eliminated the first part of the province's compulsory two-stage procedure. Goldenberg also proposed methods for the speedy arbitration of grievance cases and advocated a successor rights law allowing for the transfer of certification rights in cases where a firm was sold, leased, or transferred. Finally, in the area of protective legislation, he recommended a minimum wage, higher vacation pay, stricter safety provisions, a national joint board for settling jurisdictional disputes, and a registry of contractors.

Eventually, many of these recommendations were introduced, though subsequent developments and inquiries also contributed to the reform process. In the late 1960s another series of explosive union drives in the high-rise apartment field, where technological change was an issue, led to a second royal commission. Still, the 1962 commission was an important breakthrough in the area of government reform of the industry. Thus, the immigrant strikes led to long-term improvements in the material conditions and the collective bargaining rights of construction workers.[103]

A more immediate consequence of the strikes involved the continuing efforts of Italian workers and their allies to build on their new union base. The Brandon and old-line unions had joined forces in an effort to recruit "New Canadians" into the five residential locals represented by the Brandon Group. The council had also aimed at organizing Italian immigrants in other residential trades, in trades in the commercial and industrial field, and in road-building and paving. In the period immediately following 1961, they continued their efforts. Where Brandon locals did not exist, residential workers joined residential sections within the old-line unions. In carrying out the drives, more immigrant organizers were hired and efforts were made to recruit non-Italian immigrants in the field, most of whom were Germans and East Europeans. As the council and its member unions played a larger role among residential workers, the Brandon Group, suffering from financial problems and from internal divisions that appear to have stemmed in part from the growing dissatisfaction of local organizers and rank and file workers over the lack of democratic procedures within the organization, went into swift decline. In 1963 the group lost the crucial Bricklayers, who were fed up with repeated requests to strike in order to enforce other unions' contracts. The labourers soon followed suit, and by the end of the year the organization had effectively crumbled. [104]

By the early 1960s many contractors and workers realized that the only hope for long-term stability in the construction trades was to find a way to impose standard wages and hours on all workers and workplaces, whether or not they were unionized. The Bricklayers believed they found a way to do so in 1963. The Masonry Contractors Association and a large group of residential and commercial bricklayers successfully lobbied the provincial government, persuading the minister of labour to use his authority under the Industrial Standards Act to make it mandatory for all contractors and bricklayers in Metropolitan Toronto to abide by the terms of the union agreement (except the provision regarding the closed shop). In the eyes of some of the former Brandon organizers, including Frank Colantonio, a strong proponent of the move, it proved "a blessing all along, not only to the bricklayers themselves, but to the hundreds of legitimate and fair-minded Masonry contractors who employ them."

While the 1960 and 1961 campaigns did have long-lasting repercussions for the industry and the labour movement, it is also true that they were historic events that emerged out of the particular set of conditions that had prevailed in the two decades following the Second World War. Within less than a decade, the union structures within the construction trades in Toronto, as elsewhere, would be fundamentally challenged by technological changes in building. Beginning in the mid-1960s, developments associated with drywalling and concrete-forming challenged the skills and relative clout of unions in certain trades. A series of complex jurisdictional disputes arose, which in turn offered opportunities for new union drives. Thus began another chapter in the often turbulent labour history of Toronto's construction industry. [105]

Finally, though more difficult to pinpoint, the strikes both directly and indirectly likely solidified class differences within the Italian community in Toronto. The campaigns probably helped to draw more distinct lines between, for example, those prominent community leaders and others who were supporters of the Liberal party and those strikers and other workers who, during the years following the strikes, joined the labour movement and the NPD. Even the majority of Italian construction workers – who were probably not NDP supporters in the early 1960s – gained more political influence as immigrant workers with specific needs and demands. Their clout was evident, for instance, in the federal government's approval of funds to help establish COSTI, the retraining and rehabilitation program for Italian workers. The activism of some Italian construction workers was evident much later still with the formation of the Union of Injured Workers.

The immigrant strikes occured at a critical juncture in the history of Toronto's Italian immigrant workers and their families. For many of the men who participated in the campaign, the strikes marked the end of the greenhorn phase of immigration. They also marked the political awakening of a work force of relatively recent immigrants, most of whom were former peasants or village artisans who did not come from a trade-union background. Thus, the strikes also offer a particularly dramatic illustration of the transition that many Italian immigrants made from peasants to proletarians. For most immigrants who arrived in Toronto during the 1950s, the immigrant experience was largely working class. Both as immigrants and as workers, the strikers had engaged in major battles to end their exploitation. They had surprised everyone with their tremendous grassroots militancy and their capacity to endure lengthy disputes without benefit of formal strike funds. That militancy grew out of the peculiar combination of a shared Old World class and cultural background and a shared class and ethnic experience in postwar Toronto, and it took place within the context of an industry dominated by Italians. Furthermore, the fact that Italian workers ignored the bureaucratic restrictions on their right to strike and supported two illegal campaigns also reminds us that the postwar industrial relations system failed to contain spontaneity.[106]

The strikes not only offer a graphic illustration of immigrant militancy; they also shed light on how class, ethnicity, and gender shaped the Italian immigrant experience. The strikes were a multilayered drama in which the main actors were simultaneously men, immigrants, and workers. The union meetings were rowdy affairs; they took place in crowded, smoke-filled rooms that only men attended, and the actual organizing occurred on construction sites and in the billiard halls, cafés, and parks that Italian men frequented. Moreover, in taking part in the strikes, Italian men saw themselves as defending their own honour and the honour of their wives and children. It was simultaneously an immigrant drama; not only was the Italian language spoken at the meetings, but the strikers explained their actions as those of hard-working immigrants striving to improve the quality of their lives and those of their families. The mass rallies, unorthodox leaders, brick-throwing, and police round-ups made for a vivid working-class drama.

In the context of Canadian labour history, the strikes provide an intriguing example of immigrant influence on business unionism. As workers, these strikers had fought for job-centred demands that fit comfortably within the tradition of bread-and-butter unionism in the construction trades. As Italian immigrants, however, the strikers had chosen charismatic leaders and opted for an informal union structure (the Brandon Group) that met their needs but marked departures from patterns in the industry. Moreover, by calling for rights as Canadians, the strikers had raised a wider, democratic issue that challenged immigrant exploitation and went beyond workplace issues. Such a demand, when coupled with picket-line militancy, defiance of certification laws, jailings, and talk of deportation, gave the strikes a sharp political and social edge.[107]

Conclusion

Like their compatriots from Italy's less notoriously depressed regions, southern Italians came to postwar Toronto to make a better life for themselves and their families. They were prepared to toil at unattractive jobs, to make plenty of sacrifices, and to pursue a variety of financial strategies, including homeownership, in order to attain a degree of security. The majority of newcomers had been peasants long accustomed to earning a livelihood from highly fragmented and inferior landholdings and long victimized by an exploitative land tenure system. In short, Italians were no strangers to hard work. Nor were they strangers to living under conditions of scarcity. Within the declining economy of southern Italy their efforts had often gone unrewarded, but in Toronto's booming postwar economy many immigrants successfully exploited the new work and living opportunities available to them and achieved their goals.

In contrast to a previous era, when the immigrants had made the ocean voyage in steerage and had found few forms of support outside their own kin and community structures, the postwar Italians benefited enormously from a vastly improved transportation system and had access to an impressive range of social and welfare services. They were particularly fortunate in this latter regard because their ability to develop self-help structures had been weakened by the fascists' prohibitions on the kinds of volunteer associations that had provided models for prewar immigrants. Finally, a far larger proportion of Canada's postwar Italians came with the intention of settling permanently, and the vast majority eventually did so.

In many other respects, however, the postwar Italians, especially those who arrived before 1965, closely resembled earlier generations of southern Italians who had traded an uncertain future at home for better prospects abroad. This was true not only with respect to their regional background and religious outlook, but also with regard to the labouring role many of them played in Canada's postwar economy. As in the past, postwar Italian immigration was initially associated with the importation of a foreign, industrial proletariate. In the years immediately following the Second World War, Canadian government officials and employers alike had expected the Italians to work in industries suffering from acute labour shortages or to fill jobs shunned by Canadian workers. For their part, the immigrants responded eagerly to the job opportunities and displayed a remarkable resiliency in Toronto's often fluctuating and increasingly oversupplied labour market. Italian men played a crucial part in the city's phenomenal construction boom, while thousands of Italian women provided the fresh recruits for the city's army of female factory operatives, industrial home-sewers, and domestics.

As scholars of Italian migration to North America have regularly observed, the reality of life in southern Italy, and the strategies developed for coping with it, had oriented people to a cooperatist value system in which it was assumed that all family members must contribute their labour power to ensure the economic well-being of the family. Moreover, Italian peasants had grown highly resourceful at combining a wide range of income-generating activities to augment the farm income and sustain a family living. Their work traditions served the immigrants extremely well as they settled in early postwar Toronto. Throughout the 1950s and early 1960s the task of finding a job, of minding the children while mothers worked outside the home, and of purchasing a home were handled effectively within the context of family and kinship networks. Still, as immigrants with few financial resources, they could not expect in these early years to find in these networks of support all the solutions to their problems. Thus, the immigrants also looked beyond their multiple family households. In times of economic need, they tapped the city's various social agencies, and, in an effort to defend their interests and improve their standard of living, many of them joined unions and some also engaged in strikes. At the same time, they found ways of recreating their culture and community life in the neighbourhoods, churches, cafés, and other popular gathering places of Toronto's Little Italies.

The world of southern Italian immigrants in early postwar Toronto cannot simply be described as the transplanted family and work worlds of the old paese, for in many respects the process of migration and immigration profoundly changed the immigrants' lives, sometimes in different ways for men and women. Furthermore, their transition from the hill towns of the Mezzogiorno to the factories and construction sites of Toronto was not an entirely smooth or linear process. Even for the most successful immigrants, the early immigrant years brought a series of hardships and often painful adjustments. In any analysis of how immigrant families withstood New World pressures and carved out their lives in the host society, it ought to be remembered that success was sometimes achieved at considerable emotional and physical cost. The memories of Italian construction workers are filled with painful stories of the deaths or injuries of relatives, paesani, and co-workers. Victims of workplace accidents – described by community activist Tony Grande as "our walking wounded"[1] – continue to struggle for better social security benefits. In their recollections, Italian women recall vividly the early days of "pounding the pavement" in search of jobs, the double day of labour, and their resentment of the way employers treated them like children because they could not speak English. Still others suffered the indignity of being called a "wop" or having a social worker intrude into their homes and pass judgment on how they lived.

Ultimately, the early immigrant experiences of the Italians who came to Toronto in the years 1945–65 need to be compared with those of Italians in other Canadian locales and with those of postwar immigrants from other countries. Despite their numerical strength, the postwar Italians have not until very recently attracted the attention of scholars, save for a small group of social scientists and demographers who have been primarily interested in questions of class mobility. Like most historical studies of Italians, this book has focused on the southerners who made up the majority of Canada's, and Toronto's, postwar Italians. There is a real need for historians of Italian migration to redress the lack of attention paid to the non-southern Italian, and for meaningful comparisons to be made between the southern emigrants and their compatriots who hailed from the northern and central regions of Italy.[2]

Until more historical studies of postwar immigrants in Toronto become available, it will be equally difficult to make any valuable historical comparisons between the experiences and adjustment patterns of different immigrant groups. There are some obvious parallels between the Italians and certain other European groups that will one day need to be addressed more fully. For instance, many postwar Portuguese immigrants hailed from rural societies and sought industrial jobs in large Canadian cities such as Toronto. Many of the earliest Portuguese arrivals also came as contract workers and they, too, developed extensive chain-migration patterns. Most of the Portuguese, however, came from fishing rather than agricultural backgrounds and a larger proportion of them arrived in the 1970s –

that is, a decade after many Italians had established themselves in the city. What did such differences mean? What kind of class and ethnic relations characterized the residential construction industry, for instance, as newly arrived unskilled Portuguese men sought jobs in a sector dominated by earlier waves of Italian immigrants?[3]

These questions, and many others, can only be answered as further research into the immigrant experiences of the postwar arrivals is completed. The current monographs in the federal government's Generation Series are of limited value in developing a comparative approach because of their fundamental weaknesses and omissions. The authors of the Ukrainian volume, for example, admit that the section on the period after the Second World War is confined to a discussion of largely elite-based, political associations.[4] In the Greek and Portuguese volumes, the sections on the postwar era are largely discussions of occupational ranking and language maintenance. The authors of these studies jump quickly from a discussion of the immigrants' arrival in postwar Canada to an analysis of the contemporary position of the immigrant group.[5] Finally, the virtual absence of detailed studies of immigrants who arrived in Canada from the world's developing nations makes it impossible to contrast the Canadian immigrant experiences of the "white ethnics" with those of people of colour.

In the long run, southern Italian immigrants adjusted remarkably well to life in postwar Toronto and made their peace with the host society. As one man, a former peasant who became a certified carpenter and helped to raise two children in this country, reflects: "I didn't mind coming to Canada because it was an immigrants' country. I feel I'm one among other immigrants. Our lives were difficult, and we didn't always get the respect we deserved. But we made something of ourselves too." An Italian woman, who since arriving in Toronto with her husband in 1955 has juggled a variety of seamstress jobs and had two children, reminisces: "When we first leave for Canada, we think, its gonna be great. Especially the big city like Toronto. Work like crazy for a couple of years and then enjoy the life. It wasn't that easy. There was so much to worry about – jobs, what you're going to do for the children. But now, all these years later, we have what we want; not everybody maybe, but lots did. We have a house, lots of food on the table, a good life for our children. So we have to say that coming to Canada was the right thing."[6]

These comments, and those of the dozens of informants and others whose fascinating lives made up the central focus of this study, speak to the multilayered character of the immigrant experience.

The process of adjustment involved hardships and strains. Yet the immigrant experience was not simply a victimizing one. Despite the daily pressures of adjusting to a new life, the immigrants showed a tremendous capacity to pool their resources together and a talent for finding ways to recreate culture and community in the new environment. The immigrant experience of the early postwar era also led to acts of resistance and protest on the part of Italian workers who demanded greater recognition for their efforts and who exercised some choice over how they might live their lives in postwar Canada. The complexity of the lives that immigrants led belies any efforts to set up a dichotomy between the heroic view of immigrants and the victimization thesis; rather, it calls out for an analysis of the dialetic that goes beyond this dualism. While their pre-migration work traditions and culture helped southern Italians to reorient themselves to life in the industrial metropolis of postwar Toronto, so did the new environment lead the immigrants either to modify familiar strategies and rituals or to adopt altogether new ones.

Appendix

Table 1
Postwar Emigration to Italy and Return Migration from Italy[a]

		Emigration to					Return from			
		Eur.	US	Aust.	Canada		US	Can.	Aust.	All[b]
Year	Total	%	%	%	No.	%T[c]	No.	No.	No.	No.
1946	110,286	93	5	–	–	–	315	–	6	4,558
1947	254,144	76	9	–	58	–	3,264	40	1	65,529
1948	308,515	63	5	1	2,406	1	4,785	53	304	119,261
1949	254,469	37	5	4	5,991	2	3,202	76	193	118,626
1950	200,306	27	5	7	7,135	4	4,071	160	258	72,034
1951	293,057	51	4	6	21,467	7	3,660	152	466	91,904
1952	277,535	52	3	10	18,742	8	2,543	471	1132	96,900
1953	224,671	50	4	6	22,610	10	2,653	484	1,940	103,038
1954	250,925	43	10	7	23,440	9	2,701	848	1,623	107,200
1955	296,826	50	12	9	19,282	7	3,607	1,208	1,819	118,583
1956	344,802	60	11	7	28,008	8	5,578	1,271	2,437	155,293
1957	341,733	69	5	5	24,536	7	5,996	2,442	2,773	163,277
1958	255,459	62	10	5	28,502	11	5,987	2,908	3,420	139,038
1959	268,490	81	4	5	23,734	9	1,696	1,223	2,586	156,121
1960	383,908	81	4	5	19,011	5	450	667	1,312	192,235
1961	387,123	85	4	4	13,461	4	420	224	671	210,196
1962	365,611	86	4	4	12,528	3	284	157	521	229,088
1963	277,711	85	5	4	12,912	5	215	79	708	221,150
1964	258,482	84	3	4	17,600	7	351	168	880	190,168
1965	282,643	82	4	4	24,213	9	331	102	559	196,376
1966	296,494	74	10	4	28,591	10	298	58	743	206,486
1967	229,264	73	8	6	12,102	5	790	199	479	169,328
1968	215,713	73	10	7	16,745	8	1,203	337	1,161	150,027
1969	182,199	76	9	5	9,441	5	4,172	5,039	3,679	153,298
1970	151,854	76	10	4	7,249	5	4,422	5,161	3,844	142,503
1971	167,721	79	9	4	6,128	4	5,033	4,440	3,646	128,572
1972	141,852	79	10	3	5,207	4	5,845	4,319	4,257	138,246
1973	123,802	80	9	3	4,078	3	5,924	3,775	4,133	125,168
1974	112,020	78	8	3	4,421	4	5,623	3,001	3,178	116,708
1975	92,666	78	7	3	3,662	4	5,699	2,770	2,454	122,774
1976	97,247	75	7	3	3,586	4	5,541	2,622	2,149	115,997
1977	87,655	74	7	2	2,677	3	5,363	2,764	1,741	101,985
Total	7,535,183	69	7	5	429,523	6	101,022	47,218	55,073	4,421,667

Table 1 – Cont'd
Postwar Emigration to Italy and Return Migration from Italy

Net Migration				Return/Proportion of Emigration				
Period	Total	US	Aust.	Can.	Total	US	Aust.	Can.
1946–51	948,865	56,996	42,781	36,576	33	25	3	1
1952–61	1,589,591	168,896	169,718	209,580	48	15	10	5
1962–71	640,696	148,316	92,854	131,769	74	10	15	11
1972–77	65,636	19,317	901	4,380	110	64	95	82

[a] Condensed version of table in Clifford Jansen and Lee La Cavero, *Fact-Book on Italians in Canada* (York University 1981).

[b] Return migration from the United States, Canada, Australia, and all other countries.

[c] Represents percentage of emigrants that went to Canada.

Table 2
Postwar Immigration from Italy to Canada

Yr	To Canada	From Italy No.	From Italy %	Dependants %T	Dependants %I	Upp. Nm %T	Upp. Nm %I	Lwr. Nm %T	Lwr. Nm %I	Manual %T	Manual %I
1946	71,719	245	0.2	80.0	80.7	14.6	28.6	18.3	28.6	44.6	35.7
1947	64,127	139	0.2	38.0	46.8	7.5	6.8	19.7	37.8	58.2	43.2
1948	125,414	3,202	2.6	40.0	33.9	4.4	2.0	22.7	20.6	66.8	71.2
1949	95,217	7,742	8.1	44.4	33.6	5.0	0.6	18.0	14.7	70.5	80.8
1950	73,912	9,059	12.2	45.7	33.9	5.7	0.5	15.2	12.8	72.0	83.1
1951	194,391	24,351	12.5	41.7	25.4	4.5	0.5	28.2	19.6	63.8	72.9
1952	164,498	21,383	13.0	48.3	39.6	9.6	0.6	25.8	17.7	63.0	81.4
1953	168,868	24,293	14.4	46.0	52.3	11.0	0.9	21.8	15.1	66.1	83.7
1954	154,227	24,595	15.9	45.3	43.8	11.8	0.6	24.1	19.1	63.4	80.2
1955	109,946	20,247	18.4	47.3	49.9	14.8	0.9	21.3	26.1	63.3	72.9
1956	164,857	29,806	18.1	44.8	51.0	11.4	1.1	25.6	30.2	62.6	70.6
1957	282,164	29,443	10.4	46.3	54.7	11.4	1.1	27.3	24.3	60.9	74.4
1958	124,851	28,564	22.9	49.5	54.8	13.5	0.9	22.5	18.9	63.3	79.9
1959	106,928	26,822	25.1	49.9	54.4	14.5	1.1	20.2	18.0	64.5	80.7
1960	104,111	21,308	20.5	48.5	58.8	15.4	1.3	21.3	20.8	62.8	77.7
1961	71,689	14,630	20.4	51.4	57.8	21.8	2.5	20.5	29.2	57.5	68.2
1962	74,586	14,181	19.0	50.7	55.6	25.3	1.8	23.1	31.8	51.5	66.4
1963	93,151	15,884	15.5	50.8	52.6	23.5	2.0	25.6	34.9	50.8	63.0
1964	112,606	19,297	17.1	50.1	54.0	23.5	1.8	30.4	16.1	41.8	80.9
1965	146,758	26,398	18.0	49.4	54.0	24.8	2.3	28.7	14.6	42.8	81.2
1966	194,743	31,625	16.2	49.0	53.8	26.2	3.7	27.2	10.8	42.8	82.5
1967	222,876	30,055	13.5	46.4	51.5	28.3	4.8	27.3	13.5	41.1	78.9
1968	183,974	19,774	10.7	48.1	52.1	33.1	4.8	27.6	14.6	35.3	76.3
1969	161,531	10,383	6.4	47.8	51.9	34.9	7.5	30.2	16.4	31.6	72.8
1970	147,713	8,533	5.8	47.4	53.8	32.8	10.5	30.7	16.0	33.3	70.9
1971	121,900	5,790	4.7	49.7	57.4	32.3	9.6	31.9	15.4	31.8	72.2
1972	122,606	4,608	3.8	51.3	53.5	33.0	7.4	30.9	16.3	32.1	73.3
1973	184,200	5,468	3.0	49.9	54.2	26.6	6.6	32.8	18.1	36.9	73.1
1974	218,465	5,226	2.4	51.4	55.7	26.6	6.8	28.6	14.2	41.8	75.8
1975	187,881	5,078	2.7	56.8	62.1	31.7	20.1	27.3	16.8	38.7	61.7
1976	149,429	4,530	3.0	58.9	61.1	32.8	37.8	28.7	13.4	36.3	47.4
1977	114,914	3,411	3.0	58.6	60.3	31.8	29.4	29.3	16.6	36.1	51.8
1978	86,313	2,976	3.4	59.2	53.7	30.1	21.1	29.0	18.0	38.0	58.4
Total	4,599,965	498,946	10.8	49.2	50.9	20.4	2.8	26.3	18.1	50.3	76.9

Note: T = total; I = Italians; for 1946–61 Upper Non-manual = managers and professional technical workers; Lower Non-manual = trades and service workers; Manual = semi- and unskilled workers; for 1962–78 Upper Non-manual = managers, professionals in sciences, religion, medicine, teaching, except agricultural; Lower Non-manual = clerical sales and services; Manual = remaining occupations except agriculture. Condensed version of table compiled by Jansen and La Cavera, *Fact-Book on Italians in Canada* from data in L. Parai, *Immigration and Emigration of Professional and Skilled Manpower in the Post-War Period* (Ottawa 1965); Department of Manpower and Immigration, *Immigration* (Ottawa 1962–78).

Table 3
Italian Immigration to Canada: Destination, 1952–61

Fiscal Year-end	Total	Ontario	%	Quebec	%	BC	%
31 March 1952	28,402	17,333	61.0	8,815	31.0	1,283	4.5
31 March 1953	18,016	11,283	62.6	4,998	27.7	1,025	5.7
31 March 1954	27,477	18,019	65.6	6,722	24.5	1,335	4.9
31 Mar.–31 Dec. 1954	24,595	15,289	62.2	6,061	24.6	1,103	4.5
Calendar 1955	20,247	12,596	62.2	5,118	25.3	1,116	5.5
Calendar 1956	29,806	18,586	62.4	7,509	25.2	2,020	6.8
Calendar 1957	29,443	17,108	58.1	8,558	29.1	1,958	6.7
Calendar 1958	28,564	18,280	64.0	7,655	26.8	1,496	5.2
Calendar 1959	26,822	16,818	62.7	7,586	28.3	1,266	4.7
Calendar 1960	21,308	13,074	61.4	6,383	30.0	821	3.9
Calendar 1961	14,630	9,060	61.9	3,914	26.8	796	5.4
Total	269,310	167,446		73,319		14,219	
% of total			62.2		27.2		5.3

Source: Annual Report, Department of Citizenship and Immigration, Statistics Section, 1952–61

Table 4
Italians in Canada and Ontario

		Canada			Ontario		
		Total Population	Italian Ethnic Group	Foreign-Born Italians	Total Population	Italian Ethnic Group	Foreign-Born Italians
1941	Total	11,506,655	112,625[a]	40,432	3,787,655	60,085[a]	21,914
	Male	5,900,536	61,669	25,201	1,921,201	32,604	13,349
	Female	5,606,119	50,956	15,231	1,866,454	27,481	8,565
1951	Total	14,009,429	152,245	57,789	4,597,542	87,622	34,809[b]
	Male	7,088,873	84,914	36,778	2,314,170	48,865	22,012
	Female	6,920,556	67,331	21,011	2,283,372	38,757	12,797
1961	Total	18,238,247	450,351	265,169	6,236,092	273,864	165,576
	Male	9,218,893	240,905	146,266	3,134,528	145,412	90,451
	Female	9,019,354	209,446	118,903	3,101,564	128,452	75,125
1971	Total	21,568,310	730,820	395,880	7,703,105	463,095	259,575
	Male	10,804,130	383,955	212,540	3,843,620	243,135	138,630
	Female	10,764,180	346,865	183,340	3,859,485	219,960	120,945

Source: Canada, *Census*, 1941, 1951, 1961, 1971
[a] Population by racial origin
[b] Refers to Italy as birthplace

Table 5
Foreign-Born Italian Immigration and Population to 1961

| | Total Foreign-Born Italian Population | Period of Immigration | | | | | | Total 1946–61 | % of Total 1946–61 |
		Before 1921	1921–30	1931–45	1946–50	1951–5	1956–61		
CANADA									
Total	265,169	16,637	10,860	3,858	17,526	93,539	122,785	233,850	88.2
Male	146,266	10,555	6,274	1,736	11,640	55,602	60,495	127,737	87.3
Female	118,903	6,082	4,586	2,122	5,886	37,937	62,290	106,113	89.2
METROPOLITAN TORONTO[a]									
Total	96,080	2,879	2,044	833	5,106	36,083	49,139	90,328	94.0
Male	51,989	1,780	1,198	386	3,471	21,482	23,672	48,625	93.5
Female	44,091	1,099	846	447	1,635	14,601	25,467	41,703	94.6

Source: Canada, Census, 1961. The periodization follows the census data.
[a] Census metropolitan area

Table 6
Foreign-Born Italian Immigration and Population to 1971

| | Total Foreign-Born Italian Population | Period of Immigration | | | | | | | Total 1962–71 | % of Total 1946–61 |
		Before 1946	1946–55	1956–60	1961–5	1966–8	1969–71 [a]		
CANADA										
Total	395,880	25,680	106,455	106,120	75,325	62,595	19,705	157,625	39.8
Male	212,540	13,370	64,010	53,665	38,250	33,370	9,875	81,495	38.3
Female	183,340	12,310	42,445	52,455	37,075	29,225	9,830	76,130	41.5
METROPOLITAN TORONTO										
Total	167,735	5,635	41,935	46,360	35,045	30,125	8,635	73,805	44.0
Male	89,145	2,685	25,120	23,230	17,710	16,060	4,340	38,110	42.8
Female	78,590	2,950	16,815	23,130	17,335	14,065	4,295	35,695	45.4

Source: Canada, *Census*, 1971. The periodization follows the census data.
[a] First five months, 1971

Table 7
Italians in Metropolitan Toronto, 1941–71[a]

		Metropolitan Toronto					City of Toronto				
		Total Population	Italian Ethnic Group	% of Total	Foreign-Born Italians	% of Total	Total Population	Italian Ethnic Group	% of Total	Foreign-Born Italians	% of Total
1941	Total	900,491	17,887[b]	2.0	4,870	0.5					
	Male	436,157	9,552	2.2	2,926	0.7					
	Female	464,334	8,335	1.8	1,944	0.4					
1951	Total	1,117,470	27,962[c]	2.5			675,754	18,441	2.7	8,680	1.3
	Male	544,171	NA	0.0			326,050	10,359	3.2	5,489	1.7
	Female	573,299	NA	0.0			349,704	8,082	2.3	3,191	0.9
1961	Total	1,824,481	140,378	7.7	96,072	5.3	672,407	77,898	11.6	58,266	8.7
	Male	903,255	74,185	8.2	51,981	5.8	329,806	41,244	12.5	NA	
	Female	921,226	66,193	7.2	44,091	4.8	342,601	36,654	10.7	NA	
1971	Total	2,628,130	271,755	10.3	167,735	6.4					
	Male	1,301,375	142,265	10.9	89,145	6.9					
	Female	1,326,755	129,490	9.8	78,590	5.9					

Source: Canada, Census, 1941, 1951, 1961, 1971

[a] Census metropolitan area

[b] 1941 refers to population by racial origin

[c] Complete statistics are not available for Metropolitan Toronto

Table 8
Overseas Italian Immigrants: Intended Occupations, Unskilled Labour, 1948–61

	Farm Workers	General Labourers	Domestic Servants
Fiscal Years			
Ending 31 March			
1948–9	1,371	722	N/A
1949–50	2,785	646	N/A
1950–1	9,766	3,961	224
1951–2	8,711	5,243	1,008
1953–4	2,662	6,356	2,113
Calendar Years			
1954	2,200	6,454	1,820
1955	1,621	3,648	1,501
1956	1,541	5,290	2,094
1957	888	5,980	1,970
1958	1,324	6,199	2,779
1959	1,152	6,071	2,057
1960	745	4,094	1,495
1961	93	2,416	1,201

Source: Annual Report, Department of Mines and Resources, 1948–9; Department of Citizenship and Immigration, 1950–62

Table 9
Immigration from Italy: Sex and Dependants (Women and Children)

Fiscal Year End	Total Italian	% Sex Not Known	Sex Not Known	Men	% Men	Women	% Women	Dependent Women	% Dep. Women	Children (Assume < 15)	% Children	Dependent Women & Children	% Dependent Women & Children
03/49	5,207							828	15.9	793	15.2	1,621	31.1
03/50	7,230							1,020	14.1	1,361	18.8	2,381	32.9
03/51	9,766							1,344	13.8	2,008	20.6	3,352	34.3
03/52	28,402	0.8	219	19,860	69.9	4,377	15.4	2,649	9.3	3,946	13.9	6,595	23.2
03/53	18,016	3.4	618	7,167	39.8	5,203	28.9	3,733	20.7	5,028	27.9	8,761	48.6
03/54	27,477	4.6	1,264	10,808	39.3	8,146	29.6	5,410	19.7	7,259	26.4	12,669	46.1
12/54	24,595			12,313	50.1	6,715	27.3	4,575	18.6	5,567	22.6	10,140	41.2
12/55	20,247			8,936	44.1	6,321	31.2	4,622	22.8	4,990	24.6	9,612	47.5
12/56	29,806			12,754	42.8	9,316	31.3	6,612	22.2	7,736	26.0	14,348	48.1
12/57	29,443			12,150	41.3	9,270	31.5	6,766	23.0	8,023	27.2	14,789	50.2
12/58	28,581			12,016	42.0	9,160	32.0	6,490	22.7	7,405	25.9	13,895	48.6
12/59	26,822			11,317	42.2	8,518	31.8	6,046	22.5	6,987	26.0	13,033	48.6
12/60	21,308			8,147	38.2	7,348	34.5	5,395	25.3	5,813	27.3	11,208	52.6
12/61	14,603			4,882	33.4	6,070	41.6	4,303	29.5	3,651	25.0	7,954	54.5

Source: Calculations based on Annual Report, Department of Mines and Resources, 1948–9, Department of Citizenship and Immigration, 1950–62, Statistics Section

Table 10
Metropolitan Toronto: Average Labour Force Income by Sex, Ethnicity, and
Mother Tongue, 1960–1

Origin	Mother Tongue	Average Income ($)	
		Males	Females
British	English	5,562	2,003
	French	4,730	2,494
	Other	4,606	2,452
	All	5,557	2,602
French	English	4,614	2,431
	French	4,127	2,171
	Other	4,036	2,133
	All	4,381	2,314
German	English	5,944	2,575
	French	4,983	2,542
	Other	4,212	2,126
	All	4,770	2,263
Italian	English	4,520	2,394
	French	4,388	2,324
	Other	3,016	1,456
	All	3,189	1,592
Jewish	English	7,560	2,593
	French	4,790	2,333
	Other	5,893	2,319
	All	6,658	2,458
Ukrainian	English	4,392	2,360
	French	3,338	2,500
	Other	4,019	2,133
	All	4,086	2,188
All Others	English	5,414	2,523
	French	4,501	2,285
	Other	4,108	2,104
	All	4,542	2,268
Total Labour Force		5,080	2,437

Source: Cited in Anthony Richmond, *Immigrants and Ethnic Groups in Metropolitan Toronto* (York
University 1967), 22

Table 11

Occupations, Metro Toronto, 1951: Italian Men, Experienced Labour Force

Industry	Total	Italian — Total Italian	Italian — Italian % of Total	Italian — Distribution of Italian Total	Italian — Sector % Breakdown	British — Total British	British — British % of Total	Other Europeans — Total Other European	Other Europeans — Other European % of Total
AGRICULTURE	2,975	154	5.2	1.0		1,904	64.0	917	30.8
FORESTRY/FISH & TRAPPING/MINING	713	3	0.4			552	77.4	158	22.2
MANUFACTURING	138,812	3,199	2.3	29.0	100	96,263	69.3	39,350	28.3
Food & Beverage	13,524	365	2.7		11	9,621	71.1	3,538	26.2
Tobacco	63	5	7.9		–	23	36.5	35	55.6
Rubber	4,827	36	0.7		1	3,696	76.6	1,095	22.7
Leather	2,628	212	8.1		7	1,196	45.5	1,220	46.4
Textile (excl. clothing)	2,856	94	3.3		3	1,844	64.6	918	32.1
Clothing	9,816	381	3.9		12	2,294	23.4	7,141	72.7
Other	105,098	2,106	2.0		66	77,589	73.8	25,403	24.2
CONSTRUCTION	35,701	3,572	10.0	33.0	100	21,611	60.5	10,518	29.5
General Contractor	34,809	3,474	10.0		97	21,083	60.6	10,252	29.5
Special Trade Contractor	892	98	11.0		3	528	59.2	266	29.8
TRANSPORTATION & COMMUNICATION	31,823	751	2.4	7.0		24,799	77.9	6,273	19.7
PUBLIC UTILITIES	9,173	95	1.0	1.0		7,682	83.7	1,396	15.2
TRADE	66,859	1,611	2.4	15.0	100	47,497	71.0	17,751	26.5
Wholesale	24,437	551	2.3		34	17,804	72.9	6,082	24.9
Retail	42,422	1,060	2.5		66	29,693	70.0	11,669	27.5
Food	11,223	623	5.6		100				
Shoe & Apparel	2,954	39	1.3		59				
					4				
FINANCE	16,823	125	0.7	1.0		14,244	84.7	2,454	14.6
SERVICE	60,856	1,175	1.9	11.0	100	43,197	71.0	16,484	27.1

Gov't & Public	44,999	418	0.9	36		36,470	81.0	8,111	18.0
Personal	15,857	757	4.8	64	100	6,727	42.4	8,373	52.8
Shoe Repair	N/A	195	14.0		26				
Barbershops	1,437								
Hotel/Restaurants	9,036	373	4.0		49				
PUBLIC ADMINISTRATION/DEFENCE	N/A								
NOT STATED	3,798	192	5.0	2.0		2,086	54.9	1,519	40.0
TOTAL	367,533	10,877	3.0	100.0		259,835	70.7	96,821	26.3

Source: Dominion Bureau of Statistics, *Census of Canada*, 1951, unpublished tables

The statistics compiled in tables 11–14 refer to the Italian ethnic group.

Table 12
Occupations, Metro Toronto, 1961: Italian Men, Experienced Labour Force

Industry	Total	Italian				British		Other Europeans	
		Total Italian	Italian % of Total	Distribution of Italian Total	Sector % Breakdown	Total British	British % of Total	Total Other European	Other European % of Total
AGRICULTURE	5,944	470	7.9	1.0		3,108	52.3	2,366	39.8
FORESTRY/FISH & TRAPPING/MINING	1,713	54	3.2			1,221	71.3	438	25.6
MANUFACTURING	170,615	11,894	7.0	28.0	100	101,572	59.5	57,149	33.5
Food & Beverage	21,309	1,879	8.8	4.0	16	12,063	56.6	7,367	34.6
Tobacco	314	25	8.0		–	158	50.3	131	41.7
Rubber	3,892	109	2.8		1	2,645	68.0	1,138	29.2
Leather	2,179	427	19.6	1.0	3	742	34.1	1,010	46.4
Textile (excl. clothing)	3,662	346	9.4	1.0	3	1,953	53.3	1,363	37.2
Clothing	7,176	915	12.8	2.0	8	1,265	17.6	4,996	69.6
Other	132,083	8,193	6.2	19.0	69	82,746	62.6	41,144	31.2
CONSTRUCTION	49,174	15,560	31.6	36.0	100	18,464	37.5	15,150	30.8
General Contractor	22,289	8,278	37.1	19.0	53	7,409	33.2	6,602	29.6
Special Trade Contractor	26,885	7,282	27.1	17.0	47	11,055	41.1	8,548	31.8
TRANSPORTATION, COMMUNICATION, & PUBLIC UTILITIES	56,115	1968	3.5	5.0		40,194	71.6	13,953	24.9
TRADE	96,400	5,644	5.9	13.0	100	58,892	61.1	31,864	33.1
Wholesale	37,667	1,975	5.2	4.0	35	24,428	64.9	11,264	29.9
Retail	58,733	3,669	6.2	9.0	65	34,464	58.7	20,600	35.1
Food	12,291	1,593	12.9	4.0	43	6,755		3,953	32.2
Shoe & Apparel1	3,621	183	5.1		5	1,474		1,964	54.2
FINANCE	27,000	640	2.4	1.0		20,247	75.0	6,113	22.6
SERVICE	76,745	4,287	5.6	10.0	100	41,970	54.7	30,488	39.7

Gov't & Public	53,867	1,425	2.6	3.0	33		35,493	65.9	16,949	31.5
Personal	22,878	2,862	12.5	7.0	67	100	6,477	28.3	13,539	59.2
Shoe Repair	591	184	31.1			6				
Barbershops	2,771	1,168	42.2	3.0		41				
Hotel/Restaurants	13,956	975	7.0	2.0		34				
PUBLIC ADMINISTRATION/DEFENCE	31,713	1,057	3.3	2.0			24,401	76.9	6255	19.7
NOT STATED	13,599	1,397	10.3	3.0			7,870	57.9	4,332	31.9
TOTAL	529,018	42,971	8.1	100.0			317,939	60.1	168,108	31.8

Source: Dominion Bureau of Statistics, *Census of Canada*, 1961, unpublished tables

Table 13

Occupations, Metro Toronto, 1951: Italian Women, Experienced Labour Force

Industry	Total	Italian				British		Other Europeans	
		Total Italian	Italian % of Total	Distribution of Italian Total	Sector % Breakdown	Total British	British % of Total	Total other European	Other European % of Total
AGRICULTURE	188	6	3.2			110	58.5	72	38.3
FORESTRY/FISH & TRAPPING/MINING	167	1	0.6			140	83.8	26	15.6
MANUFACTURING	50,459	1,314	2.6	45.0	100	34,580	68.5	14,565	28.9
Food & Beverage	5,236	134	2.5	5.0	10	3,773	72.1	1,329	25.4
Tobacco	16	–	0.0		–	4	25.0	12	75.0
Rubber	995	17	1.7		1	756	76.0	222	22.3
Leather	1,146	49	4.3	2.0	4	670	58.5	427	37.3
Textile (excl. clothing)	2,200	57	2.6	2.0	4	1,464	66.5	679	30.9
Clothing	10,695	521	4.9	18.0	40	4,260	39.8	5,914	55.3
Other	30,171	536	1.8	18.0	41	23,653	78.4	5,982	19.8
CONSTRUCTION	968	32	3.3	1.0		782	80.8	154	15.9
TRANSPORTATION/STORAGE/ COMMUNICATION	6,522	67	1.0	2.0		5,495	84.3	960	14.7
PUBLIC UTILITIES	1,467	18	1.2	1.0		1,184	80.7	265	18.1
TRADE	34,247	654	1.9	23.0		26,128	76.3	7,465	21.8
FINANCE	14,902	188	1.3	7.0		12,214	82.0	2,500	16.8
SERVICE	48,928	581	1.2	20.0	100	36,889	75.4	11,458	23.4
Government/Public/Recreation/ Business	32,615	276	0.8	10.0	48	26,324	80.7	6,015	18.4
Personal	16,313	305	1.9	11.0	52 / 100	10,565	64.8	5,443	33.4
Domestic	5,789	24	0.4	1.0	8	4,077	70.4	1,688	29.2
Laundry	1,141	91	8.0	3.0	30	615	53.9	435	38.1

Other Personal	9,383	190	2.0	7.0	62	5,873	62.6	3,320	35.4
PUBLIC ADMINISTRATION/DEFENCE	N/A								
NOT STATED	1,447	43	3.0	1.0		921	63.6	483	33.4
TOTAL	159,295	2,904	1.8	100.0		118,443	74.4	37,948	23.8

Source: Dominion Bureau of Statistics, *Census of Canada*, 1951, unpublished tables

Table 14

Occupations, Metro Toronto, 1961: Italian Women, Experienced Labour Force

Industry	Total	Italian				British		Other Europeans	
		Total Italian	Italian % of Total	Distribution of Italian Total	Sector % Breakdown	Total British	British % of Total	Total other European	Other European % of Total
AGRICULTURE	580	85	14.7	1.0		285	49.1	210	36.2
FORESTRY/FISH & TRAPPING/MINING	383	4	1.0			296	77.3	83	21.7
MANUFACTURING	63,896	8,528	13.3	50.0	100	35,324	55.3	20,044	31.4
Food & Beverage	7,677	955	12.4	6.0	11	3,992	52.0	2,730	35.6
Tobacco	216	35	16.2		–	100	46.3	81	37.5
Rubber	713	50	7.0		1	485	68.0	178	25.0
Leather	1,765	697	39.5	4.0	8	448	25.4	620	35.1
Textile (excl. clothing)	4,111	968	23.5	6.0	11	1,574	38.3	1,569	38.2
Clothing	9,266	3,211	34.7	19.0	38	1,681	18.1	4,374	47.2
Other	40,148	2,612	6.5	15.0	31	27,044	67.4	10,492	26.1
CONSTRUCTION	1,881	100	5.3	1.0		1,272	67.8	509	27.1
TRANSPORTATION/STORAGE/COMMUNICATION/PUBLIC UTILITIES	12,586	248	2.0	1.0		9,252	73.5	3,086	24.5
TRADE	50,096	2,095	4.2	12.0		33,863	67.6	14,138	28.2
FINANCE	25,338	569	2.2	3.0		17,492	69.0	7,277	28.7
SERVICE	90,977	4,927	5.4	29.0	100	54,961	60.4	31,089	34.2
Government/Public/Recreation/Business	55,987	1010	1.8	6.0	20	39,609	70.7	15,368	27.4
Personal	34,990	3,917	11.2	23.0	80	15,352	43.9	15,721	44.9
Domestic	9,851	147	1.5	1.0	4	4,643	47.1	4,161	42.2
Laundry	3,832	1,075	28.1	6.0	27	1,577	41.2	1,180	30.8

Other Personal	22,207	2,695	12.1	16.0	69	9,132	41.1	10,380	46.7
PUBLIC ADMINISTRATION/DEFENCE	11,245	188	1.7	1.0		8,760	77.9	2,297	20.4
NOT STATED	3,651	246	6.7	2.0		2,187	59.9	1,218	33.4
TOTAL	260,633	16,990	6.5	100.0		163,692	62.8	79,951	30.7

Source: Dominion Bureau of Statistics, *Census of Canada*, 1961, unpublished tables

Notes

INTRODUCTION

1 John Bodnar, *The Transplanted: A History of Urban Immigrants in America* (Bloomington, Ind. 1985)
2 For statistics see Gianfausto Rosoli et al., eds., *Un secolo di emigrazione: 1876–1976* (Rome 1978). On this era see, for example, Robert Foerster, *The Italian Emigration of Our Times* (Cambridge, Mass. 1919); Humbert Nelli, *Italians in Chicago 1880–1930: A Study in Ethnic Mobility* (New York 1970); John W. Briggs, *An Italian Passage: Immigrants to Three American Cities* (New Haven 1978); Micaela di Leonardo, *The Varieties of Ethnic Experience: Kinship, Class, and Gender among California Italian-Canadians* (Ithaca 1984); John Potestio and Antonio Pucci, eds., *The Italian Immigrant Experience* (Thunder Bay, Ont. 1988); Roberto Perin and Franc Sturino, eds., *Arrangiarsi: The Italian Immigration Experience in Canada* (Montreal 1989).
3 John E. Zucchi, *Italians in Toronto: Development of a National Identity 1875–1935* (Montreal/Kingston 1988). See also Robert F. Harney and Harold Troper, *Immigrants: A Portrait of the Urban Experience 1890–1930* (Toronto 1975); Robert F. Harney, "Chiaroscuro: Italians in Toronto, 1885–1915," *Italian Americana* 1 (1975); Franc Sturino, "Inside the Chain: A Case Study in Southern Italian Immigration to North America, 1880–1930" (PhD thesis, University of Toronto, Ontario Institute for Studies in Education, 1981), and *Forging the Chain: Italian Migration to North America 1880–1930* (Toronto 1990).
4 Luigi Favero and Greziani Tassello, "Cent'anni di emigrazione Italiana (1876–1976)," in Rosoli et al., eds., *Un secolo di emigrazione*; Umberto Cassinis, "Intra-European Movements of Italian Workers," *Migration News* July–Aug. 1956; A.T. Bouscaren, *European Economic Migrations since 1945* (New York 1963), chap. 1; Ann Cornelison, *Pilgrims and*

Strangers: The Last Italian Migration (New York 1980); Jean Berger and Jean Mohr, *A Seventh Man: The Story of Migrant Workers in Europe* (Harmondsworth 1975); Antonino Mazzi, "Pasolini and Calabria as a Metaphor for the Third World," Paper presented to the Symposium on Calabrian Migration, York University, Toronto, 1986.

5 In 1953 the City of Toronto and its neighbouring municipalities became the new Metropolitan Toronto. Unless otherwise specified I have used the term Toronto loosely, to apply to the city and its suburbs.

6 Italian words are italicized only the first time they appear in the text.

7 Calculations based on statistics in *Annuario Statistico Italiano* (Rome 1960).

8 James Lemon, *Toronto since 1918: An Illustrated History* (Toronto 1985), chap. 4; K.J. Rea, *The Prosperous Years: The Economic History of Ontario* (Toronto 1985); Anthony Richmond, *Immigrants and Ethnic Groups in Metropolitan Toronto* (Toronto: York University 1967)

9 Examples include N.F. Dreisziger et al., *Struggle and Hope: The Hungarian-Canadian Experience* (Toronto 1982); Grace Anderson and David Higgs, *A Future to Inherit: The Portuguese Communities of Canada* (Toronto 1976); Peter Chimbos, *The Canadian Odyssey: The Greek Experience in Canada* (Toronto 1980); K. Aun, *The Political Refugees: Estonians in Canada* (Toronto 1983). See also Roberto Perin, "Clio as an Ethnic: The Third Force in Canadian Historiography," *Canadian Historical Review* 64 (1983).

10 Franc Sturino, "Family and Kin Cohesion among South Italian Immigrants in Toronto," in Betty Boyd Caroli et al., eds., *The Italian Immigrant Woman in North America* (Toronto 1978); the essays in Franc Sturino and John Zucchi, eds., Issue on Italians, *Polyphony* 7 (1985); Franca Iacovetta, "'Primitive Villagers and Uneducated Girls': Canada Recruits Domestics from Italy, 1951–2," *Canadian Woman Studies* 7 (1987), and "Trying to Make Ends Meet: Italian Immigrant Women, the State and Family Survival Strategies in Post-War Toronto," *Canadian Woman Studies* 8 (1987); Jeremy Boissevain, *The Italians of Montreal: Social Adjustment in a Plural Society* (Ottawa 1970); Mauro Peressini, "Stratégies migratoires et pratiques communautaires: Les Italiens du Frioul," *Recherches sociographiques* 25 (1984); Clifford Jansen, *Italians in a Multicultural Canada* (Lewiston/Queenston 1988). Unpublished works include Samuel Sidlofsky, "Post-War Immigrants in the Changing Metropolis with Special Reference to Toronto's Italian Population" (PhD thesis, University of Toronto, 1969), and Josephine Atri, "Italian Immigrant Women in Post-War Montreal" (MA thesis, Concordia University, 1980). For popular accounts see A.V. Spada, *The Italians in Canada* (Ottawa 1961), and the more recent, and superior, study by Kenneth Bagnell, *Canadese: A Portrait of the Italo-Canadians* (Toronto 1989).

11 Irving Abella and Harold Troper, *None Is Too Many: Canada and the Jews of Europe, 1933–1948* (Toronto 1983); Milda Danys, *DP: Lithuanian Immigration to Canada after the Second World War* (Toronto 1986); Reginald Whittaker, *Double Standard: The Secret History of Canadian Immigration* (Toronto 1987)

12 The most widely used works include Freda Hawkins, *Canada and Immigration: Public Policy and Public Concern* (Montreal 1972); Alan G. Green, *Immigration and the Postwar Canadian Economy* (Toronto 1976); Louis Parai, *Immigration and Emigration of Professional and Skilled Manpower during the Postwar Period* (Ottawa 1965); Raymond Breton, "Institutional Completeness and the Personal Relations of Immigrants," *American Journal of Sociology* 70 (1964); Anthony Richmond, *Postwar Immigrants in Canada* (Toronto 1967); Anthony Richmond and John Goldlust, *Multivariate Analysis of Immigrant Adaptation: A Study of Male Householders in Metropolitan Toronto* (Toronto: York University 1974); Anthony Richmond and Suzanne Ziegler, *Characteristics of Italian Householders in Metropolitan Toronto* (Toronto: York University 1977); Warren Kalback and Anthony Richmond, *Factors in the Adjustment of Immigrants and Their Descendants* (Ottawa 1980); Jean Leonard Elliot, ed., *Immigrant Groups* (Scarborough 1971). Social-psychological studies include Kurt Danziger, "The Acculturation of Italian Immigrant Girls," *International Journal of Psychology* 9 (1974); Harriet Perry, "The Metonymic Definition of the Female Concept of Honour among Italian Immigrant Families in Toronto," in Caroli et al., eds., *Italian Immigrant Woman*. For a critique see James Henretta, "Study of Social Mobility – Ideological Assumptions and Conceptual Bias," *Labor History* 18 (1977); Perin, "Clio as Ethnic"; Franc Sturino, "The Social Mobility of Italian Canadians: 'Outside' and 'Inside' Concepts of Mobility" *Polyphony* 7 (1985). See also Hawkins's recent *Critical Years in Immigration: Canada and Australia Compared* (Kingston/Montreal, 1989).

13 Rudolph Vecoli, "Contadini in Chicago: A Critique of the Uprooted," *Journal of American History* 51 (1964), "Prelates and Peasants: Italian Immigrants and the Catholic Church," *Journal of Social History* 2 (1969), "Italian American Workers, 1880–1920: Padrone Slaves or Primitive Rebels?" in S.M. Tomasi, ed., *Perspectives in Italian Immigration and Ethnicity* (New York 1977); Virginia Yans-McLaughlin, *Family and Community: Italian Immigrants in Buffalo, 1880–1930* (Ithaca 1971), "A Flexible Tradition: Southern Italian Immigrants Confront a New Work Experience," *Journal of Social History* 7 (1974); Robert F. Harney, "The Commerce of Migration," *Canadian Ethnic Studies* 9 (1977), "Men without Women: Italian Migrants in Canada, 1885–1930," in Caroli et al., eds., *Italian Immigrant Woman*, "The Padrone and the Italian Immigrant," *Canadian Review of American Studies* 5:2 (1974), "Montreal's King of Italian Labour: A Case Study of Padronism," *Labour/Le Travail-*

leur 4 (1979); "Boarding and Belonging: Thoughts on Sojourner Institutions" *Urban History Review* 2 (1978). Important recent works include Bruno Ramirez, *Les Premiers Italiens de Montréal: L'origine de la Petite Italie du Québec* (Montreal 1984); Sylvie Tashereau, *Pays et patries: Mariages et lieux d'origine des Italiens de Montréal 1906–1930* (Montreal 1987); Gary R. Mormino and George E. Pozzetta, *The Immigrant World of Ybor City: Italians and Their Latin Neighbors in Tampa, 1885–1985* (Urbana 1987).

14 Oscar Handlin, *The Uprooted* (New York 1951), *Boston's Immigrants: A Study in Acculturation* (Cambridge, Mass. 1941)

15 Vecoli, "Contadini"; Kathleen Conzen, "Immigrants, Immigrant Neighborhoods, and Ethnic Identity: Historical Issues," *Journal of American History* 66 (1979); Oliver Macdonagh, "The Irish Famine Emigration to the United States," *Perspectives in American History* 10 (1976); John Bodnar, "Immigration and Modernization: The Case of Slavic Peasants in America," *Journal of Social History* 10 (1976), *Immigration and Industrialization: Ethnicity in an American Mill Town, 1870–1940* (Pittsburg 1977); John Bodnar et al., *Lives of Their Own: Blacks, Italians and Poles in Pittsburg 1900–1960* (Urbana 1982); Yans-McLaughlin, *Family and Community*; Victor Greene, *For God and Country: The Rise of Polish and Lithuanian Consciousness in America* (Madison, Wisc. 1975); Josef Barton, *Peasants and Strangers: Italians, Roumanians, and Slovaks in an American City, 1890–1950* (Cambridge, Mass. 1975); Caroline Golab, *Immigrant Destinations* (Philadelphia 1977); Robert F. Harney and Vincenza Scarpaci, eds., *Little Italies in North America* (Toronto 1981); Donald Akenson, "Ontario: Whatever Happened to the Irish?" *Canadian Papers in Rural History* 3 (1982), and *The Irish in Ontario: A Study in Rural History* (Kingston/Montreal 1984); Robert F. Harney, ed., *Gathering Place: Peoples and Neighbourhoods of Toronto 1834–1945* (Toronto 1985)

16 Herbert Gutman, "Work, Culture, and Society in Industrializing America," *American Historical Review* 72 (1973); R.L. Ehrlich, ed., *Immigrants in Industrial America 1850–1920* (Charlottesville, Va 1977); Judith E. Smith, *Family Connections: A History of Italian and Jewish Lives in Providence, Rhode Island 1900–1940* (Albany 1985); Donna Gabaccia, *From Siciliy to Elizabeth Street: Housing and Social Change among Italian Immigrants 1880–1930* (Albany 1984); Bruno Ramirez, "Brief Encounters: Italian Immigrant Workers and the CPR, 1900–1930," *Labour/Le Travail* 17 (1980), and *On The Move: French-Canadian and Italian Migrants in the North Atlantic Economy 1860–1914* (Toronto 1990); Perin and Sturino, eds., *Arrangiarsi*

17 Peter Laslett, *The World We Have Lost* (New York 1965); Tamara Hareven, *Family Time and Industrial Time* (Cambridge, Mass. 1982). For a

useful discussion see Smith, *Family Connections*; Nancy Folbre, "Family Strategy and Feminist Theory," *Historical Methods* 20 (1987); Louise Tilly, "Beyond Family Strategies, What?" *Historical Methods* 20 (1987); Annie Phizacklea, ed., *One Way Ticket: Migration and Female Labor* (London 1983).

18 Valuable American studies include Alice Kessler-Harris, *Out To Work: A History of Wage-Earning Women in the United States* (New York 1982); Mari Jo Buhle, *Women and American Socialism* (Urbana 1981); Sarah Eisenstein, *Give Us Bread But Give Us Roses: Working Women's Consciousness in the United States, 1890 to the First World War* (London 1983); Dana Frank, "Housewives, Socialists and the Politics of Food: The 1917 Cost of Living Protests," *Feminist Studies* 11 (1985); Ruth Milkman, ed., *Women, Work and Protest: A Century of US Women's Labor History* (Boston 1985); Linda Gordon, *Heroes of Their Own Lives: The Politics and History of Family Violence* (New York 1988). On Canada see, for example, Bettina Bradbury, "Women's History and Working-Class History," *Labour/Le Travail* 19 (1987); Joan Sangster, *Dreams of Equality: Women on the Canadian Left, 1920–1950* (Toronto 1989); and Alison Prentice et al., eds., *Canadian Women: A History* (Toronto 1988).

19 American studies include Hasia R. Diner, *Erin's Daughters in America* (Baltimore 1983); Carl Ross and K. Marianne Wargelin Brown, eds., *Women Who Dared: The History of Finnish American Women* (St Paul 1986); Maxine Seller, ed., *Immigrant Women* (Philadelphia 1981), and "The Uprising of the Twenty Thousand: Sex, Class, and Ethnicity in the Shirtwaist Makers' Strike of 1910," in Dirk Hoerder, ed., *'Struggle a Hard Battle': Essays on Working-Class Immigrants* (DeKalb, Ill. 1986); Elizabeth Ewen, *Immigrant Women in the Land of Dollars: Life and Culture on the Lower East Side* (New York 1985); Evelyn Nakano Glenn, *Issei, Nisei, Warbride: Three Generations of Japanese American Women in Domestic Service* (Philadelphia 1986); Priscilla Long, "The Women of the Colorado Fuel and Iron Strike, 1913–14," in Milkman, ed., *Women, Work and Protest*; Columba Furio, "The Cultural Background of the Italian Immigrant Woman and Its Impact on Her Unionization in the New York City Garment Industry, 1880–1919," in George Pozetta, ed., *Pane e Lavoro: The Italian American Working Class* (Toronto 1980). With the notable exception of Varpu Lindstrom-Best, *Defiant Sisters: A Social History of Finnish Immigrant Women in Canada* (Toronto 1988), the Canadian literature consists of articles and picture books. Valuable collections of essays include Jean Burnet, ed., *Looking into My Sister's Eyes: An Exploration in Women's History* (Toronto 1986); *Polyphony* 8 (1986); *Canadian Woman Studies* 7 (1987). See also Marilyn Barber, "The Women Ontario Welcomed: Immigrant Domestics for Ontario Homes, 1870–1930," *Ontario History* 72 (1980); Joy Parr, "The Skilled Emigrant

and Her Kin: Gender, Culture and Labour Recruitment," *Canadian Historical Review* (1987), and *The Gender of Breadwinners: Women, Men and Change in Two Industrial Towns 1880–1950* (Toronto 1990); Ruth Frager, "Politicized Housewives in the Jewish Communist Movement of Toronto, 1929–1933," in Linda Kealey and Joan Sangster, eds., *Beyond the Vote: Women and Canadian Politics* (Toronto 1989).

20 Useful works include Sheila Arnopolous, *Problems of Immigrant Women in the Canadian Labour Force* (Ottawa 1979); Laura Johnson, *The Seam Allowance: Industrial Homesewing in Canada* (Toronto 1982); Makeda Silvera, *Silenced* (Toronto 1983); Judith Ramirez and Roxanna Ng, *Immigrant Housewives in Canada: A Report* (Toronto 1981); Charlene Gannage, *Double Day, Double Bind: Women Garment Workers* (Toronto 1986); Roxanna Ng, *The Politics of Community Services: Immigrant Women, Class and State* (Toronto 1987); the essays in *Canadian Woman Studies* 8 (1987) and 10 (1989); *Resources for Feminist Research* 16 (1987).

21 John Higham, *Strangers in the Land: Patterns of American Nativism 1860–1920* (New York 1973); Victor Greene, "The Polish American Worker to 1930: The Hunky Image in Transition," *Polish Review* 21 (1976); Ronald Takaki, *Iron Cages: Race and Culture in Nineteenth Century America* (New York 1979); Peter Ward, *White Canada Forever: Popular Attitudes and Public Policy toward Orientals in British Columbia* (Montreal 1978); Howard Palmer, *Patterns of Prejudice: A History of Nativism in Alberta* (Toronto 1982); Lita Rose Betcherman, *The Swastika and the Maple Leaf* (Toronto 1975); Ken Adachi, *The Enemy That Never Was* (Toronto 1981); Barbara Roberts, *Whence They Came: Deportation from Canada 1900–1935* (Ottawa 1988); Patricia Roy, *A White Man's Province: British Columbian Politicians and Chinese and Japanese Immigrants 1858–1914* (Vancouver 1989).

22 Gabriel Kolko, *Main Currents in Modern American History* (New York 1976), chap. 3; Edwin Fenton, *Immigrants and Unions, A Case Study: Italians and American Labor, 1870–1920* (New York 1970); see also Bodnar, *Transplanted*, chap. 3.

23 Victor Greene, *The Slavic Community on Strike* (Notre Dame 1968); Arthur Puotinen, *Finnish Radicals and Religion in Midwestern Mining Towns 1865–1914* (New York 1975); John Bodnar, *Workers' World: Kinship, Community and Protest in an Industrial Society* (Baltimore 1982); Dirk Hoerder, ed., *American Labor and Immigration 1870–1920s: Recent European Research* (Urbana 1983), and *Struggle a Hard Battle*; Donald Avery, *"Dangerous Foreigners": European Immigrant Workers and Labour Radicalism in Canada* (Toronto 1979); Varpu Lindström-Best, ed., Issue on Finns in Ontario, *Polyphony* 3 (1981); Ian Radforth, *Bushworkers and Bosses: Logging in Northern Ontario 1900–1980* (Toronto 1987); Craig Heron, *Working in Steel: The Early Years in Canada, 1883–1935* (Toronto 1988);

Carmela Patrias, "Patriots and Proletarians: The Politicization of Hungarian Immigrants in Canada, 1924–1946" (PhD thesis, University of Toronto, 1985), and *Relief Strike: Immigrant Workers and the Great Depression in Crowland, Ontario, 1930–1935* (Toronto 1990); Ramirez, *On The Move.*

24 For example see Vecoli, "Italian American Workers," and "Anthony Capraro and the Lawrence Strike of 1919," in Pozzetta, ed., *Pane e Lavoro*; Antonio Pucci, "At the Forefront of Militancy: Italians in Canada at the Turn of the Century," in Harney and Scarpaci, eds., *Little Italies*; Jean Morrison, "Ethnicity and Violence: The Lakehead Freighthandlers before World War I," in Gregory S. Kealey and Peter Warrian, eds., *Essays in Canadian Working Class History* (Toronto 1976); Allen Seager, "Class, Ethnicity and Politics in the Alberta Coalfields, 1905–1945," in Hoerder, ed., *Struggle a Hard Battle*; Donna Gabaccia, "Neither Padrone Slaves nor Primitive Rebels: Sicilians on Two Continents," in Hoerder, ed., *Struggle a Hard Battle*, and *Militants and Migrants, Rural Sicilians become American Workers* (New Brunswick, NJ 1988); Mormino and Pozetta, *Ybor City*; Potestio and Pucci, eds., *Italian Immigrant Experience*; Craig Heron and Robert Storey, "Work and Struggle in the Canadian Steel Industry," in Heron and Storey, eds., *On The Job: Confronting the Labour Process in Canada* (Kingston/Montreal 1986).

25 Zucchi, *Italians in Toronto*, preface.

CHAPTER ONE

1 Personal interview (pseudonyms in text)
2 For statistics see Luigi Favero and Greziani Tassello, "Cent'anni di emigrazione Italiana (1876–1976)," in Gianfausto Rosoli, ed., *Un secolo di emigrazione Italiana 1876–1976* (Rome 1978); Giuseppe Lucrezio Monticelli, "Italian Emigration: Basic Characteristics and Trends with Special Reference to the Post-War Years," in S.M. Tomasi and M.H. Engel, eds., *The Italian Experience in the United States* (New York 1970).
3 The literature on Italian immigration to North America in this period is extensive. Studies on the United States include Robert Foerster, *Italian Emigration of Our Times* (Cambridge 1919); Luciano Iorizzo, "The Padrone and Immigrant Distribution," in Tomasi and Engel, *Italian Experience in the United States*; John Briggs, *An Italian Passage: Immigration to Three American Cities 1890–1930* (New Haven 1978); Virginia Yans-McLaughlin, *Family and Community: Italian Immigrants in Buffalo, 1880–1920* (Ithaca 1971); Judith E. Smith, *Family Connections: A History of Italian and Jewish Immigrant Lives in Providence, Rhode Island, 1900–1940* (Albany 1985); Gary R. Mormino and George E. Pozzetta, *The Immi-*

grant World of Ybor City: Italians and Their Latin Neighbors in Tampa, *1885–1985* (Urbana and Chicago 1987). On Canada see Robert F. Harney, "Men without Women: Italian Migrants in Canada, 1885–1930," in Betty Boyd Caroli et al, eds., *The Italian Immigrant Woman in North America* (Toronto 1978); Bruno Ramirez, *Les Premiers Italiens de Montréal: L'origine de la Petite Italie du Québec* (Montreal 1984); Antonio Pucci, "Canadian Industrialization versus Italian Contadini in a Decade of Brutality, 1902–1912," in Robert F. Harney and J. Vincenza Scarpaci, eds., *Little Italies in North America* (Toronto 1981); Franc Sturino, "Italian Immigration to Canada and the Farm Labour System through the 1920s," *Studi Emigrazione* 77 (1985), and *Forging the Chair: Italian Migration to North America 1880–1930* (Toronto 1990); John Zucchi, *Italians in Toronto: Development of a National Identity, 1875–1935* (Kingston and Montreal 1988).

4 See J.P. Cole, *Italy: An Introductory Geography* (New York 1964); Robert Dickinson, *The Population Problem of Southern Italy* (Syracuse 1955), chap. 1; Russel King, *The 'Questione Meridionale' in Southern Italy* (Durham 1971); Alan B. Mountjoy, *The Mezzogiorno* (London 1973).

5 Scholars of the "meridionalisti" school offered a sustained critique of the state's role in the underdevelopment of the south. They included Giustino Fortunato, *Il Mezzogiorno e lo Stato Italiano* (Bari 1911); Francesco Nitti, *Scritti sulla questione meridionale: Saggi sulla storia del mezzogiorno, emigrazione e lavoro* (Bari 1958); Daniel Dolci, *Waste* (transl., London 1963); Antonio Gramsci, *La questione meridionale* (Rome 1966), *The Modern Prince and Other Essays* (transl. New Haven and London 1967). See also King, *'Questione Meridionale,'* chap. 2.

6 Eric Wolf, *Peasants* (Englewood Cliffs, NJ 1966) 1–17. Property was traditionally divided among offspring in the form of doweries for daughters and inheritances for sons. In response to the problems associated with subdivision among smallholders, some families, beginning in the late nineteenth century, provided only one son with land, while the others received compensation in the form of a money settlement or by having their overseas trips financed. John S. MacDonald, "Agricultural Organization, Migration and Labor Militancy in Rural Italy," *Economic History Review* 16 (1963); Rudolph Bell, *Fate and Honor, Family and Village* (Chicago 1979), 183–97.

7 Dickinson, *Population*, 39–50; Sydel Silverman, "Agricultural Organization, Social Structures and Values in Italy: Amoral Familialism Reconsidered," *American Anthropologist* 70 (1968); Macdonald, "Agricultural Organization"; Anton Block, *The Mafia of a Sicilian Village, 1860–1960: A Study of Violent Peasant Entrepreneurs* (New York 1974). On San Stefano, Sicily, see Mormino and Pozzetta, *Ybor City*, chap. 1; on Calabria, see Franc Sturino, "Inside the Chain: A Study of Southern Italian

Migration to North America, 1880–1930" (PhD thesis, University of Toronto, 1981), 148–70; on Molise, see Bruno Ramirez, *Les Premiers Italiens*, chap. 1, and *On the Move: French-Canadian and Italian Migrants in the North Atlantic Economy 1860–1914* (Toronto 1990), chap. 2.

8 Macdonald, "Agricultural Organization"; Donna Gabaccia, "Neither Padrone Slaves nor Primitive Rebels: Sicilians on Two Continents," in Dirk Hoerder, ed., *'Struggle a Hard Battle': Essays on Working-Class Immigrants* (DeKalb, Ill. 1976); Mormino and Pozzetta, *Ybor City*, chap. 2; Sydney Tarrow, *Peasant Communism in Southern Italy* (New Haven 1967), 275–80; See also Lucia Chaivola Birnbaum, *liberazione della donna: feminism in Italy* (Middletown, Conn. 1986), chap. 2; Alan Cassels, *Facist Italy* (New York 1968).

9 Drawing on parliamentary enquiries, Ramirez documents these changes for Molise in *On the Move*. For a contemporary account see Adolfo Rossi, "Vantaggi e danni dell'emigrazione nel mezzogiorno d'Italia" (Note di un viaggio fatto in Basilicata e in Calabria), *Bollettino dell'emigrazione* 13 (1908). See also Sturino, "Inside the Chain," 201–18; R.F. Harney, "The Padrone System and Sojourners in the Canadian North, 1885–1920," in George Pozzetta, ed., *Pane e Lavoro: The Italian American Working Class* (Toronto 1980), 137 n31.

10 Philip Canistraro and Gianfausto Rosoli, "Fascist Emigration Policy in the 1920s: An Interpretive Framework," *International Migration Review* 13 (1979); William G. Welk, *Fascist Economic Policy: An Analysis of Italy's Economic Experiment* (Cambridge, Mass. 1938), 182–93. See also J.P. Diggins, *Mussolini and Fascism: The View from America* (Princeton 1972); Philip Canistraro, "Fascism and Italian Americans," in S.M. Tomasi, ed., *Perspectives in Italian Immigration and Ethnicity* (New York 1977); Luigi Bruti Liberatti, *Il Canada, l'Italia e il fascismo, 1919–1945* (Rome 1984); Zucchi, *Italians in Toronto*, chap. 7; Roberto Perrin, "Making Good Fascists and Good Canadians: Consular Propoganda and the Italian Community in Montreal in the 1930s," in Gerald L. Gold, ed., *Minorities and Mother Country Imagery* (St John's 1984).

11 Canistraro and Rosoli, "Fascist Emigration Policy"; Welk, *Fascist Economic Policy*, 188; Dickinson, *Population*, 6–8; Russell King, *The Industrial Geography of Italy* (London 1985), 69–72, 72–98, 300–2. See also Joseph Lopreato, *Peasants No More! Social Change in an Underdeveloped Society* (Scranton, Penn. 1967), 40–8; Constance Cronin, *The Sting of Change: Sicilians in Sicily and Australia* (Chicago 1970), 35–40.

12 King, *Industrial Geography*, 62–98, 285–305; Dickinson, *Population*, 6–10. See also Vera C. Lutz, *A Study on Economic Development* (London 1962), 92–6; Shepard Clough, *Economic History of Modern Italy* (New York 1964), 305–7.

13 Mountjoy, *Mezzogiorno*, 8–10

14 Government statistic cited in ibid.; Carlo Levi, *Christ Stopped at Eboli* (New York 1946, rpr. 1963), 85–6; on literacy see Cronin, *Sting of Change*, 35–7, 40–2; Margaret Carlyle, *The Awakening of Southern Italy* (London 1962), 32–6.

15 Sydney Tarrow, *Peasant Communism in Southern Italy* (New Haven 1967), 272–99. See also King, 'Questione Meridionale,' 30–54; Mountjoy *Mezzogiorno*, 19–22.

16 Franc Sturino, "Family and Kin Cohesion among South Italian Immigrants," in Caroli et al., *Italian Immigrant Woman*

17 Anthropological studies include Charlotte Gower Chapman, *Milocca: A Sicilian Village* (Cambridge, Mass. 1971); A. Maraspini, *A Study of an Italian Village* (Paris 1968); Bell, *Fate and Honor*; Jan Brogger, *Montavarese: A Study of a Peasant Society and Culture in Southern Italy* (Oslo 1971). See also Rudolph Vecoli, "Contadini in Chicago: A Critique of the Uprooted," *Journal of American History* 51 (1964); Donna Gabaccia, *From Sicily to Elizabeth Street: Housing and Social Change among Italian Immigrants, 1880–1930* (Albany 1984), chap. 2; Yans-McLaughlin, *Family and Community*, chap. 2; Louise Tilly, "Comments on the McLaughlin and Davidoff Papers," *Journal of Social History* 7 (1974).

18 Vecoli, "Contadini"; "Yans-McLaughlin, *Family and Community*, 26–8; Smith, *Family Connections*, 23–5; Sturino, "Inside the Chain", 42–9, 66–78; personal interviews.

19 Josef Barton, *Peasants and Strangers: Italians, Roumanians, and Slovaks in an American City 1890–1950* (Cambridge, Mass. 1975), 40. The discussion is based on the literature in note 17 above and on personal interviews.

20 Silverman, "Agricultural Organization"; Smith, *Family Connections*, 26–8, 182–3; Cronin, *Sting of Change*, chap. 4–6; Bell, *Fate and Honor*, 2–3, 72–6; Leonard W. Moss and Stephen S. Cappannari, "Patterns of Kinship, Comparaggio and Community in a South Italian Village," *Anthropological Quarterly* 33 (1960); John Davis, *Land and Family in Pisticci* (London 1964), 22–39, 60–1. Interviews confirm this view.

21 On "backwardness" see Edward Banfield, *The Moral Basis of a Backward Society* (New York 1958). For emphasis on "economic maximizers" see Barton, *Peasants and Strangers*, chap. 1.

22 Basil Kerbay, "Chayanov and the Theory of the Peasant Economy as a Specific Type of Economy," in Theodor Shanin, ed., *Peasant Societies: Selected Readings* (London 1971); Wolf, *Peasants*, 1–17. For a valuable discussion of peasants see also Allan Greer, *Peasant, Lord and Merchant: Rural Society in Three Quebec Parishes 1740–1840* (Toronto 1985).

23 Small owner-cultivators (*coltivatore diretto*) owned their plots outright, but small tenant farmers (*affittuario*) paid a fixed rent on their land – usually half of the produce grown and often one-half to two-thirds of

the olives, figs, or other cash crops available on the land. In the latter case, the full risk of agricultural investment passed from the landowner to the tenant farm family. The sharecropping contract (*colonia parziaria*) was a hybrid of the classical sharecropping (*mezzadria*) system that dominated parts of central Italy. Under the system, a peasant family, usually an extended family living on the property, cultivated the land in return for a share, usually one-half, of the produce grown. The landlord furnished most of the capital required to run the farm and both landlord and tenant shared the risks involved. In the south, however, a substantial portion of the produce, including cash crops, was divided not according to some fixed ratio but, rather, a fixed rent – which meant that the landlord was far less committed to increasing agricultural productivity. See Silverman, "Agricultural organization"; David I. Kertzer, *Family Life in Central Italy 1880–1910: Sharecropping, Wage Labor, and Coresidence* (New Brunswick, NJ 1984), chap. 3.

24 On the agricultural cycles see Brogger, *Montavarese*.

25 Gabaccia, "Neither Padrone Slaves nor Primitive Rebels;" Lopreato, *Peasants No More*, 48–9, 150–3, 181–2; Chapman, *Milocca*, 58–60; personal interviews.

26 Smith, *Family Connections*, 85–8; Cronin, *Sting of Change*, chaps 4–6; Leonard W. Moss and Walter H. Thompson, "The South Italian Family: Literature and Observation," *Human Organization* 18 (1959)

27 Chapman, *Milocca*, 40–85; Moss and Camppannari, "Kinship"; Bell, *Fate and Honor*, 2–3, 72–6; Davis, *Land and Family*, 22–39; see also note 26 above.

28 Banfield, *Moral Basis*; Gabaccia, *Sicily to Elizabeth Street*, chaps 3 and 6. See also John Davis, "Moral and Backward Societies," *Comparative Studies in Society and History* (July 1970).

29 Briggs, *Italian Passage*, chap. 2; Edwin Fenton, *Immigrants and Unions: A Case Study, Italians and American Labor, 1870–1920* (New York), chap. 1. See also Smith, *Family Connections*, 125–8; David Horowitz, *The Italian Labor Movement* (Cambridge, Mass. 1963)

30 Chapman, *Milocca*, 48, 5–10, 73, 161; Tarrow, *Peasant Communism*, chap. 8

31 Bell, *Fate and Honor*, 3–4; personal interview. See also L. Moss and S. Cappannari, "Estate and Class in a South Italian Hill Village," *American Anthropologist* 64 (1964).

32 Personal interviews. Similar examples emerged in the oral testimonies of many of the informants.

33 Tarrow, *Peasant Communism*, chap. 8; Maraspini, *Italian Village*, 10, 106–10; Chapman, *Milocca*, 139; Lopreato, *Peasants No More*, 80–1, 170

34 National Archives of Canada, Immigration Records, Accession No. 83–

84/349, box 40, file 5195-1-575, A/Chief Operations to Attaché, Visa Office, Rome, "Immigration Agents – Italy," 12 March 1964

35 Personal interview

36 Ibid.; Tarrow, *Peasant Communism*, 162–77; Banfield, *Moral Basis*, 24–31; Sturino, *Forging the Chain*, chap. 1

37 This discussion draws on interviews and the following: Rudolph Vecoli, "Peasants and Prelates: Italian Immigrants and the Catholic Church," *Journal of Social History* 2 (1969), "Cult and Occult in Italian American Culture: The Persistence of a Religious Heritage," in Randall M. Miller and Thomas D. Marzik, eds., *Immigrants and Religion in Urban America* (Philadelphia 1977); Phylis H. Williams, *South Italian Folkways in Europe and America* (New Haven 1938); Chapman, *Milocca*.

38 Cited in Chapman, *Milocca*, 124

39 Personal interviews. See also Enrico Cumbo, "The Feast of Madonna del Monte," *Polyphony* 5 (1983); Levi, *Christ*, 116, 117–20; Robert Orsi, *The Madonna of 115th Street: Faith and Community in Italian Harlem 1880–1950* (New Haven 1985).

40 See note 37 and chapter 5.

41 Personal interview. See also Alan Cassels, *Fascist Italy* (New York 1968); Ivone Kirkpatrick, *Mussolini: A Study in Power* (New York 1964); Jane Kramer, *Unsettling Europe* (New York 1972).

42 Tarrow, *Peasant Communism*, chap. 8; Dennis Mack Smith, *Italy: A Modern History* (Ann Arbor 1969), 494–6; P.A. Allum, "The South and National Politics, 1945–50," in J.S. Wolf, ed., *The Rebirth of Italy* (New York 1973). See also J.W. Pickersgill, *The Mackenzie King Record*, vol. 4 (Toronto 1970); Reginald Whittaker, *Double Standard: The Secret History of Canadian Immigration* (Toronto 1978), 61–3; Michael Ledeen, *Italy in Crisis* [The Washington Papers] (Beverly Hills 1977).

43 Tarrow, *Peasant Communism*, chap. 8; Banfield, *Moral Basis*, 24–31; John Davis, *Land and Family in Pisticci* (London 1964), chap. 1

CHAPTER TWO

1 Personal interview (pseudonyms)

2 For a valuable synthesis of the numerous works dealing with the mass era of immigration to the United States see John Bodnar, *The Transplanted: A History of Immigrants in Urban America* (Bloomington, Ind. 1985). On postwar Canada see Freda Hawkins, *Canada and Immigration: Public Policy and Public Concern* (Montreal 1972); Alan G. Green, *Immigration and the Postwar Canadian Economy* (Toronto 1976); D.C. Corbett, *Canada's Immigration Policy: A Critique* (Toronto 1957); Louis Parai, *Immigration and Emigration of Professional and Skilled Manpower during the Postwar Period* (Ottawa 1965).

3 Canadian Institute of Public Opinion, Special Releases, 25 April and 30 Oct. 1946. In the October poll, people were asked: "If Canada does allow more immigrants are there any … nationalities you would like to keep out?" The results were Japanese 60 per cent, Jewish 49 per cent, Germans 34 per cent, Russian 33 per cent, Negro 31 per cent, Italian 25 per cent, Chinese 24 per cent, Middle European 16 per cent, Ukrainian 15 per cent, Polish 14 per cent, Other 3 per cent, None 18 per cent, No Answer 3 per cent. On Canada's hesitation to admit Italians, see National Archives of Canada (NA), Immigration Records (IR), vol. 131, file 28885, A.L. Jolliffe to P.T. Baldwin, 21 June 1946.

4 Donald Avery, "Canadian Immigration Policy and the Foreign Navvy, 1886–1914," *Historical Papers 1972*, and *"Dangerous Foreigners": European Immigrant Workers and Labour Radicalism* (Toronto 1979); Robert F. Harney, "Montreal's King of Italian Labour: A Case Study of Padronism," *Labour/Le Travailleur* 5 (1979), and "Men without Women: Italian Migrants in Canada, 1885–1935," in B.B. Caroli et al., eds., *The Italian Immigrant Woman in North America* (Toronto 1978); Robert Craig Brown and Ramsay Cook, *Canada, 1896–1921: A Nation Transformed* (Toronto 1974), chap. 4; Jaroslav Petrushyn, *Peasants in the Promised Land: Canada and the Ukrainians 1891–1914* (Toronto 1985); N.F. Dreisziger et al., *Struggle and Hope: The Hungarian-Canadian Experience* (Toronto 1982)

5 Archives of Ontario (AO), Ontario Department of Planning and Development, Immigration Branch (IB), Church of England, Bulletin Council for Social Service, No. 104, 15 Oct. 1941

6 NA, IR, vol. 131, file 28885, Laval Fortier, Memorandum, "Italian Immigration," 4 October 1949; AO, IB, E.H. Gurton to Fortier, 1 June 1951. From 1946 to 1950 the ministers responsible for immigration were J.A. Glen, C.D. Howe (briefly), and Colin Gibson. The Department of Immigration and Citizenship was created in 1950. The first minister was Walter Harris, who was replaced by J.W. Pickersgill in 1954. The deputy ministers were Hugh Keenleyside (1947–9), Fortier (1950–60), and George Davidson (1960–3).

7 NA, IR, vol. 130, file 28885, Carlo Fecia Di Cossato to Glen, 23 Aug. 1946; Di Cossato to Prime Minister's Office, 23 Aug. 1946; Willis George (CMA) to MacNamara, 6 June 1944; C.E.S. Smith to Glen, 21 May 1947. See also John Potestio, "From Navvies to Contractors: The History of Vincenzo and Giovani Veltri, Founders of the R.F. Welch Limited, 1885–1931" (MA thesis, Lakehead University, 1982), and Postestio, ed., *The Memoirs of Giovanni Veltri* (Toronto 1987).

8 NA, IR, vol. 130, file 28885, Smith to H.D. Ovendum, veterans' officer, March 1947, 26 Nov. 1946, 4 Jan. 1947; Roberto Riccardi, Italian vice-counsul, Toronto, to A.D. Adamson, 6 Oct. 1947; A. Spada, Canadian Aid to Italy, to Major-General H.F.G. Letson, 4 Nov. 1949;

C.D. Howe to L.W. Sky, 18 Oct. 1947; J.R. Robillard to Fortier, 28 Oct. 1948; House of Commons, *Debates*, 14 Dec. 1945, 13 June 1950

9 NA, IR, vol. 130, file 28885, Ovendum to Glen, 21 March 1947; Letson to Jolliffe, nd; Department of External Affairs (DEA), vol. 147, file 3–33–18, A.D.P. Heeney, Memorandum, 1 March 1949

10 DEA, vol. 147, file 3–33–18, J.W. Holmes to R.G. Riddle, External Affairs, 27 Feb. 1946

11 *Symposium on Population Growth and Immigration into Canada* (Hamilton: McMaster University, 1949); Hawkins, *Canada and Immigration*; Irving Abella and Harold Troper, *None Is Too Many: Canada and the Jews of Europe, 1933–1948* (Toronto 1983), chaps 7–8; Milda Danys, *DP: Lithuanian Immigration to Canada after the Second World War* (Toronto 1986), chap. 4; Corbett, *Policy*; Franca Iacovetta, "The Political Career of Senator Cairine Wilson," *Atlantis* 11 (1985)

12 PC 1734 (1 May 1947) admitted as close relatives the husband or wife, fiance(e), the son, daughter, brother, or sister, together with husband or wife and unmarried children, if any, of any person legally resident in Canada "who is in a position to receive and care for such relatives." A list of orders-in-council is in Green, *Immigration*.

13 Robert F. Harney, "'So Great a Heritage as Ours': Immigration and the Survival of the Canadian Polity," *Daedalus* 117 (1988). See also Howard Palmer, *Patterns of Prejudice* (Toronto 1982); Reginald Whittaker, *Double Standard: The Secret History of Canadian Immigration Policy* (Toronto 1987).

14 Immigration Branch, *Annual Report* 1951; Abella and Troper, *None Is Too Many*, chap. 8; Danys, *DP*; Gerald Dirks, *Canada's Refugee Policy: Indifference or Opportunism?* (Montreal 1977); Ian Radforth, *Bushworkers and Bosses: Logging in Northern Ontario 1900–1980* (Toronto 1987); Rachel Epstein, "Domestic Workers: The Experience in B.C.," in Linda Briskin and Lynda Yanz, eds., *Union Sisters: Women in the Labour Movement* (Toronto 1984); Mikeda Silvera *Silenced* (Toronto 1983), introduction

15 NA, IR, vol. 130, file 28885, Robillard to Joliffe, 24 March 1947; Fortier to Cogdon, 29 Sept. 1948; Ronald Brooks to Canadian Embassy, Rome, 10 Jan. 1949; W.J. Bambrick to Smith, 12 Jan. 1949. For more details consult this file. See also NA, Department of Labour (DOL), vol. 147, file 3–33–18, Heeney, Memorandum, 23 Feb. and 1 March 1949.

16 DEA, vol. 147, file 3–33–18, Leslie Chance to Raymond Ranger, Immigration-Labour Committee, 18 March 1949; personal interviews. See also Franc Sturino, "Post World War Two Canadian Immigration Policy towards Italians," *Polyphony* 7 (1985); Constance Cronin, *Sting of Change: Sicilians in Sicily and Australia* (Chicago 1970).

17 *Debates*, 13 June 1950; NA, IR, vol. 130, file 28885; on Quebec, see
   A.W. Mackenzie to Smith, 14 March 1949; Senator Gouin, "Quebec
   and Immigration," in *Symposium*; W.R. Greening, "Is the French Canadian Attitude towards Immigration Changing?" *Dalhousie Review* 27
   (Oct. 1947).
18 NA, IR, vol. 130, file 28885, James F. Manion, Report on Italy, to L.B.
   Pearson, External Affairs, 11 April 1947. For the Ontario report see ibid.
19 Ibid., vol. 674, file 92652, United Nations Bulletins, sections on Italy
   and Canada, 1 Nov. 1948, 1 Feb. 1952. On the Marshall Plan see DEA,
   vol. 147, file 3–33–18, Chance to Keenleyside, 26 July 1949; Keenleyside to Chance, 8 Aug. 1949; Canadian ambassador, Washington, Dis-
   patches, 20 July and 6 Aug. 1949.
20 NA, IR, vol. 130, file 28885, Manion to Pearson, 11 April 1947; DEA,
   vol. 147, file 3–33–1–575, L.D. Currie, Report on Italy, to Louis
   St Laurent, 10 Sept. 1949; Chance to Ranger, 18 March 1949; Canadian
   Embassy, Rome, to External Affairs, 8 March 1949; IR, vol. 130,
   file 5195–1–575, DEA, Confidential Memorandum and Briefs on Prime
   Minister Mario Scelba's visit to Canada, 1955
21 NA, IR, vol. 130, file 28885, Fortier, Memorandum: "Italian Immigration," 4 Oct. 1949
22 Ibid., Aide-memoire on Italian Immigration, 25 Oct. 1950. While the
   London office stayed open during the war, the first postwar office
   was opened in The Hague in January 1947 to oversee the movement
   of farm families. In 1948 posts went up in Brussels, Stockholm, and
   Rome; in 1949, in Salsburg, Dublin, Athens, Berne, and Liverpool.
23 NA, IR, vol. 131, file 28885, MacNamara to Di Stefano, 7 Nov. 1951.
   Much of the information on these movements is available in the detailed correspondence contained in this file and in the following files:
   IR, vol. 674, file 92655; ibid., vol. 408, file 594511; DOL, vol. 290,
   files 1–26–52–3, 1–26–3, 1–26–52–4, and 1–26–52–5.
24 For details on 1950 see IR, vol. 674, file 92655. On 1951 see DOL,
   vol. 290, file 1–26–52–5, Sharrer to MacNamara, 26 April 1951; ibid.,
   Sharrer to Dawson, 4 May 1951.
25 NA, IR, vol. 674, file 92655, J.L. Anfossi to MacNamara, 11 April 1951
26 NA, DOL, vol. 290, file 1–26–52–5, Sharrer to R. Lamarre (ILO),
   Karlsruhe, 22 March 1951 (copy to MacNamara)
27 NA, IR, vol. 408, file 594511, Rome cable to Ottawa, 29 June 1950;
   DOL, vol. 674, file 92655, shipping lists for 1950 and 1951
28 For details see IR, vol. 408, file 594511; vol. 674, file 92655.
29 Ibid., vol. 408, file 594511, J.E. Mckenna, Immigration-Labour Committee, to P.T. Baldwin, 19 Feb. 1950; H.C.P. Cresswell to G.R. Benoit, 15 March 1951; Benoit to Cresswell, 22 March 1951; Anfossi to
   Benoit, 9 April 1951

30 Ibid., vol. 408, file 594511, Baldwin, Memorandum, 5 Dec. 1951; Immigration-Labour Committee to MacNamara, 17 Dec. 1951; officer-in-charge, Stolkholm, to Benoit, 12 March and 24 April 1952

31 For details see NA, DOL, vol. 290, file 1–26–52–3 and file 1–26–52–5. On the BC order see ibid., file 1–26–52–3, MacNamara to Lamarre, 24 Oct. 1950; V.C. Wansbrough, REO, to Dawson, 20 Nov. 1950.

32 Ibid., file 1–26–52–5, MacNamara to Sharrer, 2 and 15 May, 26 July 1951

33 Ibid., file 1–26–52–3, Vittorio Bifulco, emigration attaché, Ottawa, to Dawson, 24 Sept. 1951; Dawson to Bifulco, 1 Oct. 1951. On Italians who did settle in the area see Valerie Sestieri Lee, "From Tuscany to the North West Territories: The Italian Community of Yellowknife," *Canadian Ethnic Studies* 19 (1987).

34 NA, IR, vol. 674, file 92655, Anfosi to D. McFarlane, 17 July 1950; acting director, Memorandum, 10 Aug. 1950; DOL, vol. 290, file 1–26–52–5, Dawson to Sharrer, 25 May 1951; Dawson to MacNamara, 17 Aug. 1951

35 NA, IR, vol. 131, file 28885, Sharrer (Trieste) to MacNamara, 17 Oct. 1951

36 The movement of Italians to logging jobs was comparatively small and mostly involved men who had been directly sponsored by Canadian companies. For example, see NA, IR, vol. 674, file 92655, Anfossi to Benoit, 5 and 9 April 1951; vol. 408, file 594511, Benoit to McKenna, 6 April 1951, Rome cable to Ottawa, 28 March 1951; DOL, vol. 290, file 1–26–52–3, Sharrer to Walter Harris, 4 May 1951.

37 For details on this scheme see DOL, vol. 290, file 1–26–52–4/5.

38 Ibid., MacNamara to G.B. Sullivan, 6 and 16 March, 10 and 20 April 1951; Sullivan to MacNamara, 15 June 1951; E.P. Laberge, ILO Rome Section, to MacNamara, 11 June 1951

39 Ibid., Laberge to Rome office, 16 July 1951

40 Ibid., Sharrer to M. Coté, Rome office, 2 Aug. 1951

41 Ibid., Finsider to Anfossi, 13 April 1952 (Solari Menotti's report on Canada, 17 March 1952, attached); RCMP Commissioners' Report, file D–935–302, 9 Oct. 1952; H.C. Brown, Canadian Locomotive Company, to External Affairs, 13 and 26 May 1952. See also ibid., J.F. Dwyer, "Italian Mechanics at Ajax," to Sullivan, 28 Jan. 1952; Sharrer, "Placement Report on Italian Mechanics," 29 April 1952.

42 NA, DOL, vol. 290, file 1–26–52–5, MacNamara to Chance, 8 Aug. 1949; D.C. Tait, ILO, to V.C. Phelan, 20 April 1949; Phelan to MacNamara, 26 April 1949

43 Ibid., MacNamara to premier of Ontario, 28 Sept. 1949

44 For details see DOL, vol. 290, file 1–26–52–5.

45 The assisted-passage scheme, passed in 1950, provided immigrants whose services were considered "urgently required" in Canada with no-interest loans to cover travel costs to their destination. The loan had to be repaid within twenty-five months after the immigrant's arrival. The subsidy was considered a compromise between no help and Australia's offer of free transportation to certain occupational categories of immigrants. In 1955 and 1956 the scheme was extended to include the family dependants of residents in Canada. Green, *Immigrant* 26–7

46 NA, DOL, vol. 290, file 1–26–52–5, Anfossi to Smith, 18 Nov. 1951; Anfossi to Smith, 4 June 1951

47 Ibid., file 1–26–52–4, Italy, "Report on Canada – Recruiting of Domestics," 24 July 1951

48 Ibid., Anfossi to director of immigration, 4 June 1951

49 Ibid., F.M. Hereford to MacNamara, 24 Nov. 1951

50 Ibid., Edith Cornell to H.L. Tosland, 19 Dec. 1951

51 Ibid., Dawson to Tosland, 18 Dec. 1951, 8 Jan. 1952; Fortier to MacNamara, 18 Jan. 1952; MacNamara to Fortier, 12 April 1952

52 Personal interview (pseudonym). The following discussion on frontier and farm conditions is drawn from interviews; Danys, *DP*, chaps 5–8; Radforth, *Bushworkers and Bosses*

53 Personal interview (pseudonym)

54 Personal interview (pseudonym)

55 Personel interview (pseudonym)

56 Personal interview (pseudonym); NA, DOL, vol. 290, file 1–26–52–3, William Horrobin, UIC, Vancouver, to Dawson, 12 Aug. 1951

57 NA, DOL, vol. 290, file 1–26–52–3, manager, Van Roi Mines, to Fortier, 12 Sept. 1951

58 Ibid., George Wallach to Horrobin, 13 Sept. 1951

59 Gianni Grohovaz, "Toronto's Italian Press after the Second World War," *Polyphony* 4 (1982); personal interview (pseudonym)

60 Personal interview (pseudonym). On an earlier period see Bruno Ramirez, "Brief Encounters: Italian Immigrant Workers and the CPR, 1900–1930," *Labour/Le Travail* 17 (1985); Antonio Pucci, "Canadian Industrialization versus the Italian Contadini in a Decade of Brutality, 1902–1912," in Robert F. Harney and J. Vincenza Scarpaci, eds., *Little Italies in North America* (Toronto 1981); Jean Morrison, "Ethnicity and Violence: The Lakehead Freighthandlers before World War I," in Gregory S. Kealey and Peter Warrian, eds., *Essays in Canadian Working-Class History* (Toronto 1976); Craig Heron and Robert Storey, "Work and Struggle in the Canadian Steel Industry, 1900–1950," in Heron and Storey, eds., *On the Job: Confronting the Labour Process in Canada*

(Kingston/Montreal 1986); Craig Heron, *Working in Steel* (Toronto 1988).

61 NA, DOL, vol. 290, file 1–26–52–5, Dawson to Sharrer, 25 May 1951

62 NA, IR, vol. 131, file 28885, Baldwin, Memorandum, "Italian Farm Labour Cases," 24 April 1950; Fortier to Di Stefano, 17 April 1950

63 Ibid., Antonietti Report, 26 Sept. 1951

64 Ibid., Anfossi to Benoit, 25 Nov. 1951

65 NA, DOL, vol. 290, file 1–26–52–3, H.H. Wright (CMMA), to Dawson, 26 Sept. 1951; manager, Western Exploration Company, to Henry Johns, UIC, Salmo, BC, nd; Wright to Dawson, 28 July 1951; Dawson to Wright, 8 Aug. 1951

66 NA, IR, vol. 131, file 28885, MacNamara to Di Stefano, 7 Nov. 1951

67 Ibid., Baldwin, Memorandum, "Eastern District Superintendant, Travelling Inspector's Report," to chief of settlement services, 24 April 1950; personal interviews.

68 NA, DOL, vol. 290, file 1–26–52–4, L.G. Simmons, Rome, to Lamarre, 11 Jan. 1952

69 Ibid., Dwyer to NES Toronto office, 5 Feb. 1952; NES Labour Survey, Jan. 1952; V. Coyne to MacNamara, 8 Jan. 1952; R. McGuire to Mac-Namara, 15 Jan. 1952

70 Ibid., Dwyer, quoting P. Gravely's report to Miss Irvine, NES, Toronto, Ottawa, 12 Jan. 1952

71 Ibid., J. Hamilton to MacNamara, 12 Jan. 1952; C. Kristjansson to Dawson, 12 Jan. 1952. On skipping, see Cornell to Tosland, 30 April 1952. Further details are contained in this file.

72 Personal interviews (pseudonyms). PAO, International Institute of Metropolitan Toronto (IIMT), Confidential case files, MU6519, 1962 (pseudonym). Other files of miners who later arrived in Toronto confirm this pattern. Since these are confidential case files, the identities of clients are not revealed.

73 Personal interview. The employment files contained in IIMT, MU6518–22 refer to dozens of men who arrived in Toronto each year because of seasonal layoffs in resource–industry jobs.

74 Personal interview (pseudonym)

75 NA, DOL, vol. 279, file 1–26–10–1, Lewis to Dawson, 10 Aug. 1951, cited in Danys, *DP*, 334, n29

76 Ninth Annual Federal-Provincial Conference, *Labour Gazette*, Feb. 1952, 145–52; NA, IR, vol. 131, file 28885, Fortier, Memorandum, 15 Sept. 1951. For an earlier period see Franc Sturino, "Italian Immigration and the Farm Labour System through the 1920s," *Studi Emigrazione* 77 (1985).

77 Personal interview (pseudonym). For comparative purposes see

Danys, *DP*; Radforth, *Bushworkers* and Bosses; and Abella and Troper, *None Is Too Many*.

78 *Debates*, 23 Aug. 1958, 23 April 1959; Samuel Sidlofsky, "Postwar Immigrants in the Changing Metropolis with Special Reference to Toronto's Italian Population" (PhD thesis, University of Toronto, 1969), chap. 2

79 NA, DOL, vol. 290, file 1–26–52–4, Dwyer to Irvine, 8 Jan. 1952; Dunham to Hamilton, 9 Jan. 1952; Cornell to Tosland, 30 April 1952

80 Personal interview (pseudonym)

81 The only detailed community study available on the postwar Italians in a Canadian city is Jeremy Boissevain's *The Italians of Montreal: Social Adjustment in a Plural Society* (Ottawa 1970), undertaken as part of the studies of the Royal Commission on Bilingualism and Biculturalism. Statistics for regions are compiled from *Annuario Statistico Italiano* (Rome 1956, 1960), cited in Sturino, "Family and Kin Cohesion among South Italian Immigrants in Toronto," in Caroli et al., eds., *Italian Immigrant Woman*; data on major provinces of origin are compiled from *Annuario Di Statictiche del Lavoro* (Rome 1959), and figures supplied by Italian consulate are cited in Sidlofsky, "Postwar Immigrants," 110–12.

82 Personal interviews. The impact of emigration on Italian towns has only recently attracted the attention of scholars in Italy. See, for example, the articles in *Altreitalie* 1–4 (1989–90).

83 L.D. MacDonald, "Chain Migration, Ethnic Neighborhood Formation and Social Networks," *Millbank Memorial Fund Quarterly* 13 (1964); Harvey Choldin, "Kinship Networks in the Migration Process," *International Migration Review* 7 (1973); Sturino, "Family and Kin Cohesion." On boarding arrangements in Toronto see chapters 3 and 4.

84 NA, IR, vol. 131, file 28885, Smith to Benoit, 18 oct. 1951; Robillard to Fortier, 15 Sept. 1948; H.B. Jeffs, chief medical officer, Rome, to C.P. Brown, 20 Sept. 1948; Anfossi to acting director, 28 Oct. 1950; Robillard, Memorandum, 27 Dec. 1950

85 Ibid., vol. 349, file 5195–1–575, acting chief of operations to Canadian Embassy, Rome, "Immigration Agents – Italy," 12 March 1964; director, Memorandum, "Investigation of Settlement Arrangements – Immigration from Italy," to Fortier, 19 Dec. 1960

86 Ibid., vol. 131, file 28885, Benoit to Bifulco, 15 May 1951; chief admissions officer to Robillard, 11 May 1951

87 Ibid., Memorandum, "Curtailment of Movement of Immigrants from Italy," 30 May 1952; Benoit to Smith, 31 May 1952. These restrictions worried External Affairs officials keen to improve relations with Italy. See also ibid., Heeney, Memorandum, 18 Aug. 1952; Smith to Fortier, 28 Sept. 1953, 18 May 1956; DEA, vol. 147, file 3–33–18, Fortier to Har-

ris, 25 May 1954; Ocupational List, Jan. 1955; acting director to Fortier, 8 May 1956; *Debates*, 26 June 1954, 30 Jan. 1958, 5 March 1959; Blair Fraser, "Can the Immigration Issue Lick the Liberals?" *Maclean's*, 10 Dec. 1955.

88 DEA, vol. 128, file 3–33–16, Cabinet Committee on Immigration, Memorandum, 15 Aug. 1958; Fortier to Ellen Fairclough, 24 June 1958; *Debates*, 30 June 1958, 22 and 23 April 1959; NA, IR, vol. 349, file 5195–1–575, W.R. Baskerville, Memorandum, 19 Dec. 1960

89 Hawkins, *Canada and Immigration*, 121–5; Peter C. Newman, *Renegade in Power: The Diefenbaker Years* (Toronto 1963), 100

90 For details see especially Hawkins, *Canada and Immigration*, chaps 1 and 2.

CHAPTER THREE

1 Valentini cited in Toronto *Telegram*, 18 March 1960; Toronto, *Globe and Mail*, 18 March 1960

2 *Globe and Mail*, 18 March 1960. For details of events, subsequent inquiry, and responses see *Telegram*, 18 and 19 March, 2, 4, and 6 April 1960; Toronto *Star*, 18 March, 4 April 1960; *Corriere Canadese* 22 March, 5 and 12 April 1960.

3 *Corriere Canadese*, 22 March 1960

4 Judith E. Smith, *Family Connections: A History of Italian and Jewish Immigrant Lives in Providence, Rhode Island 1990–1940* (Albany 1985). See also Virginia Yans-McLaughlin, *Family and Community: Italian Immigrants in Buffalo, 1880–1920* (Ithaca 1971); John Bodnar et al., *Lives of Their Own: Blacks, Italians and Poles in Pittsburgh, 1900–1960*; Miriam Cohen, "From Workshop to Office: Italian Women and Family Strategies in New York City, 1900–1950" (PhD thesis, University of Michigan, 1978).

5 Personal interview (pseudonym). Postwar immigrants tended to be fairly young; the average for all ethnic orgins was 24.9. For Italians the figure was 23.7. W. Kalback and W. McKey, *The Impact of Immigration on Canada* (Ottawa 1970), 50

6 *Report of the Royal Commission on Labour-Management Relations in the Construction Industry* (Ontario 1962); Samuel Sidlofsky, "Postwar Immigrants in the Changing Metropolis with Special Reference to Toronto's Italian Population" (PhD thesis, University of Toronto, 1969). For a detailed look at the construction industry see chapter 7 in this book.

7 Robert F. Harney, "Boarding and Belonging: Thoughts on Sojourner Institutions," *Urban History Review* 2 (1978); personal interview

8 Jeremy Boissevain, *The Italians of Montreal: Social Adjustment in a Plural Society* (Ottawa 1970), 9–18. For contemporary accounts of Italian households in Toronto see also Edith Ferguson, *Newcomers in Transi-*

tion (Toronto 1962–4); Department of Citizenship and Immigration, Report EG–2, Martin Greenwood, "Some Observations of Italian Immigrants in Toronto," (Ottawa 1962). I would like to thank the late Robert F. Harney for lending me a copy of this report.

9 James Lemon, *Toronto since 1918: An Illustrated History* (Toronto 1985), chap. 4

10 Anthony Richmond, *Immigrants and Ethnic Groups in Metropolitan Toronto* (Toronto: York University 1967); Anthony Richmond and Suzanne Ziegler, *Characteristics of Italian Householders* (Toronto: York University 1972). Immigration Branch data on intended occupations reveal that with few industrial skills, most Italians were slotted for low-level jobs. The statistics are cited in the appendix. For a discussion see Louis Parai, *Emigration and Immigration of Professional and Skilled Manpower during the Postwar Period* (Ottawa 1965); Clifford Jansen, *Italians in a Multicultural Canada* (Lewiston/Queenston 1988).

11 The case studies are in Archives of Ontario (AO), International Institute of Metropolitan Toronto (IIMT) MU6399, Italian Immigrant Aid Society (IIAS), *Annual Report*, 1963–4; ibid., IIMT, MU6515, Confidential Case files, 1969 H–I (pseudonym); MU6519, 1962 C. To protect confidentiality, the names of institute clients who appear in the text have been changed, and some details of each case history have been modified. See also ibid, MU6399, IIAS, *Monthly Report*, March 1955; AO, Microfilm, 54-1, IIAS, Minutes of Executive Meetings, 20 May 1959.

12 Personal interview (pseudonym); AO, IIMT, MU6520, 1962 F (pseudonym); case file in ibid., 1962 C

13 Personal interviews; census statistics do not provide a breakdown of jobs. For a sample, see AO, IIMT, MU6513–20; MU6399, IIAS, *Monthly Reports*, 1954–64.

14 Personal interviews; Franc Sturino, "Contours of Postwar Italian Immigration to Toronto," *Polyphony* 6 (1984)

15 *Corriere Canadese*, 6 Oct. 1954; personal interviews

16 See John E. Zucchi, *Italians in Toronto: Development of a National Identity 1875–1935* (Kingston/Montreal 1988); Franc Sturino, *Forging the Chain: Italian Migration to North America, 1880–1930* (Toronto 1990); Franc Sturino and John Zucchi, guest eds., Special Issue on Italians, *Polyphony* 7 (1985).

17 On average, construction labourers earned $2000–$2499, an income that was comparable with that earned by service workers (cleaners/cooks, waiters), food and beverage workers, and landscape workers. The wages of construction tradesmen, which ranged between $3000 and $3500, compared favourably with those earned by tradesmen in industry. Self-employed building tradesmen, or subcontractors, could

potentially earn still higher wages. Calculations based on Canada, *Census*, 1961, vol. 4, table B:4. See also chapter 7.

18 Yans-McLaughlin, *Family and Community*. See also Smith, *Family Connections*; Edwin Fenton, *Immigrants and Unions: A Case Study, Italians and American Labor* (New York 1975); Bruno Ramirez, *Les Premiers Italiens de Montréal: L'origine de la Petite Italie du Québec* (Montreal 1980).

19 Personal interview (pseudonym). On the value of kin networks to rural migrants and immigrants see Michael Anderson, *Family Structure in Nineteenth Century Lancashire* (London 1971); Gordon Darroch, "Migrants in the Nineteenth Century: Fugitives or Families in Motion," *Journal of Family History* 6 (1981); John Bodnar, *Workers' World: Kinship, Community and Protest in an Industrial City* (Baltimore 1982).

20 Personal interviews (pseudonyms). Similar stories were told by other man who had been artisans.

21 Personal interview (pseudonym); interviews

22 Elizabeth Ewen, *Immigrant Women in the Land of Dollars: Life and Culture on the Lower East Side* (New York 1985). On immigrant marketplaces see also Moses Rischin, *The Promised City: New York's Jews, 1870–1914* (New York 1962); John Bodnar, *The Transplanted: A History of Immigrants in Urban America* (Bloomington, Ind. 1985).

23 Bruno Ramirez, "Brief Encounters: Italian Immigrant Workers and the CPR, 1900–1930," *Labour/Le Travail* 17 (1986). See also Robert F. Harney, "Toronto's Little Italy, 1885–1945," in Harney and J. Vincenza Scarpaci, *Little Italies in North America* (Toronto 1981); Zucchi, *Italians in Toronto*.

24 AO, IIMT, MU6399, IIAS, *Monthly Report*, Nov. 1960; ibid., *Annual Report*, 1963–4; IIMT, Case files, MU6514–6523

25 Case files involving complaints are in AO, IIMT, MU6514, 1962 D, 1962 E–F; MU6509, 1957.

26 Ibid., MU 6513, 1959 C (pseudonym)

27 Ibid., 1962 B (pseudonym)

28 *Labour Gazette*, May 1957, 555–60; Report on Injury and Fatalities in Ontario for 1956, *Labour Gazette*, May 1957, 558, 555–60; *Report of the Royal Commission on Industrial Safety* (Toronto 1971), 11–13, 27, appendix F, 74; Paul Malle, *Employment Insecurity and Industrial Relations in Construction* (Ottawa 1975), table 7.1, 58

29 *Telegram*, 5, 7, 8, and 9 April 1960; *Report of the Royal Commission on Industrial Safety* 13, 19–20, 35–6. See also H.C. Goldenberg and J.H. Crispo, *Construction Labour Relations* (Toronto 1968), 587.

30 Samuel Sidlofsky and Stephen Hellman, *The Delivery of Safety Services to New Canadian Workers* (Prepared for the Joint Project of Canadian Construction Association and Locals 506 and 183 of the International

Laborers' International Union of America, New Canadian Workers' Project, Ontario Ministry of Labour, 1975), 30–7. My thanks to Stephan Hellman for making the report available to me.

31 *Corriere Canadese*, 29 Sept. 1954, 1 March 1955, 9 Sept. 1958
32 Ibid., 10 Feb. 1959, 3 June 1958
33 Ibid., 27 May 1958
34 Ibid., 2 July 1957
35 Personal interview
36 On wcb cases see, for example, the cases contained in ao, iimt, mu6516, 1961 h–i; mu6515, 1962–5 v; mu6515, 1963–6 t; mu6517, 1961 p, q; mu6514, 1960–6 m; mu6523, 1962–4 f, g; mu6523, 1963 c. See also Ferguson, *Newcomers in Transition*, 61–3.
37 The case file is in ao, immt, mu6514, 1960–6 l.
38 Ibid., mu6416, file on costi, *Star*, 10 Feb. 1973 (clippings). On costi see chapter 6.
39 Labour historians have shown little interest in the relations between male workers and their families, but a recent correction is Mark Rosenfeld, "'It Was a Hard Life': Class and Gender in the Work and Family Rhythms of a Railway Town, 1920–1950," *Historical Papers*, 1988, and Joy Parr's pathbreaking work, *The Gender of Breadwinners: Women, Men and Industrial Change in Two Industrial Towns* (Toronto 1990). Immigration historians have done better in this regard, mainly because they have tried to understand men's actions at least in part by reference to family strategies. For Canadian examples see Lilian Petroff, "Sojourner and Settler: The Macedonian Presence in the City, 1903–1940," in Robert F. Harney, ed., *Gathering Place: Peoples and Neighbourhoods of Toronto, 1834–1945* (Toronto 1985); Carmela Patrias, "Patriots and Proletarians: The Politicization of Hungarian Immigrants in Canada, 1924–1946" (PhD thesis, University of Toronto, 1985), while Bruce S. Elliot's illuminating *Irish Migrants in the Canadas: A New Approach* (Kingston/Montreal 1988) is an example of how a family focus can obscure women's lives at the same time as it illuminates men's experiences. A useful discussion of the literature on Canadian working women is Bettina Bradbury, "Women's History and Working-Class History," *Labour/Le Travail* 19 (1987). Valuable American studies include Alice Kessler-Harris, *Out To Work: A History of Wage-Earning Women in the United States* (New York 1982); Sarah Eisenstein, *Give Us Bread But Give Us Roses: Working Women's Consciousness in the United States, 1890 to the First World War* (London 1983).
40 Personal interview
41 Calculations based on Canada, *Census*, 1961, vol 1.3, table 107
42 Calculations from Lydio Tomasi, "The Italian Community in Toronto:

A Demographic Profile," *International Migration Review* 11 (1977): 197–8. The data refers to Italians as an ethnic group and thus includes Italian-born and Canadian-born Italians.

43 Ferguson, *Newcomers in Transition*, 69, 35–8

44 Anthony Richmond and Warren Kalback, *Factors in the Adjustment of Immigrants and Their Descendents* (Ottawa 1980), 404–7. The data refers to Italian ethnic origin. On immigrant homeownership for an earlier period see Stephen Thernstrom's work on Italians and Irish in *The Other Bostonians: Poverty and Progress in the American Metropolis, 1880–1970* (Cambridge, Mass. 1973). See also Franc Sturino, "The Social Mobility of Italian Canadians: 'Outside' and 'Inside' Concepts of Mobility," *Polyphony* 7 (1985).

45 Ferguson, *Newcomers in Transition*, 35

46 As previously noted, in 1961 Italian-speaking men earned on average $3016. That same year, Statistics Canada produced poverty lines of $1500 for a single person, $2500 for a family of two, $3000 for a family of three, and $500 for each additional person. See the Report on the Special Senate Committee on Poverty, *Poverty in Canada* (Ottawa 1976), 6. Families on unemployment benefits could face considerable hardship. In 1955, for example, a bricklayer employed for one week might earn $114; the benefits paid to him and his dependants might amount to only $30. In the same year, a labourer might earn $39, but his weekly benefits would be $17 if he were single and $24 if he had dependants. (The calculations assume an estimated bricklayer's hourly wage of $2.40 and a labourer's of 90 cents.) The schedule of benefits is contained in Gary Dingle, *A Chronolgy of Response: The Evolution of Unemployment Insurance from 1940–1980* (Ottawa 1981).

47 AO, IIMT, MU6521, 1963 D (pseudonym)

48 Ibid., MU6514, 1964, F, G (pseudonym). Other cases reveal injured men trying to find work for their wives. For example see ibid., MU6514, F, G; 1962 D.

49 The file is in ibid., MU6519, 1962 C (pseudonym); interview (pseudonym).

50 Cited in Clifford Jansen and Lee R Cavera, *Fact-Book on Italians in Canada* (Toronto: York University 1981), table 4.8, 39. (This data refers to ethnic origin.) On the schools see Loren Lind, "New Canadianism: Melting the Ethnics in Toronto Schools," in George Martell, ed., *The Politics of the Canadian Public School* (Toronto 1971).

51 AO, IIMT, MU6515, 1960 J-P (pseudonym)

52 Personel interview. The Italians (as an ethnic group) did not experience upward mobility with respect to education, occupation, and income until the 1980s, which reflects mobility among the second and third generation. See Jansen, *Italians in a Multicultural Canada*, chap. 5.

Such findings concur with the lagged mobility of earlier Italians to the United States. See Stephen Thernstrom, *Poverty and Progress: Social Mobility in a Nineteenth Century City* (Cambridge, Mass. 1964).

53 The debate concerns the importance of the "family wage" to the survival of the working-class family, and to women's secondary status in the labour movement. For example, see Jane Humphries, "Class Struggle and the Persistence of the Working Class Family," *Cambridge Journal of Economics* 1 (1977); Michele Barrett and Mary McIntosh, "'The Family Wage': Some Problems for Socialists and Feminists," *Capital and Class* 11 (1980); Martha May, "'Bread before Roses: American Workingmen, Labor Unions and the Family Wage," in Ruth Milkman, ed., *Woman, Work and Protest: A Century of U.S. Women's Labor History* (London 1985).

54 Personal interview

55 Personal interview

56 Personal interview. Similar views were expressed by other informants. See also Franc Sturino, "Family and Kin Cohesion among South Italian Immigrants in Toronto," in Betty Boyd Caroli et al., eds., *The Italian Immigrant Woman in North America* (Toronto 1978).

57 AO, IIMT, MU6521, 1962 V–Z (pseudonym)

58 The case file is in ibid., MU6519, 1962 C; personal interview.

59 *Corriere Canadese*, 9 March 1960; interview

60 Cynthia Cockburn, *Brothers* (London 1983); Stan Gray, "Sharing the Shop Floor," in Michael Kaufman, ed., *Beyond Patriarchy: Essays by Men on Pleasure, Power and Change* (Toronto 1987); Mark Rosenfeld, "It Was a Hard Life"; D.W. Livingstone and Meg Luxton, "Gender Consciousness at Work: Modification of the Male Breadwinner Norm among Steelworkers and Their Spouses," *Canadian Review of Sociology and Anthropology* 26 (1989). See also Meg Luxton, *More Than a Labour of Love* (Toronto 1980); Parr, *Gender of Breadwinners*.

61 For a more detailed discussion see chapter 5.

CHAPTER FOUR

1 Personal interview (pseudonym)

2 National Archives of Canada (NA), Immigration Branch Records (IR), vol. 131, file 28885, G.H. McGee, "Some Observations Respecting ... Italian Farm Workers," 4 April 1952

3 NA, Department of External Affairs, Statement, 29 March 1950; A.D.P. Heeney, Memorandum, 30 March 1950; House of Commons, *Debates*, 28 March 1960

4 Alan G. Green, *Immigration and the Postwar Canadian Economy* (Toronto 1976), 89–90; Monica Boyd, "The Status of Immigrant Women in Can-

ada," in Marylee Stephenson, ed., *Women in Canada* (Don Mills 1977).
See also Sheila Arnopolous, *Problem of Immigrant Women in the Canadian Labour Force* (Ottawa 1979); Laura Johnson, *The Seam Allowance: Industrial Home Sewing in Canada* (Toronto 1982); Alejandra Cumsille et al., "Tripple Oppression: Immigrant Women in the Labour Force," in Linda Briskin and Lynda Yanz, eds., *Union Sisters: Women in the Labour Movement* (Toronto 1983); Roxanna Ng and Tania Das Gupta, "Nation-Builders? The Captive Labour Force of Non-English Speaking Immigrant Women," *Canadian Woman's Studies* 3 (1981); Mikeda Silvera, *Silenced* (Toronto 1983).

5 Jan Brogger, *Montavarese: A Study of a Peasant Society and Culture in Southern Italy* (Oslo 1971); John Davis, *Land and Family in Pisticci* (New York 1973) 94–5

6 Constance Cronin, *The Sting of Change: Sicilians in Sicily and Australia* (Chicago 1970), chap. 4; Brogger, *Montaverese*, 106–20; Davis, *Pisticci*, chap. 2; Charlotte Gower Chapman, *Milocca: A Sicilian Village* (Cambridge, Mass. 1971), 41, 72–80, 109–10; A.L. Maraspini, *The Study of an Italian Village* (Paris 1968), 17–18, 73–8, 142–50

7 Personal interview (pseudonym); Leonard W. Moss and Walter H. Thompson, "The South Italian Family: Literature and Observation," *Human Organization* 18 (1959)

8 Personal interview (pseudonym); interviews. See also Judith E. Smith, *Family Connections: A History of Italian and Jewish Immigrant Lives in Providence, Rhode Island 1900–1940* (Albany 1985), chap. 2; Donna Gabbaccia, *From Sicily to Elizabeth Street: Housing and Social Change among Italian Immigrants* (Albany 1984), chap. 2; Edward Banfield, *The Moral Basis of a Backward Society* (New York 1958), 53–4, 63; Davis, *Pisticci*, 46–7; Chapman, *Milocca*, 23–5.

9 Rudolph Bell, *Fate and Honor, Family and Village* (Chicago 1979), 40, 124–7; references in note 8

10 Personal interview. On Sicily see Cronin, *Sting of Change*, 92–4; Chapman, *Milocca*, 32–3; for other regions see interviews and Ann Cornelisen, *Women of the Shadows: A Study of the Wives and Mothers of Southern Italy* (New York 1977), 24, 157–60; Davis, *Pisticci*, chap. 3.

11 Personal interviews; Chapman, *Milocca*, 23–4, 32–4, 64; Bell, *Fate and Honour*, 124–34; Banfield, *Backward Society*, 50

12 Personal interviews; Chapman, *Milocca*, 16–17. See also Thomas Kessner and Betty Boyd Caroli, "New Immigrant Woman at Work: Italians and Jews in New York City, 1880–1905," *Journal of Ethnic Studies* 5 (1978).

13 Personal interview (pseudonym); interviews; Cronin, *Sting of Change*, 92–5

14 Banfield, *Backward Society*, 53; Maraspini, *Italian Village*, 14–15; Ann

Cornelisen, *Women of the Shadows*, 44–5; Lucia Chiavola Birnbaum, *liberazione della donna: feminism in Italy* (Middletown, Conn. 1986), 242

15 Personal interview (pseudonym)

16 Personal interviews (pseudonyms); Gabbaccia, *From Sicily to Elizabeth Street*, 40–5

17 Cornelisen, *Women of the Shadows*, 222–4, 57–93; Chapman, *Milocca*, 32–40. Oral informants made the same point. By contrast, contemporary studies, such as Harriet Perry, "The Metonymic Definition of the Female and Concept of Honour among Italian Immigrant Families in Toronto," in Caroli et al., *Italian Immigrant Woman*, stress Italian women's subordination within the family. See also Vincenza Scarpaci, "La Contadina, the Plaything of the Middle Class Woman Historian," *Journal of Ethnic Studies* 9 (1981).

18 Personal interview (pseudonyms). See also Davis, *Pisticci*, 31–2.

19 Chapman, *Milocca*, 40; Personal interview (pseudonym)

20 Personal interview (pseudonym)

21 Ann Bravo, "Solidarity and Loneliness: Piedmontese Peasant Women at the Turn of the Century," *International Journal of Oral History* 3 (1982)

22 Personal interviews; Cornelisen, *Women of the Shadows*, 61–3; Gabbaccia, *From Sicily to Elizabeth Street*, 44–9; Chapman, *Milocca*, 83–4, 116–28

23 Personal interview (pseudonym); interviews. See also Gabaccia, *From Sicily to Elizabeth Street*, chap. 3; Davis, *Pisticci*, 71–2.

24 Cited in Gabbaccia, *From Sicily to Elizabeth Street*, 48

25 Personal interviews (pseudonyms)

26 Personal interview (pseudonym)

27 Personal interview (pseudonym). This pattern was also pronounced among postwar Portuguese immigrants. See David Higgs, *The Portuguese in Canada* (Saint John, NB 1982).

28 Personal interviews (pseudonyms). Valuable discussions of women and migration include Mirjana Morokvasic, "Why Do Women Migrate? Towards an Understanding of the Sex-Selectivity in the Migratory Movements of Labour," *Studi Emigrazione* 20 (1983); Annie Phizacklea, ed., *One Way Ticket: Migration and Female Labour* (London 1983).

29 Personal interviews

30 Personal interviews

31 Personal interviews (pseudonyms)

32 Personal interview (pseudonym). For a contemporary account of boarding among Italian families see Edith Ferguson, *Newcomers in Transition: A Project of the International Institute of Metropolitan Toronto 1962–1964* (Toronto 1964).

33 Personal interviews. On domestic labour see Wally Secombe, "The Housewife and Her Labour under Capitalism," *New Left Review* 83

(1974); Meg Luxton, *More than a Labour of Love: Three Generations of Women's Work in the Home* (Toronto 1980); Bonnie Fox, *Hidden in the Household: Women's Domestic Labour under Capitalism* (Toronto 1980). For an earlier period see Ruth Shwartz Cowan, *More Work for Mother: The Ironics of Household Technology from the Open Hearth to the Microwave* (New York 1983); Veronica Strong-Boag, "Keeping House in God's Country": Canadian Women at Work in the Home," in Craig Heron and Robert Storey, eds., *On the Job* (Montreal/Kingston 1986).

34 Personal interview

35 Personal interview (pseudonym); personal interview. See also Mark Rosenfeld. "It Was a Hard Life": Class and Gender in the Work and Family Rhythms of a Railway Town," *Historical Papers* (1988).

36 Personal interviews (pseudonyms). On nativism see also chapter 5.

37 Ferguson, *Newcomers in Transition*, 7–8; personal interviews

38 Married women's statistics cited in Julie White, *Women and Unions* (Ottawa 1980), 37; Toronto data in Canada, *Census*, 1961. See also Patricia Connelly, *Last Hired First Fired: Women and the Canadian Work Force* (Toronto 1978); Pat and Hugh Armstrong, *The Double Ghetto: Canadian Women and Their Segregated Work* (Toronto 1978).

39 This calculation was arrived at by dividing the total number of Italian women in the Metropolitan work force into the total number of women in the Italian ethnic group aged 15–64 in Metropolitan Toronto. Using the same method of calculation, the percentage of women in the work force by ethnic group was as follows: all groups, 44.6; British Isles, 45.0; German, 51.0; Netherlands, 18.9; Polish, 41.5; Ukrainian, 48.5. Canada, *Census* 1961; Dominion Bureau of Statistics, Unpublished Tables on Labour Force, Metropolitan Toronto, 1961

40 Canada, *Census*, 1961. See also Arnopolous, *Immigrant Women;* Monica Boyd, "At a Disadvantage: The Occupational Attainment of Foreign-Born Women in Canada," *International Migration Review* 18 (1984) and "The Status of Immigrant Women in Canada," *Canadian Review of Sociology and Anthropology* 12:4 (1975); Charlene Gannage, *Double Day, Double Bind: Women Garment Workers* (Toronto 1986); Margueritte Andersen, ed., *Histoires d'immigrées* (Montreal 1987); Catherine E. Warren, ed., *Vignettes of Life: Experiences and Self-Perceptions of New Canadian Women* (Calgary 1986); Barbara Roberts et al., *Looking for Greener Pastures: Immigrant Women in the Winnipeg Garment Industry* (Toronto, forthcoming).

41 Archives of Ontario (AO), International Institute of Metropolitan Toronto (IIMT), MU6399, Italian Immigrant Aid Society, *Annual Report*, 1962, 1962–4; MU6461, files on sewing courses; Ferguson, *Newcomers in Transition* 81

42 Personal interview (pseudonym); interviews; Ferguson, *Newcomers in Transition*, 54–5. On female kin networks see also Varpu Lindstrom-Best, *Defiant Sisters: A Social History of Finnish Immigrant Women in Canada* (Toronto 1988); Marilyn Barber, "Sunny Ontario for British Girls, 1900–1930," in Jean Burnett, ed., *Looking into My Sister's Eyes: An Exploration in Women's History* (Toronto 1986); Joy Parr, "Rethinking Work and Kinship in a Canadian Hosiery Town, 1900–1950," *Feminist Studies* 1 (1987), and "The Skilled Emigrant and Her Kin: Gender, Culture and Labour Recruitment," *Canadian Historical Review* 68 (1987).

43 Virginia Yans-McLaughlin, "Patterns of Work and Family Organization: Buffalo's Italians," *Journal of Interdisciplinary History* 2 (1971), *Family and Community: Italian Immigrants in Buffalo, 1880–1930* (Urbana 1982), chap. 7, and "Italian Women and Work: Experience and Perception," in Milton Cantor and Bruce Laurie, eds., *Class, Sex and the Woman Worker* (Westport, Conn. 1977). On Canada see Franc Sturino, "The Role of Women in Italian Immigration to the New World," in Burnet, ed., *My Sister's Eyes*; Josephine Atri, "Italian Immigrant Women in Post-War Montreal" (MA thesis, Concordia University, 1980).

44 Personal interviews with oral informants; Louise Tilly, "Comments on the Yans-McLaughlin and Davidoff Papers," *Journal of Social History* 7 (1974)

45 Personal interview

46 Giuliana Colalillo, "Culture Conflict in the Adolescent Italian Girl" (MA thesis, University of Toronto, 1974), 82–8; Roxana Ng and Judith Ramirez, *Immigrant Housewives: A Report* (Toronto 1981)

47 For a similar argument on an earlier period see Bettina Bradury, "The Fragmented Family: Family Strategies in the Face of Death, Illness and Poverty, Montreal, 1860–1885," in Joy Parr, ed., *Childhood and Family in Canadian History* (Toronto 1982).

48 Personal interviews; AO, IIMT, MU6522, 1963 D, F D; MU6518, 1962 A, A A. For a comparison see Fernanda Nunes, "Portuguese-Canadian Women: Problems and Prospects," *Polyphony* 8 (1986); Roberts et al., *Greener Pastures*.

49 Personal interviews; Ferguson, *Newcomers in Transition*, 127

50 White, *Women and Unions*, chap. 3; personal interviews. See also Sheila Arnopolous, "Immigrants and Women: Sweatshops of the 1970s," in Irving Abella and David Miller, eds., *The Canadian Worker in the Twentieth Century* (Toronto 1983); Rachel Epstein, "Domestic Workers: The Experience in BC," in Briskin and Yanz, eds., *Union Sisters*

51 Ferguson, *Newcomers in Transition*, 122–5; personal interviews (pseudonyms)

52 Personal interview; AO, IIMT, MU6522, 1963 C (pseudonym); personal interview (pseudonym); AO, IIMT, MU6522, 1963 B.

53 Ferguson, *Newcomers in Transition*, 125

54 Personal interview (pseudonym); the case file is in AO, IIMT, MU6517, 1961 P, Q; MU6522, 1963 C.

55 Personal interview; Ferguson, *Newcomers in Transition*, 126

56 Personal interview; AO, IMMT, MU6514, 1962 D; Johnson, *The Seam Allowance*

57 Personal interviews

58 Personal interviews; Stuart Marshall Jamieson, *Times of Trouble: Labour Unrest and Industrial Conflict in Canada, 1900–66* (Ottawa 1968), chap. 7; White, *Women and Unions*, 36–45

59 Judith Adler Hellman, "The Italian Communists, the Woman's Question, and the Challenge of Feminism," *Studies in Political Economy* 13 (1985); and *Journeys Among Women: Feminism in Five Italian Cities* (New York 1987); Birnbaum, *Liberazione della donna*

60 Roman Catholic Archdiocese of Toronto Archives, Parish files, St Mary of the Angels, Father Benjamin Basetti to Monsignor Fulton, 24 Sept. 1961; *Corriere Canadese*, 14 July 1954, 15 Feb. 1955, 31 Jan. and 3 Feb. 1956

61 Personal interview; personal interview (pseudonym)

62 Cited in Drea, "Garment Jungle Hit by Unionist," *Telegram*, 5 and 16 May 1960. In 1960 the female minimum wage in Ontario was $30 per week (about 62 cents per hour) for experienced workers and $26–$27 per week (or 54–56 cents per hour) for inexperienced workers for a week of not more than 48 hours. In 1955 the figures were $22 and $19–$20 per week, respectively. *Labour Gazette* 1960, 720; 1955, 330

63 *Corriere Canadese*, 21 and 31 May 1957; Drea, "Immigrants Thrive in Fur Industry," *Telegram*, 12 April 1960; Toronto *Star*, 5 and 10 May 1960; NA, MU31, Marino Toppan Papers, file on Boot and Shoe Workers Union, Speeches for *Voce del Lavoro* (Voice of Labour) radio broadcasts, 16 March and 10 June 1965; *Star*, 20 Sept. 1960

64 Personal interview (pseudonym); *Telegram*, 5 May 1960. See also Costanza Allevato, "The Status of Italian Immigrant Women in Canada," *Canadian Woman Studies* 8 (1987).

CHAPTER FIVE

1 Robert T. Allen, "Portrait of Little Italy," *Maclean's*, 21 March 1964

2 On Canadian patterns of racism and nativism see, for example, Howard Palmer, *Patterns of Prejudice: A History of Nativism in Alberta* (Toronto 1982); Donald Avery, *Dangerous Foreigners: European Immigrant Workers and Labour Radicalism* (Toronto 1979); Marilyn Barber,

"Nationalism, Nativism, and the Social Gospel: The Protestant Church Response to Foreign Immigrants in Western Canada," in A.R. Allen, ed., *The Social Gospel in Canada* (Ottawa 1975); Peter Ward, *White Canada Forever: Popular Attitudes and Public Policy Toward Orientals in British Columbia* (Montreal 1979); Patricia Roy, *A White Man's Province: British Columbian Politicians and Chinese and Japanese Immigrants 1858–1914* (Vancouver 1989); Lita-Rose Betcherman, *The Swastika and the Maple Leaf: Fascist Movements in the Thirties* (Don Mills 1975); Irving Abella and Harold Troper, *None Is Too Many: Canada and the Jews of Europe 1933–1948* (Toronto 1983). On the United States see especially John Higham, *Strangers in the Land: Patterns of American Nativism* (New York 1973); Ronald Takaki, *Iron Cages: Race and Culture in Nineteenth Century America* (New York 1979); and Ronald Takaki, ed., *From Different Shores: Perspectives in Race and Ethnicity in America* (New York 1987).

3 Robert F. Harney, "Italophobia: An English-speaking Malady?" *Polyphony* 7 (1985); Salvatore J. La Gumina, ed., *WOP! A Documentary History of Anti-Italian Discrimination in the United States* (New York 1973); Higham, *Strangers in the Land*, 90–1, 160–2, 168–9; Franc Sturino, *Forging the Chain: Italian Migration to North America, 1880–1930* (Toronto 1990); Virginia Yans-McLaughlin, *Family and Community: Italian Immigrants in Buffalo, 1880–1930* (Ithaca 1971); Elizabeth Ewen, *Immigrant Women in the Land of Dollars: Life and Culture on the Lower East Side* (New York 1985); George Pozzetta, ed., *Pane e Lavoro: The Italian American Working Class* (Toronto 1980)

4 N. Tienhaara, *Canadian Views on Immigration and Population: An Analysis of Post-war Gallup Polls* (Ottawa 1971), 59. On Italians and fascism see John Zucchi, *Italians in Toronto: Development of a National Identity, 1875–1935* (Montreal/Kingston 1988); Roberto Perrin, "Making Good Fascists and Good Canadians: Consular Propoganda and the Italian Community in Montreal in the 1930s," in Gerald Gold, ed., *Minorities and Mother Image Country Imagery* (St John's 1984); Luigi Pennacchio, "The Canadian Government and Italian Fascists in World War II," Paper presented to the Elia Chair in Italian Canadian Studies Lecture Series, Columbus Centre, Toronto, Feb. 1989

5 Archives of Ontario (AO), Department of Planning and Development, Immigration Branch Files, F.J. Love to Premier Leslie Frost, 1 Sept. 1954; H.C. Warrender to Love, 2 Sept. 1954; Allen, "Portrait of Little Italy," 18

6 Personal interview; interviews; on school children see AO, International Institute of Metropolitan Toronto (IIMT), file on Italian Immigrant Aid Society (IIAS), *Annual Report*, 1963–4.

7 *Corriere Canadese*, 25 May 1956, 24 June 1958. On police at Italian soccer games see ibid., 20 July 1956, 13 Oct. 1959.

8 Quoted in ibid., 19 May 1959
9 *Telegram*, 6 July 1961 (B. Carlesimo). Another wrote, "I am an Italian bricklayer and I say we Italians are here to stay. Those who are against us are against justice. We are working hard to beautify this city." See also ibid. (C. Rocco); *Corriere Canadese*, 8 Sept. 1954 (T. De-Felicia); 25 Jan. 1960 (C. Romano).
10 *Telegram*, 6 July 1961 (M.S. Walsh)
11 Ibid., 1 April 1960 (J. Wilson); 1 April 1960 (H.C. McLean). See also ibid., 12 April 1960 (F. Hegon); 20 April 1960 (W. Sherman); and chapter 7.
12 *Globe and Mail*, 17 June 1961 (A.E. Burt)
13 Ibid., 7 June 1961 (R.A. Meagan). On negative response to the strikers see chapter 7.
14 *Telegram*, 20 April 1960 (R.C. Anderson); 1 April 1960 (M.I. McLean); 29 March 1960 (F. Speer)
15 *Star*, 11 Aug. 1960 (no name given); National Archives of Canada (NA), Department of External Affairs (DEA), vol. 128, file 3–33–18, Memorandum, "Prospects on Italian Immigration to Canada," 23 March 1955
16 W.H.S. Macklin, "Canada Doesn't Need More People," *Maclean's*, 27 oct. 1956, 6, 71–4
17 DEA, vol. 18, file 3–33–18, Memorandum, "Prospects on Italian Immigration to Canada." See also file 3–33–16, George Davidson to Ellen Fairclough, 23 March 1962.
18 Department of Citizenship and Immigration, Report EG–2, Martin Greewood, "Some Observations of Italian Immigrants in Toronto," 1961. These themes are developed more fully in my essay, "Making New Canadians: Social Workers, Women, and the Reshaping of Immigrant Families," in Franca Iacovetta and Mariana Valverde, eds., *Gender Conflicts: New Essays in Women's History* (Toronto 1992).
19 *Telegram*, 6 July 1961 (C.E.A. Laker). See also *Star*, 30 June 1961 (L. Hendrick).
20 *Telegram*, 20 April 1960 (Mrs "Mad"); 8 July 1961 (J. Hodgson). See also 12 and 20 April 1960.
21 *Telegram*, 6 July 1961 (Laker); personal interviews
22 Ibid., 6 July 1961 (C.E.A. Laker); *Star*, 30 June 1961 (L. Hendricks). See also *Telegram*, 4, 12, and 19 July 1961. On "curb-cruising" see Samuel Sidlofsky, "Post-War Immigrants in the Changing Metropolis with Special Reference to Toronto's Italian Population" (PhD thesis, University of Toronto, 1969), 246–8.
23 DEA, vol. 126, file 1–33—16, Ferio Carosi, consul general of Italy, to A.A. Wishert, attorney-general of Ontario, 29 Sept. 1964
24 Department of Citizenship and Immigration, Criminality Rates for Canadian and Foreign-Born in Canada (1951–1954), 1955

25 *Corriere Canadese*, 13 oct., 24 November 1954; *Telegram*, 5 and 13 Aug. 1960; *Teledominica*, 16 Sept. 1962; *Corriere Canadese*, 27 April 1956

26 The literature on violence against women is vast. For an historical treatment that raises class and race issues see, for example, Linda Gordon, *Heroes of Their Own Lives: The Politics and History of Family Violence* (New York 1988), and Mariana Valverde, *The Age of Light, Soap and Water: Moral Reform in Canada, 1880s–1920s* (Toronto 1991). See also Franca Iacovetta, "Trying to Make Ends Meet; Italian Immigrant Women, the State and Family Survival Strategies in Post-War Toronto," *Canadian Woman Studies* 8 (1987).

27 Reginald Whitaker, *Double Standard: The Secret History of Canadian Immigration* (Toronto 1987), 63–5; Blair Fraser, "Can the Immigration Issue Lick the Liberals? *Maclean's*, 10 Dec. 1955

28 NA, Immigration Records, vol. 674, file 92655, F.B. Costworth, Memorandum for Chief of Amissions, 25 and 26 April 1951. For other cases see DEA, vol. 147, file 3–33–18, E.P. Beasely to Italian Embassy, 10 April 1964; director of immigration to deputy minister, 10 April 1964; Fred Bodsworth, "What Kinds of Canadians Are We Getting?" *Maclean's*, 15 Feb. 1952, 52.

29 Goldsmith quoted in DEA, vol. 349, file 5230–1–575, G.R. Benoit to director of immigration, 15 June 1955

30 Greenwood, "Some Observations of Italian Immigrants in Toronto"

31 See Alan Philips's five-part series for *Maclean's*, 24 Aug., 21 Sept., 5 Oct., 2 Dec. 1963, 4 April 1964. See also Harlow Unger, "American Report," *Canadian Business*, Feb. 1965; and "The Mafia Moves In on Legitimate Business," ibid., June 1965.

32 Philips, "Give the Police More Power," *Maclean's*, 4 April 1963. Such interest in the Mafia culminated in the "Connections" television specials of the early 1970s. They evoked angry responses from Senator Peter Bosa and other prominent Italian Canadians. Harney, "Italophobia"

33 Pierre Berton (with Henry Rossier), *The New City: A Prejudiced View of Toronto* (Toronto 1961), "Italian Town"; *Telegram*, 8 July 1961 (J. Hodgson); see chapter 6.

34 Allen, "Little Italy," 43–4, 46

35 *Telegram*, 31 March 1960

36 *Star*, 30 July 1960

37 Ibid., 18 April 1960; *Telegram*, 24 June 1961. See chapter 7.

38 *Telegram*, 8 April 1960 (Mrs Grobiki)

39 Ibid., 20 April 1960 (M. Van Rorie); 27 June 1961 (Mrs Walsh and O.W. Breen)

40 Jean Belliveau, "How are Canada's Italians Making Out," *Star Weekly*, 17 March 1956

41 *Star*, 8 July 1961; *Corriere Canadese*, 3 May 1957

42 Pierre Berton, "A Strange Interlude," *Star*, 12 July 1961
43 Peter C. Newman, "Are New Canadians Hurting Canada?" *Maclean's* 18 July 1959; Hugh Garner, "An Old Canadian Assesses the New Canadians' Case Against Us," *Maclean's*, 18 July 1959
44 Allen, "Little Italy," 19
45 Rod McQueen, "The New Italian Super-Rich," *Toronto Life*, Dec. 1985
46 Dionne Brand and Krisantha Sri Bhaggiyadatta, *Rivers Have Sources, Trees Have Roots: Speaking of Racism* (Toronto 1986); Mikeda Silvera, *Silenced* (Toronto 1983)

CHAPTER SIX

1 A useful list of agencies is in Peter C. Newman, "Are We Doing Enough To Help Our Immigrants," *Financial Post*, 2 Aug. 1952; City of Toronto Archives (CTA), Special Collections (SC), vol. 40, Social Planning Council of Metropolitan Toronto, Immigration Section; James Lemon, *Toronto since 1918: An Illustrated History* (Toronto 1985), chap. 4.
2 Department of Citizenship and Immigration, Report EG–2, Martin Greenwood, "Some Observations on Italian Immigrants in Toronto, 1961"; Edith Ferguson, *Newcomers in Transition* (Toronto 1962–4), 59–68; Edith Ferguson, *Newcomers and New Learning* (Toronto 1964–6), 21–4
3 Archives of Ontario (AO), International Institute of Metropolitan Toronto (IIMT), MU6413, file on Ethnic Occasions, Report on 1961 Conference; MU6399, file on Italian Immigrant Aid Society (IIAS), IIAS *Monthly Report*, May 1955; *Annual Report*, 1962, on failure to attract Italians to home nursing course run by Red Cross staff; Ferguson, *Newcomers in Transition*, 96–105
4 AO, IIMT Confidential Case files, MU6522, file 1962 D, MD: ibid., SD
5 Ibid., MU6380, file on incorporation, 30 Oct. 1952; MU6399, file on IIAS, Pamphlet, "Our Story," 1962. For further details see Enrico Cumbo, "The Italian Immigrant Aid Society," (graduate paper, Department of History, University of Toronto 1986).
6 AO, IIMT, MU6380, file on Ethnic Occasions, John Hadad, St Christopher's House, to Jean Shek, SPC, 12 April 1961; MU6399, file on IIAS, IIAS *Annual Report*, 1955–62, especially Ladies Auxiliary reports; on activities and citizenship classes see MU6413–14, files on Ethnic Groups; MU3517, YWCA, box 1, file on Immigrants; box 22, clippings. On an earlier era see Richard Juliani, "The Settlement House and the Italian Family," in Betty Boyd Caroli et al., eds., *The Italian Immigrant Woman in North America* (Toronto 1978); Maxine Seller, "Protestant Evangelism and the Italian Immigrant Woman," in ibid.; Mary Ellen Mancina Battinich, "The Interaction between Italian Immigrant

Women and the Chicago Commons Settlement House, 1909–1914," in ibid.; on Toronto, Franc Sturino, "Inside the Chain: A Case Study in Southern Italian Migration to North America, 1880–1930" (PhD thesis, University of Toronto, Ontario Institute for Studies in Education, 1981), chap. 4; Robert F. Harney and Harold Troper, *Immigrants: A Portrait of the Urban Experience* (Toronto 1975).

7 CTA, SC, vol. 40, SPC, box 6, file on Immigrants, A. Cecilia Pope, RN, to Doris Clark, Immigrant Section, SPC, 15 April 1958

8 The case file is in AO, IIMT, MU6520, 1957–8 B; MU6399, file on IIAS, IIAS *Monthy Report*, Feb. 1955; MU6519, 1962 D. On an earlier era see Virginia Yans-McLaughlin, *Family and Community: Italian Immigrants in Buffalo, 1880–1930* (Ithaca 1971); Elizabeth Ewen, *Immigrant Women in the Land of Dollars: Life and Culture on the Lower East Side, 1890–1925* (New York 1985), chap. 5; Linda Gordon, *Heroes of Their Own Lives: The Politics and History of Family Violence* (New York 1988).

9 AO, MU6399, file on IIAS, *Annual Report*, Feb./March 1955; the case file is in MU6519, 1959 D. Officials normally did not deport people who became public charges unless it occurred in combination with "some other undesirable features," such as mental illness. See National Archives of Canada (NA), Immigration Records (IR), vol. 349, file 5230–1–575, George Davidson to director of immigration, 3 May 1962; Expulsion and Exclusion Section, Memorandum, 20 Oct. 1965.

10 The relevant case files are in the following records: AO, IMMT, MU6520, 1961 C; MU6522, 1966 C; and MU6520, file 1962 Q–R. Deserted wives could be deported as public charges if they had no means of support except welfare. See NA, IR, vol. 349, file 5230–1–575, C.E.S. Smith, director, to undersecretary of state for external affairs, 7 Dec. 1955.

11 AO, IIMT, MU6521, 1965 S

12 Ferguson, *Newcomers in Transition*, chaps. 3 and 6; Ferguson, *Newcomers and New Learning*; Greenwood, "Some Observations"

13 Rudolph Vecoli, "Prelates and Peasants: Italian Immigrants and the Catholic Church," *Journal of Social History* 2 (1969), "Cult and Occult in Italian American Culture," in *Immigrants and Religion in Urban America*, ed. Randall M. Miller and Thomas D. Marzik (Philadelphia 1977), "Italian Religious Organizations in Minnesota," *Studi Emigrazione* 66 (June 1982): 191–202

14 Archdiocese Archives of Toronto (AAT), Our Lady of Mount Carmel, file on Photos, Clippings, Text of broadcast, 29 June 1957; Cardinal McGuigan speech, delivered at St Mary of the Angels, cited in *Corriere Canadese* 7 July 1954

15 AAT, Holy Rosary, file on Photos, Clippings, St Alphonsus Church, Parish Bulletin, Oct. 1966. On the prewar activities of the Methodists see John Zucchi, *Italians in Toronto: Development of a National Identity,*

1875–1935 (Kingston and Montreal 1988), chap. 5; Enrico Cumbo, "Impediments to the Harvest: The Limitations of Methodist Proselytization of Toronto's Italians 1905–1925," paper presented to the Catholic Archdiocese of Toronto Conference, June 1990. On the postwar period see also AAT, St Pascal Baylon, file on Photos, Clippings, Parish Bulletin, 20 Oct. 1957; ibid., St Helen's, Father Joseph Carraro to Archbishop F. Pocock, 3 April 1963.

16 AAT, A. McQuillan and Richard Teixeira, *The Roman Catholic and United Churches' Progress with the Italian Community of St. John's Ward 1885–1920* (Toronto: United Church Archives, 1961), 12–18; ibid., Parish files, St Agnes, file on Photos, Clippings, Booklet, *Silver Jubilee Celebration of the Fransiscan Fathers of the Immaculate Conception*, 16 Nov. 1959; Father Ezio Marchetto, "The Catholic Church and Italian Immigration to Toronto: An Overview," *Polyphony* 7 (1985). On prewar Toronto see Zucchi, *Italians in Toronto*, chap. 5; Michael Di Stassi, *The Story of St Paul's United Church* (Toronto: United Church Archives 1955), *Fifty Years of Italian Evangelicalism* (Toronto: United Church Archives 1955).

17 Details are contained in the AAT parish files and in Franca Iacovetta, "Working-Class Immigrants: Southern Italians in Post-War Toronto, 1947–65" (PhD thesis, York University, 1988). The Italian congregation St Agnes grew so large that in 1967 it was moved into the larger neighbouring church of St Francis of Assisi. As in the case of Mount Carmel, St Agnes became a Portuguese national parish.

18 Lydio Tomasi, *The Other Catholics: A Preliminary Partial Report on the Italian Apostolate in Toronto's Archdiocese; 11: Priests' Survey* (New York: Centre for Migration Studies, 1975). On recruiting, see, for example, AAT, St Thomas Aquinas, file on General Correspondence, Father McGuin to Very Rev. Adelmo Custos, superior, Fransiscan Fathers, St Lawrence Monastery, Beacon, New York, 20 May 1961; AAT, St Agnes, file on Photos, Clippings, Booklet, *Silver Jubilee of the Fransiscans*, 16 Nov. 1959; Very Rev. Charles Tallarico, minister of provincial, Fransiscan Fathers, to Fulton, 28 May 1958, 19 June 1959; AAT, Holy Angels, Father Kosak, Oblate Fathers, to Pocock, 8 July 1963; AAT, Holy Rosary, file on Photos, Clippings, "St. Alphonsus Serves 600 Italian Families," *Canadian Register*, 4 May 1968 (clipping); AAT, St Francis of Assisi, Booklet, *Diamond Jubilee, 1903–1978*, 11 May 1979.

19 Tomasi, *The Other Catholics*, 24–6; McQuillan and Texeira, *Roman Catholic and United Churches' Progress*, 16

20 Tomasi, *The Other Catholics*; AAT, Immaculate Conception, file on Photos, Clippings, *Dedication Book*, 1 Dec. 1957; AAT, St Pascal Baylon, file on General Correspondence, Parish Bulletin, 20 oct. 1957; Father LoSavio to Archibishop Pocock, 20 Oct. 1962, 15 Aug. 1963, 27 Nov. 1964; parish history

21 AAT, St Agnes, file on Photos, Clippings, Parish History; ibid.,
St Mary of the Angels, Rev. Benjamin Bassetti to Fulton, 24 Sept.
1961; ibid., St Gabriel of the Sorrowful Virgin, file on General Correspondence, Rev. Gossart to Fulton, 31 Aug. 1964, 8 Nov. 1965. At St Sebastien's, public health nurses complained about the overcrowded
conditions and unsatisfactory facilities available for the baby clinic.
Church leaders agreed to improve matters. See ibid., St Sebastien, file
on General Correspondence, A.R. Boyd to Fulton, 19 June 1967; Fulton to E.N. Cryderman, 21 June 1967; Fulton to Father Borhgi, 21 June
1967. See also ibid., St Anthony, Rev. O'Neil to Fulton, 12 Nov. 1965;
and correspondence in file on Petitions, 1973.

22 Vecoli, "Priests and Prelates"

23 AAT, Holy Angels, Rev. M.J. Smith to Archibishop Pocock, Petition
dated spring 1961; personal interview. See also AAT, St Thomas Aquinas, file on General Correspondence, Rev. McGuin to Fulton, 26 Feb.
1962; AAT, St Agnes, file on General Correspondence, Memorandum,
6 Sept. 1963; AAT, St Alphonsus, Father Carraro to Pocock, 14 Sept.
1966; *Corriere Canadese*, 9 June and 28 July 1954

24 AAT, St Thomas Aquinas, file on General Correspondence, Giovanna
Mortellari to Pocock, 22 April 1965. Others letters are contained in this
file.

25 Ibid., Petition to Pocock, 22 April 1965; St Charles Borromeo, file on
General Correspondence, Petition to Father Thomas Hayes, 29 Nov.
1968

26 Ibid., Sister Pina Vivona to Pocock, 30 March 1968; Pocock to Hayes,
4 April 1968; Pocock to Vivona, 4 April 1968

27 Ibid., St Clare, file on General Correspondence, Thomas Donahue to
Chancery Office, 2 Jan. 1968

28 Ibid., St Thomas Aquinas, file on General Correspondence, Nan Anderson to Pocock, 22 May 1966; ibid., 24 Feb. 1966, 7 July 1967

29 Ibid., St Clare, file on General Correspondence, Attillio Martellacio
(nd)

30 Ibid., St Thomas Aquinas, file on General Correspondence, Ann
Hughes to Pocock, 8 Dec. 1966; Pocock to Hughes, 12 Dec. 1966. See
also responses to Anderson in ibid., Pocock to Anderson, 24 Feb.
1966, 30 May 1966.

31 Ibid., Holy Angels, file on General Correspondence, Father Iuculano
to Fulton, 24 Sept. 1968. See also ibid., St Alphonsus, Rev. Pierre Pel-
lase to Pocock, 10 Dec. 1966; ibid., St Matthew, file on Photos, Clippings, Parish Bulletin, 11 Jan. 1959

32 Ibid., St Catherine of Sienna, file on General Correspondence, Father
Mauro Mastrodicasa to Pocock, 26 April 1963. See also ibid., St Mary
of the Angels, file on General Correspondence, Father Bassetti to Fulton, 7 June 1962; ibid., St Pascal Baylon, file on General Correspon-

dence, Father LoSavio to McGuigan (nd); ibid., St Alphonsus, file on
General Correspondence, Archibishop Pocock to Father Pellas, 16 Dec.
1966

33 Tomasi, *The Other Catholics*, 49–52, 109
34 Ibid.; on parish activities see, for example, AAT, Parish Files, St Pascal
Baylon, file on General Correspondence, Parish Bulletin, 12 April
1959; AAT, St Clare, file on Parish Records, Parish Bulletin, 2 Aug.
1962; List of Parish Organizations, 1955–6. On the North American
character of some of the organizations see Samuel Sidlofsky, "Postwar Immigrants in the Changing Metropolis with Special Reference to
Toronto's Italian Population" (PhD thesis, University Toronto 1969),
254; Zucchi, *Italians in Toronto*, 135–9.
35 Personal interview
36 Personal interview; Ferguson, *Newcomers in Transition*, 50–1
37 Personal interviews. See also Ewen, *Immigrant Women*.
38 AAT, St Francis of Assisi, file on General Correspondence, Booklet,
Festa della Madonna del Pietra; ibid., St Agnes, Parish files, file on Photos, Clippings, *Toronto Telegram*, 6 Feb. 1950 (clipping)
39 AAT, St Pascal, file on General Correspondence, George Hulme,
Toronto Humane Society, to Cardinal McGuigan, 17 Aug. 1962; ibid.,
St Mary of the Angels, file on General Correspondence, Frances Phillips to Archbishop Pocock, 12 July 1965
40 Ibid., "A group of young people" to Monsignor Fulton, 30 May 1960.
It was written in anticipation of the up-coming feast of St Nicola of
Bari. A section reads: "The young people in Canada are surprised in
front of these superstitions; the good Catholics remain silent and suffer so much and the bad Catholics are laughing and do not care. We
are ... asking to stop the Procession ... [or] at least to reduce the
Procession around the church and to make it a matter of devotion and
gravity ... because we know very well that the Protestant[s] are com-
plaining very much on these matters."
41 Ibid., Pocock to Phillips, 26 July 1965
42 *Corriere Canadese*, 7 July 1954. There had been considerable interest in
starting up a paper before Dan Ianuzzi, the Canadian-born son of Italian immigrants in Montreal who had established a small newspaper
empire, provided the funding. In 1955 Luigi Petrucci, newly arrived
from Bogota, Columbia, set a up a rival paper, *Panarama*, but it floun-
dered for a few years and then disappeared. The Communist party
occasionaly published an Italian newspaper entitled *Lotta Saria*, but
there are no surviving copies at the CCP Archives in Toronto. *La Gio-
vanne Fiamme*, established in 1964, was the organ of the Italian Canadian Youth Club, an organization set up by Peter Bosa. It was not
until 1972 that several Italian socialists and social democrats who had

joined the NDP – Odoardo Di Santo, Tony Lupusella, and Tony Grande – created a working-class organ, *Forze Nouve*. As Di Santo put it, its mandate was to keep a vigil on the "self-proclaimed leaders," to moblize parents against the steaming of immigrant children into vocational schools, and to lobby for better benefits for injured workers. Inadequate funding meant that the paper came out only periodically until the late 1970s. Odoardo Di Santo, "Forze Nouvo," in *Polyphony* 4 (1982); Gianni Grohovas, "Toronto's Italian Press after the Second World War," *Polyphony* 4 (1982); personal interviews with oral informants.

43 On mutual benefit societies see, for example, Josef Barton, *Peasants and Strangers: Italians, Roumanians, and Slovaks in an American City, 1880–1950* (Cambridge, Mass. 1975); John Briggs, *An Italian Passage: Immigrants to Three American Cities, 1890–1930* (New Haven 1978); Humbert Nelli, *The Italians in Chicago, 1880–1930: A Study in Ethnic Mobility* (New York 1970); on political representatives initiating patriotic clubs within immigrant colonies see, for example, Carmela Patrias, "Patriots and Proletarians: The Politicization of Hungarian Immigrants in Canada, 1900–1939" (PhD thesis, University of Toronto, 1985); Roberto Perin, "Making Good Fascists and Good Canadians: Consular Propoganda and the Italian Community in Montreal in the 1930s," in Gerald Gold, ed., *Minorities and Mother Country Imagery* (St John's 1984); Luigi Bruti Liberati, *Il Canada, l'Italia and il fascismo 1919–1945* (Rome 1984).

44 Zucchi, *Italians in Toronto*. On the fascist era see also Antonio Principe, "The Italo-Canadian Anti-fascist Press in Toronto, 1922–40," *Nemla Italian Studies* 4 (1980); Luigi Pennacchio, "The Canadian Government and Italian Fascists in World War II," paper presented to the Italian Migration Lecture Series, sponsored by the Elia Chair in Italian Canadian Studies, Columbus Centre, Toronto, Feb. 1989.

45 Gianni Grohovaz, "See You at Brandon Hall ... Oh! ... I Mean the Italian-Canadian Recreation Club," *Polyphony* 7 (1985). Most of the links between the prewar and postwar period remain fuzzy because the wartime era, and the role played by Italian-Canadian elites in the wartime and postwar periods, have not been closely examined. Luigi Pennacchio's forthcoming University of Toronto (OISE) PhD thesis, "Ethnics in Crisis: Italians in Canada during World War Two," promises to fill an important gap.

46 Jeremy Boissevain, *The Italians of Montreal: Social Adjustment in a Plural Society* (Ottawa 1970), chap. 3; Sidlofsky, "Postwar Immigrants in the Changing Metropolis," 247–64; 285–6; Martin Greenwood, "Some Observations"; personal interviews. Father Jeremiah Hayes spoke to the issue in 1959 when he wrote about tensions at his parish bowley al-

leys: "It is like trying to mix oil and water. The older and established parishioners are the bowlers. The newly arrived come in and the older parishioners retire into the background." AAT, Mount Carmel, file on General Correspondence, Hayes to Cardinal McGuigan, 29 Oct. 1959. On tensions between earlier and later arriving immigrants see, for example, Henry Radecki (with Benedykt Heydenkorn), *A Member of a Distinguished Family: The Polish Group in Canada* (Toronto 1976); Milda Danys, *DP: Lithuanian Immigration to Canada after the Second World War* (Toronto 1986); the essays on Ukrainians, Romanians, and Jews in Howard Palmer and Tamara Palmer, eds., *Peoples of Alberta: Portraits ofCultural Diversity* (Saskatoon 1985); for an earlier period see also Stephen Speisman, *The Jews of Toronto: A History of 1937* (Toronto 1979), and, for the United States, Irving Howe, *World of Our Fathers* (New York 1976).

47 *Corriere Canadese*, 6 May 1958; Sidlofsky, "Post-war Immigrants in the Changing Metropolis," 244–65. See also J.M. Craig, "Associations of Persons of Italian Origin in Toronto, 1956–57" (MA thesis, University of Toronto 1957).

48 Example cited in Sidlofsky, "Post-war Immigrants in the Changing Metropolis," 259; personal interviews

49 Robert F. Harney, "How To Write a History of Postwar Toronto Italia," *Polyphony* 7 (1985). See also Craig, "Associations"; AO, MU6399, IIMT, file on Order of the Sons of Italy; ibid., IIMT, MU6413, file on Ethnic Associations; *Corriere Canadese*, 22 Sept. 1954.

50 Grohovaz, "See You at Brandon Hall"; personal interviews; Sidlofsky, "Post-war Immigrants in the Changing Metropolis," 80–1; on Palermo, *Corriere Canadese*, 23 June 1954

51 MHSO, Donald Di Giulio Papers, J.D. Carrier to Prime Minister Louis St Laurent, 15 Sept. 1953. This brief history draws largely on the following sources: correspondence and minutes of meetings contained in the Di Giulio Papers; newspapers; Nick Forte, "Return of the Casa d'Italia: The Seeds of Unity of the Italian Community of Toronto, 1950–62" (research paper, Department of History, University of Toronto); Harney, "Postwar Toronto Italia." I would like to thank Nick Forte for sharing his research findings.

52 In addition to the references in the note above, see also *Corriere Canadese*, 29 Nov. 1955, 4 Aug. 1954, 29 Sept. 1954, and 6 Jan. 63; A.V. Spada, *The Italians in Canada* (Ottawa 1969); AO, MU6319, B–4, IIMT, file on ICBPA.

53 Harney, "Postwar Toronto Italia"; Forte, "Return of the Casa d'Italia"

54 The discussion of the IIAS draws on the following sources: AO, MU6399, B–4, IIMT, file on CIBPA; ibid., file on IIAS, IIAS *Annual Reports* 1954–60; ibid., microfilm 54–1/2, IIAS, Minutes of Executive

Meetings, 1954–62; *Corriere Canadese*, 29 Sept. 1954, 6 Dec. 1955, 23 Sept. 1958, 9 March 1956, 17 and 24 March 1959, 5 Jan. 1960; Enrico Cumbo, "The Italian Immigrant Aid society" (research paper, Department of History, University of Toronto). I would like thank Enrico Cumbo for making this paper available to me.

55 Cumbo, "Italian Immigrant Aid Society"
56 Toronto *Star*, 9 June 1960; Toronto *Telegram*, 9 June 1960; *Corriere Canadese*, 14 June 1960. See also Cumbo, "Italian Immigrant Aid Society" and, for details on Lollabrigida's visit: *Star* 6, 7, 8 June 1960; *Telegram* 3, 4, 7 June 1960; *Corriere Canadese* 3, 10 May 1960, 7, 21 June 1960. On ethnic elites see, for example, Zucchi, *Italians in Toronto*; John Higham, ed., *Ethnic Leadership in America* (Baltimore 1978); John Bodnar, *The Transplanted: A History of Immigrants in Urban America* (Bloomington, Ind. 1985); Patrias, "Peasants and Proletarians."
57 Cumbo, "Italian Immigrant Aid society"; personal interviews; Kenneth Bagnell, *Canadese: A Portrait of the Italian Canadians* (Toronto 1989), 174–6; Edith Ferguson, *Newcomers and New Learning* 22, 53–5, 63, 79. On COSTI–IIAS see Angelo Delfino, "Italian Immigrant Aid Society: An Historical Outline," *Polyphony* 7 (1985); Gregory Grande, "COSTI–IIAS: Social Services in the Italian Community, 1952–1985," *Italian Canadiana* 3 (1987).
58 Clifford Jansen, "Leadership in the Toronto Italian Ethnic Group," *International Migration Review* 14 (1969). See also his "Community organizations of Italians in Toronto," in Leo Driedger ed., *The Canadian Ethnic Mosaic* (Toronto 1978).
59 Personal interviews; for a useful bibliography of organizations see MHSO, Ethnocultural Directory of Ontario, 1982; on Brandon Hall, see Grohovaz, "See You at Brandon Hall," and Grohavaz, ed., *Fammee Furlane: The First Half Century* (Toronto 1982); J. McKay, "Entity Vs. Process Approaches to Ethnic Relations and Ethnic Identity: A Case Study of Ethnic Soccer Clubs in Toronto's Italian Community," *Canadian Ethnic Studies* 8 (1980).

CHAPTER SEVEN

1 Toronto *Telegram*, 26 June 1961; Toronto *Star*, 26 June 1961. The 1960 strike was illegal because it was a recognition strike. Under the Ontario Labour Relations Act, strikes are prohibited until a union has been certified or voluntarily recognized by the employer and until conciliation procedures have been completed. The 1961 strike was a recognition strike for some and hence illegal; for those under contract, the strike was illegal because the Labour Relations Act prohibited strikes during the life of a collective agreement.

2 For brief discussions of the strikes see John Crispo, "Labour-Management Relations in the Construction Industry: The Goldenberg Report," *Canadian Journal of Economics and Political Science* 29 (1963); *Report of the Royal Commission on Labour-Management Relations in the Construction Industry* (hereafter *Goldenberg Report*) (Ottawa 1962), 15–18; Stuart Marshall Jamieson, *Times of Trouble: Labour Unrest and Industrial Conflict in Canada, 1900–66* (Ottawa 1968), 395–405, 408–9. A popular and cynical account is in Catherine Wismer, *Sweethearts: The Builders, the Mob and the Men* (Toronto 1968), chap. 8. For a more sympathetic popular account see Kenneth Bagnell, *Canadese: A Portrait of the Italian Canadians* (Toronto 1989).

3 K.J. Rea, *The Prosperous Years: The Economic History of Ontario 1939–75* (Toronto 1985), 43–55; *Goldenberg Report*, 1–2

4 For statistics see chapter 3; on Italians in the residential field see W. Stefanovitch [Ontario regional director, United Brotherhood of Carpenters and Joiners of America], "Historic Organizing Campaign," *Canadian Labour* [Canadian Labour Congress] 6 (March 1961): personal interviews.

5 *Goldenberg Report*, 5–7, 15–20. On the structure of the industry see ibid.; Crispo, "Labour-Management Relations"; H.C. Goldenberg and J.H. Crispo, eds., *Construction Labour Relations* (Toronto 1968); Samuel Sidlofsky, "Post-war Immigrants in the Changing Metropolis with Special Emphasis on Italians" (PhD thesis, University of Toronto, 1969).

6 Archives of Ontario (AO), Royal Commission on Industrial Relations, 1961, Submissions, vol. 10, 1535–54, 2280–392

7 Personal interviews; Sidlofsky, "Post-war Immigrants," chaps 3 and 4; Crispo, "Labour-Management Relations"; C. Ross Ford, "Training Requirements and Methods," in Crispo and Goldenberg, eds., *Construction Labour Relations*

8 Crispo, "Labour-Management Relations"; *Goldenberg Report*, 15–24; Stefanovitch, "Historic Organizing Campaign"; Joseph Carraro, "Unions and the Italian Community," *Polyphony* 7 (1985); Bagnell, *Canadese*, chaps. 7 and 8

9 *Telegram*, 5 April 1960 (A.E. Chapman et al.); personal interview; *Telegram*, 16 May 1960. See also *Telegram*, letters to the editor, 29 March 1960 (C. Gardiner); *Telegram*, 16 April 1960; *Star* editorial, 18 April 1960.

10 By contrast, the Canadian firms dominated the more technical trades, such as electrical work, plumbing, and tinsmithing. *Goldenberg Report*, 3–5, 8–15; personal interviews; D.G. Chutter, "The Canadian Construction Industry," *Canadian Labour* 5 (June 1960). On builders and developers see James Lemon, *Toronto since 1918: An Illustrated History* (Toronto 1985), 122–4, 164–86; Sidlofsky, "Post-war Immigrants" 182–

222; Wismer, *Sweehearts*, chaps 4–7; on the large Italian-Canadian contractors see A.V. Spada, *The Italians in Canada* (Ottawa 1969).

11 Pedoni's brief, cited in *Goldenberg Report*, 13. See also Bagnell, *Canadese*, chap. 7.

12 Brandon Union Group's and Toronto and District Trade Contractors
Council's briefs, cited in *Goldenberg Report*, 10–12; Frank Colantonio,
"The Italian Immigrants in Toronto's Construction Industry" (unpublished manuscript in author's possession), 5–7. Another similar version of this manuscript, with the same title, is available at the
Multicultural History Society of Ontario. *Telegram* 31 March and
3 April 1960; *Star*, 5 and 18 April 1960

13 Pedoni's brief, cited in *Goldenberg Report*, 10

14 *Telegram*, 16 May 1960. See also Frank Drea's columns in ibid.,
31 March, 12 and 21 April 1960; *Goldenberg Report*, 11–13, 45–7; *Telegram* editorial, 27 June 1961.

15 *Goldenberg Report*, 12; *Telegram*, 31 March, 21 April, and 18 May 1960;
Toronto *Globe and Mail*, 8 Aug. 1960; *Corriere Canadese*, 12 April 1960

16 Personal interview

17 Personal interview (pseudonym). On falling wages see *Telegram*,
24 June 1960; *Globe and Mail*, 31 March and 2 Aug. 1960; *Star*, 28 May
1960. In April 1960 the Plaster Contractors' Association claimed that
some employers were paying workers well below the minimum standard ($2.80) set for the trade under the Industrial Standards Act (ISA).
The plasterers and painters were the only two trades affected by the
ISA. *Telegram*, 21 April 1960

18 Ontario Legislative Assembly, *Debates*, 18 and 24 March, 4 and 8 April
1960; *Telegram*, 19 and 30 May 1960, 1, 3, 4, 6, 11, and 21 April 1960;
Star, 23 March, 12 May, and 4 April 1960; *Globe and Mail*, 29 March,
22 and 27 April 1960; *Corriere Canadese*, 22 March, 5 and 12 April 1960

19 See references note 18 above and chapter 3.

20 AO, Leslie Frost Papers, General Correspondence, box 70, file 131 G,
Ernesto Valentini (with a petition from 400 Italians) to Frost, 8 April
1960; T.M. Eberlee, cabinet secretary, to Valentini, 21 April 1960;
Eberlee to Frost, 7 April 1960; Frost to W.K. Warrender, minister of
municipal affairs, 25 April 1960; *Telegram*, 5 April 1960; Legislative Assembly, *Debates*, 8 April 1960

21 *Telegram*, 28 March, 6, 19, and 20 April 1960; *Star*, 29 March, 4 and
7 April 1960; *Globe and Mail*, 8 April 1960

22 See, for example, the essays in Dirk Hoerder, ed., *"Struggle a Hard
Battle"; Essays on Working-Class Immigrants* (DeKalb, Ill. 1986); George
E. Pozzetta, ed., *Pane e Lavoro: The Italian-American Working-Class* (To-
ronto 1980).

23 *Star*, 18 and 19 Oct. 1955; letters to the editor, 21 and 24 Oct. 1955;

Globe and Mail, 19 Oct. 1955; *Corriere Canadese*, 21 and 25 Oct. 1955;
letters to the editor, 18 Nov. (Francescuti), 25 Jan. (A. Forius), 11 Feb.
1955 (S. Fernando, B. Lilibato); Drea, "Suicide Five Years Ago Led to
Present Strike," *Telegram*, 9 Aug. 1960

24 Interviews with Zanini in Wismer, *Sweethearts*, 45–8; Stefanovitch,
"Historic Organizing Campaign," 17; *Corriere Canadese*, 11 Nov. 1955,
6 Jan. 1956, 12 April 1960, 15 May 1957; personal interview; G.G.
Cushing, "Building the Building Trades Labour Force and its Organization," *Canadian Labour* 2 (1957); Bagnell, *Canadese*, 154

25 *Labour Gazette*, Nov. 1957, 1401; Martin Goodman, *Star*, 8 Aug. 1960;
Telegram, 28 March 1960

26 Colantonio, "Italian Immigrants in Toronto's Construction Industry,"
8–10

27 *Star*, 8 Aug. 1960; *Globe and Mail*, 16 April 1960, 22 June 1961; Wismer,
Sweathearts, 9, 12, 15; personal interviews; Wismer, *Sweethearts*, con-
tains unsubstantiated accusations about Zanini's later associations
with crime figures.

28 See references in note 27 above. Some contemporary observers considered Irvine an opportunist. One incident recorded in the press indicates how some media reports intimated that Irvine was motivated
in part by a desire to protect Canadian workers from losing their jobs
to lower-paid Italian immigrants. During a dispute with a plaster contractor in Windsor, Irvine's Windsor local, an old-line union that included residential workers, was said to have demanded that the
employer keep the proportion of Italian workers to 50 per cent of his
work force. Since 90 per cent of the contractors' work force was Italian, this would have meant replacing 40 per cent of the Italian workers (many of whom were not organized) with Canadian workers.
Globe and Mail, 4 March 1960; *Star* 4 May 1960

29 Personal interview

30 *Goldenberg Report*, 15–18, 42–5; National Archives of Canada (NA), MG
31, vol. 1, Marino Toppan Papers, Curriculum Vitae, 10 July 1966;
personal interviews

31 Personal interviews with oral informants; Wismer, *Sweethearts*, 75–98.
The Brandon locals were: Bricklayers, Masons, and Plasterers' International Union of America, Local 40; International Hod Carriers, Building and Common Laborers' Union of America, Local 811; United
Brotherhood of Carpenters and Joiners of America, Local 1190; Operative Plasterers and Cement Masons' International Association of the
United States and Canada, Local 117 (Plasterers) and Local 117–C (Cement Masons).

32 Personal interviews; Colantonio, "Italian Immigrants in Toronto's
Construction Industry," 10–12; Irvine cited in *Telegram*, 16 April 1960.
Telegram, 1 and 3 April 1960; *Globe and Mail*, 16 April 1960

33 *Telegram*, 2 Aug. 1960

34 Ibid.

35 *Corriere Canadese*, "The story of Mario S. Striker," 8 Aug. 1961. See also note 91.

36 Personal interview (pseudonym). For contemporary portraits of other strikers see *Telegram*, 31 March 1960; *Star*, 30 July, 5 and 18 April 1960.

37 Personal interviews; *Star*, 12 May 1960; *Goldenberg Report*, 13–14. It proved very difficult to convince Italian workers to testify before the Royal Commission on Industrial Safety, and only four men did so. See AO, Royal Commission, Submissions, vol. 10, 2280–5, 2342–8, 2393–434.

38 *Corriere Canadese*, 19, 5 and 20 April 1960. See also ibid., 12 April and 11 Nov. 1960

39 *Star*, 29 March 1960; *Telegram*, 30 March 1960

40 *Telegram*, 31 March 1960; *Star*, 4 and 7 April 1960. On further outbreaks between the elite and strikers see *Star*, 8 April 1960; *Corriere Canadese*, 12 April 1960; *Telegram*, 8 April 1960.

41 *Star*, 19 Aug. 1960 (Vice Versa); see also other letters in *Telegram*, 29 March, 12 and 20 April 1960; see also chapter 5.

42 *Telegram*, 19 March 1960; *Star*, 18 April 1960; Goodman in *Star*, 8 Aug. 1960; *Globe and Mail*, 8 Aug. 1960. For sympathetic coverage of the Hogg's Hollow tragedy see *Star*, 23 March and 18 April 1960; *Telegram*, 2, 4, and 5 April 1960.

43 For example, see Drea's columns in *Telegram*, 31 March, 3, 5, 8, 11, and 16 April 1960.

44 On skirmishes, see *Telegram*, 2 and 3 Aug. 1960; *Star*, 2 and 3 Aug. 1960; *Globe and Mail*, 2 and 3 Aug. 1960.

45 Personal interviews. See also note 64.

46 *Telegram*, 3 and 4 Aug. 1960; *Star*, 4 Aug. 1960; *Globe and Mail*, 4 and 6 Aug. 1960

47 *Telegram*, 5 Aug. 1960; *Globe and Mail*, 5 Aug. 1960

48 *Star*, 6 Aug. 1960; *Globe and Mail*, 6, 9 and 10 Aug. 1960

49 *Globe and Mail*, 9 and 10 Aug. 1960; *Telegram*, 11 Aug. 1960

50 *Telegram*, 10 and 11 Aug. 1960; *Star*, 11 Aug. 1960; *Globe and Mail*, 12 Aug. 1960

51 *Star*, 15 and 16 Aug. 1960; *Telegram*, 15 Aug. 1960; *Globe and Mail*, 15 and 16 Aug. 1960. On other skirmishes see *Telegram*, 12, 13, 17, 18 Aug. 1960; *Globe and Mail*, 17, 18, and 20 Aug. 1960.

52 H. Simon (CLC regional director for Ontario), "Toronto Building Trades Launch Organizing Campaign," *Canadian Labour* 5 (Sept. 1960); 54; *Star*, 30 July 1960; *Telegram*, 16 Aug. 1960; *Globe and Mail*, 17 Aug. 1960

53 *Globe and Mail*, 19 Aug. 1960; *Star*, 19 and 20 Aug. 1960

54 *Star*, 8 Aug. 1960; *Labour Gazette*, Aug. 1960, 1094; *Goldenberg Report*, 16. The wage rates assumed a two-year period of accumulation. They were bricklayers, $3.15; plasterers, $3.08; carpenters, $2.90; cement masons, $2.57; and labourers, $2.00.

55 Colantonio, "Italian Immigrants in Toronto's Construction Industry," 13

56 Personal interview; H. Simon, "Successful Organizing Campaign Conducted by the Toronto Building Trades Council," *Canadian Labour* 5 (Oct. 1960); *Telegram*, 22 Aug., 3 Sept. 1960; *Star*, 2 Sept. 1960

57 *Goldenberg Report*, 17; *Labour Gazette*, July 1962, 777–8; Bagnell, *Canadese*, 156

58 *Globe and Mail*, 29 May 1961; *Star*, 3 June 1961; Colantonio, "The Italian Immigrants in Toronto's Construction Industry," 15–16. See also the interview with John Stefanini in Bagnell's *Canadese*, 156–61.

59 *Telegram*, 27 May 1961

60 Ibid., 29 May 1961

61 *Globe and Mail*, 30 and 31 May 1960; *Telegram*, 30 and 31 May 1960

62 *Telegram*, 1 and 2 June 1960; *Star*, 1 and 2 June 1960; Stefanini interview in Bagnell, *Canadese*, chap. 7

63 Personal interview (pseudonym); *Star*, 3 and 7 June 1960

64 *Star*, 7 June 1960 (journeyman electrician); ibid., 2 June 1961; *Telegram*, 2 June 1960

65 *Globe and Mail*, 2 June 1960; *Telegram*, 3 June 1960

66 *Star*, 3 June 1961; *Telegram*, 3 and 6 June 1961; editorial, *Canadian Labour* 6 (Sept. 1961): 4

67 *Globe and Mail*, 12 June 1961 (D. Allen); ibid., 17 June 1961 (A.E. Burt). See also *Star*, 6, 7, and 16 June 1961; *Telegram*, 4 and 24 July 1960.

68 *Star*, 3 and 7 June 1961

69 *Globe and Mail*, 7 June 1961; Martin Goodman, "Deportation Unlikely," in *Telegram*, 23 July 1961

70 *Globe and Mail*, 16 June 1961 (Dust); *Telegram*, 5 July 1961 (Braithwaite); *Star*, 24 June 1961 (sheet metal worker). See also *Star*, 3 and 10 June 1961; *Telegram*, 3, 6, 7, and 27 June 1961.

71 *Telegram*, 5 June 1960

72 Ibid., 8 and 9 June 1961; *Globe and Mail*, 7 June 1961

73 *Star*, 5 June 1961; *Telegram*, 7 and 8 June 1961; *Globe and Mail*, 8 June 1961

74 *Telegram*, 10 June 1961; *Star*, 10 June 1961; *Globe and Mail*, 10 June 1961

75 See references in note 74 above.

76 Colantonio, "The Italian Immigrants in Toronto's Construction Industry," 21–3; personal interviews; Bagnell, *Canadese*, 158–9

77 *Telegram*, 11, 12, and 15 June 1961; *Star*, 13, 14, 15, and 19 June 1961

78 *Telegram*, 20 and 21 June 1961; *Star*, 20 June 1961

79 See references in note 78 above.

80 *Telegram*, 22 June 1961

81 Ibid.; *Globe and Mail*, 22 June 1961

82 *Globe and Mail*, 22 and 23 June 1961; *Telegram*, 22 June 1961; *Star*, 22 June 1961; on Stefanini see also Bagnell, *Canadese*, 159–60. In personal interviews, on all informants recalled the great fear that Stefanini's horse sentence had instilled in them.

83 *Globe and Mail*, 9 June 1961; *Canadian Tribune*, 5, 12, 19, and 26 June, 3, 10, 17 and 24 July, and 4 Sept. 1961. Copies of *Il Lavoratore*, whose editor of this time was Ernesto Valentino, are not available. My discussion is also drawn from personal interviews.

84 Grohovaz in *Telegram*, 23 July 1961; see *Corriere Canadese*, 14 June, and 7, 8, 12, and 19 July 1961. See also letters to editor, 31 May 1961 (L. Bresciani); 21 June 1961 (PD); 28 June 1961 (M. Muccione).

85 *Telegram*, 26 June 1961; *Star*, 24 and 26 June 1961

86 *Star*, 27 and 30 June 1961; *Telegram*, 28, 29, and 30 June 1961

87 *Telegram*, 30 June and 3 July 1961; *Star*, 3 July 1961. The Toronto Building Trades Council represented nineteen member unions and 25,000 workers.

88 *Star*, 6 July 1961

89 Ibid., 7 July 1961

90 Personal interview; *Telegram*, 4 March 1961

91 Personal interview; personal interview (pseudonym); see contemporary interviews with strikers and their families, especially Dominic Moscone, in *Telegram*, 31 March 1960, and Angelo DeCastro and his father-in-law, in *Star*, 30 July 1960.

92 *Telegram*, 24 June 1961

93 NA, MG 31, vol. 1, Marino Toppan Papers, file on Correspondence and Memoirs, 1961–8, Toppan to Thomas Murphy, Washington, 7 July 1961

94 *Telegram*, 9 July 1961

95 Ibid.; personal interview

96 *Telegram*, 11 and 12 July 1961

97 Ibid., 13 July 1961

98 Ibid., 15 July 1961; *Star*, 15 July 1961; *Canadian Labour* 6 (Nov. 1961) and (Sept. 1961): 29

99 *Telegram*, 17 July 1961; *Star*, 17 July 1961

100 This theme emerges in the testimonies of former participants, some of whom attribute the demise of the Brandon Group to the tight control that Irvine and Zanini (and a few of their closest colleagues) exerted over the organization. It is a topic that requires further attention, but since most of the criticism concerns the men's handling of the Brandon Group in the years after the 1960 and 1961 cam-

paigns, the issue is not covered in detail here. See also Bagnell, *Canadese*, chaps. 7 and 8; Wismer, *Sweathearts*.

101 *Canadian Labour* 6 (Sept. 1961); *Labour Gazette*, Sept. 1961, 986 (estimate is 5000 workers); *Goldenberg Report*, 17 (6000 workers)

102 *Goldenberg Report*, 15. For details about the Labour Relations Act and the recommendations see especially 25–77. See *Labour Gazette*, July 1962, 781–3; Crispo, "Labour-Management Relations."

103 For details see, for example, Gerard Hebert, "Labour Standards Legislation," in Crispo and Goldenberg, eds., *Construction Labour Relations*; A.W.R. Carothers, "Labour Relations Acts," in ibid: Gerard Dion, "Jurisdictional Disputes," in ibid.

104 On later developments see, for example, Hebert, "Labour Standards Legislation"; on the demise of the Brandon Group see, for example, Stefanini interview material in Bagnell, *Canadese*, especially 168–9; Colantonio, "Italian Immigrants in Toronto's Construction Industry"; Toppan Papers, vol. 1, Curriculum Vitae

105 Colantonio, "Italian Immigrants in Toronto's Construction Industry"; see also Toppan's fairly lengthy account of his past union activities in Toppan Papers, Curriculum Vitae.

106 Laurel Sefton MacDowell, "The Formation of the Canadian Industrial Relations System during World War II," *Labour/Le Travail* 3 (1978); Leo Panitch and Donald Swartz, "Towards Permanent Exceptionalism: Coercion and Consent in Canadian Industrial Relations," ibid. 13 (1984)

107 Harold Logan, *Trade Unions in Canada* (Toronto 1948); E.A. Forsey, *Trade Unions in Canada, 1812–1902* (Toronto 1982)

CONCLUSION

1 Tony Grande, Panel Discussion on Italian Workers in Toronto, Workers and Their Communities Conference, York University, 1989

2 For the postwar era, a recent exception is Mauro Peressini's historically informed sociological research on Montreal's Italians from Friuli. See his "Stratégies migratoire et pratiques communautaires: Les Italiens du Frioul," *Recherches Sociographiques* 25 (1984).

3 Grace Anderson and David Higgs, *A Future to Inherit: The Portuguese Communities of Canada* (Toronto 1976)

4 M.R. Lupul, ed., *A Heritage in Transition: Essays in the History of Ukrainians in Canada* (Toronto 1982)

5 Peter Chimbos, *The Canadian Odyssey: The Greek Experience in Canada* (Toronto 1980); Anderson and Higgs, *Future to Inherit*. On the series see Roberto Perin, "Clio as an Ethnic: The Third Force in Canadian Historiography," *Canadian Historical Review* 64 (1983); recent research

on the Portuguese is contained in David Higgs, ed., *Portuguese Migration in Global Perspective* (Toronto 1990).

6 Personal interviews

Index